1996 STATUTORY SUPPL

to

FOOD AND DRUG LAW

Cases and Materials

SECOND EDITION

By

PETER BARTON HUTT
Covington & Burling, Washington, D.C.

and

RICHARD A. MERRILL
Professor of Law, University of Virginia
and Special Counsel, Covington & Burling

Westbury, New York
THE FOUNDATION PRESS, INC.
1996

TEXT IS PRINTED ON 10% POST CONSUMER RECYCLED PAPER

Printed with **Printwise**
Environmentally Advanced Water Washable Ink

TABLE OF CONTENTS

*

PREFACE

This Supplement contains in full or partial text the principal statutes pertinent to the study of federal food and drug law. The Food, Drug, and Cosmetic Act of 1938, is reproduced in full text. This version includes all amendments made by Congress through June 30, 1995, including the Radiation for Safety and Health Act, which was originally part of the Public Health Service Act. Also reproduced in full are the 1906 Food and Drugs Act and the Fair Packaging and Labeling Act. Other related stat-utes whose enforcement is delegated to the Food and Drug Administra-tion or that apply to food and drugs and related products but are administered by another agency, such as the Federal Trade Commission Act, are included in partial text only. The complete current versions of these laws, as well as other federal health and safety statutes, are reproduced in a useful compilation published biennially as a Committee Print of the Committee on Interstate and Foreign Commerce of the U.S. House of Representatives.

All provisions of statutes currently in force are included in their amended form as of June 30, 1995. It is not feasible to reproduce or il-lustrate each amendment of these laws, particularly the much-amended Federal Food, Drug, and Cosmetic Act, since their original enactment. The principal amendments to the 1906 Food and Drugs Act and the 1938 Food, Drug, and Cosmetic Act are set out in a compilation published peri-odically by the Superintendent of the Document Room, U.S. House of Representatives.

This Supplement does not reproduce many laws of general applicabil-ity to which the Food and Drug Administration is subject. It does in-clude most sections of the Administrative Procedure Act, including the Freedom of Information Act, but among the other important general laws we have omitted are the Federal Advisory Committee Act; the Pa-perwork Reduction Act; and the National Environmental Policy Act. For a comprehensive listing of regulatory statutes that are potentially applic-able to producers of food, drugs, medical devices, cosmetics, biologics, and electronic products, *see* Appendix A of Hutt and Merrill, FOOD AND DRUG LAW: CASES AND MATERIALS (Second Edition, 1991), pub-lished by The Foundation Press, Inc.

The statutory provisions included in this Supplement are lengthy and in many places complex. They represent nearly a century of Con-gressional draftsmanship. While not even seasoned lawyers have mas-tered every detail of these intricate enactments, it is important for stu-dents and practitioners alike to understand the basic concepts embodied

v

in the law and to appreciate the broad array of statutory powers that FDA can rely upon in carrying out its responsibilities.

PETER BARTON HUTT
RICHARD A. MERRILL

December 1995

1996 STATUTORY SUPPLEMENT

to

FOOD AND DRUG LAW

Cases and Materials

*

FEDERAL FOOD, DRUG, AND COSMETIC ACT

TITLE 21, U.S.C.A

SUBCHAPTER I—SHORT TITLE

§ 301. Short title

This chapter may be cited as the Federal Food, Drug, and Cosmetic Act.

SUBCHAPTER II—DEFINITIONS

§ 321. Definitions; generally

For the purposes of this chapter—

(a)(1) The term "State", except as used in the last sentence of section 372(a) of this title, means any State or Territory of the United States, the District of Columbia, and the Commonwealth of Puerto Rico.

(2) The term "Territory" means any Territory or possession of the United States, including the District of Columbia, and excluding the Commonwealth of Puerto Rico and the Canal Zone.

(b) The term "interstate commerce" means (1) commerce between any State or Territory and any place outside thereof, and (2) commerce within the District of Columbia or within any other Territory not organized with a legislative body.

(c) The term "Department" means the Department of Health and Human Services.

(d) The term "Secretary" means the Secretary of Health and Human Services.

(e) The term "person" includes individual, partnership, corporation, and association.

(f) The term "food" means (1) articles used for food or drink for man or other animals, (2) chewing gum, and (3) articles used for components of any such article.

(g)(1) The term "drug" means (A) articles recognized in the official United States Pharmacopoeia, official Homeopathic Pharmacopoeia of the United States, or official National Formulary, or any supplement to any of them; and (B) articles intended for use in the diagnosis, cure, mitigation, treatment, or prevention of disease in man or other animals; and (C) articles (other than food) intended to affect the structure or any function of the body of man or other animals; and (D) articles intended

1

for use as a component of any article specified in clauses (A), (B), or (C) of this paragraph. A food or dietary supplement for which a claim, subject to sections 343(r)(1)(B) and 343(r)(3) of this title or sections 343(r)(1)(B) and 343(r)(5)(D) of this title, is made in accordance with the requirements of section 343(r) of this title is not a drug solely because the label or the labeling contains such a claim. A food, dietary ingredient, or dietary supplement for which a truthful and not misleading statement is made in accordance with section 343(r)(6) of this title is not a drug under clause (C) solely because the label or the labeling contains such a statement.

(2) The term "counterfeit drug" means a drug which, or the container or labeling of which, without authorization, bears the trademark, trade name, or other identifying mark, imprint, or device, or any likeness thereof, of a drug manufacturer, processor, packer, or distributor other than the person or persons who in fact manufactured, processed, packed, or distributed such drug and which thereby falsely purports or is represented to be the product of, or to have been packed or distributed by, such other drug manufacturer, processor, packer, or distributor.

(h) The term "device" (except when used in paragraph (n) of this section and in sections 331(i), 343(f), 352(c), and 362(c) of this title) means an instrument, apparatus, implement, machine, contrivance, implant, in vitro reagent, or other similar or related article, including any component, part, or accessory, which is—

> (1) recognized in the official National Formulary, or the United States Pharmacopeia, or any supplement to them,

> (2) intended for use in the diagnosis of disease or other conditions, or in the cure, mitigation, treatment, or prevention of disease, in man or other animals, or

> (3) intended to affect the structure or any function of the body of man or other animals, and

which does not achieve its primary intended purposes through chemical action within or on the body of man or other animals and which is not dependent upon being metabolized for the achievement of its primary intended purposes.

(i) The term "cosmetic" means (1) articles intended to be rubbed, poured, sprinkled, or sprayed on, introduced into, or otherwise applied to the human body or any part thereof for cleansing, beautifying, promoting attractiveness, or altering the appearance, and (2) articles intended for use as a component of any such articles; except that such term shall not include soap.

(j) The term "official compendium" means the official United States Pharmacopoeia, official Homeopathic Pharmacopoeia of the United States, official National Formulary, or any supplement to any of them.

(k) The term "label" means a display of written, printed, or graphic matter upon the immediate container of any article; and a requirement made by or under authority of this chapter that any word, statement, or other information appear on the label shall not be considered to be complied with unless such word, statement, or other information also appears on the outside container or wrapper, if any there be, of the retail package of such article, or is easily legible through the outside container or wrapper.

(*l*) The term "immediate container" does not include package liners.

(m) The term "labeling" means all labels and other written, printed, or graphic matter (1) upon any article or any of its containers or wrappers, or (2) accompanying such article.

(n) If an article is alleged to be misbranded because the labeling or advertising is misleading, then in determining whether the labeling or advertising is misleading there shall be taken into account (among other things) not only representations made or suggested by statement, word, design, device, or any combination thereof, but also the extent to which the labeling or advertising fails to reveal facts material in the light of such representations or material with respect to consequences which may result from the use of the article to which the labeling or advertising relates under the conditions of use prescribed in the labeling or advertising thereof or under such conditions of use as are customary or usual.

(o) The representation of a drug, in its labeling, as an antiseptic shall be considered to be a representation that it is a germicide, except in the case of a drug purporting to be, or represented as, an antiseptic for inhibitory use as a wet dressing, ointment, dusting powder, or such other use as involves prolonged contact with the body.

(p) The term "new drug" means—

(1) Any drug (except a new animal drug or an animal feed bearing or containing a new animal drug) the composition of which is such that such drug is not generally recognized, among experts qualified by scientific training and experience to evaluate the safety and effectiveness of drugs, as safe and effective for use under the conditions prescribed, recommended, or suggested in the labeling thereof, except that such a drug not so recognized shall not be deemed to be a "new drug" if at any time prior to the enactment of this chapter it was subject to the Food and Drugs Act of June 30, 1906, as amended, and if at such time its labeling contained the same representations concerning the conditions of its use; or

(2) Any drug (except a new animal drug or an animal feed bearing or containing a new animal drug) the composition of which is such that such drug, as a result of investigations to determine its safety and effectiveness for use under such conditions, has become so recognized, but which has not, otherwise than in such investiga-

3

tions, been used to a material extent or for a material time under such conditions.

(q) The term "pesticide chemical" means any substance which, alone, in chemical combination or in formulation with one or more other substances, is "a pesticide" within the meaning of the Federal Insecticide, Fungicide, and Rodenticide Act [7 U.S.C.A. § 136 et seq.] as now in force or as hereafter amended, and which is used in the production, storage, or transportation of raw agricultural commodities.

(r) The term "raw agricultural commodity" means any food in its raw or natural state, including all fruits that are washed, colored, or otherwise treated in their unpeeled natural form prior to marketing.

(s) The term "food additive" means any substance the intended use of which results or may reasonably be expected to result, directly or indirectly, in its becoming a component or otherwise affecting the characteristics of any food (including any substance intended for use in producing, manufacturing, packing, processing, preparing, treating, packaging, transporting, or holding food; and including any source of radiation intended for any such use), if such substance is not generally recognized, among experts qualified by scientific training and experience to evaluate its safety, as having been adequately shown through scientific procedures (or, in the case of a substance used in food prior to January 1, 1958, through either scientific procedures or experience based on common use in food) to be safe under the conditions of its intended use; except that such term does not include—

(1) a pesticide chemical in or on a raw agricultural commodity; or

(2) a pesticide chemical to the extent that it is intended for use or is used in the production, storage, or transportation of any raw agricultural commodity; or

(3) a color additive; or

(4) any substance used in accordance with a sanction or approval granted prior to September 6, 1958 pursuant to this chapter, the Poultry Products Inspection Act (21 U.S.C. 451 and the following) or the Meat Inspection Act of March 4, 1907, as amended and extended;

(5) a new animal drug; or

(6) an ingredient described in paragraph (ff) in, or intended for use in, a dietary supplement.

(t)(1) The term "color additive" means a material which—

(A) is a dye, pigment, or other substance made by a process of synthesis or similar artifice, or extracted, isolated, or otherwise derived, with or without intermediate or final change of identity, from a vegetable, animal, mineral, or other source, and

(B) when added or applied to a food, drug, or cosmetic, or to the human body or any part thereof, is capable (alone or through reaction with other substance) of imparting color thereto;

except that such term does not include any material which the Secretary, by regulation, determines is used (or intended to be used) solely for a purpose or purposes other than coloring.

(2) The term "color" includes black, white, and intermediate grays.

(3) Nothing in subparagraph (1) of this paragraph shall be construed to apply to any pesticide chemical, soil or plant nutrient, or other agricultural chemical solely because of its effect in aiding, retarding, or otherwise affecting, directly or indirectly, the growth or other natural physiological processes of produce of the soil and thereby affecting its color, whether before or after harvest.

(u) The term "safe" as used in paragraph (s) of this section and in sections 348, 360b, and 379e of this title, has reference to the health of man or animal.

(v) The term "new animal drug" means any drug intended for use for animals other than man, including any drug intended for use in animal feed but not including such animal feed,—

(1) the composition of which is such that such drug is not generally recognized, among experts qualified by scientific training and experience to evaluate the safety and effectiveness of animal drugs, as safe and effective for use under the conditions prescribed, recommended, or suggested in the labeling thereof; except that such a drug not so recognized shall not be deemed to be a "new animal drug" if at any time prior to June 25, 1938, it was subject to the Food and Drug Act of June 30, 1906, as amended, and if at such time its labeling contained the same representations concerning the conditions of its use; or

(2) the composition of which is such that such drug, as a result of investigations to determine its safety and effectiveness for use under such conditions, has become so recognized but which has not, otherwise than in such investigations, been used to a material extent or for a material time under such conditions.

(w) The term "animal feed", as used in paragraph (w) of this section, in section 360b of this title, and in provisions of this chapter referring to such paragraph or section, means an article which is intended for use for food for animals other than man and which is intended for use as a substantial source of nutrients in the diet of the animal, and is not limited to a mixture intended to be the sole ration of the animal.

(x) The term "informal hearing" means a hearing which is not subject to section 554, 556, or 557 of Title 5 and which provides for the following:

(1) The presiding officer in the hearing shall be designated by the Secretary from officers and employees of the Department who have not participated in any action of the Secretary which is the subject of the hearing and who are not directly responsible to an officer or employee of the Department who has participated in any such action.

(2) Each party to the hearing shall have the right at all times to be advised and accompanied by an attorney.

(3) Before the hearing, each party to the hearing shall be given reasonable notice of the matters to be considered at the hearing, including a comprehensive statement of the basis for the action taken or proposed by the Secretary which is the subject of the hearing and a general summary of the information which will be presented by the Secretary at the hearing in support of such action.

(4) At the hearing the parties to the hearing shall have the right to hear a full and complete statement of the action of the Secretary which is the subject of the hearing together with the information and reasons supporting such action, to conduct reasonable questioning, and to present any oral or written information relevant to such action.

(5) The presiding officer in such hearing shall prepare a written report of the hearing to which shall be attached all written material presented at the hearing. The participants in the hearing shall be given the opportunity to review and correct or supplement the presiding officer's report of the hearing.

(6) The Secretary may require the hearing to be transcribed. A party to the hearing shall have the right to have the hearing transcribed at his expense. Any transcription of a hearing shall be included in the presiding officer's report of the hearing.

(y) The term "saccharin" includes calcium saccharin, sodium saccharin, and ammonium saccharin.

(z) The term "infant formula" means a food which purports to be or is represented for special dietary use solely as a food for infants by reason of its simulation of human milk or its suitability as a complete or partial substitute for human milk.

(aa) The term "abbreviated drug application" means an application submitted under section 355(j) or 357 of this title for the approval of a drug that relies on the approved application of another drug with the same active ingredient to establish safety and efficacy, and—

(1) in the case of section 335a of this title, includes a supplement to such an application for a different or additional use of the drug but does not include a supplement to such an application for other than a different or additional use of the drug, and

(2) in the case of sections 335b and 335c of this title, includes any supplement to such an application.

(bb) The term "knowingly" or "knew" means that a person, with respect to information—

(1) has actual knowledge of the information, or

(2) acts in deliberate ignorance or reckless disregard of the truth or falsity of the information.

(cc) For purposes of section 335a of this title, the term "high managerial agent"—

(1) means—

(A) an officer or director of a corporation or an association,

(B) a partner of a partnership, or

(C) any employee or other agent of a corporation, association, or partnership,

having duties such that the conduct of such officer, director, partner, employee, or agent may fairly be assumed to represent the policy of the corporation, association, or partnership, and

(2) includes persons having management responsibility for—

(A) submissions to the Food and Drug Administration regarding the development or approval of any drug product,

(B) production, quality assurance, or quality control of any drug product, or

(C) research and development of any drug product.

(dd) For purposes of sections 335a and 335b of this title, the term "drug product" means a drug subject to regulation under section 355, 357, 360b, or 382 of this title or under section 262 of Title 42.

(ee) The term "Commissioner" means the Commissioner of Food and Drugs.

(ff) The term "dietary supplement"—

(1) means a product (other than tobacco) intended to supplement the diet that bears or contains one or more of the following dietary ingredients:

(A) a vitamin;

(B) a mineral;

(C) an herb or other botanical;

(D) an amino acid;

(E) a dietary substance for use by man to supplement the diet by increasing the total dietary intake; or

(F) a concentrate, metabolite, constituent, extract, or combination of any ingredient described in clause (A), (B), (C), (D), or (E);

(2) means a product that—

(A)(i) is intended for ingestion in a form described in section 350(c)(1)(B)(i) of this title; or

(ii) complies with section 350(c)(1)(B)(ii) of this title;

(B) is not represented for use as a conventional food or as a sole item of a meal or the diet; and

(C) is labeled as a dietary supplement; and

(3) does—

(A) include an article that is approved as a new drug under section 355 of this title, certified as an antibiotic under section 357 of this title, or licensed as a biologic under section 262 Title 42, and was, prior to such approval, certification, or license, marketed as a dietary supplement or as a food unless the Secretary has issued a regulation, after notice and comment, finding that the article, when used as or in a dietary supplement under the conditions of use and dosages set forth in the labeling for such dietary supplement, is unlawful under section 342(f) of this title; and

(B) not include—

(i) an article that is approved as a new drug under section 355 of this title, certified as an antibiotic under section 357 of this title, or licensed as a biologic under section 262 of Title 42, or

(ii) an article authorized for investigation as a new drug, antibiotic, or biological for which substantial clinical investigations have been instituted and for which the existence of such investigations has been made public,

which was not before such approval, certification, licensing, or authorization marketed as a dietary supplement or as a food unless the Secretary, in the Secretary's discretion, has issued a regulation, after notice and comment, finding that the article would be lawful under this chapter.

Except for purposes of paragraph (g), a dietary supplement shall be deemed to be a food within the meaning of this chapter.

SUBCHAPTER III—PROHIBITED ACTS AND PENALTIES

§ 331. Prohibited acts

The following acts and the causing thereof are prohibited:

(a) The introduction or delivery for introduction into interstate commerce of any food, drug, device, or cosmetic that is adulterated or misbranded.

(b) The adulteration or misbranding of any food, drug, device, or cosmetic in interstate commerce.

(c) The receipt in interstate commerce of any food, drug, device, or cosmetic that is adulterated or misbranded, and the delivery or proffered delivery thereof for pay or otherwise.

(d) The introduction or delivery for introduction into interstate commerce of any article in violation of section 344 or 355 of this title.

(e) The refusal to permit access to or copying of any record as required by section 350a or 373 of this title; or the failure to establish or maintain any record, or make any report, required under section 350a, 355(i) or (k), 357(d) or (g), 360b(a)(4)(C), 360b(j), (*l*), or (m), 360e(f), or 360i of this title, or the refusal to permit access to or verification or copying of any such required record.

(f) The refusal to permit entry or inspection as authorized by section 374 of this title.

(g) The manufacture within any Territory of any food, drug, device, or cosmetic that is adulterated or misbranded.

(h) The giving of a guaranty or undertaking referred to in section 333(c)(2) of this title which guaranty or undertaking is false, except by a person who relied upon a guaranty or undertaking to the same effect signed by, and containing the name and address of, the person residing in the United States from whom he received in good faith the food, drug, device, or cosmetic; or the giving of a guaranty or undertaking referred to in section 333(c)(3) of this title which guaranty or undertaking is false.

(i)(1) Forging, counterfeiting, simulating, or falsely representing, or without proper authority using any mark, stamp, tag, label, or other identification device authorized or required by regulations promulgated under the provisions of section 344, 356, 357, or 379e of this title.

(2) Making, selling, disposing of, or keeping in possession, control, or custody, or concealing any punch, die, plate, stone, or other thing designed to print, imprint, or reproduce the trademark, trade name, or other identifying mark, imprint, or device of another or any likeness of any of the foregoing upon any drug or container or labeling thereof so as to render such drug a counterfeit drug.

(3) The doing of any act which causes a drug to be a counterfeit drug, or the sale or dispensing, or the holding for sale or dispensing, of a counterfeit drug.

(j) The using by any person to his own advantage, or revealing, other than to the Secretary or officers or employees of the Department, or to the courts when relevant in any judicial proceeding under this chapter, any information acquired under authority of section 344, 348, 350a, 355, 356, 357, 360, 360b, 360c, 360d, 360e, 360f, 360h, 360i, 360j, 374, 379, or 379e of this title concerning any method or process which as a trade secret is entitled to protection. This paragraph does not authorize the withholding of information from either House of Congress or from, to the extent of matter within its jurisdiction, any committee or subcommittee of such committee or any joint committee of Congress or any subcommittee of such joint committee.

(k) The alteration, mutilation, destruction, obliteration, or removal of the whole or any part of the labeling of, or the doing of any other act with respect to, a food, drug, device, or cosmetic, if such act is done while such article is held for sale (whether or not the first sale) after shipment in interstate commerce and results in such article being adulterated or misbranded.

(*l*) The using, on the labeling of any drug or device or in any advertising relating to such drug or device, of any representation or suggestion that approval of an application with respect to such drug or device is in effect under section 355, 360e, or 360j(g) of this title, as the case may be, or that such drug or device complies with the provisions of such section.

(m) The sale or offering for sale of colored oleomargarine or colored margarine, or the possession or serving of colored oleomargarine or colored margarine in violation of subsections (b) or (c) of section 347 of this title.

(n) The using, in labeling, advertising or other sales promotion of any reference to any report or analysis furnished in compliance with section 374 of this title.

(o) In the case of a prescription drug distributed or offered for sale in interstate commerce, the failure of the manufacturer, packer, or distributor thereof to maintain for transmittal, or to transmit, to any practitioner licensed by applicable State law to administer such drug who makes written request for information as to such drug, true and correct copies of all printed matter which is required to be included in any package in which that drug is distributed or sold, or such other printed matter as is approved by the Secretary. Nothing in this paragraph shall be construed to exempt any person from any labeling requirement imposed by or under other provisions of this chapter.

(p) The failure to register in accordance with section 360 of this title, the failure to provide any information required by section 360(j) or 360(k) of this title, or the failure to provide a notice required by section 360(j)(2) of this title.

(q)(1) The failure or refusal to (A) comply with any requirement prescribed under section 360h or 360j(g) of this title, (B) furnish any notification or other material or information required by or under section 360i or 360j(g) of this title, or (C) comply with a requirement under section 360l of this title.

(2) With respect to any device, the submission of any report that is required by or under this chapter that is false or misleading in any material respect.

(r) The movement of a device in violation of an order under section 334(g) of this title or the removal or alteration of any mark or label required by the order to identify the device as detained.

(s) The failure to provide the notice required by section 350a(c) of this title or 350a(e) of this title, the failure to make the reports required by section 350a(f)(1)(B) of this title, the failure to retain the records required by section 350a(b)(4) of this title, or the failure to meet the requirements prescribed under section 350a(f)(3) of this title.

(t) The importation of a drug in violation of section 381(d)(1) of this title, the sale, purchase, or trade of a drug or drug sample or the offer to sell, purchase, or trade a drug or drug sample in violation of section 353(c) of this title, the sale, purchase, or trade of a coupon, the offer to sell, purchase, or trade such a coupon, or the counterfeiting of such a coupon in violation of section 353(c)(2) of this title, the distribution of a drug sample in violation of section 353(d) of this title or the failure to otherwise comply with the requirements of section 353(d) of this title, or the distribution of drugs in violation of section 353(e) of this title or the failure to otherwise comply with the requirements of section 353(e) of this title.

(u) The failure to comply with any requirements of the provisions of, or any regulations or orders of the Secretary, under section 360b(a)(4)(A), 360b(a)(4)(D), or 360b(a)(5) of this title.

§ 332. Injunction proceedings

(a) Jurisdiction of courts

The district courts of the United States and the United States courts of the Territories shall have jurisdiction, for cause shown [1] to restrain violations of section 331 of this title, except paragraphs (h)-(j) of said section.

(b) Violation of injunction

In case of violation of an injunction or restraining order issued under this section, which also constitutes a violation of this chapter, trial shall be by the court, or, upon demand of the accused, by a jury.

§ 333. Penalties

(a) Violation of section 331 of this title; second violation; intent to defraud or mislead

(1) Any person who violates a provision of section 331 of this title shall be imprisoned for not more than one year or fined not more than $1,000, or both.

---

1. So in original. Probably should have a comma.

(2) Notwithstanding the provisions of paragraph (1), if any person commits such a violation after a conviction of him under this section has become final, or commits such a violation with the intent to defraud or mislead, such person shall be imprisoned for not more than three years or fined not more than $10,000, or both.

(b) Prescription drug marketing violations

(1) Notwithstanding subsection (a) of this section, any person who violates section 331(t) of this title by—

(A) knowingly importing a drug in violation of section 381(d)(1) of this title,

(B) knowingly selling, purchasing, or trading a drug or drug sample or knowingly offering to sell, purchase, or trade a drug or drug sample, in violation of section 353(c)(1) of this title,

(C) knowingly selling, purchasing, or trading a coupon, knowingly offering to sell, purchase, or trade such a coupon, or knowingly counterfeiting such a coupon, in violation of section 353(c)(2) of this title, or

(D) knowingly distributing drugs in violation of section 353(e)(2)(A) of this title,

shall be imprisoned for not more than 10 years or fined not more than $250,000, or both.

(2) Any manufacturer or distributor who distributes drug samples by means other than the mail or common carrier whose representative, during the course of the representative's employment or association with that manufacturer or distributor, violated section 331(t) of this title because of a violation of section 353(c)(1) of this title or violated any State law prohibiting the sale, purchase, or trade of a drug sample subject to section 353(b) of this title or the offer to sell, purchase, or trade such a drug sample shall, upon conviction of the representative for such violation, be subject to the following civil penalties:

(A) A civil penalty of not more than $50,000 for each of the first two such violations resulting in a conviction of any representative of the manufacturer or distributor in any 10–year period.

(B) A civil penalty of not more than $1,000,000 for each violation resulting in a conviction of any representative after the second conviction in any 10–year period.

For the purposes of this paragraph, multiple convictions of one or more persons arising out of the same event or transaction, or a related series of events or transactions, shall be considered as one violation.

(3) Any manufacturer or distributor who violates section 331(t) of this title because of a failure to make a report required by section 353(d)(3)(E) of this title shall be subject to a civil penalty of not more than $100,000.

(4)(A) If a manufacturer or distributor or any representative of such manufacturer or distributor provides information leading to the institution of a criminal proceeding against, and conviction of, any representative of that manufacturer or distributor for a violation of section 331(t) of this title because of a sale, purchase, or trade or offer to purchase, sell, or trade a drug sample in violation of section 353(c)(1) of this title or for a violation of State law prohibiting the sale, purchase, or trade or offer to sell, purchase, or trade a drug sample, the conviction of such representative shall not be considered as a violation for purposes of paragraph (2).

(B) If, in an action brought under paragraph (2) against a manufacturer or distributor relating to the conviction of a representative of such manufacturer or distributor for the sale, purchase, or trade of a drug or the offer to sell, purchase, or trade a drug, it is shown, by clear and convincing evidence—

(i) that the manufacturer or distributor conducted, before the institution of a criminal proceeding against such representative for the violation which resulted in such conviction, an investigation of events or transactions which would have led to the reporting of information leading to the institution of a criminal proceeding against, and conviction of, such representative for such purchase, sale, or trade or offer to purchase, sell, or trade, or

(ii) that, except in the case of the conviction of a representative employed in a supervisory function, despite diligent implementation by the manufacturer or distributor of an independent audit and security system designed to detect such a violation, the manufacturer or distributor could not reasonably have been expected to have detected such violation,

the conviction of such representative shall not be considered as a conviction for purposes of paragraph (2).

(5) If a person provides information leading to the institution of a criminal proceeding against, and conviction of, a person for a violation of section 331(t) of this title because of the sale, purchase, or trade of a drug sample or the offer to sell, purchase, or trade a drug sample in violation of section 353(c)(1) of this title, such person shall be entitled to one-half of the criminal fine imposed and collected for such violation but not more than $125,000.

(c) Exceptions in certain cases of good faith, etc.

No person shall be subject to the penalties of subsection (a)(1) of this section, (1) for having received in interstate commerce any article and delivered it or proffered delivery of it, if such delivery or proffer was made in good faith, unless he refuses to furnish on request of an officer or employee duly designated by the Secretary the name and address of the person from whom he purchased or received such article and copies of all documents, if any there be, pertaining to the delivery of the article to him; or (2) for having violated section 331(a) or (d) of this title, if he

13

establishes a guaranty or undertaking signed by, and containing the name and address of, the person residing in the United States from whom he received in good faith the article, to the effect, in case of an alleged violation of section 331(a) of this title, that such article is not adulterated or misbranded, within the meaning of this chapter designating this chapter or to the effect, in case of an alleged violation of section 331(d) of this title, that such article is not an article which may not, under the provisions of section 344 or 355 of this title, be introduced into interstate commerce; or (3) for having violated section 331(a) of this title, where the violation exists because the article is adulterated by reason of containing a color additive not from a batch certified in accordance with regulations promulgated by the Secretary under this chapter, if such person establishes a guaranty or undertaking signed by, and containing the name and address of, the manufacturer of the color additive, to the effect that such color additive was from a batch certified in accordance with the applicable regulations promulgated by the Secretary under this chapter; or (4) for having violated section 331(b), (c) or (k) of this title by failure to comply with section 352(f) of this title in respect to an article received in interstate commerce to which neither section 353(a) nor 353(b)(1) of this title is applicable, if the delivery or proffered delivery was made in good faith and the labeling at the time thereof contained the same directions for use and warning statements as were contained in the labeling at the time of such receipt of such article; or (5) for having violated section 331(i)(2) of this title if such person acted in good faith and had no reason to believe that use of the punch, die, plate, stone, or other thing involved would result in a drug being a counterfeit drug, or for having violated section 331(i)(3) of this title if the person doing the act or causing it to be done acted in good faith and had no reason to believe that the drug was a counterfeit drug.

(d) Exceptions involving misbranded food

No person shall be subject to the penalties of subsection (a)(1) of this section for a violation of section 331 of this title involving misbranded food if the violation exists solely because the food is misbranded under section 343(a)(2) of this title because of its advertising.

(e) Prohibited distribution of anabolic steroids

(1) Except as provided in paragraph (2), any person who distributes or possesses with the intent to distribute any anabolic steroid for any use in humans other than the treatment of disease pursuant to the order of a physician shall be imprisoned for not more than three years or fined under Title 18, or both.

(2) Any person who distributes or possesses with the intent to distribute to an individual under 18 years of age, any anabolic steroid for any use in humans other than the treatment of disease pursuant to the order of a physician shall be imprisoned for not more than six years or fined under Title 18, or both.

(f) Prohibited distribution of human growth hormones

(1) Except as provided in paragraph (2), whoever knowingly distributes, or possesses with intent to distribute, human growth hormone for any use in humans other than the treatment of a disease or other recognized medical condition, where such use has been authorized by the Secretary of Health and Human Services under section 355 of this title and pursuant to the order of a physician, is guilty of an offense punishable by not more than 5 years in prison, such fines as are authorized by Title 18, or both.

(2) Whoever commits any offense set forth in paragraph (1) and such offense involves an individual under 18 years of age is punishable by not more than 10 years imprisonment, such fines as are authorized by Title 18, or both.

(3) Any conviction for a violation of paragraphs (1) and (2) of this subsection shall be considered a felony violation of the Controlled Substances Act [21 U.S.C.A. § 801 et seq.] for the purposes of forfeiture under section 413 of such Act [21 U.S.C.A. § 853].

(4) As used in this subsection the term "human growth hormone" means somatrem, somatropin, or an analogue of either-of them.

(5) The Drug Enforcement Administration is authorized to investigate offenses punishable by this subsection.

(g) Violations related to devices

(1)(A) Except as provided in subparagraph (B), any person who violates a requirement of this chapter which relates to devices shall be liable to the United States for a civil penalty in an amount not to exceed $15,000 for each such violation, and not to exceed $1,000,000 for all such violations adjudicated in a single proceeding.

(B) Subparagraph (A) shall not apply—

(i) to any person who violates the requirements of section 360i(a) or 360j(f) of this title unless such violation constitutes (I) a significant or knowing departure from such requirements, or (II) a risk to public health.

(ii) to any person who commits minor violations of section 360i(e) or 360i(f) of this title (only with respect to correction reports) if such person demonstrates substantial compliance with such section, or

(iii) to violations of section 351(a)(2)(A) of this title which involve one or more devices which are not defective.

(2)(A) A civil penalty under paragraph (1) shall be assessed by the Secretary by an order made on the record after opportunity for a hearing provided in accordance with this subparagraph and section 554 of Title 5. Before issuing such an order, the Secretary shall give written notice to the person to be assessed a civil penalty under such order of the

Secretary's proposal to issue such order and provide such person an opportunity for a hearing on the order. In the course of any investigation, the Secretary may issue subpoenas requiring the attendance and testimony of witnesses and the production of evidence that relates to the matter under investigation.

(B) In determining the amount of a civil penalty, the Secretary shall take into account the nature, circumstances, extent, and gravity of the violation or violations and, with respect to the violator, ability to pay, effect on ability to continue to do business, any history of prior such violations, the degree of culpability, and such other matters as justice may require.

(C) The Secretary may compromise, modify, or remit, with or without conditions, any civil penalty which may be assessed under paragraph (1). The amount of such penalty, when finally determined, or the amount agreed upon in compromise, may be deducted from any sums owing by the United States to the person charged.

(3) Any person who requested, in accordance with paragraph (2)(A), a hearing respecting the assessment of a civil penalty and who is aggrieved by an order assessing a civil penalty may file a petition for judicial review of such order with the United States Court of Appeals for the District of Columbia Circuit or for any other circuit in which such person resides or transacts business. Such a petition may only be filed within the 60–day period beginning on the date the order making such assessment was issued.

(4) If any person fails to pay an assessment of a civil penalty—

(A) after the order making the assessment becomes final, and if such person does not file a petition for judicial review of the order in accordance with paragraph (3), or

(B) after a court in an action brought under paragraph (3) has entered a final judgment in favor of the Secretary,

the Attorney General shall recover the amount assessed (plus interest at currently prevailing rates from the date of the expiration of the 60–day period referred to in paragraph (3) or the date of such final judgment, as the case may be) in an action brought in any appropriate district court of the United States. In such an action, the validity, amount, and appropriateness of such penalty shall not be subject to review.

§ 333a.   Repealed. Pub.L. 101–647, Title XIX, § 1905, Nov. 29, 1990, 104 Stat. 4853

§ 334.   Seizure

(a) Grounds and jurisdiction

(1) Any article of food, drug, or cosmetic that is adulterated or misbranded when introduced into or while in interstate commerce or

while held for sale (whether or not the first sale) after shipment in interstate commerce, or which may not, under the provisions of section 344 or 355 of this title, be introduced into interstate commerce, shall be liable to be proceeded against while in interstate commerce, or at any time thereafter, on libel of information and condemned in any district court of the United States or United States court of a Territory within the jurisdiction of which the article is found. No libel for condemnation shall be instituted under this chapter, for any alleged misbranding if there is pending in any court a libel for condemnation proceeding under this chapter based upon the same alleged misbranding, and not more than one such proceeding shall be instituted if no such proceeding is so pending, except that such limitations shall not apply (A) when such misbranding has been the basis of a prior judgment in favor of the United States, in a criminal, injunction, or libel for condemnation proceeding under this chapter, or (B) when the Secretary has probable cause to believe from facts found, without hearing, by him or any officer or employee of the Department that the misbranded article is dangerous to health, or that the labeling of the misbranded article is fraudulent, or would be in a material respect misleading to the injury or damage of the purchaser or consumer. In any case where the number of libel for condemnation proceedings is limited as above provided the proceeding pending or instituted shall, on application of the claimant, seasonably made, be removed for trial to any district agreed upon by stipulation between the parties, or, in case of failure to so stipulate within a reasonable time, the claimant may apply to the court of the district in which the seizure has been made, and such court (after giving the United States attorney for such district reasonable notice and opportunity to be heard) shall by order, unless good cause to the contrary is shown, specify a district of reasonable proximity to the claimant's principal place of business, to which the case shall be removed for trial.

(2) The following shall be liable to be proceeded against at any time on libel of information and condemned in any district court of the United States or United States court of a Territory within the jurisdiction of which they are found: (A) Any drug that is a counterfeit drug, (B) Any container of a counterfeit drug, (C) Any punch, die, plate, stone, labeling, container, or other thing used or designed for use in making a counterfeit drug or drugs, and (D) Any adulterated or misbranded device.

(3)(A) Except as provided in subparagraph (B), no libel for condemnation may be instituted under paragraph (1) or (2) against any food which—

(i) is misbranded under section 343(a)(2) of this title because of its advertising, and

(ii) is being held for sale to the ultimate consumer in an establishment other than an establishment owned or operated by a manufacturer, packer, or distributor of the food.

(B) A libel for condemnation may be instituted under paragraph (1) or (2) against a food described in subparagraph (A) if—

(i)(I) the food's advertising which resulted in the food being misbranded under section 343(a)(2) of this title was disseminated in the establishment in which the food is being held for sale to the ultimate consumer,

(II) such advertising was disseminated by, or under the direction of, the owner or operator of such establishment, or

(III) all or part of the cost of such advertising was paid by such owner or operator; and

(ii) the owner or operator of such establishment used such advertising in the establishment to promote the sale of the food.

(b) Procedure; multiplicity of pending proceedings

The article, equipment, or other thing proceeded against shall be liable to seizure by process pursuant to the libel, and the procedure in cases under this section shall conform, as nearly as may be, to the procedure in admiralty; except that on demand of either party any issue of fact joined in any such case shall be tried by jury. When libel for condemnation proceedings under this section, involving the same claimant and the same issues of adulteration or misbranding, are pending in two or more jurisdictions, such pending proceedings, upon application of the claimant seasonably made to the court of one such jurisdiction, shall be consolidated for trial by order of such court, and tried in (1) any district selected by the claimant where one of such proceedings is pending; or (2) a district agreed upon by stipulation between the parties. If no order for consolidation is so made within a reasonable time, the claimant may apply to the court of one such jurisdiction, and such court (after giving the United States attorney for such district reasonable notice and opportunity to be heard) shall by order, unless good cause to the contrary is shown, specify a district of reasonable proximity to the claimant's principal place of business, in which all such pending proceedings shall be consolidated for trial and tried. Such order of consolidation shall not apply so as to require the removal of any case the date for trial of which has been fixed. The court granting such order shall give prompt notification thereof to the other courts having jurisdiction of the cases covered thereby.

(c) Availability of samples of seized goods prior to trial

The court at any time after seizure up to a reasonable time before trial shall by order allow any party to a condemnation proceeding, his attorney or agent, to obtain a representative sample of the article seized and a true copy of the analysis, if any, on which the proceeding is based and the identifying marks or numbers, if any, of the packages from which the samples analyzed were obtained.

(d) Disposition of goods after decree of condemnation; claims for remission or mitigation of forfeitures

(1) Any food, drug, device, or cosmetic condemned under this section shall, after entry of the decree, be disposed of by destruction or sale as the court may, in accordance with the provisions of this section, direct and the proceeds thereof, if sold, less the legal costs and charges, shall be paid into the Treasury of the United States; but such article shall not be sold under such decree contrary to the provisions of this chapter or the laws of the jurisdiction in which sold. After entry of the decree and upon the payment of the costs of such proceedings and the execution of a good and sufficient bond conditioned that such article shall not be sold or disposed of contrary to the provisions of this chapter or the laws of any State or Territory in which sold, the court may by order direct that such article be delivered to the owner thereof to be destroyed or brought into compliance with the provisions of this chapter under the supervision of an officer or employee duly designated by the Secretary, and the expenses of such supervision shall be paid by the person obtaining release of the article under bond. If the article was imported into the United States and the person seeking its release establishes (A) that the adulteration, misbranding, or violation did not occur after the article was imported, and (B) that he had no cause for believing that it was adulterated, misbranded, or in violation before it was released from customs custody, the court may permit the article to be delivered to the owner for exportation in lieu of destruction upon a showing by the owner that all of the conditions of section 381(e) of this title can and will be met. The provisions of this sentence shall not apply where condemnation is based upon violation of section 342(a)(1), (2), or (6), section 351(a)(3), section 352(j), or section 361(a) or (d) of this title. Where such exportation is made to the original foreign supplier, then paragraphs (1) and (2) of section 381(e) of this title and the preceding sentence shall not be applicable; and in all cases of exportation the bond shall be conditioned that the article shall not be sold or disposed of until the applicable conditions of section 381(e) of this title have been met. Any article condemned by reason of its being an article which may not, under section 344 or 355 of this title, be introduced into interstate commerce, shall be disposed of by destruction.

(2) The provisions of paragraph (1) of this subsection shall, to the extent deemed appropriate by the court, apply to any equipment or other thing which is not otherwise within the scope of such paragraph and which is referred to in paragraph (2) of subsection (a) of this section.

(3) Whenever in any proceeding under this section, involving paragraph (2) of subsection (a) of this section, the condemnation of any equipment or thing (other than a drug) is decreed, the court shall allow the claim of any claimant, to the extent of such claimant's interest, for remission or mitigation of such forfeiture if such claimant proves to the satisfaction of the court (i) that he has not committed or caused to be

committed any prohibited act referred to in such paragraph (2) and has no interest in any drug referred to therein, (ii) that he has an interest in such equipment or other thing as owner or lienor or otherwise, acquired by him in good faith, and (iii) that he at no time had any knowledge or reason to believe that such equipment or other thing was being or would be used in, or to facilitate, the violation of laws of the United States relating to counterfeit drugs.

(e) Costs

When a decree of condemnation is entered against the article, court costs and fees, and storage and other proper expenses, shall be awarded against the person, if any, intervening as claimant of the article.

(f) Removal of case for trial

In the case of removal for trial of any case as provided by subsection (a) or (b) of this section—

(1) The clerk of the court from which removal is made shall promptly transmit to the court in which the case is to be tried all records in the case necessary in order that such court may exercise jurisdiction.

(2) The court to which such case was removed shall have the powers and be subject to the duties, for purposes of such case, which the court from which removal was made would have had, or to which such court would have been subject, if such case had not been removed.

(g) Administrative restraint; detention orders

(1) If during an inspection conducted under section 374 of this title of a facility or a vehicle, a device which the officer or employee making the inspection has reason to believe is adulterated or misbranded is found in such facility or vehicle, such officer or employee may order the device detained (in accordance with regulations prescribed by the Secretary) for a reasonable period which may not exceed twenty days unless the Secretary determines that a period of detention greater than twenty days is required to institute an action under subsection (a) of this section or section 332 of this title, in which case he may authorize a detention period of not to exceed thirty days. Regulations of the Secretary prescribed under this paragraph shall require that before a device may be ordered detained under this paragraph the Secretary or an officer or employee designated by the Secretary approve such order. A detention order under this paragraph may require the labeling or marking of a device during the period of its detention for the purpose of identifying the device as detained. Any person who would be entitled to claim a device if it were seized under subsection (a) of this section may appeal to the Secretary a detention of such device under this paragraph. Within five days of the date an appeal of a detention is filed with the Secretary, the Secretary shall after affording opportunity for an informal hearing by order confirm the detention or revoke it.

(2)(A) Except as authorized by subparagraph (B), a device subject to a detention order issued under paragraph (1) shall not be moved by any person from the place at which it is ordered detained until—

(i) released by the Secretary, or

(ii) the expiration of the detention period applicable to such order,

whichever occurs first.

(B) A device subject to a detention order under paragraph (1) may be moved—

(i) in accordance with regulations prescribed by the Secretary, and

(ii) if not in final form for shipment, at the discretion of the manufacturer of the device for the purpose of completing the work required to put it in such form.

§ 335. Hearing before report of criminal violation

Before any violation of this chapter is reported by the Secretary to any United States attorney for institution of a criminal proceeding, the person against whom such proceeding is contemplated shall be given appropriate notice and an opportunity to present his views, either orally or in writing, with regard to such contemplated proceeding.

§ 335a. Debarment, temporary denial of approval, and suspension

(a) Mandatory debarment

(1) Corporations, partnerships, and associations

If the Secretary finds that a person other than an individual has been convicted, after May 13, 1992, of a felony under Federal law for conduct relating to the development or approval, including the process for development or approval, of any abbreviated drug application, the Secretary shall debar such person from submitting, or assisting in the submission of, any such application.

(2) Individuals

If the Secretary finds that an individual has been convicted of a felony under Federal law for conduct—

(A) relating to the development or approval, including the process for development or approval, of any drug product, or

(B) otherwise relating to the regulation of any drug product under this chapter, the Secretary shall debar such individual from providing services in any capacity to a person that has an approved or pending drug product application.

(b) Permissive debarment

(1) In general

The Secretary, on the Secretary's own initiative or in response to a petition, may, in accordance with paragraph (2), debar—

(A) a person other than an individual from submitting or assisting in the submission of any abbreviated drug application, or

(B) an individual from providing services in any capacity to a person that has an approved or pending drug product application.

(2) Persons subject to permissive debarment

The following persons are subject to debarment under paragraph (1):

(A) Corporations, partnerships, and associations

Any person other than an individual that the Secretary finds has been convicted—

(i) for conduct that—

(I) relates to the development or approval, including the process for the development or approval, of any abbreviated drug application; and

(II) is a felony under Federal law (if the person was convicted before May 13, 1992), a misdemeanor under Federal law, or a felony under State law, or (ii) of a conspiracy to commit, or aiding or abetting, a criminal offense described in clause (i) or a felony described in subsection (a)(1) of this section,

if the Secretary finds that the type of conduct which served as the basis for such conviction undermines the process for the regulation of drugs.

(B) Individuals

(i) Any individual whom the Secretary finds has been convicted of—

(I) a misdemeanor under Federal law or a felony under State law for conduct relating to the development or approval, including the process for development or approval, of any drug product or otherwise relating to the regulation of drug products under this chapter, or

(II) a conspiracy to commit, or aiding or abetting, such criminal offense or a felony described in subsection (a)(2) of this section, if the Secretary finds that the type of conduct which served as the basis for such conviction undermines the process for the regulation of drugs.

(ii) Any individual whom the Secretary finds has been convicted of—

(I) a felony which is not described in subsection (a)(2) of this section or clause (i) of this subparagraph and which involves bribery, payment of illegal gratuities, fraud, perjury, false statement, racketeering, blackmail, extortion, falsification or destruction of records, or interference with, obstruction of an investigation into, or prosecution of, any criminal offense, or

(II) a conspiracy to commit, or aiding or abetting, such felony,

if the Secretary finds, on the basis of the conviction of such individual and other information, that such individual has demonstrated a pattern of conduct sufficient to find that there is reason to believe that such individual may violate requirements under this chapter relating to drug products.

(iii) Any individual whom the Secretary finds materially participated in acts that were the basis for a conviction for an offense described in subsection (a) of this section or in clause (i) or (ii) for which a conviction was obtained, if the Secretary finds, on the basis of such participation and other information, that such individual has demonstrated a pattern of conduct sufficient to find that there is reason to believe that such individual may violate requirements under this chapter relating to drug products.

(iv) Any high managerial agent whom the Secretary finds—

(I) worked for, or worked as a consultant for, the same person as another individual during the period in which such other individual took actions for which a felony conviction was obtained and which resulted in the debarment under subsection (a)(2) of this section, or clause (i), of such other individual,

(II) had actual knowledge of the actions described in subclause (I) of such other individual, or took action to avoid such actual knowledge, or failed to take action for the purpose of avoiding such actual knowledge.

(III) knew that the actions described in subclause (I) were violative of law, and

(IV) did not report such actions, or did not cause such actions to be reported, to an officer, employee, or agent of the Department or to an appropriate law enforcement officer, or failed to take other appropriate action that would have ensured that the process for the regulation of drugs was not undermined, within a reasonable time after such agent first knew of such actions,

if the Secretary finds that the type of conduct which served as the basis for such other individual's conviction undermines the process for the regulation of drugs.

(3) Stay of certain orders

An order of the Secretary under clause (iii) or (iv) of paragraph (2)(B) shall not take effect until 30 days after the order has been issued.

(c) Debarment period and considerations

(1) Effect of debarment

The Secretary—

(A) shall not accept or review (other than in connection with an audit under this section) any abbreviated drug application submitted by or with the assistance of a person debarred under subsection (a)(1) or (b)(2)(A) of this section during the period such person is debarred,

(B) shall, during the period of a debarment under subsection (a)(2) or (b)(2)(B) of this section, debar an individual from providing services in any capacity to a person that has an approved or pending drug product application and shall not accept or review (other than in connection with an audit under this section) an abbreviated drug application from such individual, and

(C) shall, if the Secretary makes the finding described in paragraph (6) or (7) of section 335b(a) of this title, assess a civil penalty in accordance with section 335b of this title.

(2) Debarment periods

(A) In general

The Secretary shall debar a person under subsection (a) or (b) of this section for the following periods:

(i) The period of debarment of a person (other than an individual) under subsection (a)(1) of this section shall not be less than 1 year or more than 10 years, but if an act leading to a subsequent debarment under subsection (a) of this section occurs within 10 years after such person has been debarred under subsection (a)(1) of this section, the period of debarment shall be permanent.

(ii) The debarment of an individual under subsection (a)(2) of this section shall be permanent.

(iii) The period of debarment of any person under subsection (b)(2) of this section shall not be more than 5 years.

The Secretary may determine whether debarment periods shall run concurrently or consecutively in the case of a person debarred for multiple offenses.

(B) Notification

Upon a conviction for an offense described in subsection (a) or (b) of this section or upon execution of an agreement with the United States to plead guilty to such an offense, the person involved may notify the Secretary that the person acquiesces to debarment and such person's debarment shall commence upon such notification.

(3) Considerations

In determining the appropriateness and the period of a debarment of a person under subsection (b) of this section and any period of debarment beyond the minimum specified in subparagraph (A)(i) of paragraph (2), the Secretary shall consider where applicable—

(A) the nature and seriousness of any offense involved,

(B) the nature and extent of management participation in any offense involved, whether corporate policies and practices encouraged the offense, including whether inadequate institutional controls contributed to the offense,

(C) the nature and extent of voluntary steps to mitigate the impact on the public of any offense involved, including the recall or the discontinuation of the distribution of suspect drugs, full cooperation with any investigations (including the extent of disclosure to appropriate authorities of all wrongdoing), the relinquishing of profits on drug approvals fraudulently obtained, and any other actions taken to substantially limit potential or actual adverse effects on the public health,

(D) whether the extent to which changes in ownership, management, or operations have corrected the causes of any offense involved and provide reasonable assurances that the offense will not occur in the future,

(E) whether the person to be debarred is able to present adequate evidence that current production of drugs subject to abbreviated drug applications and all pending abbreviated drug applications are free of fraud or material false statements, and

(F) prior convictions under this chapter or under other Acts involving matters within the jurisdiction of the Food and Drug Administration.

(d) Termination of debarment

(1) Application

Any person that is debarred under subsection (a) of this section (other than a person permanently debarred) or any person that is debarred under subsection (b) of this section may apply to the Secretary for termination of the debarment under this subsection. Any information submitted to the Secretary under this paragraph does not constitute an amendment or supplement to pending or approved abbreviated drug applications.

(2) Deadline

The Secretary shall grant or deny any application respecting a debarment which is submitted under paragraph (1) within 180 days of the date the application is submitted.

(3) Action by the Secretary

(A) Corporations

(i) Conviction reversal

If the conviction which served as the basis for the debarment of a person under subsection (a)(1) or (b)(2)(A) of this section is reversed, the Secretary shall withdraw the order of debarment.

(ii) Application

Upon application submitted under paragraph (1), the Secretary shall terminate the debarment of a person if the Secretary finds that—

(I) changes in ownership, management, or operations have fully corrected the causes of the offense involved and provide reasonable assurances that the offense will not occur in the future, and

(II) sufficient audits, conducted by the Food and Drug Administration or by independent experts acceptable to the Food and Drug Administration, demonstrate that pending applications and the development of drugs being tested before the submission of an application are free of fraud or material false statements.

In the case of persons debarred under subsection (a)(1) of this section, such termination shall take effect no earlier than the expiration of one year from the date of the debarment.

(B) Individuals

(i) Conviction reversal

If the conviction which served as the basis for the debarment of an individual under subsection (a)(2) of this section or clause (i), (ii), (iii), or (iv) of subsection (b)(2)(B) of this section is reversed, the Secretary shall withdraw the order of debarment.

(ii) Application

Upon application submitted under paragraph (1), the Secretary shall terminate the debarment of an individual who has been debarred under subsection (b)(2)(B) of this section if such termination serves the interests of justice and adequately protects the integrity of the drug approval process.

(4) Special termination

(A) Application

Any person that is debarred under subsection (a)(1) of this section (other than a person permanently debarred under subsection (c)(2)(A)(i) of this section) or any individual who is debarred under subsection (a)(2) of this section may apply to the Secretary for special termination of debarment under this subsection. Any information submitted to the Secretary under this subparagraph does not constitute an amendment or supplement to pending or approved abbreviated drug applications.

(B) Corporations

Upon an application submitted under subparagraph (A), the Secretary may take the action described in subparagraph (D) if the Secretary, after an informal hearing, finds that—

(i) the person making the application under subparagraph (A) has demonstrated that the felony conviction which was the basis for such person's debarment involved the commission of an offense which was not authorized, requested, commanded, performed, or recklessly tolerated by the board of directors or by a high managerial agent acting on behalf of the person within the scope of the board's or agent's office or employment,

(ii) all individuals who were involved in the commission of the offense or who knew or should have known of the offense have been removed from employment involving the development or approval of any drug subject to sections 355 or 357 of this title,

(iii) the person fully cooperated with all investigations and promptly disclosed all wrongdoing to the appropriate authorities, and

(iv) the person acted to mitigate any impact on the public of any offense involved, including the recall, or the discontinuation of the distribution, of any drug with respect to which the Secretary requested a recall or discontinuation of distribution due to concerns about the safety or efficacy of the drug.

(C) Individuals

Upon an application submitted under subparagraph (A), the Secretary may take the action described in subparagraph (D) if the Secretary, after an informal hearing, finds that such individual has provided substantial assistance in the investigations or prosecutions of offenses which are described in subsection (a) or (b) of this section or which relate to any matter under the jurisdiction of the Food and Drug Administration.

(D) Secretarial action

The action referred to in subparagraphs (B) and (C) is—

(i) in the case of a person other than an individual—

(I) terminating the debarment immediately, or

(II) limiting the period of debarment to less than one year, and

(ii) in the case of an individual, limiting the period of debarment to less than permanent but to no less than 1 year,

whichever best serves the interest of justice and protects the integrity of the drug approval process.

(e) Publication and list of debarred persons

The Secretary shall publish in the Federal Register the name of any person debarred under subsection (a) or (b) of this section, the effective date of the debarment, and the period of the debarment. The Secretary shall also maintain and make available to the public a list, updated no less often than quarterly, of such persons, of the effective dates and minimum periods of such debarments, and of the termination of debarments.

(f) Temporary denial of approval

(1) In general

The Secretary, on the Secretary's own initiative or in response to a petition, may, in accordance with paragraph (3), refuse by order, for the period prescribed by paragraph (2), to approve any abbreviated drug application submitted by any person—

(A) if such person is under an active Federal criminal investigation in connection with an action described in subparagraph (B),

(B) if the Secretary finds that such person—

(i) has bribed or attempted to bribe, has paid or attempted to pay an illegal gratuity, or has induced or attempted to induce another person to bribe or pay an illegal gratuity to any officer, employee, or agent of the Department of Health and Human Services or to any other Federal, State, or local official in connection with any abbreviated drug application, or has conspired to commit, or aided or abetted, such actions, or

(ii) has knowingly made or caused to be made a pattern or practice of false statements or misrepresentations with respect to material facts relating to any abbreviated drug application, or the production of any drug subject to an abbreviated drug application, to any officer, employee, or agent of the Department of Health and Human Services, or has conspired to commit, or aided or abetted, such actions, and

(C) if a significant question has been raised regarding—

(i) the integrity of the approval process with respect to such abbreviated drug application, or

(ii) the reliability of data in or concerning such person's abbreviated drug application.

Such an order may be modified or terminated at any time.

(2) Applicable period

(A) In general

Except as provided in subparagraph (B), a denial of approval of an application of a person under paragraph (1) shall be in effect for a period determined by the Secretary but not to exceed 18 months beginning on the date the Secretary finds that the conditions described in subparagraphs (A), (B), and (C) of paragraph (1) exist. The Secretary shall terminate such denial—

(i) if the investigation with respect to which the finding was made does not result in a criminal charge against such person, if criminal charges have been brought and the charges have been dismissed, or if a judgment of acquittal has been entered, or

(ii) if the Secretary determines that such finding was in error.

(B) Extension

If, at the end of the period described in subparagraph (A), the Secretary determines that a person has been criminally charged for an action described in subparagraph (B) of paragraph (1), the Secretary may extend the period of denial of approval of an application for a period not to exceed 18 months. The Secretary shall terminate such extension if the charges have been dismissed, if a judgment of acquittal has been entered, or if the Secretary determines that the finding described in subparagraph (A) was in error.

(3) Informal hearing

Within 10 days of the date an order is issued under paragraph (1), the Secretary shall provide such person with an opportunity for an informal hearing, to be held within such 10 days, on the decision of the Secretary to refuse approval of an abbreviated drug application. Within 60 days of the date on which such hearing is held, the Secretary shall notify the person given such hearing whether the Secretary's refusal of approval will be continued, terminated, or otherwise modified. Such notification shall be final agency action.

(g) Suspension authority

(1) In general

If—

(A) the Secretary finds—

(i) that a person has engaged in conduct described in subparagraph (B) of subsection (f)(1) of this section in connection with 2 or more drugs under abbreviated drug applications, or

(ii) that a person has engaged in flagrant and repeated, material violations of good manufacturing practice or good laboratory practice in connection with the development, manufacturing, or distribution of one or more drugs approved under an abbreviated drug application during a 2-year period, and—

(I) such violations may undermine the safety and efficacy of such drugs, and

(II) the causes of such violations have not been corrected within a reasonable period of time following notice of such violations by the Secretary, and

(B) such person is under an active investigation by a Federal authority in connection with a civil or criminal action involving conduct described in subparagraph (A),

the Secretary shall issue an order suspending the distribution of all drugs the development or approval of which was related to such conduct described in subparagraph (A) or suspending the distribution of all drugs approved under abbreviated drug applications of such person if the Secretary finds that such conduct may have affected the development or approval of a significant number of drugs which the Secretary is unable to identify. The Secretary shall exclude a drug from such order if the Secretary determines that such conduct was not likely to have influenced the safety or efficacy of such drug.

(2) Public health waiver

The Secretary shall, on the Secretary's own initiative or in response to a petition, waive the suspension under paragraph (1)(involving an action described in paragraph (1)(A)(i)) with respect to any drug if the Secretary finds that such waiver is necessary to protect the public health because sufficient quantities of the drug would not otherwise be available. The Secretary shall act on any petition seeking action under this paragraph within 180 days of the date the petition is submitted to the Secretary.

(h) Termination of suspension

The Secretary shall withdraw an order of suspension of the distribution of a drug under subsection (g) of this section if the person with respect to whom the order was issued demonstrates in a petition to the Secretary—

(1)(A) on the basis of an audit by the Food and Drug Administration or by experts acceptable to the Food and Drug Administration, or on the basis of other information, that the development, approval, manufacturing, and distribution of such drug is in substantial compliance with the applicable requirements of this chapter, and

(B) changes in ownership, management, or operations—

(i) fully remedy the patterns or practices with respect to which the order was issued, and

(ii) provide reasonable assurances that such actions will not occur in the future, or

(2) the initial determination was in error.

The Secretary shall act on a submission of a petition under this subsection within 180 days of the date of its submission and the Secretary may consider the petition concurrently with the suspension proceeding. Any information submitted to the Secretary under this subsection does not constitute an amendment or supplement to a pending or approved abbreviated drug application.

(i) Procedure

The Secretary may not take any action under subsection (a), (b), (c), (d)(3), (g), or (h) of this section with respect to any person unless the Secretary has issued an order for such action made on the record after opportunity for an agency hearing on disputed issues of material fact. In the course of any investigation or hearing under this subsection, the Secretary may administer oaths and affirmations, examine witnesses, receive evidence, and issue subpoenas requiring the attendance and testimony of witnesses and the production of evidence that relates to the matter under investigation.

(j) Judicial review

(1) In general

Except as provided in paragraph (2), any person that is the subject of an adverse decision under subsection (a), (b), (c), (d), (f), (g), or (h) of this section may obtain a review of such decision by the United States Court of Appeals for the District of Columbia or for the circuit in which the person resides, by filing in such court (within 60 days following the date the person is notified of the Secretary's decision) a petition requesting that the decision be modified or set aside.

(2) Exception

Any person that is the subject of an adverse decision under clause (iii) or (iv) of subsection (b)(2)(B) of this section may obtain a review of such decision by the United States District Court for the District of Columbia or a district court of the United States for the district in which the person resides, by filing in such court (within 30 days following the date the person is notified of the Secretary's decision) a complaint requesting that the decision be modified or set aside. In such an action, the court shall determine the matter de novo.

(k) Certification

Any application for approval of a drug product shall include—

(1) a certification that the applicant did not and will not use in any capacity the services of any person debarred under subsection (a) or (b) of this section, in connection with such application, and

(2) if such application is an abbreviated drug application, a list of all convictions, described in subsections (a) and (b) of this section which occurred within the previous 5 years, of the applicant and affiliated persons responsible for the development or submission of such application.

(*l*) Applicability

(1) Conviction

For purposes of this section, a person is considered to have been convicted of a criminal offense—

(A) when a judgment of conviction has been entered against the person by a Federal or State court, regardless of whether there is an appeal pending,

(B) when a plea of guilty or nolo contendere by the person has been accepted by a Federal or State court, or

(C) when the person has entered into participation in a first offender, deferred adjudication, or other similar arrangement or program where judgment of conviction has been withheld.

(2) Effective dates

Subsection (a) of this section, subparagraph (A) of subsection (b)(2) of this section, and clauses (i) and (ii) of subsection (b)(2)(B) of this section shall not apply to a conviction which occurred more than 5 years before the initiation of an agency action proposed to be taken under subsection (a) or (b) of this section. Clauses (iii) and (iv) of subsection (b)(2)(B) of this section and subsections (f) and (g) of this section shall not apply to an act or action which occurred more than 5 years before the initiation of an agency action proposed to be taken under subsection (b), (f), or (g) of this section. Clause (iv) of subsection (b)(2)(B) of this section shall not apply to an action which occurred before June 1, 1992. Subsection (k) of this section shall not apply to applications submitted to the Secretary before June 1, 1992.

§ 335b. Civil penalties

(a) In general

Any person that the Secretary finds—

(1) knowingly made or caused to be made, to any officer, employee, or agent of the Department of Health and Human Services, a false

statement or misrepresentation of a material fact in connection with an abbreviated drug application,

(2) bribed or attempted to bribe or paid or attempted to pay an illegal gratuity to any officer, employee, or agent of the Department of Health and Human Services in connection with an abbreviated drug application,

(3) destroyed, altered, removed, or secreted, or procured the destruction, alteration, removal, or secretion of, any material document or other material evidence which was the property of or in the possession of the Department of Health and Human Services for the purpose of interfering with that Department's discharge of its responsibilities in connection with an abbreviated drug application,

(4) knowingly failed to disclose, to an officer or employee of the Department of Health and Human Services, a material fact which such person had an obligation to disclose relating to any drug subject to an abbreviated drug application,

(5) knowingly obstructed an investigation of the Department of Health and Human Services into any drug subject to an abbreviated drug application,

(6) is a person that has an approved or pending drug product application and has knowingly—

(A) employed or retained as a consultant or contractor, or

(B) otherwise used in any capacity the services of,

a person who was debarred under section 335a of this title, or

(7) is an individual debarred under section 335a of this title and, during the period of debarment, provided services in any capacity to a person that had an approved or pending drug product application,

shall be liable to the United States for a civil penalty for each such violation in an amount not to exceed $250,000 in the case of an individual and $1,000,000 in the case of any other person.

(b) Procedure

(1) In general

(A) Action by the Secretary

A civil penalty under subsection (a) of this section shall be assessed by the Secretary on a person by an order made on the record after an opportunity for an agency hearing on disputed issues of material fact and the amount of the penalty. In the course of any investigation or hearing under this subparagraph, the Secretary may administer oaths and affirmations, examine witnesses, receive evidence, and issue subpoenas requiring the attendance and testimony of witnesses and the production of evidence that relates to the matter under investigation.

(B) Action by the Attorney General

In lieu of a proceeding under subparagraph (A), the Attorney General may, upon request of the Secretary, institute a civil action to recover a civil money penalty in the amount and for any of the acts set forth in subsection (a) of this section. Such an action may be instituted separately from or in connection with any other claim, civil or criminal, initiated by the Attorney General under this chapter.

(2) Amount

In determining the amount of a civil penalty under paragraph (1), the Secretary or the court shall take into account the nature, circumstances, extent, and gravity of the act subject to penalty, the person's ability to pay, the effect on the person's ability to continue to do business, any history of prior, similar acts, and such other matters as justice may require.

(3) Limitation on actions

No action may be initiated under this section—

(A) with respect to any act described in subsection (a) of this section that occurred before May 13, 1992, or

(B) more than 6 years after the date when facts material to the act are known or reasonably should have been known by the Secretary but in no event more than 10 years after the date the act took place.

(c) Judicial review

Any person that is the subject of an adverse decision under subsection (b)(1)(A) of this section may obtain a review of such decision by the United States Court of Appeals for the District of Columbia or for the circuit in which the person resides, by filing in such court (within 60 days following the date the person is notified of the Secretary's decision) a petition requesting that the decision be modified or set aside.

(d) Recovery of penalties

The Attorney General may recover any civil penalty (plus interest at the currently prevailing rates from the date the penalty became final) assessed under subsection (b)(1)(A) of this section in an action brought in the name of the United States. The amount of such penalty may be deducted, when the penalty has become final, from any sums then or later owing by the United States to the person against whom the penalty has been assessed. In an action brought under this subsection, the validity, amount, and appropriateness of the penalty shall not be subject to judicial review.

(e) Informants

The Secretary may award to any individual (other than an officer or employee of the Federal Government or a person who materially participated in any conduct described in subsection (a) of this section) who provides information leading to the imposition of a civil penalty under this section an amount not to exceed—

    (1) $250,000, or

    (2) one-half of the penalty so imposed and collected,

whichever is less. The decision of the Secretary on such award shall not be reviewable.

§ 335c. Authority to withdraw approval of abbreviated drug applications

(a) In general

    The Secretary—

    (1) shall withdraw approval of an abbreviated drug application if the Secretary finds that the approval was obtained, expedited, or otherwise facilitated through bribery, payment of an illegal gratuity, or fraud or material false statement, and

    (2) may withdraw approval of an abbreviated drug application if the Secretary finds that the applicant has repeatedly demonstrated a lack of ability to produce the drug for which the application was submitted in accordance with the formulations or manufacturing practice set forth in the abbreviated drug application and has introduced, or attempted to introduce, such adulterated or misbranded drug into commerce.

(b) Procedure

    The Secretary may not take any action under subsection (a) of this section with respect to any person unless the Secretary has issued an order for such action made on the record after opportunity for an agency hearing on disputed issues of material fact. In the course of any investigation or hearing under this subsection, the Secretary may administer oaths and affirmations, examine witnesses, receive evidence, and issue subpoenas requiring the attendance and testimony of witnesses and the production of evidence that relates to the matter under investigation.

(c) Applicability

    Subsection (a) of this section shall apply with respect to offenses or acts regardless of when such offenses or acts occurred.

(d) Judicial review

    Any person that is the subject of an adverse decision under subsection (a) of this section may obtain a review of such decision by the United States Court of Appeals for the District of Columbia or for the circuit in which the person resides, by filing in such court (within 60 days following the date the person is notified of the Secretary's decision) a petition requesting that the decision be modified or set aside.

§ 336. Report of minor violations

Nothing in this chapter shall be construed as requiring the Secretary to report for prosecution, or for the institution of libel or injunction proceedings, minor violations of this chapter whenever he believes that the public interest will be adequately served by a suitable written notice or warning.

§ 337. Proceedings in name of United States; provision as to subpoenas

(a) Except as provided in subsection (b) of this section, all such proceedings for the enforcement, or to restrain violations, of this chapter shall be by and in the name of the United States. Subpoenas for witnesses who are required to attend a court of the United States, in any district, may run into any other district in any such proceeding under this section.

(b)(1) A State may bring in its own name and within its jurisdiction proceedings for the civil enforcement, or to restrain violations, of section 341 of this title, sections 343(b), 343(c), 343(d), 343(e), 343(f), 343(g), 343(h), 343(i), 343(k), 343(q) or 343(r) of this title if the food that is the subject of the proceedings is located in the State.

(2) No proceeding may be commenced by a State under paragraph (1)—

(A) before 30 days after the State has given notice to the Secretary that the State intends to bring such proceeding,

(B) before 90 days after the State has given notice to the Secretary of such intent if the Secretary has, within such 30 days, commenced an informal or formal enforcement action pertaining to the food which would be the subject of such proceeding, or

(C) if the Secretary is diligently prosecuting a proceeding in court pertaining to such food, has settled such proceeding, or has settled the informal or formal enforcement action pertaining to such food.

In any court proceeding described in subparagraph (C), a State may intervene as a matter of right.

SUBCHAPTER IV—FOOD

§ 341. Definitions and standards for food

Whenever in the judgment of the Secretary such action will promote honesty and fair dealing in the interest of consumers, he shall promulgate regulations fixing and establishing for any food, under its common or usual name so far as practicable, a reasonable definition and standard of identity, a reasonable standard of quality, or reasonable standards of fill of container. No definition and standard of identity and no standard of quality shall be established for fresh or dried fruits, fresh or dried vegetables, or butter, except that definitions and standards of identity may be established for avocadoes, cantaloupes, citrus fruits, and melons. In prescribing any standard of fill of container, the Secretary shall give due consideration to the natural shrinkage in storage and in transit of fresh natural food and to need for the necessary packing and protective material. In the prescribing of any standard of quality for any canned fruit or canned vegetable, consideration shall be given and due allowance made for the differing characteristics of the several varieties of such fruit or vegetable. In prescribing a definition and standard of identity for any food or class of food in which optional ingredients are permitted, the Secretary shall, for the purpose of promoting honesty and fair dealing in the interest of consumers, designate the optional ingredients which shall be named on the label. Any definition and standard of identity prescribed by the Secretary for avocadoes, cantaloupes, citrus fruits, or melons shall relate only to maturity and to the effects of freezing.

§ 342. Adulterated food

A food shall be deemed to be adulterated—

(a) Poisonous, insanitary, etc., ingredients

(1) If it bears or contains any poisonous or deleterious substance which may render it injurious to health; but in case the substance is not an added substance such food shall not be considered adulterated under this clause if the quantity of such substance in such food does not ordinarily render it injurious to health. (2)(A) if it bears or contains any added poisonous or added deleterious substance (other than one which is (i) a pesticide chemical in or on a raw agricultural commodity; (ii) a food additive; (iii) a color additive; or (iv) a new animal drug) which is unsafe within the meaning of section 346 of this title, or (B) if it is a raw agricultural commodity and it bears or contains a pesticide chemical which is unsafe within the meaning of section 346a(a) of this title, or (C) if it is, or it bears or contains, any food additive which is unsafe within the meaning of section 348 of this title: Provided, That where a pesticide chemical has been used in or on a raw agricultural commodity in conformity with an exemption granted or a tolerance prescribed under section 346a of this title and such raw agricultural commodity has been subjected to processing such as canning, cooking, freezing, dehydrating, or milling, the residue of such pesticide chemical remaining in or on such processed food shall, notwithstanding the provisions of sections 346 and 348 of this title, not be deemed unsafe if such residue in or on the raw agricultural commodity has been removed to the extent possible in good manufacturing practice and the concentration of such residue in the processed food when ready to eat is not greater than the tolerance prescribed for the raw agricultural commodity; or (D) if it is, or it bears or contains, a new animal drug (or conversion product thereof) which is unsafe within the meaning of section 360b of this title. (3) If it consists

in whole or in part of any filthy, putrid, or decomposed substance, or if it is otherwise unfit for food; or (4) if it has been prepared, packed, or held under insanitary conditions whereby it may have become contaminated with filth, or whereby it may have been rendered injurious to health; or (5) if it is, in whole or in part, the product of a diseased animal or of an animal which has died otherwise than by slaughter; or (6) if its container is composed, in whole or in part, of any poisonous or deleterious substance which may render the contents injurious to health; or (7) if it has been intentionally subjected to radiation, unless the use of the radiation was in conformity with a regulation or exemption in effect pursuant to section 348 of this title.

(b) Absence, substitution, or addition of constituents

(1) If any valuable constituent has been in whole or in part omitted or abstracted therefrom; or (2) if any substance has been substituted wholly or in part therefor; or (3) if damage or inferiority has been concealed in any manner; or (4) if any substance has been added thereto or mixed or packed therewith so as to increase its bulk or weight, or reduce its quality or strength, or make it appear better or of greater value than it is.

(c) Color additives

If it is, or it bears or contains, a color additive which is unsafe within the meaning of section 379e(a) of this title.

(d) Confectionery containing alcohol or nonnutritive substance

If it is confectionery, and—

(1) has partially or completely imbedded therein any nonnutritive object, except that this subparagraph shall not apply in the case of any nonnutritive object if, in the judgment of the Secretary as provided by regulations, such object is of practical functional value to the confectionery product and would not render the product injurious or hazardous to health;

(2) bears or contains any alcohol other than alcohol not in excess of one- half of 1 per centum by volume derived solely from the use of flavoring extracts except that this clause shall not apply to confectionery which is introduced or delivered for introduction into, or received or held for sale in, interstate commerce if the sale of such confectionery is permitted under the laws of the State in which such confectionery is intended to be offered for sale; or

(3) bears or contains any nonnutritive substance, except that this subparagraph shall not apply to a safe nonnutritive substance which is in or on confectionery by reason of its use for some practical functional purpose in the manufacture, packaging, or storage of such confectionery if the use of the substance does not promote deception of the consumer or otherwise result in adulteration or misbranding in violation of any provision of this chapter, except that the Secretary may, for the purpose

of avoiding or resolving uncertainty as to the application of this subparagraph, issue regulations allowing or prohibiting the use of particular nonnutritive substances.

(e) Oleomargarine containing filthy, putrid, etc., matter

If it is oleomargarine or margarine or butter and any of the raw material used therein consisted in whole or in part of any filthy, putrid, or decomposed substance, or such oleomargarine or margarine or butter is otherwise unfit for food.

(f) Dietary supplement or ingredient: safety

(1) If it is a dietary supplement or contains a dietary ingredient that—

(A) presents a significant or unreasonable risk of illness or injury under—

(i) conditions of use recommended or suggested in labeling, or

(ii) if no conditions of use are suggested or recommended in the labeling, under ordinary conditions of use;

(B) is a new dietary ingredient for which there is inadequate information to provide reasonable assurance that such ingredient does not present a significant or unreasonable risk of illness or injury;

(C) the Secretary declares to pose an imminent hazard to public health or safety, except that the authority to make such declaration shall not be delegated and the Secretary shall promptly after such a declaration initiate a proceeding in accordance with sections 554 and 556 of Title 5, to affirm or withdraw the declaration; or

(D) is or contains a dietary ingredient that renders it adulterated under paragraph (a)(1) under the conditions of use recommended or suggested in the labeling of such dietary supplement.

In any proceeding under this subparagraph, the United States shall bear the burden of proof on each element to show that a dietary supplement is adulterated. The court shall decide any issue under this paragraph on a de novo basis.

(2) Before the Secretary may report to a United States attorney a violation of paragraph (1)(A) for a civil proceeding, the person against whom such proceeding would be initiated shall be given appropriate notice and the opportunity to present views, orally and in writing, at least 10 days before such notice, with regard to such proceeding.

(g) Dietary supplement: manufacturing practices

(1) If it is a dietary supplement and it has been prepared, packed, or held under conditions that do not meet current good manufacturing

practice regulations, including regulations requiring, when necessary, expiration date labeling, issued by the Secretary under subparagraph (2).

(2) The Secretary may by regulation prescribe good manufacturing practices for dietary supplements. Such regulations shall be modeled after current good manufacturing practice regulations for food and may not impose standards for which there is no current and generally available analytical methodology. No standard of current good manufacturing practice may be imposed unless such standard is included in a regulation promulgated after notice and opportunity for comment in accordance with chapter 5 of Title 5.

§ 343. Misbranded food

A food shall be deemed to be misbranded—

(a) False or misleading label

If (1) its labeling of false or misleading in any particular, or (2) in the case of a food to which section 350 of this title applies, its advertising is false or misleading in a material respect or its labeling is in violation of section 350(b)(2) of this title.

(b) Offer for sale under another name

If it is offered for sale under the name of another food.

(c) Imitation of another food

If it is an imitation of another food, unless its label bears, in type of uniform size and prominence, the word "imitation" and, immediately thereafter, the name of the food imitated.

(d) Misleading container

If its container is so made, formed, or filled as to be misleading.

(e) Package form

If in package form unless it bears a label containing (1) the name and place of business of the manufacturer, packer, or distributor; and (2) an accurate statement of the quantity of the contents in terms of weight, measure, or numerical count, except that under clause (2) of this paragraph reasonable variations shall be permitted, and exemptions as to small packages shall be established, by regulations prescribed by the Secretary.

(f) Prominence of information on label

If any word, statement, or other information required by or under authority of this chapter to appear on the label or labeling is not prominently placed thereon with such conspicuousness (as compared with other words, statements, designs, or devices, in the labeling) and in such terms as to render it likely to be read and understood by the ordinary individual under customary conditions of purchase and use.

(g) Representation as to definition and standard of identity

If it purports to be or is represented as a food for which a definition and standard of identity has been prescribed by regulations as provided by section 341 of this title, unless (1) it conforms to such definition and standard, and (2) its label bears the name of the food specified in the definition and standard, and, insofar as may be required by such regulations, the common names of optional ingredients (other than spices, flavoring, and coloring) present in such food.

(h) Representation as to standards of quality and fill of container

If it purports to be or is represented as—

(1) a food for which a standard of quality has been prescribed by regulations as provided by section 341 of this title, and its quality falls below such standard, unless its label bears, in such manner and form as such regulations specify, a statement that it falls below such standard; or

(2) a food for which a standard or standards of fill of container have been prescribed by regulations as provided by section 341 of this title, and it falls below the standard of fill of container applicable thereto, unless its label bears, in such manner and form as such regulations specify, a statement that it falls below such standard.

(i) Label where no representation as to definition and standard of identity

Unless its label bears (1) the common or usual name of the food, if any there be, and (2) in case it is fabricated from two or more ingredients, the common or usual name of each such ingredient and if the food purports to be a beverage containing vegetable or fruit juice, a statement with appropriate prominence on the information panel of the total percentage of such fruit or vegetable juice contained in the food; except that spices, flavorings, and colors not required to be certified under section 379e(c) of this title, unless sold as spices, flavorings, or such colors, may be designated as spices, flavorings, and colorings without naming each. To the extent that compliance with the requirements of clause (2) of this paragraph is impracticable, or results in deception or unfair competition, exemptions shall be established by regulations promulgated by the Secretary.

(j) Representation for special dietary use

If it purports to be or is represented for special dietary uses, unless its label bears such information concerning its vitamin, mineral, and other dietary properties as the Secretary determines to be, and by regulations prescribes as, necessary in order fully to inform purchasers as to its value for such uses.

(k) Artificial flavoring, artificial coloring, or chemical preservatives

If it bears or contains any artificial flavoring, artificial coloring, or chemical preservative, unless it bears labeling stating that fact, except that to the extent that compliance with the requirements of this paragraph is impracticable, exemptions shall be established by regulations promulgated by the Secretary. The provisions of this paragraph and paragraphs (g) and (i) with respect to artificial coloring shall not apply in the case of butter, cheese, or ice cream. The provisions of this paragraph with respect to chemical preservatives shall not apply to a pesticide chemical when used in or on a raw agricultural commodity which is the produce of the soil.

(*l*) Pesticide chemicals on raw agricultural commodities

If it is a raw agricultural commodity which is the produce of the soil, bearing or containing a pesticide chemical applied after harvest, unless the shipping container of such commodity bears labeling which declares the presence of such chemical in or on such commodity and the common or usual name and the function of such chemical, except that no such declaration shall be required while such commodity, having been removed from the shipping container, is being held or displayed for sale at retail out of such container in accordance with the custom of the trade.

(m) Color additives

If it is a color additive, unless its packaging and labeling are in conformity with such packaging and labeling requirements, applicable to such color additive, as may be contained in regulations issued under section 379e of this title.

(n) Packaging or labeling of drugs in violation of regulations

If its packaging or labeling is in violation of an applicable regulation issued pursuant to section 1472 or 1473 of Title 15.

(o) Saccharin for immediate consumption

(1) If it contains saccharin, unless, except as provided in subparagraph (2), its label and labeling bear the following statement: "USE OF THIS PRODUCT MAY BE HAZARDOUS TO YOUR HEALTH. THIS PRODUCT CONTAINS SACCHARIN WHICH HAS BEEN DETERMINED TO CAUSE CANCER IN LABORATORY ANIMALS". Such statement shall be located in a conspicuous place on such label and labeling as proximate as possible to the name of such food and shall appear in conspicuous and legible type in contrast by typography, layout, and color with other printed matter on such label and labeling.

(2) The Secretary may by regulation review and revise or remove the requirement of subparagraph (1) if the Secretary determines such action is necessary to reflect the current state of knowledge concerning saccharin.

(p) Saccharin not for immediate consumption

(1) If it contains saccharin and is offered for sale, but not for immediate consumption, at a retail establishment, unless such retail establishment displays prominently, where such food is held for sale,

notice (provided by the manufacturer of such food pursuant to subparagraph (2)) for consumers respecting the information required by paragraph (*o*) to be on food labels and labeling.

(2) Each manufacturer of food which contains saccharin and which is offered for sale by retail establishments but not for immediate consumption shall, in accordance with regulations promulgated by the Secretary pursuant to subparagraph (4), take such action as may be necessary to provide such retail establishments with the notice required by subparagraph (1).

(3) The Secretary may by regulation review and revise or remove the requirement of subparagraph (1) if he determines such action is necessary to reflect the current state of knowledge concerning saccharin.

(4) The Secretary shall by regulation prescribe the form, text, and manner of display of the notice required by subparagraph (1) and such other matters as may be required for the implementation of the requirements of that subparagraph and subparagraph (2). Regulations of the Secretary under this subparagraph shall be promulgated after an oral hearing but without regard to the National Environmental Policy Act of 1969 [42 U.S.C.A. § 4321 et seq.] and chapter 5 of Title 5. In any action brought for judicial review of any such regulation, the reviewing court may not postpone the effective date of such regulation.

(q) Nutrition information

(1) Except as provided in subparagraphs (3), (4), and (5), if it is a food intended for human consumption and is offered for sale, unless its label or labeling bears nutrition information that provides—

(A)(i) the serving size which is an amount customarily consumed and which is expressed in a common household measure that is appropriate to the food, or

(ii) if the use of the food is not typically expressed in a serving size, the common household unit of measure that expresses the serving size of the food,

(B) the number of servings or other units of measure per container,

(C) the total number of calories—

(i) derived from any source, and

(ii) derived from the total fat,

in each serving size or other unit of measure of the food,

(D) the amount of the following nutrients: Total fat, saturated fat, cholesterol, sodium, total carbohydrates, complex carbohydrates, sugars, dietary fiber, and total protein contained in each serving size or other unit of measure,

(E) any vitamin, mineral, or other nutrient required to be placed on the label and labeling of food under this chapter before October 1, 1990, if the Secretary determines that such information will assist consumers in maintaining healthy dietary practices.

The Secretary may by regulation require any information required to be placed on the label or labeling by this subparagraph or subparagraph (2)(A) to be highlighted on the label or labeling by larger type, bold type, or contrasting color if the Secretary determines that such highlighting will assist consumers in maintaining healthy dietary practices.

(2)(A) If the Secretary determines that a nutrient other than a nutrient required by subparagraph (1)(C), (1)(D), or (1)(E) should be included in the label or labeling of food subject to subparagraph (1) for purposes of providing information regarding the nutritional value of such food that will assist consumers in maintaining healthy dietary practices, the Secretary may by regulation require that information relating to such additional nutrient be included in the label or labeling of such food.

(B) If the Secretary determines that the information relating to a nutrient required by subparagraph (1)(C), (1)(D), or (1)(E) or clause (A) of this subparagraph to be included in the label or labeling of food is not necessary to assist consumers in maintaining healthy dietary practices, the Secretary may by regulation remove information relating to such nutrient from such requirement.

(3) For food that is received in bulk containers at a retail establishment, the Secretary may, by regulation, provide that the nutrition information required by subparagraphs (1) and (2) be displayed at the location in the retail establishment at which the food is offered for sale.

(4)(A) The Secretary shall provide for furnishing the nutrition information required by subparagraphs (1) and (2) with respect to raw agricultural commodities and raw fish by issuing voluntary nutrition guidelines, as provided by clause (B) or by issuing regulations that are mandatory as provided by clause (D).

(B)(i) Upon the expiration of 12 months after November 8, 1990, the Secretary, after providing an opportunity for comment, shall issue guidelines for food retailers offering raw agricultural commodities or raw fish to provide nutrition information specified in subparagraphs (1) and (2). Such guidelines shall take into account the actions taken by food retailers during such 12-month period to provide to consumers nutrition information on raw agricultural commodities and raw fish. Such guidelines shall only apply—

(I) in the case of raw agricultural commodities, to the 20 varieties of vegetables most frequently consumed during a year and the 20 varieties of fruit most frequently consumed during a year, and

(II) to the 20 varieties of raw fish most frequently consumed during a year.

The vegetables, fruits, and raw fish to which such guidelines apply shall be determined by the Secretary by regulation and the Secretary may apply such guidelines regionally.

(ii) Upon the expiration of 12 months after November 8, 1990, the Secretary shall issue a final regulation defining the circumstances that constitute substantial compliance by food retailers with the guidelines issued under subclause (i). The regulation shall provide that there is not substantial compliance if a significant number of retailers have failed to comply with the guidelines. The size of the retailers and the portion of the market served by retailers in compliance with the guidelines shall be considered in determining whether the substantial-compliance standard has been met.

(C)(i) Upon the expiration of 30 months after November 8, 1990, the Secretary shall issue a report on actions taken by food retailers to provide consumers with nutrition information for raw agricultural commodities and raw fish under the guidelines issued under clause (A). Such report shall include a determination of whether there is substantial compliance with the guidelines.

(ii) If the Secretary finds that there is substantial compliance with the guidelines, the Secretary shall issue a report and make a determination of the type required in subclause (i) every two years.

(D)(i) If the Secretary determines that there is not substantial compliance with the guidelines issued under clause (A), the Secretary shall at the time such determination is made issue proposed regulations requiring that any person who offers raw agricultural commodities or raw fish to consumers to provide, in a manner prescribed by regulations, the nutrition information required by subparagraphs (1) and (2). The Secretary shall issue final regulations imposing such requirements 6 months after issuing the proposed regulations. The final regulations shall become effective 6 months after the date of their promulgation.

(ii) Regulations issued under subclause (i) may require that the nutrition information required by subparagraphs (1) and (2) be provided for more than 20 varieties of vegetables, 20 varieties of fruit, and 20 varieties of fish most frequently consumed during a year if the Secretary finds that a larger number of such products are frequently consumed. Such regulations shall permit such information to be provided in a single location in each area in which raw agricultural commodities and raw fish are offered for sale. Such regulations may provide that information shall be expressed as an average or range per serving of the same type of raw agricultural commodity or raw fish. The Secretary shall develop and make available to the persons who offer such food to consumers the information required by subparagraphs (1) and (2).

(iii) Regulations issued under subclause (i) shall permit the required information to be provided in each area of an establishment in which raw agricultural commodities and raw fish are offered for sale. The regulations shall permit food retailers to display the required information by supplying copies of the information provided by the Secretary, by making the information available in brochure, notebook or leaflet form, or by posting a sign disclosing the information. Such regulations shall also permit presentation of the required information to be supplemented by a video, live demonstration, or other media which the Secretary approves.

(E) For purposes of this subparagraph, the term "fish" includes freshwater or marine fin fish, crustaceans, and mollusks, including shellfish, amphibians, and other forms of aquatic animal life.

(F) No person who offers raw agricultural commodities or raw fish to consumers may be prosecuted for minor violations of this subparagraph if there has been substantial compliance with the requirements of this paragraph.

(5)(A) Subparagraphs (1), (2), (3), and (4) shall not apply to food—

(i) which is served in restaurants or other establishments in which food is served for immediate human consumption or which is sold for sale or use in such establishments,

(ii) which is processed and prepared primarily in a retail establishment, which is ready for human consumption, which is of the type described in subclause (i), and which is offered for sale to consumers but not for immediate human consumption in such establishment and which is not offered for sale outside such establishment,

(iii) which is an infant formula subject to section 350a of this title,

(iv) which is a medical food as defined in section 360ee(b) of this title, or

(v) which is described in section 345(2) of this title.

(B) Subparagraphs (1) and (2) shall not apply to the label of a food if the Secretary determines by regulations that compliance with such subparagraphs is impracticable because the package of such food is too small to comply with the requirements of such subparagraphs and if the label of such food does not contain any nutrition information.

(C) If a food contains insignificant amounts, as determined by the Secretary, of all the nutrients required by subparagraphs (1) and (2) to be listed in the label or labeling of food, the requirements of such subparagraphs shall not apply to such food if the label, labeling, or advertising of such food does not make any claim with respect to the nutritional value of such food. If a food contains insignificant amounts, as determined by the Secretary, of more than one-half the nutrients required by subparagraphs (1) and (2) to be in the label or labeling of the food, the Secretary shall require the amounts of such nutrients to be stated in a simplified form prescribed by the Secretary.

(D) If a person offers food for sale and has annual gross sales made or business done in sales to consumers which is not more than $500,000 or has annual gross sales made or business done in sales of food to consumers which is not more than $50,000, the requirements of subparagraphs (1), (2), (3), and (4) shall not apply with respect to food sold by such person to consumers unless the label or labeling of food offered by such person provides nutrition information or makes a nutrition claim.

(E)(i) During the 12–month period for which an exemption from subparagraphs (1) and (2) is claimed pursuant to this subclause, the requirements of such subparagraphs shall not apply to any food product if—

(I) the labeling for such product does not provide nutrition information or make a claim subject to paragraph (r),

(II) the person who claims for such product an exemption from such subparagraphs employed fewer than an average of 100 full-time equivalent employees,

(III) such person provided the notice described in subclause (iii), and

(IV) in the case of a food product which was sold in the 12–month period preceding the period for which an exemption was claimed, fewer than 100,000 units of such product were sold in the United States during such preceding period, or in the case of a food product which was not sold in the 12–month period preceding the period for which such exemption is claimed, fewer than 100,000 units of such product are reasonably anticipated to be sold in the United States during the period for which such exemption is claimed.

(ii) During the 12–month period after the applicable date referred to in this sentence, the requirements of subparagraphs (1) and (2) shall not apply to any food product which was first introduced into interstate commerce before May 8, 1994, if the labeling for such product does not provide nutrition information or make a claim subject to paragraph (r), if such person provided the notice described in subclause (iii), and if—

(I) during the 12–month period preceding May 8, 1994, the person who claims for such product an exemption from such subparagraphs employed fewer than an average of 300 full-time equivalent employees and fewer than 600,000 units of such product were sold in the United States,

(II) during the 12–month period preceding May 8, 1995, the person who claims for such product an exemption from such subparagraphs employed fewer than an average of 300 full-time equivalent employees and fewer than 400,000 units of such product were sold in the United States, or

(III) during the 12–month period preceding May 8, 1996, the person who claims for such product an exemption from such subparagraphs employed fewer than an average of 200 full-time equivalent employees and fewer than 200,000 units of such product were sold in the United States.

(iii) The notice referred to in subclauses (i) and (ii) shall be given to the Secretary prior to the beginning of the period during which the exemption under subclause (i) or (ii) is to be in effect, shall state that the person claiming such exemption for a food product has complied with the applicable requirements of subclause (i) or (ii), and shall—

(I) state the average number of full-time equivalent employees such person employed during the 12 months preceding the date such person claims such exemption,

(II) state the approximate number of units the person claiming the exemption sold in the United States,

(III) if the exemption is claimed for a food product which was sold in the 12–month period preceding the period for which the exemption was claimed, state the approximate number of units of such product which were sold in the United States during such preceding period, and, if the exemption is claimed for a food product which was not sold in such preceding period, state the number of units of such product which such person reasonably anticipates will be sold in the United States during the period for which the exemption was claimed, and

(IV) contain such information as the Secretary may require to verify the information required by the preceding provisions of this subclause if the Secretary has questioned the validity of such information.

If a person is not an importer, has fewer than 10 full-time equivalent employees, and sells fewer than 10,000 units of any food product in any year, such person is not required to file a notice for such product under this subclause for such year.

(iv) In the case of a person who claimed an exemption under subclause (i) or (ii), if, during the period of such exemption, the number of full-time equivalent employees of such person exceeds the number in such subclause or if the number of food products sold in the United States exceeds the number in such subclause, such exemption shall extend to the expiration of 18 months after the date the number of full-time equivalent employees or food products sold exceeded the applicable number.

(v) For any food product first introduced into interstate commerce after May 8, 2002, the Secretary may by regulation lower the employee or units of food products requirement of subclause (i) if the Secretary determines that the cost of compliance with such lower requirement will not place an undue burden on persons subject to such lower requirement.

(vi) For purposes of subclauses (i), (ii), (iii), (iv), and (v)—

(I) the term "unit" means the packaging or, if there is no packaging, the form in which a food product is offered for sale to consumers,

(II) the term "food product" means food in any sized package which is manufactured by a single manufacturer or which bears the same brand name, which bears the same statement of identity, and which has similar preparation methods, and

(III) the term "person" in the case of a corporation includes all domestic and foreign affiliates of the corporation.

(F) A dietary supplement product (including a food to which section 350 of this title applies) shall comply with the requirements of subparagraphs (1) and (2) in a manner which is appropriate for the product and which is specified in regulations of the Secretary which shall provide that—

(i) nutrition information shall first list those dietary ingredients that are present in the product in a significant amount and for which a recommendation for daily consumption has been established by the Secretary, except that a dietary ingredient shall not be required to be listed if it is not present in a significant amount, and shall list any other dietary ingredient present and identified as having no such recommendation;

(ii) the listing of dietary ingredients shall include the quantity of each such ingredient (or of a proprietary blend of such ingredients) per serving;

(iii) the listing of dietary ingredients may include the source of a dietary ingredient; and

(iv) the nutrition information shall immediately precede the ingredient information required under subclause (i), except that no ingredient identified pursuant to subclause (i) shall be required to be identified a second time.

(G) Subparagraphs (1), (2), (3), and (4) shall not apply to food which is sold by a food distributor if the food distributor principally sells food to restaurants or other establishments in which food is served for immediate human consumption and does not manufacture, process, or repackage the food it sells.

(r) Nutrition levels and health-related claims

(1) Except as provided in clauses (A) through (C) of subparagraph (5), if it is a food intended for human consumption which is offered for

sale and for which a claim is made in the label or labeling of the food which expressly or by implication—

(A) characterizes the level of any nutrient which is of the type required by paragraph (q)(1) or (q)(2) to be in the label or labeling of the food unless the claim is made in accordance with subparagraph (2), or

(B) characterizes the relationship of any nutrient which is of the type required by subsec. (q)(1) or (q)(2) of this section to be in the label or labeling of the food to a disease or a health-related condition unless the claim is made in accordance with subparagraph (3) or (5)(D).

A statement of the type required by subsec. (q) of this section that appears as part of the nutrition information required or permitted by such paragraph is not a claim which is subject to this paragraph and a claim subject to clause (A) is not subject to clause (B).

(2)(A) Except as provided in subparagraphs (4)(A)(ii) and (4)(A)(iii) and clauses (A) through (C) of subparagraph (5), a claim described in subparagraph (1)(A)—

(i) may be made only if the characterization of the level made in the claim uses terms which are defined in regulations of the Secretary,

(ii) may not state the absence of a nutrient unless—

(I) the nutrient is usually present in the food or in a food which substitutes for the food as defined by the Secretary by regulation, or

(II) the Secretary by regulation permits such a statement on the basis of a finding that such a statement would assist consumers in maintaining healthy dietary practices and the statement discloses that the nutrient is not usually present in the food,

(iii) may not be made with respect to the level of cholesterol in the food if the food contains, as determined by the Secretary by regulation, fat or saturated fat in an amount which increases to persons in the general population the risk of disease or a health related condition which is diet related unless—

(I) the Secretary finds by regulation that the level of cholesterol is substantially less than the level usually present in the food or in a food which substitutes for the food and which has a significant market share, or the Secretary by regulation permits a statement regarding the absence of cholesterol on the basis of a finding that cholesterol is not usually present in the food and that such a statement would assist consumers in maintaining healthy dietary practices and the regulation requires that the statement disclose that cholesterol is not usually present in the food, and

(II) the label or labeling of the food discloses the level of such fat or saturated fat in immediate proximity to such claim and with appropriate prominence which shall be no less than one-half the size of the claim with respect to the level of cholesterol,

(iv) may not be made with respect to the level of saturated fat in the food if the food contains cholesterol unless the label or labeling of the food discloses the level of cholesterol in the food in immediate proximity to such claim and with appropriate prominence which shall be no less than one-half the size of the claim with respect to the level of saturated fat,

(v) may not state that a food is high in dietary fiber unless the food is low in total fat as defined by the Secretary or the label or labeling discloses the level of total fat in the food in immediate proximity to such statement and with appropriate prominence which shall be no less than one- half the size of the claim with respect to the level of dietary fiber, and

(vi) may not be made if the Secretary by regulation prohibits the claim because the claim is misleading in light of the level of another nutrient in the food.

(B) If a claim described in subparagraph (1)(A) is made with respect to a nutrient in a food, the label or labeling of such food shall contain, prominently and in immediate proximity to such claim, the following statement: "See _____ for nutrition information.". In the statement—

(i) the blank shall identify the panel on which the information described in the statement may be found, and

(ii) if the Secretary determines that the food contains a nutrient at a level which increases to persons in the general population the risk of a disease or health-related condition which is diet related, taking into account the significance of the food in the total daily diet, the statement shall also identify such nutrient.

(C) Subparagraph (2)(A) does not apply to a claim described in subparagraph (1)(A) and contained in the label or labeling of a food if such claim is contained in the brand name of such food and such brand name was in use on such food before October 25, 1989, unless the brand name contains a term defined by the Secretary under subparagraph (2)(A)(i). Such a claim is subject to paragraph (a).

(D) Subparagraph (2) does not apply to a claim described in subparagraph (1)(A) which uses the term "diet" and is contained in the label or labeling of a soft drink if (i) such claim is contained in the brand name of such soft drink, (ii) such brand name was in use on such soft drink before October 25, 1989, and (iii) the use of the term "diet" was in conformity with section 105.66 of title 21 of the Code of Federal Regulations. Such a claim is subject to paragraph (a).

(E) Subclauses (i) through (v) of subparagraph (2)(A) do not apply to a statement in the label or labeling of food which describes the percentage of vitamins and minerals in the food in relation to the amount of such vitamins and minerals recommended for daily consumption by the Secretary.

(F) Subclause (i) clause (A) does not apply to a statement in the labeling of a dietary supplement that characterizes the percentage level of a dietary ingredient for which the Secretary has not established a reference daily intake, daily recommended value, or other recommendation for daily consumption.

(3)(A) Except as provided in subparagraph (5), a claim described in subparagraph (1)(B) may only be made—

(i) if the claim meets the requirements of the regulations of the Secretary promulgated under clause (B), and

(ii) if the food for which the claim is made does not contain, as determined by the Secretary by regulation, any nutrient in an amount which increases to persons in the general population the risk of a disease or health-related condition which is diet related, taking into account the significance of the food in the total daily diet, except that the Secretary may by regulation permit such a claim based on a finding that such a claim would assist consumers in maintaining healthy dietary practices and based on a requirement that the label contain a disclosure of the type required by subparagraph (2)(B).

(B)(i) The Secretary shall promulgate regulations authorizing claims of the type described in subparagraph (1)(B) only if the Secretary determines, based on the totality of publicly available scientific evidence (including evidence from well-designed studies conducted in a manner which is consistent with generally recognized scientific procedures and principles), that there is significant scientific agreement, among experts qualified by scientific training and experience to evaluate such claims, that the claim is supported by such evidence.

(ii) A regulation described in subclause (i) shall describe—

(I) the relationship between a nutrient of the type required in the label or labeling of food by paragraph (q)(1) or (q)(2) and a disease or health- related condition, and

(II) the significance of each such nutrient in affecting such disease or health-related condition.

(iii) A regulation described in subclause (i) shall require such claim to be stated in a manner so that the claim is an accurate representation of the matters set out in subclause (ii) and so that the claim enables the public to comprehend the information provided in the claim and to understand the relative significance of such information in the context of a total daily diet.

(4)(A)(i) Any person may petition the Secretary to issue a regulation under subparagraph (2)(A)(i) or (3)(B) relating to a claim described in subparagraph (1)(A) or (1)(B). Not later than 100 days after the petition is received by the Secretary, the Secretary shall issue a final decision denying the petition or file the petition for further action by the Secretary. If the Secretary denies the petition, the petition shall not be made available to the public. If the Secretary files the petition, the Secretary shall deny the petition or issue a proposed regulation to take the action requested in the petition not later than 90 days after the date of such decision.

(ii) Any person may petition the Secretary for permission to use in a claim described in subparagraph (1)(A) terms that are consistent with the terms defined by the Secretary under subparagraph (2)(A)(i). Within 90 days of the submission of such a petition, the Secretary shall issue a final decision denying the petition or granting such permission.

(iii) Any person may petition the Secretary for permission to use an implied claim described in subparagraph (1)(A) in a brand name. After publishing notice of an opportunity to comment on the petition in the Federal Register and making the petition available to the public, the Secretary shall grant the petition if the Secretary finds that such claim is not misleading and is consistent with terms defined by the Secretary under subparagraph (2)(A)(i). The Secretary shall grant or deny the petition within 100 days of the date it is submitted to the Secretary and the petition shall be considered granted if the Secretary does not act on it within such 100 days.

(B) A petition under clause (A)(i) respecting a claim described in subparagraph (1)(A) or (1)(B) shall include an explanation of the reasons why the claim meets the requirements of this paragraph and a summary of the scientific data which supports such reasons.

(C) If a petition for a regulation under subparagraph (3)(B) relies on a report from an authoritative scientific body of the United States, the Secretary shall consider such report and shall justify any decision rejecting the conclusions of such report.

(5)(A) This paragraph does not apply to infant formulas subject to section 350a(h) of this title and medical foods as defined in section 360ee(b) of this title.

(B) Subclauses (iii) through (v) of subparagraph (2)(A) and subparagraph (2)(B) do not apply to food which is served in restaurants or other establishments in which food is served for immediate human consumption or which is sold for sale or use in such establishments.

(C) A subparagraph (1)(A) claim made with respect to a food which claim is required by a standard of identity issued under section 341 of this title shall not be subject to subparagraph (2)(A)(i) or (2)(B).

(D) A subparagraph (1)(B) claim made with respect to a dietary supplement of vitamins, minerals, herbs, or other similar nutritional substances shall not be subject to subparagraph (3) but shall be subject to a procedure and standard, respecting the validity of such claim, established by regulation of the Secretary.

(6) For purposes of paragraph (r)(1)(B), a statement for a dietary supplement may be made if—

 (A) the statement claims a benefit related to a classical nutrient deficiency disease and discloses the prevalence of such disease in the United States, describes the role of a nutrient or dietary ingredient intended to affect the structure or function in humans, characterizes the documented mechanism by which a nutrient or dietary ingredient acts to maintain such structure or function, or describes general well-being from consumption of a nutrient or dietary ingredient,

 (B) the manufacturer of the dietary supplement has substantiation that such statement is truthful and not misleading, and

 (C) the statement contains, prominently displayed and in boldface type, the following: "This statement has not been evaluated by the Food and Drug Administration. This product is not intended to diagnose, treat, cure, or prevent any disease.".

A statement under this subparagraph may not claim to diagnose, mitigate, treat, cure, or prevent a specific disease or class of diseases. If the manufacturer of a dietary supplement proposes to make a statement described in the first sentence of this subparagraph in the labeling of the dietary supplement, the manufacturer shall notify the Secretary no later than 30 days after the first marketing of the dietary supplement with such statement that such a statement is being made.

(s) Dietary supplements

 If—

 (1) it is a dietary supplement; and

 (2)(A) the label or labeling of the supplement fails to list—

  (i) the name of each ingredient of the supplement that is described in section 321(ff) of this title; and

  (ii)(I) the quantity of each such ingredient; or

  (II) with respect to a proprietary blend of such ingredients, the total quantity of all ingredients in the blend;

 (B) the label or labeling of the dietary supplement fails to identify the product by using the term "dietary supplement", which term may be modified with the name of such an ingredient;

(C) the supplement contains an ingredient described in section 321(ff)(1)(C) of this title, and the label or labeling of the supplement fails to identify any part of the plant from which the ingredient is derived;

(D) the supplement—

(i) is covered by the specifications of an official compendium;

(ii) is represented as conforming to the specifications of an official compendium; and

(iii) fails to so conform; or

(E) the supplement—

(i) is not covered by the specifications of an official compendium; and

(ii)(I) fails to have the identity and strength that the supplement is represented to have; or

(II) fails to meet the quality (including tablet or capsule disintegration), purity, or compositional specifications, based on validated assay or other appropriate methods, that the supplement is represented to meet.

A dietary supplement shall not be deemed misbranded solely because its label or labeling contains directions or conditions of use or warnings.

§ 343–1. National uniform nutrition labeling; State prohibitions and exemptions

(a) Except as provided in subsection (b) of this section, no State or political subdivision of a State may directly or indirectly establish under any authority or continue in effect as to any food in interstate commerce—

(1) any requirement for a food which is the subject of a standard of identity established under section 341 of this title that is not identical to such standard of identity or that is not identical to the requirement of section 343(g) of this title, except that this paragraph does not apply to a standard of identity of a State or political subdivision of a State for maple syrup that is of the type required by sections 341 and 343(g) of this title,

(2) any requirement for the labeling of food of the type required by section 343(c), 343(e) or 343(i)(2) of this title that is not identical to the requirement of such section, except that this paragraph does not apply to a requirement of a State or political subdivision of a State that is of the type required by section 343(c) of this title and that is applicable to maple syrup,

(3) any requirement for the labeling of food of the type required by section 343(b), (d), (f), (h), (i)(1) or (k) of this title that is not identical to the requirement of such section, except that this paragraph does not apply to a requirement of a State or political

subdivision of a State that is of the type required by section 343(h)(1) of this title and that is applicable to maple syrup,

(4) any requirement for nutrition labeling of food that is not identical to the requirement of section 343(q) of this title, except a requirement for nutrition labeling of food which is exempt under subclause (i) or (ii) of section 343(q)(5)(A) of this title, or

(5) any requirement respecting any claim of the type described in section 343(r)(1) of this title, made in the label or labeling of food that is not identical to the requirement of section 343(r) of this title, except a requirement respecting a claim made in the label or labeling of food which is exempt under section 343(r)(5)(B) of this title.

Paragraph (3) shall take effect in accordance with section 6(b) of the Nutrition Labeling and Education Act of 1990.

(b) Upon petition of a State or a political subdivision of a State, the Secretary may exempt from subsection (a) of this section, under such conditions as may be prescribed by regulation, any State or local requirement that—

(1) would not cause any food to be in violation of any applicable requirement under Federal law,

(2) would not unduly burden interstate commerce, and

(3) is designed to address a particular need for information which need is not met by the requirements of the sections referred to in subsection (a) of this section.

§ 343–2.   Dietary supplement labeling exemptions

(a) In general

A publication, including an article, a chapter in a book, or an official abstract of a peer-reviewed scientific publication that appears in an article and was prepared by the author or the editors of the publication, which is reprinted in its entirety, shall not be defined as labeling when used in connection with the sale of a dietary supplement to consumers when it—

(1) is not false or misleading;

(2) does not promote a particular manufacturer or brand of a dietary supplement;

(3) is displayed or presented, or is displayed or presented with other such items on the same subject matter, so as to present a balanced view of the available scientific information on a dietary supplement;

(4) if displayed in an establishment, is physically separate from the dietary supplements; and

(5) does not have appended to it any information by sticker or any other method.

(b) Application

Subsection (a) of this section shall not apply to or restrict a retailer or wholesaler of dietary supplements in any way whatsoever in the sale of books or other publications as a part of the business of such retailer or wholesaler.

(c) Burden of proof

In any proceeding brought under subsection (a) of this section, the burden of proof shall be on the United States to establish that an article or other such matter is false or misleading.

§ 343a. Health risks presented by use of saccharin

(a) Statement on vending machines dispensing food containing saccharin respecting health risk; regulations

The Secretary may by regulation require vending machines through which food containing saccharin is sold to bear a statement of the risks to health which may be presented by the use of saccharin. A regulation under this subsection shall require such statement to be located in a conspicuous place on such vending machine and as proximate as possible to the name of each food containing saccharin which is sold through such machine. Any food containing saccharin which is sold in a vending machine which does not meet any applicable requirement promulgated under this subsection shall, for purposes of this chapter, be considered a misbranded food.

(b) Availability and distribution of information; review and revision

The Secretary shall (1) prepare information respecting the nature of the controversy surrounding the use of food containing saccharin, and (2) provide for the distribution of such information for display by retail establishments where such food is sold but not for immediate consumption. The Secretary may review and revise such information if he determines such action is necessary to reflect the current state of knowledge concerning the risks to health presented by the use of saccharin.

§ 344. Emergency permit control

(a) Conditions on manufacturing, processing, etc., as health measure

Whenever the Secretary finds after investigation that the distribution in interstate commerce of any class of food may, by reason of contamination with micro-organisms during the manufacture, processing, or packing thereof in any locality, be injurious to health, and that such injurious nature cannot be adequately determined after such articles have entered interstate commerce, he then, and in such case only,

57

shall promulgate regulations providing for the issuance, to manufacturers, processors, or packers of such class of food in such locality, of permits to which shall be attached such conditions governing the manufacture, processing, or packing of such class of food, for such temporary period of time, as may be necessary to protect the public health; and after the effective date of such regulations, and during such temporary period, no person shall introduce or deliver for introduction into interstate commerce any such food manufactured, processed, or packed by any such manufacturer, processor, or packer unless such manufacturer, processor, or packer holds a permit issued by the Secretary as provided by such regulations.

(b) Violation of permit; suspension and reinstatement

The Secretary is authorized to suspend immediately upon notice any permit issued under authority of this section if it is found that any of the conditions of the permit have been violated. The holder of a permit so suspended shall be privileged at any time to apply for the reinstatement of such permit, and the Secretary shall, immediately after prompt hearing and an inspection of the establishment, reinstate such permit if it is found that adequate measures have been taken to comply with and maintain the conditions of the permit, as originally issued or as amended.

(c) Inspection of permit-holding establishments

Any officer or employee duly designated by the Secretary shall have access to any factory or establishment, the operator of which holds a permit from the Secretary, for the purpose of ascertaining whether or not the conditions of the permit are being complied with, and denial of access for such inspection shall be ground for suspension of the permit until such access is freely given by the operator.

§ 345. Regulations making exemptions

The Secretary shall promulgate regulations exempting from any labeling requirement of this chapter (1) small open containers of fresh fruits and fresh vegetables and (2) food which is, in accordance with the practice of the trade, to be processed, labeled, or repacked in substantial quantities at establishments other than those where originally processed or packed, on condition that such food is not adulterated or misbranded under the provisions of this chapter upon removal from such processing, labeling, or repacking establishment. This section does not apply to the labeling requirements of sections 343(q) and 343(r) of this title.

§ 346. Tolerances for poisonous or deleterious substances in food; regulations

Any poisonous or deleterious substance added to any food, except where such substance is required in the production thereof or cannot be avoided by good manufacturing practice shall be deemed to be unsafe for purposes of the application of clause (2)(A) of section 342(a) of this title; but when such substance is so required or cannot be so avoided, the Secretary shall promulgate regulations limiting the quantity therein or thereon to such extent as he finds necessary for the protection of public health, and any quantity exceeding the limits so fixed shall also be deemed to be unsafe for purposes of the application of clause (2)(A) of section 342(a) of this title. While such a regulation is in effect limiting the quantity of any such substance in the case of any food, such food shall not, by reason of bearing or containing any added amount of such substance, be considered to be adulterated within the meaning of clause (1) of section 342(a) of this title. In determining the quantity of such added substance to be tolerated in or on different articles of food the Secretary shall take into account the extent to which the use of such substance is required or cannot be avoided in the production of each such article, and the other ways in which the consumer may be affected by the same or other poisonous or deleterious substances.

§ 346a. Tolerances for pesticide chemicals in or on raw agricultural commodities

(a) Conditions of safety

Any poisonous or deleterious pesticide chemical, or any pesticide chemical which is not generally recognized, among experts qualified by scientific training and experience to evaluate the safety of pesticide chemicals, as safe for use, added to a raw agricultural commodity, shall be deemed unsafe for the purposes of the application of clause (2) of section 342(a) of this title unless—

(1) a tolerance for such pesticide chemical in or on the raw agricultural commodity has been prescribed by the Administrator of the Environmental Protection Agency (hereinafter in this section referred to as the "Administrator") under this section and the quantity of such pesticide chemical in or on the raw agricultural commodity is within the limits of the tolerance so prescribed; or

(2) with respect to use in or on such raw agricultural commodity, the pesticide chemical has been exempted from the requirement of a tolerance by the Administrator under this section.

While a tolerance or exemption from tolerance is in effect for a pesticide chemical with respect to any raw agricultural commodity, such raw agricultural commodity shall not, by reason of bearing or containing any added amount of such pesticide chemical, be considered to be adulterated within the meaning of clause (1) of section 342(a) of this title.

(b) Establishment of tolerances

The Administrator shall promulgate regulations establishing tolerances with respect to the use or on raw agricultural commodities of poisonous or deleterious pesticide chemicals and of pesticide chemicals which are not generally recognized, among experts qualified by scientific training and experience to evaluate the safety of pesticide chemicals, as safe for use, to the extent necessary to protect the public health. In establishing any such regulation, the Administrator shall give appropriate consideration, among other relevant factors, (1) to the necessity for the production of an adequate, wholesome, and economical food supply; (2) to the other ways in which the consumer may be affected by the same pesticide chemical or by other related substances that are poisonous or deleterious; and (3) to the opinion submitted with a certification of usefulness under subsection (*l*)f this section. Such regulations shall be promulgated in the manner prescribed in subsection (d) or (e) of this section. In carrying out the provisions of this section relating to the establishment of tolerances, the Administrator may establish the tolerance applicable with respect to the use of any pesticide chemical in or on any raw agricultural commodity at zero level if the scientific data before the Administrator does not justify the establishment of a greater tolerance.

(c) Exemptions

The Administrator shall promulgate regulations exempting any pesticide chemical from the necessity of a tolerance with respect to use in or on any or all raw agricultural commodities when such a tolerance is not necessary to protect the public health. Such regulations shall be promulgated in the manner prescribed in subsection (d) or (e) of this section.

(d) Regulations pursuant to petition; publication of notice; time for issuance; referral to advisory committees; effective date; hearings

(1) Any person who has registered, or who has submitted an application for the registration of, a pesticide under the Federal Insecticide, Fungicide, and Rodenticide Act [7 U.S.C.A. § 136 et seq.] may file with the Administrator a petition proposing the issuance of a regulation establishing a tolerance for a pesticide chemical which constitutes, or is an ingredient of, such pesticide, or exempting the pesticide chemical from the requirement of a tolerance. The petition shall contain data showing—

(A) the name, chemical identity, and composition of the pesticide chemical;

(B) the amount, frequency, and time of application of the pesticide chemical;

(C) full reports of investigations made with respect to the safety of the pesticide chemical;

(D) the results of tests on the amount of residue remaining, including a description of the analytical methods used;

(E) practicable methods for removing residue which exceeds any proposed tolerance;

(F) proposed tolerances for the pesticide chemical if tolerances are proposed; and

(G) reasonable grounds in support of the petition.

Samples of the pesticide chemical shall be furnished to the Administrator upon request. Notice of the filing of such petition shall be published in general terms by the Administrator within thirty days after filing. Such notice shall include the analytical methods available for the determination of the residue of the pesticide chemical for which a tolerance or exemption is proposed.

(2) Within ninety days after a certification of usefulness under subsection (*l*)f this section with respect to the pesticide chemical named in the petition, the Administrator shall, after giving due consideration to the data submitted in the petition or otherwise before him, by order make public a regulation—

(A) establishing a tolerance for the pesticide chemical named in the petition for the purposes for which it is so certified as useful, or

(B) exempting the pesticide chemical from the necessity of a tolerance for such purposes,

unless within such ninety-day period the person filing the petition requests that the petition be referred to an advisory committee or the Administrator within such period otherwise deems such referral necessary, in either of which events the provisions of paragraph (3) of this subsection shall apply in lieu hereof.

(3) In the event that the person filing the petition requests, within ninety days after a certification of usefulness under subsection (*l*)f this section with respect to the pesticide chemical named in the petition, that the petition be referred to an advisory committee, or in the event the Administrator within such period otherwise deems such referral necessary, the Administrator shall forthwith submit the petition and other data before him to an advisory committee to be appointed in accordance with subsection (g) of this section. As soon as practicable after such referral, but not later than sixty days thereafter, unless extended as hereinafter provided, the committee shall, after independent study of the data submitted to it by the Administrator and other data before it, certify to the Administrator a report and recommendations on the proposal in the petition to the Administrator, together with all underlying data and a statement of the reasons or basis for the recommendations. The sixty-day period provided for herein may be extended by the advisory committee for an additional thirty days if the advisory committee deems this necessary. Within thirty days after such certification, the Administrator shall, after giving due consideration to all data then

before him, including such report, recommendations, underlying data, and statement, by order make public a regulation—

(A) establishing a tolerance for the pesticide chemical named in the petition for the purposes for which it is so certified as useful; or

(B) exempting the pesticide chemical from the necessity of a tolerance for such purposes.

(4) The regulations published under paragraph (2) or (3) of this subsection will be effective upon publication.

(5) Within thirty days after publication, any person adversely affected by a regulation published pursuant to paragraph (2) or (3) of this subsection, or pursuant to subsection (e) of this section, may file objections thereto with the Administrator, specifying with particularity the provisions of the regulation deemed objectionable, stating reasonable grounds therefor, and requesting a public hearing upon such objections. A copy of the objections filed by a person other than the petitioner shall be served on the petitioner, if the regulation was issued pursuant to a petition. The petitioner shall have two weeks to make a written reply to the objections. The Administrator shall thereupon, after due notice, hold such public hearing for the purpose of receiving evidence relevant and material to the issues raised by such objections. Any report, recommendations, underlying data, and reasons certified to the Administrator by an advisory committee shall be made a part of the record of the hearing, if relevant and material, subject to the provisions of section 556(c) of Title 5. The National Academy of Sciences shall designate a member of the advisory committee to appear and testify at any such hearing with respect to the report and recommendations of such committee upon request of the Administrator, the petitioner, or the officer conducting the hearing: Provided, That this shall not preclude any other member of the advisory committee from appearing and testifying at such hearing. As soon as practicable after completion of the hearing, the Administrator shall act upon such objections and by order made public a regulation. Such regulation shall be based only on substantial evidence of record at such hearing, including any report, recommendations, underlying data, and reasons certified to the Administrator by an advisory committee, and shall set forth detailed findings of fact upon which the regulation is based. No such order shall take effect prior to the ninetieth day after its publication, unless the Administrator finds that emergency conditions exist necessitating an earlier effective date, in which event the Administrator shall specify in the order his findings as to such conditions.

(e) Regulations pursuant to Administrator's proposals

The Administrator may at any time, upon his own initiative or upon the request of any interested person, propose the issuance of a regulation establishing a tolerance for a pesticide chemical or exempting it from the necessity of a tolerance. Thirty days after publication of such a proposal, the Administrator may by order publish a regulation based upon the proposal which shall become effective upon publication unless within such thirty-day period a person who has registered, or who has submitted an application for the registration of, a pesticide under the Federal Insecticide, Fungicide, and Rodenticide Act containing the pesticide chemical named in the proposal, requests that the proposal be referred to an advisory committee. In the event of such a request, the Administrator shall forthwith submit the proposal and other relevant data before him to an advisory committee to be appointed in accordance with subsection (g) of this section. As soon as practicable after such referral, but not later than sixty days thereafter, unless extended as hereinafter provided, the committee shall, after independent study of the data submitted to it by the Administrator and other data before it, certify to the Administrator a report and recommendations on the proposal together with all underlying data and a statement of the reasons or basis for the recommendations. The sixty-day period provided for herein may be extended by the advisory committee for an additional thirty days if the advisory committee deems this necessary. Within thirty days after such certification, the Administrator may, after giving due consideration to all data before him, including such report, recommendations, underlying data and statement, by order publish a regulation establishing a tolerance for the pesticide chemical named in the proposal or exempting it from the necessity of a tolerance which shall become effective upon publication. Regulations issued under this subsection shall upon publication be subject to paragraph (5) of subsection (d) of this section.

(f) Data submitted as confidential

All data submitted to the Administrator or to an advisory committee in support of a petition under this section shall be considered confidential by the Administrator and by such advisory committee until publication of a regulation under paragraph (2) or (3) of subsection (d) of this section. Until such publication, such data shall not be revealed to any person other than those authorized by the Administrator or by an advisory committee in the carrying out of their official duties under this section.

(g) Advisory committees; appointment; composition; compensation; clerical assistance

Whenever the referral of a petition or proposal to an advisory committee is requested under this section, or the Administrator otherwise deems such referral necessary the Administrator shall forthwith appoint a committee of competent experts to review the petition or proposal and to make a report and recommendations thereon. Each such advisory committee shall be composed of experts, qualified in the subject matter of the petition and of adequately diversified professional background selected by the National Academy of Sciences and shall include one or more representatives from land-grant colleges. The size of the committee shall be determined by the Administrator. Members of an advisory committee shall receive compensation and travel expenses in accordance with section 379e(b)(5)(D) of this title. The members shall not be subject to any other provisions of law regarding the appointment and compensation of employees of the United States. The Administrator shall furnish the committee with adequate clerical and other assistance, and shall by rules and regulations prescribe the procedure to be followed by the committee.

(h) Right of consultation

A person who has filed a petition or who has requested the referral of a proposal to an advisory committee in accordance with the provisions of this section, as well as representatives of the Environmental Protection Agency, shall have the right to consult with any advisory committee provided for in subsection (g) of this section in connection with the petition or proposal.

(i) Judicial review

(1) In a case of actual controversy as to the validity of any order under subsection (d)(5), (e), or (*l*)f this section any person who will be adversely affected by such order may obtain judicial review by filing in the United States Court of Appeals for the circuit wherein such person resides or has his principal place of business, or in the United States Court of Appeals for the District of Columbia Circuit, within sixty days after the entry of such order, a petition praying that the order be set aside in whole or in part.

(2) In the case of a petition with respect to an order under subsection (d)(5) or (e) of this section, a copy of the petition shall be forthwith transmitted by the clerk of the court to the Administrator, or any officer designated by him for that purpose, and thereupon the Administrator shall file in the court the record of the proceedings on which he based his order, as provided in section 2112 of Title 28. Upon the filing of such petition, the court shall have exclusive jurisdiction to affirm or set aside the order complained of in whole or in part. The findings of the Administrator with respect to questions of fact shall be sustained if supported by substantial evidence when considered on the record as a whole, including any report and recommendation of an advisory committee.

(3) In the case of a petition with respect to an order under subsection (*l*)f this section, a copy of the petition shall be forthwith transmitted by the clerk of the court to the Administrator, or any officer designated by him for that purpose, and thereupon the Administrator shall file in the court the record of the proceedings on which he based his order, as provided in section 2112 of Title 28. Upon the filing of such petition, the court shall have exclusive jurisdiction to affirm or set aside the order complained of· in whole or in part. The findings of the Administrator with respect to questions of fact shall be sustained if supported by substantial evidence when considered on the record as a whole.

(4) If application is made to the court for leave to adduce additional evidence, the court may order such additional evidence to be taken before the Administrator and to be adduced upon the hearing in such manner and upon such terms and conditions as to the court may seem proper, if such evidence is material and there were reasonable grounds for failure to adduce such evidence in the proceedings below. The Administrator may modify his findings as to the facts and order by reason of the additional evidence so taken, and shall file with the court such modified findings and order.

(5) The judgment of the court affirming or setting aside, in whole or in part, any order under this section shall be final, subject to review by the Supreme Court of the United States upon certiorari or certification as provided in section 1254 of Title 28. The commencement of proceedings under this section shall not, unless specifically ordered by the court to the contrary, operate as a stay of an order.

(j) Temporary tolerances

The Administrator may, upon the request of any person who has obtained an experimental permit for a pesticide chemical under the Federal Insecticide, Fungicide, and Rodenticide Act or upon his own initiative, establish a temporary tolerance for the pesticide chemical for the uses covered by the permit whenever in his judgment such action is deemed necessary to protect the public health, or may temporarily exempt such pesticide chemical from a tolerance. In establishing such a tolerance, the Administrator shall give due regard to the necessity for experimental work in developing an adequate, wholesome, and economical food supply and to the limited hazard to the public health involved in such work when conducted in accordance with applicable regulations under the Federal Insecticide, Fungicide, and Rodenticide Act.

(k) Regulations based on public hearings before January 1, 1953

Regulations affecting pesticide chemicals in or on raw agricultural commodities which are promulgated under the authority of section 346(a) of this title upon the basis of public hearings instituted before January 1, 1953, in accordance with section 371(a) of this title, shall be deemed to be regulations under this section and shall be subject to amendment or repeal as provided in subsection (m) of this section.

(l) Pesticides under Federal Insecticide, Fungicide, and Rodenticide Act; functions of Administrator of the Environmental Protection Agency; certifications; hearing; time limitation; opinion; regulations

The Administrator, upon request of any person who has registered, or who has submitted an application for the registration of, a pesticide under the Federal Insecticide, Fungicide, and Rodenticide Act [7 U.S.C.A. § 136 et seq.], and whose request is accompanied by a copy of a petition filed by such person under subsection (d)(1) of this section with respect to a pesticide chemical which constitutes, or is an ingredient of, such pesticide, shall, within thirty days or within sixty days if upon notice prior to the termination of such thirty days the Administrator deems it necessary to postpone action for such period, on the basis of data before him, either—

(1) certify that such pesticide chemical is useful for the purpose for which a tolerance or exemption is sought; or

(2) notify the person requesting the certification of his proposal to certify that the pesticide chemical does not appear to be useful for the purpose for which a tolerance or exemption is sought, or appears to be useful for only some of the purposes for which a tolerance or exemption is sought.

In the event that the Administrator takes the action described in clause (2) of the preceding sentence, the person requesting the certification, within one week after receiving the proposed certification, may either (A) request the Administrator to certify on the basis of the proposed certification; (B) request a hearing on the proposed certification or the parts thereof objected to; or (C) request both such certification and such hearing. If no such action is taken, the Administrator may by order make the certification as proposed. In the event that the action described in clause (A) or (C) is taken, the Administrator shall by order make the certification as proposed with respect to such parts thereof as are requested. In the event a hearing is requested, the Administrator shall provide opportunity for a prompt hearing. The certification of the Administrator as the result of such hearing shall be made by order and shall be based only on substantial evidence of record at the hearing and shall set forth detailed findings of fact. In no event shall the time elapsing between the making of a request for a certification under this subsection and final certification by the Administrator exceed one hundred and sixty days. The Administrator shall submit with any certification of usefulness under this subsection an opinion, based on the data before him, whether the tolerance or exemption proposed by the petitioner reasonably reflects the amount of residue likely to result when the pesticide chemical is used in the manner proposed for the purpose for which the certification is made. The Administrator, after due notice and opportunity for public hearing, is authorized to promulgate rules and regulations for carrying out the provisions of this subsection.

(m) Amendment of regulations

The Administrator shall prescribe by regulations the procedure by which regulations under this section may be amended or repealed, and such procedure shall conform to the procedure provided in this section for the promulgation of regulations establishing tolerances, including the appointment of advisory committees and the procedure for referring petitions to such committees.

(n) Guaranties

The provisions of section 333(c) of this title with respect to the furnishing of guaranties shall be applicable to raw agricultural commodities covered by this section.

(*o*) Payment of fees; services or functions as conditioned on; waiver or refund of fees

The Administrator shall by regulation require the payment of such fees as will in the aggregate, in the judgment of the Administrator, be sufficient over a reasonable term to provide, equip, and maintain an adequate service for the performance of the Administrator's functions under this section. Under such regulations, the performance of the Administrator's services or other functions pursuant to this section, including any one or more of the following, may be conditioned upon the payment of such fees: (1) The acceptance of filing of a petition submitted under subsection (d) of this section; (2) the promulgation of a regulation establishing a tolerance, or an exemption from the necessity of a tolerance, under this section, or the amendment or repeal of such a regulation; (3) the referral of a petition or proposal under this section to an advisory committee; (4) the acceptance for filing of objections under subsection (d)(5) of this section; or (5) the certification and filing in court of a transcript of the proceedings and the record under subsection (i)(2) of this section. Such regulations may further provide for waiver or refund of fees in whole or in part when in the judgment of the Administrator such waiver or refund is equitable and not contrary to the purposes of this subsection.

§ 346b. Same; appropriations

There are authorized to be appropriated, out of any moneys in the Treasury not otherwise appropriated, such sums as may be necessary for the purpose and administration of sections 321(q), (r), 342(a)(2), and 346a of this title.

§ 347. Intrastate sales of colored oleomargarine

(a) Law governing

Colored oleomargarine or colored margarine which is sold in the same State or Territory in which it is produced shall be subject in the same manner and to the same extent to the provisions of this chapter as if it had been introduced in interstate commerce.

(b) Labeling and packaging requirements

No person shall sell, or offer for sale, colored oleomargarine or colored margarine unless—

(1) such oleomargarine or margarine is packaged,

(2) the net weight of the contents of any package sold in a retail establishment is one pound or less,

(3) there appears on the label of the package (A) the word "oleomargarine" or "margarine" in type or lettering at least as large as any other type or lettering on such label, and (B) a full and accurate statement of all the ingredients contained in such oleomargarine or margarine, and

(4) each part of the contents of the package is contained in a wrapper which bears the word "oleomargarine" or "margarine" in type or lettering not smaller than 20–point type.

The requirements of this subsection shall be in addition to and not in lieu of any of the other requirements of this chapter.

(c) Sales in public eating places

No person shall possess in a form ready for serving colored oleomargarine or colored margarine at a public eating place unless a notice that oleomargarine or margarine is served is displayed prominently and conspicuously in such place and in such manner as to render it likely to be read and understood by the ordinary individual being served in such eating place or is printed or is otherwise set forth on the menu in type or lettering not smaller than that normally used to designate the serving of other food items. No person shall serve colored oleomargarine or colored margarine at a public eating place, whether or not any charge is made therefor, unless (1) each separate serving bears or is accompanied by labeling identifying it as oleomargarine or margarine, or (2) each separate serving thereof is triangular in shape.

(d) Same; exemption from labeling requirements

Colored oleomargarine or colored margarine when served with meals at a public eating place shall at the time of such service be exempt from the labeling requirements of section 343 of this title (except subsection (a) and (f) of section 343 of this title) if it complies with the requirements of subsection (b) of this section.

(e) Color content of oleomargarine

For the purpose of this section colored oleomargarine or colored margarine is oleomargarine or margarine having a tint or shade containing more than one and six-tenths degrees of yellow, or of yellow and red collectively, but with an excess of yellow over red, measured in terms of Lovibond tintometer scale or its equivalent.

§ 347a. Congressional declaration of policy regarding oleomargarine sales

The Congress finds and declares that the sale, or the serving in public eating places, of colored oleomargarine or colored margarine without clear identification as such or which is otherwise adulterated or misbranded within the meaning of this chapter depresses the market in interstate commerce for butter and for oleomargarine or margarine clearly identified and neither adulterated nor misbranded, and constitutes a burden on interstate commerce in such articles. Such burden exists, irrespective of whether such oleomargarine or margarine originates from an interstate source or from the State in which it is sold.

§ 347b. Contravention of State laws

Nothing in sections 331(m), 342(e), and 347 to 347b of this title, and sections 45(*l*) and 55(a), (f) of Title 15 shall be construed as authorizing the possession, sale, or serving of colored oleomargarine or colored margarine in any State or Territory in contravention of the laws of such State or Territory.

§ 348. Food additives

(a) Unsafe food additives; exception for conformity with exemption or regulation

A food additive shall, with respect to any particular use or intended use of such additives, be deemed to be unsafe for the purposes of the application of clause (2)(C) of section 342(a) of this title, unless—

(1) it and its use or intended use conform to the terms of an exemption which is in effect pursuant to subsection (i) of this section; or

(2) there is in effect, and it and its use or intended use are in conformity

with, a regulation issued under this section prescribing the conditions under which such additive may be safely used.

While such a regulation relating to a food additive is in effect, a food shall not, by reason of bearing or containing such an additive in accordance with the regulation, be considered adulterated within the meaning of clause (1) of section 342(a) of this title.

(b) Petition for regulation prescribing conditions of safe use; contents; description of production methods and controls; samples; notice of regulation

(1) Any person may, with respect to any intended use of a food additive, file with the Secretary a petition proposing the issuance of a regulation prescribing the conditions under which such additive may be safely used.

(2) Such petition shall, in addition to any explanatory or supporting data, contain—

(A) the name and all pertinent information concerning such food additive, including, where available, its chemical identity and composition;

(B) a statement of the conditions of the proposed use of such additive, including all directions, recommendations, and suggestions proposed for the use of such additive, and including specimens of its proposed labeling;

(C) all relevant data bearing on the physical or other technical effect such additive is intended to produce, and the quantity of such additive required to produce such effect;

(D) a description of practicable methods for determining the quantity of such additive in or on food, and any substance formed in or on food, because of its use; and

(E) full reports of investigations made with respect to the safety for use of such additive, including full information as to the methods and controls used in conducting such investigations.

(3) Upon request of the Secretary, the petitioner shall furnish (or, if the petitioner is not the manufacturer of such additive, the petitioner shall have the manufacturer of such additive furnish, without disclosure to the petitioner) a full description of the methods used in, and the facilities and controls used for, the production of such additive.

(4) Upon request of the Secretary, the petitioner shall furnish samples of the food additive involved, or articles used as components thereof, and of the food in or on which the additive is proposed to be used.

(5) Notice of the regulation proposed by the petitioner shall be published in general terms by the Secretary within thirty days after filing.

(c) Approval or denial of petition; time for issuance of orders; evaluation of data; factors

(1) The Secretary shall—

(A) by order establish a regulation (whether or not in accord with that proposed by the petitioner) prescribing, with respect to one or more proposed uses of the food additive involved, the conditions under which such additive may be safely used (including, but not limited to, specifications as to the particular food or classes of food in or in which such additive may be used, the maximum quantity which may be used or permitted to remain in or on such food, the manner in which such additive may be added to or used in or on such food, and any directions or other labeling or packaging requirements for such additive deemed necessary by him to assure the safety of such use), and shall notify the petitioner of such order and the reasons for such action; or

(B) by order deny the petition, and shall notify the petitioner of such order and of the reasons for such action.

(2) The order required by paragraph (1)(A) or (B) of this subsection shall be issued within ninety days after the date of filing of the petition, except that the Secretary may (prior to such ninetieth day), by written

notice to the petitioner, extend such ninety-day period to such time (not more than one hundred and eighty days after the date of filing of the petition) as the Secretary deems necessary to enable him to study and investigate the petition.

(3) No such regulation shall issue if a fair evaluation of the data before the Secretary—

(A) fails to establish that the proposed use of the food additive, under the conditions of use to be specified in the regulation, will be safe: Provided, That no additive shall be deemed to be safe if it is found to induce cancer when ingested by man or animal, or if it is found, after tests which are appropriate for the evaluation of the safety of food additives, to induce cancer in man or animal, except that this proviso shall not apply with respect to the use of a substance as an ingredient of feed for animals which are raised for food production, if the Secretary finds (i) that, under the conditions of use and feeding specified in proposed labeling and reasonably certain to be followed in practice, such additive will not adversely affect the animals for which such feed is intended, and (ii) that no residue of the additive will be found (by methods of examination prescribed or approved by the Secretary by regulations, which regulations shall not be subject to subsections (f) and (g) of this section) in any edible portion of such animal after slaughter or in any food yielded by or derived from the living animal; or

(B) shows that the proposed use of the additive would promote deception of the consumer in violation of this chapter or would otherwise result in adulteration or in misbranding of food within the meaning of this chapter.

(4) If, in the judgment of the Secretary, based upon a fair evaluation of the data before him, a tolerance limitation is required in order to assure that the proposed use of an additive will be safe, the Secretary—

(A) shall not fix such tolerance limitation at a level higher than he finds to be reasonably required to accomplish the physical or other technical effect for which such additive is intended; and

(B) shall not establish a regulation for such proposed use if he finds upon a fair evaluation of the data before him that such data do not establish that such use would accomplish the intended physical or other technical effect.

(5) In determining, for the purposes of this section, whether a proposed use of a food additive is safe, the Secretary shall consider among other relevant factors—

(A) the probable consumption of the additive and of any substance formed in or on food because of the use of the additive;

(B) the cumulative effect of such additive in the diet of man or animals, taking into account any chemically or pharmacologically related substance or substances in such diet; and

(C) safety factors which in the opinion of experts qualified by scientific training and experience to evaluate the safety of food additives are generally recognized as appropriate for the use of animal experimentation data.

(d) Regulation issued on Secretary's initiative

The Secretary may at any time, upon his own initiative, propose the issuance of a regulation prescribing, with respect to any particular use of a food additive, the conditions under which such additive may be safely used, and the reasons therefor. After the thirtieth day following publication of such a proposal, the Secretary may by order establish a regulation based upon the proposal.

(e) Publication and effective date of orders

Any order, including any regulation established by such order, issued under subsection (c) or (d) of this section, shall be published and shall be effective upon publication, but the Secretary may stay such effectiveness if, after issuance of such order, a hearing is sought with respect to such order pursuant to subsection (f) of this section.

(f) Objections and public hearing; basis and contents of order; statement

(1) Within thirty days after publication of an order made pursuant to subsection (c) or (d) of this section, any person adversely affected by such an order may file objections thereto with the Secretary, specifying with particularity the provisions of the order deemed objectionable, stating reasonable grounds therefor, and requesting a public hearing upon such objections. The Secretary shall, after due notice, as promptly as possible hold such public hearing for the purpose of receiving evidence relevant and material to the issues raised by such objections. As soon as practicable after completion of the hearing, the Secretary shall by order act upon such objections and make such order public.

(2) Such order shall be based upon a fair evaluation of the entire record at such hearing, and shall include a statement setting forth in detail the findings and conclusions upon which the order is based.

(3) The Secretary shall specify in the order the date on which it shall take effect, except that it shall not be made to take effect prior to the ninetieth day after its publication, unless the Secretary finds that emergency conditions exist necessitating an earlier effective date, in which event the Secretary shall specify in the order his findings as to such conditions.

(g) Judicial review

(1) In a case of actual controversy as to the validity of any order issued under subsection (f) of this section, including any order thereunder with respect to amendment or repeal of a regulation issued under this section, any person who will be adversely affected by such order may obtain judicial review by filing in the United States Court of Appeals for the circuit wherein such person resides or has his principal place of business, or in the United States Court of Appeals for the District of Columbia Circuit, within sixty days after the entry of such order, a petition praying that the order be set aside in whole or in part.

(2) A copy of such petition shall be forthwith transmitted by the clerk of the court to the Secretary, or any officer designated by him for that purpose, and thereupon the Secretary shall file in the court the record of the proceedings on which he based his order, as provided in section 2112 of Title 28. Upon the filing of such petition the court shall have jurisdiction, which upon the filing of the record with it shall be exclusive, to affirm or set aside the order complained of in whole or in part. Until the filing of the record the Secretary may modify or set aside his order. The findings of the Secretary with respect to questions of fact shall be sustained if based upon a fair evaluation of the entire record at such hearing.

(3) The court, on such judicial review, shall not sustain the order of the Secretary if he failed to comply with any requirement imposed on him by subsection (f)(2) of this section.

(4) If application is made to the court for leave to adduce additional evidence, the court may order such additional evidence to be taken before the Secretary and to be adduced upon the hearing in such manner and upon such terms and conditions as to the court may seem proper, if such evidence is material and there were reasonable grounds for failure to adduce such evidence in the proceedings below. The Secretary may modify his findings as to the facts and order by reason of the additional evidence so taken, and shall file with the court such modified findings and order.

(5) The judgment of the court affirming or setting aside, in whole or in part, any order under this section shall be final, subject to review by the Supreme Court of the United States upon certiorari or certification as provided in section 1254 of Title 28. The commencement of proceedings under this section shall not, unless specifically ordered by the court to the contrary, operate as a stay of an order.

(h) Amendment or repeal of regulations

The Secretary shall by regulation prescribe the procedure by which regulations under the foregoing provisions of this section may be amended or repealed, and such procedure shall conform to the procedure provided in this section for the promulgation of such regulations.

(i) Exemptions for investigational use

Without regard to subsections (b) to (h), inclusive, of this section, the Secretary shall by regulation provide for exempting from the requirements of this section any food additive, and any food bearing or containing such additive, intended solely for investigational use by qualified experts when in his opinion such exemption is consistent with the public health.

§ 349. Bottled drinking water standards; publication in Federal Register

Whenever the Administrator of the Environmental Protection Agency prescribes interim or revised national primary drinking water regulations under section 300g–1 of Title 42, the Secretary shall consult with the Administrator and within 180 days after the promulgation of such drinking water regulations either promulgate amendments to regulations under this chapter applicable to bottled drinking water or publish in the Federal Register his reasons for not making such amendments.

§ 350. Vitamins and minerals

(a) Authority and limitations of Secretary; applicability

(1) Except as provided in paragraph (2)—

(A) the Secretary may not establish, under section 321(n), 341, or 343 of this title, maximum limits on the potency of any synthetic or natural vitamin or mineral within a food to which this section applies;

(B) the Secretary may not classify any natural or synthetic vitamin or mineral (or combination thereof) as a drug solely because it exceeds the level of potency which the Secretary determines is nutritionally rational or useful;

(C) the Secretary may not limit, under section 321(n), 341, or 343 of this title, the combination or number of any synthetic or natural—

(i) vitamin,

(ii) mineral, or

(iii) other ingredient of food,

within a food to which this section applies.

(2) Paragraph (1) shall not apply in the case of a vitamin, mineral, other ingredient of food, or food, which is represented for use by individuals in the treatment or management of specific diseases or disorders, by children, or by pregnant or lactating women. For purposes of this subparagraph, the term "children" means individuals who are under the age of twelve years.

(b) Labeling and advertising requirements for foods

(1) A food to which this section applies shall not be deemed under section 343 of this title to be misbranded solely because its label bears, in accordance with section 343(i)(2) of this title, all the ingredients in the food or its advertising contains references to ingredients in the food which are not vitamins or minerals.

(2) The labeling for any food to which this section applies may not list its ingredients which are not dietary supplement ingredients described in section 321(ff) of this title (i) except as a part of a list of all the ingredients of such food, and (ii) unless such ingredients are listed in accordance with applicable regulations under section 343 of this title. To the extent that compliance with clause (i) of this subparagraph is impracticable or results in deception or unfair competition, exemptions shall be established by regulations promulgated by the Secretary.

(c) Definitions

(1) For purposes of this section, the term "food to which this section applies" means a food for humans which is a food for special dietary use—

(A) which is or contains any natural or synthetic vitamin or mineral, and

(B) which—

(i) is intended for ingestion in tablet, capsule, powder, softgel, gelcap, or liquid form, or

(ii) if not intended for ingestion in such a form, is not represented as conventional food and is not represented for use as a sole item of a meal or of the diet.

(2) For purposes of paragraph (1)(B)(i), a food shall be considered as intended for ingestion in liquid form only if it is formulated in a fluid carrier and it is intended for ingestion in daily quantities measured in drops or similar small units of measure.

(3) For purposes of paragraph (1) and of section 343(j) of this title insofar as that section is applicable to food to which this section applies, the term "special dietary use" as applied to food used by man means a particular use for which a food purports or is represented to be used, including but not limited to the following:

(A) Supplying a special dietary need that exists by reason of a physical, physiological, pathological, or other condition, including but not limited to the condition of disease, convalescence, pregnancy, lactation, infancy, allergic hypersensitivity to food, underweight, overweight, or the need to control the intake of sodium.

(B) Supplying a vitamin, mineral, or other ingredient for use by man to supplement his diet by increasing the total dietary intake.

(C) Supplying a special dietary need by reason of being a food for use as the sole item of the diet.

§ 350a. Infant formulas

(a) Adulteration

An infant formula, including an infant formula powder, shall be deemed to be adulterated if—

(1) such infant formula does not provide nutrients as required by subsection (i),

(2) such infant formula does not meet the quality factor requirements prescribed by the Secretary under subsection (b)(1), or

(3) the processing of such infant formula is not in compliance with the good manufacturing practices and the quality control procedures prescribed by the Secretary under subsection (b)(2).

(b) Regulations for quality factors and manufacturing practices

(1) The Secretary shall by regulation establish requirements for quality factors for infant formulas to the extent possible consistent with current scientific knowledge, including quality factor requirements for the nutrients required by subsection (i).

(2)(A) The Secretary shall by regulation establish good manufacturing practices for infant formulas, including quality control procedures that the Secretary determines are necessary to assure that an infant formula provides nutrients in accordance with this subsection and subsection (i) and is manufactured in a manner designed to prevent adulteration of the infant formula.

(B) The good manufacturing practices and quality control procedures prescribed by the Secretary under subparagraph (A) shall include requirements for—

(i) the testing, in accordance with paragraph (3) and by the manufacturer of an infant formula or an agent of such manufacturer, of each batch of infant formula for each nutrient required by subsection (i) before the distribution of such batch,

(ii) regularly scheduled testing, by the manufacturer of an infant formula or an agent of such manufacturer, of samples of infant formulas during the shelf life of such formulas to ensure that such formulas are in compliance with this section,

(iii) in-process controls including, where necessary, testing required by good manufacturing practices designed to prevent adulteration of each batch of infant formula, and

(iv) the conduct by the manufacturer of an infant formula or an agent of such manufacturer of regularly scheduled audits to determine that such manufacturer has complied with the regulations prescribed under subparagraph (A).

In prescribing requirements for audits under clause (iv), the Secretary shall provide that such audits be conducted by appropriately trained individuals who do not have any direct responsibility for the manufacture or production of infant formula.

(3)(A) At the final product stage, each batch of infant formula shall be tested for vitamin A, vitamin B1, vitamin C, and vitamin E to ensure that such infant formula is in compliance with the requirements of this subsection and subsection (i) relating to such vitamins.

(B) Each nutrient premix used in the manufacture of an infant formula shall be tested for each relied upon nutrient required by subsection (i) which is contained in such premix to ensure that such premix is in compliance with its specifications or certifications by a premix supplier.

(C) During the manufacturing process or at the final product stage and before distribution of an infant formula, an infant formula shall be tested for all nutrients required to be included in such formula by subsection (i) for which testing has not been conducted pursuant to subparagraph (A) or (B). Testing under this subparagraph shall be conducted to—

    (i) ensure that each batch of such infant formula is in compliance with the requirements of subsection (i) relating to such nutrients, and

    (ii) confirm that nutrients contained in any nutrient premix used in such infant formula are present in each batch of such infant formula in the proper concentration.

(D) If the Secretary adds a nutrient to the list of nutrients in the table in subsection (i), the Secretary shall by regulation require that the manufacturer of an infant formula test each batch of such formula for such new nutrient in accordance with subparagraph (A), (B), or (C).

(E) For purposes of this paragraph, the term "final product stage" means the point in the manufacturing process, before distribution of an infant formula, at which an infant formula is homogenous and is not subject to further degradation.

(4)(A) The Secretary shall by regulation establish requirements respecting the retention of records. Such requirements shall provide for—

    (i) the retention of all records necessary to demonstrate compliance with the good manufacturing practices and quality control procedures prescribed by the Secretary under paragraph (2), including records containing the results of all testing required under paragraph (2)(B),

(ii) the retention of all certifications or guarantees of analysis by premix suppliers.[2]

(iii) the retention by a premix supplier of all records necessary to confirm the accuracy of all premix certifications and guarantees of analysis,

(iv) the retention of—

(I) all records pertaining to the microbiological quality and purity of raw materials used in infant formula powder and in finished infant formula, and

(II) all records pertaining to food packaging materials which show that such materials do not cause an infant formula to be adulterated within the meaning of section 402(a)(2)(C),

(v) the retention of all records of the results of regularly scheduled audits conducted pursuant to the requirements prescribed by the Secretary under paragraph (2)(B)(iv), and

(vi) the retention of all complaints and the maintenance of files with respect to, and the review of, complaints concerning infant formulas which may reveal the possible existence of a hazard to health.

(B)(i) Records required under subparagraph (A) with respect to an infant formula shall be retained for at least one year after the expiration of the shelf life of such infant formula. Except as provided in clause (ii), such records shall be made available to the Secretary for review and duplication upon request of the Secretary.

(ii) A manufacturer need only provide written assurances to the Secretary that the regularly scheduled audits required by paragraph (2)(B)(iv) are being conducted by the manufacturer, and need not make available to the Secretary the actual written reports of such audits.

(c) Introduction of infant formula into interstate commerce

(1) No person shall introduce or deliver for introduction into interstate commerce any new infant formula unless—

(A) such person has, before introducing such new infant formula, or delivering such new infant formula for introduction, into interstate commerce, registered with the Secretary the name of such person, the place of business of such person, and all establishments at which such person intends to manufacture such new infant formula, and

(B) such person has at least 90 days before marketing such new infant formula, made the submission to the Secretary required by subsection (c)(1).

2. So in original.

(2) For purposes of paragraph (1), the term "new infant formula" includes—

(A) an infant formula manufactured by a person which has not previously manufactured an infant formula, and

(B) an infant formula manufactured by a person which has previously manufactured infant formula and in which there is a major change, in processing or formulation, from a current or any previous formulation produced by such manufacturer.

For purposes of this paragraph, the term "major change" has the meaning given to such term in section 106.30(c)(2) of title 21, Code of Federal Regulations (as in effect on August 1, 1986), and guidelines issued thereunder.

(d) Submissions to Secretary

(1) A person shall, with respect to any infant formula subject to subsection (c), make a submission to the Secretary which shall include—

(A) the quantitative formulation of the infant formula,

(B) a description of any reformulation of the formula or change in processing of the infant formula,

(C) assurances that the infant formula will not be marketed unless it meets the requirements of subsections (b)(1) and (i), as demonstrated by the testing required under subsection (b)(3), and

(D) assurances that the processing of the infant formula complies with subsection (b)(2).

(2) After the first production of an infant formula subject to subsection (c), and before the introduction into interstate commerce of such formula, the manufacturer of such formula shall submit to the Secretary, in such form as may be prescribed by the Secretary, a written verification which summarizes test results and records demonstrating that such formula complies with the requirements of subsections (b)(1), (b)(2)(A), (b)(2)(B)(i), (b)(2)(B)(iii), (b)(3)(A), (b)(3)(C), and (i).

(3) If the manufacturer of an infant formula for commercial or charitable distribution for human consumption determines that a change in the formulation of the formula or a change in the processing of the formula may affect whether the formula is adulterated under subsection (a), the manufacturer shall, before the first processing of such formula, make the submission to the Secretary required by paragraph (1).

(e) Notification of adulteration

(1) If the manufacturer of an infant formula has knowledge which reasonably supports the conclusion that an infant formula which has been processed by the manufacturer and which has left an establishment subject to the control of the manufacturer—

(A) may not provide the nutrients required by subsection (i), or

(B) may be otherwise adulterated or misbranded,

the manufacturer shall promptly notify the Secretary of such knowledge. If the Secretary determines that the infant formula presents a risk to human health, the manufacturer shall immediately take all actions necessary to recall shipments of such infant formula from all wholesale and retail establishments, consistent with recall regulations and guidelines issued by the Secretary.

(2) For purposes of paragraph (1), the term "knowledge" as applied to a manufacturer means (A) the actual knowledge that the manufacturer had, or (B) the knowledge which a reasonable person would have had under like circumstances or which would have been obtained upon the exercise of due care.

(f) Recall of infant formula

(1) If a recall of infant formula is begun by a manufacturer, the recall shall be carried out in accordance with such requirements as the Secretary shall prescribe under paragraph (2) and—

(A) the Secretary shall, not later than the 15th day after the beginning of such recall and at least once every 15 days thereafter until the recall is terminated, review the actions taken under the recall to determine whether the recall meets the requirements prescribed under paragraph (2), and

(B) the manufacturer shall, not later than the 14th day after the beginning of such recall and at least once every 14 days thereafter until the recall is terminated, report to the Secretary the actions taken to implement the recall.

(2) The Secretary shall by regulation prescribe the scope and extent of recalls of infant formulas necessary and appropriate for the degree of risks to human health presented by the formula subject to the recall.

(3) The Secretary shall by regulation require each manufacturer of an infant formula who begins a recall of such formula because of a risk to human health to request each retail establishment at which such formula is sold or available for sale to post at the point of purchase of such formula a notice of such recall at such establishment for such time that the Secretary determines necessary to inform the public of such recall.

(g) Recordkeeping requirements for manufacturer; regulatory oversight and enforcement

(1) Each manufacturer of an infant formula shall make and retain such records respecting the distribution of the infant formula through any establishment owned or operated by such manufacturer as may be necessary to effect and monitor recalls of the formula. Such records shall be retained for at least one year after the expiration of the shelf life of the infant formula.

(2) To the extent that the Secretary determines that records are not being made or maintained in accordance with paragraph (1), the Secretary may by regulation prescribe the records required to be made under paragraph (1) and requirements respecting the retention of such records under such paragraph. Such regulations shall take effect on such date as the Secretary prescribes but not sooner than the 180th day after the date such regulations are promulgated. Such regulations shall apply only with respect to distributions of infant formulas made after such effective date.

(h) Exemptions; regulatory oversight

(1) Any infant formula which is represented and labeled for use by an infant—

(A) who has an inborn error of metabolism or a low birth weight, or

(B) who otherwise has an unusual medical or dietary problem,

is exempt from the requirements of subsections (a), (b) and (c) of this section. The manufacturer of an infant formula exempt under this paragraph shall, in the case of the exempt formula, be required to provide the notice required by subsection (e)(1) of this section, only with respect to adulteration or misbranding described in subsection (e)(1)(B) of this section, and to comply with the regulations prescribed by the Secretary under paragraph (2).

(2) The Secretary may by regulation establish terms and conditions for the exemption of an infant formula from the requirements of subsections (a), (b) and (c) of this section. An exemption of an infant formula under paragraph (1) may be withdrawn by the Secretary if such formula is not in compliance with applicable terms and conditions prescribed under this paragraph.

(i) Nutrient requirements

(1) An infant formula shall contain nutrients in accordance with the table set out in this subsection or, if revised by the Secretary under paragraph (2) of this section, as so revised.

(2) The Secretary may by regulation—

(A) revise the list of nutrients in the table in this subsection, and

(B) revise the required level for any nutrient required by the table.

NUTRIENTS

Nutrient	Minimum [3]	Maximum [4]
Protein (gm)	1.8 [5]	4.5

3. Stated per 100 kilocalories.
4. Stated per kilocalories.

5. The source of protein shall be at least nutritionally equivalent to casein.

Nutrient	Minimum [3]	Maximum [4]
Fat:		
gm	3.3	6.0.
percent cal	30.0	54.0.
Essential fatty acids (linoleate):		
percent cal	2.7	
mg	300.0	
Vitamins:		
A (IU)	250.0 (75 µg) [6]	750.0 (225 µg).[7]
D (IU)	40.0	100.0.
K (µg)	4.0	
E (IU)	0.7 (with 0.7 IU/gm linoleic acid).	
C (ascorbic acid)(mg)	8.0	
B_1 (thiamine)(µg)	40.0	
B_2 (riboflavin)(µg)	60.0	
B_6 (pyridoxine)(µg)	35.0 (with 15 µg/gm of protein in formula).	
B_{12} (µg)	0.15	
Niacin (µg)	250.0	
Folic acid (µg)	4.0	
Pantothenic acid (µg)	300.0	
Biotin (µg)	1.5 [8]	
Choline (mg)	7.0 [9]	
Inositol (mg)	4.0 [10]	
Minerals:		
Calcium (mg)	50.0 [11]	
Phosphorus (mg)	25.0 [12]	
Magnesium (mg)	6.0	
Iron (mg)	0.15	
Iodine (µg)	5.0	
Zinc (mg)	0.5	
Copper (µg)	60.0	
Manganese (µg)	5.0	
Sodium (mg)	20.0	60.0.
Potassium (mg)	80.0	200.0.
Chloride (mg)	55.0	150.0.

§ 350b. New dietary ingredients

(a) In general

A dietary supplement which contains a new dietary ingredient shall be deemed adulterated under section 342(f) of this title unless it meets one of the following requirements:

6. Retinol equivalents.

7. Retinol equivalents.

8. Required to be included in this amount only in formulas which are not milk-based.

9. Required to be included in this amount only in formulas which are not milk-based.

10. Required to be included in this amount only in formulas which are not milk-based.

11. Calcium to phosphorus ratio must be less than 1.1 nor more than 2.0.

12. Calcium to phosphorus ratio must be less than 1.1 nor more than 2.0.

(1) The dietary supplement contains only dietary ingredients which have been present in the food supply as an article used for food in a form in which the food has not been chemically altered.

(2) There is a history of use or other evidence of safety establishing that the dietary ingredient when used under the conditions recommended or suggested in the labeling of the dietary supplement will reasonably be expected to be safe and, at least 75 days before being introduced or delivered for introduction into interstate commerce, the manufacturer or distributor of the dietary ingredient or dietary supplement provides the Secretary with information, including any citation to published articles, which is the basis on which the manufacturer or distributor has concluded that a dietary supplement containing such dietary ingredient will reasonably be expected to be safe.

The Secretary shall keep confidential any information provided under paragraph (2) for 90 days following its receipt. After the expiration of such 90 days, the Secretary shall place such information on public display, except matters in the information which are trade secrets or otherwise confidential, commercial information.

(b) Petition

Any person may file with the Secretary a petition proposing the issuance of an order prescribing the conditions under which a new dietary ingredient under its intended conditions of use will reasonably be expected to be safe. The Secretary shall make a decision on such petition within 180 days of the date the petition is filed with the Secretary. For purposes of chapter 7 of Title 5, the decision of the Secretary shall be considered final agency action.

(c) Definition

For purposes of this section, the term "new dietary ingredient" means a dietary ingredient that was not marketed in the United States before October 15, 1994 and does not include any dietary ingredient which was marketed in the United States before October 15, 1994.

SUBCHAPTER V—DRUGS AND DEVICES

PART A—DRUGS AND DEVICES

§ 351. Adulterated drugs and devices

A drug or device shall be deemed to be adulterated—

(a) Poisonous, insanitary, etc., ingredients; adequate controls in manufacture

(1) If it consists in whole or in part of any filthy, putrid, or decomposed substance; or (2)(A) if it has been prepared, packed, or held under insanitary conditions whereby it may have been contaminated with filth, or whereby it may have been rendered injurious to health; or

(B) if it is a drug and the methods used in, or the facilities or controls used for, its manufacture, processing, packing, or holding do not conform to or are not operated or administered in conformity with current good manufacturing practice to assure that such drug meets the requirements of this chapter as to safety and has the identity and strength, and meets the quality and purity characteristics, which it purports or is represented to possess; or (3) if its container is composed, in whole or in part, of any poisonous or deleterious substance which may render the contents injurious to health; or (4) if (A) it bears or contains, for purposes of coloring only, a color additive which is unsafe within the meaning of section 379e(a) of this title, or (B) it is a color additive the intended use of which in or on drugs or devices is for purposes of coloring only and is unsafe within the meaning of section 379e(a) of this title; or (5) if it is a new animal drug which is unsafe within the meaning of section 360b of this title; or (6) if it is an animal feed bearing or containing a new animal drug, and such animal feed is unsafe within the meaning of section 360b of this title.

(b) Strength, quality, or purity differing from official compendium

If it purports to be or is represented as a drug the name of which is recognized in an official compendium, and its strength differs from, or its quality or purity falls below, the standard set forth in such compendium. Such determination as to strength, quality, or purity shall be made in accordance with the tests or methods of assay set forth in such compendium, except that whenever tests or methods of assay have not been prescribed in such compendium, or such tests or methods of assay as are prescribed are, in the judgment of the Secretary, insufficient for the making of such determination, the Secretary shall bring such fact to the attention of the appropriate body charged with the revision of such compendium, and if such body fails within a reasonable time to prescribe tests or methods of assay which, in the judgment of the Secretary, are sufficient for purposes of this paragraph, then the Secretary shall promulgate regulations prescribing appropriate tests or methods of assay in accordance with which such determination as to strength, quality, or purity shall be made. No drug defined in an official compendium shall be deemed to be adulterated under this paragraph because it differs from the standard of strength, quality, or purity therefor set forth in such compendium, if its difference in strength, quality, or purity from such standard is plainly stated on its label. Whenever a drug is recognized in both the United States Pharmacopoeia and the Homeopathic Pharmacopoeia of the United States it shall be subject to the requirements of the United States Pharmacopoeia unless it is labeled and offered for sale as a homeopathic drug, in which case it shall be subject to the provisions of the Homeopathic Pharmacopoeia of the United States and not to those of the United States Pharmacopoeia.

(c) Misrepresentation of strength, etc., where drug is unrecognized in compendium

If it is not subject to the provisions of paragraph (b) and its strength differs from, or its purity or quality falls below, that which it purports or is represented to possess.

(d) Mixture with or substitution of another substance .

If it is a drug and any substance has been (1) mixed or packed therewith so as to reduce its quality or strength or (2) substituted wholly or in part therefor.

(e) Devices not in conformity with performance standards

If it is, or purports to be or is represented as, a device which is subject to a performance standard established under section 360d of this title, unless such device is in all respects in conformity with such standard.

(f) Certain class III devices

(1) If it is a class III device—

(A)(i) which is required by a regulation promulgated under subsection (b) of section 360e of this title to have an approval under such section of an application for premarket approval and which is not exempt from section 360e of this title under section 360j(g) of this title, and

(ii)(I) for which an application for premarket approval or a notice of completion of a product development protocol was not filed with the Secretary within the ninety-day period beginning on the date of the promulgation of such regulation, or

(II) for which such an application was filed and approval of the application has been denied, suspended, or withdrawn, or such a notice was filed and has been declared not completed or the approval of the device under the protocol has been withdrawn;

(B)(i) which was classified under section 360c(f) of this title into class III, which under section 360e(a) of this title is required to have in effect an approved application for premarket approval, and which is not exempt from section 360e of this title under section 360j(g) of this title, and

(ii) which has an application which has been suspended or is otherwise not in effect; or

(C) which was classified under section 360j(*l*) of this title into class III, which under such section is required to have in effect an approved application under section 360e of this title, and which has an application which has been suspended or is otherwise not in effect.

(2)(A) In the case of a device classified under section 360c(f) of this title into class III and intended solely for investigational use, paragraph (1)(B) shall not apply with respect to such device during the period ending on the ninetieth day after the date of the promulgation of the regulations prescribing the procedures and conditions required by section 360j(g)(2) of this title.

(B) In the case of a device subject to a regulation promulgated under subsection (b) of section 360e of this title, paragraph (1) shall not apply with respect to such device during the period ending—

> (i) on the last day of the thirtieth calendar month beginning after the month in which the classification of the device in class III became effective under section 360c of this title, or

> (ii) on the ninetieth day after the date of the promulgation of such regulation, whichever occurs later.

(g) Banned devices

If it is a banned device.

(h) Manufacture, packing, storage, or installation of device not in conformity with applicable requirements or conditions

If it is a device and the methods used in, or the facilities or controls used for, its manufacture, packing, storage, or installation are not in conformity with applicable requirements under section 360j(f)(1) of this title or an applicable condition prescribed by an order under section 360j(f)(2) of this title.

(i) Failure to comply with requirements under which device was exempted for investigational use

If it is a device for which an exemption has been granted under section 360j(g) of this title for investigational use and the person who was granted such exemption or any investigator who uses such device under such exemption fails to comply with a requirement prescribed by or under such section.

§ 352. Misbranded drugs and devices

A drug or device shall be deemed to be misbranded—

(a) False or misleading label

If its labeling is false or misleading in any particular.

(b) Package form; contents of label

If in package form unless it bears a label containing (1) the name and place of business of the manufacturer, packer, or distributor; and (2) an accurate statement of the quantity of the contents in terms of weight, measure, or numerical count: Provided, That under clause (2) of this paragraph reasonable variations shall be permitted, and exemptions as to small packages shall be established, by regulations prescribed by the Secretary.

(c) Prominence of information on label

If any word, statement, or other information required by or under authority of this chapter to appear on the label or labeling is not prominently placed thereon with such conspicuousness (as compared with other words, statements, designs, or devices, in the labeling) and in such terms as to render it likely to be read and understood by the ordinary individual under customary conditions of purchase and use.

(d) Habit forming substances

If it is for use by man and contains any quantity of the narcotic or hypnotic substance alpha eucaine, barbituric acid, betaeucaine, bromal, cannabis, carbromal, chloral, coca, cocaine, codeine, heroin, marihuana, morphine, opium, paraldehyde, peyote, or sulphonmethane; or any chemical derivative of such substance, which derivative has been by the Secretary, after investigation, found to be, and by regulations designated as, habit forming; unless its label bears the name and quantity or proportion of such substance or derivative and in juxtaposition therewith the statement "Warning—May be habit forming."

(e) Designation of drugs or devices by established names

(1) If it is a drug, unless (A) its label bears, to the exclusion of any other nonproprietary name (except the applicable systematic chemical name or the chemical formula), (i) the established name (as defined in subparagraph (3))of the drug, if such there be, and (ii), in case it is fabricated from two or more ingredients, the established name and quantity of each active ingredient, including the quantity, kind, and proportion of any alcohol, and also including, whether active or not, the established name and quantity or proportion of any bromides, ether, chloroform, acetanilid, acetphenetidin, amidopyrine, antipyrine, atropine, hyoscine, hyoscyamine, arsenic, digitalis, digitalis glucosides, mercury, ouabain, strophanthin, strychnine, thyroid, or any derivative or preparation of any such substances, contained therein; Provided, That the requirement for stating the quantity of the active ingredients, other than the quantity of those specifically named in this paragraph, shall apply only to prescription drugs; and (B) for any prescription drug the established name of such drug or ingredient, as the case may be, on such label (and on any labeling on which a name for such drug or ingredient is used) is printed prominently and in type at least half as large as that used thereon for any proprietary name or designation for such drug or ingredient: Provided, That to the extent that compliance with the requirements of clause (A)(ii) or clause (B) of this paragraph is impracticable, exemptions shall be established by regulations promulgated by the Secretary.

(2) If it is a device and it has an established name, unless its label bears, to the exclusion of any other nonproprietary name, its established

name (as defined in subparagraph (4))prominently printed in type at least half as large as that used thereon for any proprietary name or designation for such device, except that to the extent compliance with the requirements of this subparagraph is impracticable, exemptions shall be established by regulations promulgated by the Secretary.

(3) As used in subparagraph (1), the term "established name", with respect to a drug or ingredient thereof, means (A) the applicable official name designated pursuant to section 358 of this title, or (B), if there is no such name and such drug, or such ingredient, is an article recognized in an official compendium, then the official title thereof in such compendium, or (C) if neither clause (A) nor clause (B) of this subparagraph applies, then the common or usual name, if any, of such drug or of such ingredient, except that where clause (B) of this subparagraph applies to an article recognized in the United States Pharmacopeia and in the Homeopathic Pharmacopoeia under different official titles, the official title used in the United States Pharmacopeia shall apply unless it is labeled and offered for sale as a homeopathic drug, in which case the official title used in the Homeopathic Pharmacopoeia shall apply.

(4) As used in paragraph (2), the term "established name" with respect to a device means (A) the applicable official name of the device designated pursuant to section 358 of this title, (B) if there is no such name and such device is an article recognized in an official compendium, then the official title thereof in such compendium, or (C) if neither clause (A) nor clause (B) of this paragraph applies, then any common or usual name of such device.

(f) Directions for use and warnings on label

Unless its labeling bears (1) adequate directions for use; and (2) such adequate warnings against use in those pathological conditions or by children where its use may be dangerous to health, or against unsafe dosage or methods or duration of administration or application, in such manner and form, as are necessary for the protection of users, except that where any requirement of clause (1) of this paragraph, as applied to any drug or device, is not necessary for the protection of the public health, the Secretary shall promulgate regulations exempting such drug or device from such requirement.

(g) Representations as recognized drug; packing and labeling; inconsistent requirements for designation of drug

If it purports to be a drug the name of which is recognized in an official compendium, unless it is packaged and labeled as prescribed therein. The method of packing may be modified with the consent of the Secretary.

Whenever a drug is recognized in both the United States Pharmacopoeia and the Homeopathic Pharmacopoeia of the United States, it shall be subject to the requirements of the United States Pharmacopoeia with respect to packaging and labeling unless it is labeled and offered for sale as a homeopathic drug, in which case it shall be subject to the provisions of the Homeopathic Pharmacopoeia of the United States, and not to those of the United States Pharmacopoeia, except that in the event of inconsistency between the requirements of this paragraph and those of paragraph (e) as to name by which the drug or its ingredients shall be designated, the requirements of paragraph (e) shall prevail.

(h) Deteriorative drugs; packing and labeling

If it has been found by the Secretary to be a drug liable to deterioration, unless it is packaged in such form and manner, and its label bears a statement of such precautions, as the Secretary shall by regulations require as necessary for the protection of the public health. No such regulation shall be established for any drug recognized in an official compendium until the Secretary shall have informed the appropriate body charged with the revision of such compendium of the need for such packaging or labeling requirements and such body shall have failed within a reasonable time to prescribe such requirements.

(i) Drug; misleading container; imitation; offer for sale under another name

(1) If it is a drug and its container is so made, formed, or filled as to be misleading; or (2) if it is an imitation of another drug; or (3) if it is offered for sale under the name of another drug.

(j) Health-endangering when used as prescribed

If it is dangerous to health when used in the dosage or manner, or with the frequency or duration prescribed, recommended, or suggested in the labeling thereof.

(k) Insulin not properly certified

If it is, or purports to be, or is represented as a drug composed wholly or partly of insulin, unless (1) it is from a batch with respect to which a certificate or release has been issued pursuant to section 356 of this title, and (2) such certificate or release is in effect with respect to such drug.

(l) Antibiotic drugs improperly certified

If it is, or purports to be, or is represented as a drug (except a drug for use in animals other than man) composed wholly or partly of any kind of penicillin, streptomycin, chlortetracycline, chloramphenicol, bacitracin, or any other antibiotic drug, or any derivative thereof, unless (1) it is from a batch with respect to which a certificate or release has been issued pursuant to section 357 of this title, and (2) such certificate or release is in effect with respect to such drug: Provided, That this subsection shall not apply to any drug or class of drugs exempted by regulations promulgated under section 357(c) or (d) of this title.

(m) Color additives; packing and labeling

If it is a color additive the intended use of which is for the purpose of coloring only, unless its packaging and labeling are in conformity with such packaging and labeling requirements applicable to such color additive, as may be contained in regulations issued under section 379e of this title.

(n) Prescription drug advertisements; established name; quantitative formula; side effects, contraindications, and effectiveness; prior approval; false advertising; labeling; construction of the Convention on Psychotropic Substances

In the case of any prescription drug distributed or offered for sale in any State, unless the manufacturer, packer, or distributor thereof includes in all advertisements and other descriptive printed matter issued or caused to be issued by the manufacturer, packer, or distributor with respect to that drug a true statement of (1) the established name as defined in paragraph (e), printed prominently and in type at least half as large as that used for any trade or brand name thereof, (2) the formula showing quantitatively each ingredient of such drug to the extent required for labels under paragraph (e), and (3) such other information in brief summary relating to side effects, contraindications, and effectiveness as shall be required in regulations which shall be issued by the Secretary in accordance with the procedure specified in section 371(e) of this title, except that (A) except in extraordinary circumstances, no regulation issued under this subsection shall require prior approval by the Secretary of the content of any advertisement, and (B) no advertisement of a prescription drug, published after the effective date of regulations issued under this subsection applicable to advertisements of prescription drugs, shall with respect to the matters specified in this subsection or covered by such regulations, be subject to the provisions of sections 52 to 57 of Title 15. This paragraph (n) shall not be applicable to any printed matter which the Secretary determines to be labeling as defined in section 321(m) of this title. Nothing in the Convention on Psychotropic Substances, signed at Vienna, Austria, on February 21, 1971, shall be construed to prevent drug price communications to consumers.

(o) Drugs or devices from nonregistered establishments

If it was manufactured, prepared, propagated, compounded, or processed in an establishment in any State not duly registered under section 360 of this title, if it was not included in a list required by section 360(j) of this title, if a notice or other information respecting it was not provided as required by such section or section 360(k) of this title, or if it does not bear such symbols from the uniform system for identification of devices prescribed under section 360(e) of this title as the Secretary by regulation requires.

(p) Packaging or labeling of drugs in violation of regulations

If it is a drug and its packaging or labeling is in violation of an applicable regulation issued pursuant to section 1472 or 1473 of Title 15.

(q) Restricted devices using false or misleading advertising or used in violation of regulations

In the case of any restricted device distributed or offered for sale in any State, if (1) its advertising is false or misleading in any particular, or (2) it is sold, distributed, or used in violation of regulations prescribed under section 360j(e) of this title.

(r) Restricted devices not carrying requisite accompanying statements in advertisements and other descriptive printed matter

In the case of any restricted device distributed or offered for sale in any State, unless the manufacturer, packer, or distributor thereof includes in all advertisements and other descriptive printed matter issued or caused to be issued by the manufacturer, packer, or distributor with respect to that device (1) a true statement of the device's established name as defined in paragraph (e), printed prominently and in type at least half as large as that used for any trade or brand name thereof, and (2) a brief statement of the intended uses of the device and relevant warnings, precautions, side effects, and contraindications and, in the case of specific devices made subject to a finding by the Secretary after notice and opportunity for comment that such action is necessary to protect the public health, a full description of the components of such device or the formula showing quantitatively each ingredient of such device to the extent required in regulations which shall be issued by the Secretary after an opportunity for a hearing. Except in extraordinary circumstances, no regulation issued under this paragraph shall require prior approval by the Secretary of the content of any advertisement and no advertisement of a restricted device, published after the effective date of this paragraph shall, with respect to the matters specified in this paragraph or covered by regulations issued hereunder, be subject to the provisions of sections 52 through 55 of Title 15. This paragraph shall not be applicable to any printed matter which the Secretary determines to be labeling as defined in section 321(m) of this title.

(s) Devices subject to performance standards not bearing requisite labeling

If it is a device subject to a performance standard established under section 360d of this title, unless it bears such labeling as may be prescribed in such performance standard.

(t) Devices for which there has been a failure or refusal to give required notification or to furnish required material or information

If it is a device and there was a failure or refusal (1) to comply with any requirement prescribed under section 360h of this title respecting the device, (2) to furnish any material or information required by or under section 360i of this title respecting the device, or (3) to comply with a requirement under section 360l of this title.

§ 353. Exemptions and consideration for certain drugs, devices, and biological products

(a) Regulations for goods to be processed, labeled, or repacked elsewhere

The Secretary is directed to promulgate regulations exempting from any labeling or packaging requirement of this chapter drugs and devices which are, in accordance with the practice of the trade, to be processed, labeled, or repacked in substantial quantities at establishments other than those where originally processed or packed, on condition that such drugs and devices are not adulterated or misbranded under the provisions of this chapter upon removal from such processing, labeling, or repacking establishment.

(b) Prescription by physician; exemption from labeling and prescription requirements; misbranded drugs; compliance with narcotic and marihuana laws

(1) A drug intended for use by man which—

(A) is a habit-forming drug to which section 352(d) of this title applies; or

(B) because of its toxicity or other potentiality for harmful effect, or the method of its use, or the collateral measures necessary to its use, is not safe for use except under the supervision of a practitioner licensed by law to administer such drug; or

(C) is limited by an approved application under section 355 of this title to use under the professional supervision of a practitioner licensed by law to administer such drug,

shall be dispensed only (i) upon a written prescription of a practitioner licensed by law to administer such drug, or (ii) upon an oral prescription of such practitioner which is reduced promptly to writing and filed by the pharmacist, or (iii) by refilling any such written or oral prescription if such refilling is authorized by the prescriber either in the original prescription or by oral order which is reduced promptly to writing and filed by the pharmacist. The act of dispensing a drug contrary to the provisions of this paragraph shall be deemed to be an act which results in the drug being misbranded while held for sale.

(2) Any drug dispensed by filling or refilling a written or oral prescription of a practitioner licensed by law to administer such drug shall be exempt from the requirements of section 352 of this title, except paragraphs (a), (i)(2) and (3), (k), and (l), and the packaging requirements of paragraphs (g), (h), and (p), if the drug bears a label containing the name and address of the dispenser, the serial number and date of the prescription or of its filling, the name of the prescriber, and, if stated in

the prescription, the name of the patient, and the directions for use and cautionary statements, if any, contained in such prescription. This exemption shall not apply to any drug dispensed in the course of the conduct of a business of dispensing drugs pursuant to diagnosis by mail, or to a drug dispensed in violation of paragraph (1) of this subsection.

(3) The Secretary may by regulation remove drugs subject to sections 352(d) and 355 of this title from the requirements of paragraph (1) of this subsection when such requirements are not necessary for the protection of the public health.

(4) A drug which is subject to paragraph (1) of this subsection shall be deemed to be misbranded if at any time prior to dispensing its label fails to bear the statement "Caution: Federal law prohibits dispensing without prescription". A drug to which paragraph (1) of this subsection does not apply shall be deemed to be misbranded if at any time prior to dispensing its label bears the caution statement quoted in the preceding sentence.

(5) Nothing in this subsection shall be construed to relieve any person from any requirement prescribed by or under authority of law with respect to drugs now included or which may hereafter be included within the classifications stated in section 3220 of Title 26, or to marihuana as defined in section 3238(b) of Title 26.

(c) Sales restrictions

(1) No person may sell, purchase, or trade or offer to sell, purchase, or trade any drug sample. For purposes of this paragraph and subsection (d) of this section, the term "drug sample" means a unit of a drug, subject to subsection (b) of this section, which is not intended to be sold and is intended to promote the sale of the drug. Nothing in this paragraph shall subject an officer or executive of a drug manufacturer or distributor to criminal liability solely because of a sale, purchase, trade, or offer to sell, purchase, or trade in violation of this paragraph by other employees of the manufacturer or distributor.

(2) No person may sell, purchase, or trade, offer to sell, purchase, or trade, or counterfeit any coupon. For purposes of this paragraph, the term "coupon" means a form which may be redeemed, at no cost or at a reduced cost, for a drug which is prescribed in accordance with subsection (b) of this section.

(3)(A) No person may sell, purchase, or trade, or offer to sell, purchase, or trade, any drug—

(i) which is subject to subsection (b) of this section, and

(ii)(I) which was purchased by a public or private hospital or other health care entity, or

(II) which was donated or supplied at a reduced price to a charitable organization described in section 501(c)(3) of Title 26.

(B) Subparagraph (A) does not apply to—

(i) the purchase or other acquisition by a hospital or other health care entity which is a member of a group purchasing organization of a drug for its own use from the group purchasing organization or from other hospitals or health care entities which are members of such organization,

(ii) the sale, purchase, or trade of a drug or an offer to sell, purchase, or trade a drug by an organization described in subparagraph (A)(ii)(II) to a nonprofit affiliate of the organization to the extent otherwise permitted by law,

(iii) a sale, purchase, or trade of a drug or an offer to sell, purchase, or trade a drug among hospitals or other health care entities which are under common control,

(iv) a sale, purchase, or trade of a drug or an offer to sell, purchase, or trade a drug for emergency medical reasons, or

(v) a sale, purchase, or trade of a drug, an offer to sell, purchase, or trade a drug, or the dispensing of a drug pursuant to a prescription executed in accordance with subsection (b) of this section.

For purposes of this paragraph, the term "entity" does not include a wholesale distributor of drugs or a retail pharmacy licensed under State law and the term "emergency medical reasons" includes transfers of a drug between health care entities or from a health care entity to a retail pharmacy undertaken to alleviate temporary shortages of the drug arising from delays in or interruptions of regular distribution schedules.

(d) Distribution of drug samples

(1) Except as provided in paragraphs (2) and (3), no person may distribute any drug sample. For purposes of this subsection, the term "distribute" does not include the providing of a drug sample to a patient by a—

(A) practitioner licensed to prescribe such drug,

(B) health care professional acting at the direction and under the supervision of such a practitioner, or

(C) pharmacy of a hospital or of another health care entity that is acting at the direction of such a practitioner and that received such sample pursuant to paragraph (2) or (3).

(2)(A) The manufacturer or authorized distributor of record of a drug subject to subsection (b) of this section may, in accordance with this paragraph, distribute drug samples by mail or common carrier to practitioners licensed to prescribe such drugs or, at the request of a licensed practitioner, to pharmacies of hospitals or other health care entities. Such a distribution of drug samples may only be made—

(i) in response to a written request for drug samples made on a form which meets the requirements of subparagraph (B), and

(ii) under a system which requires the recipient of the drug sample to execute a written receipt for the drug sample upon its delivery and the return of the receipt to the manufacturer or authorized distributor of record.

(B) A written request for a drug sample required by subparagraph (A)(i) shall contain—

(i) the name, address, professional designation, and signature of the practitioner making the request,

(ii) the identity of the drug sample requested and the quantity requested,

(iii) the name of the manufacturer of the drug sample requested, and

(iv) the date of the request.

(C) Each drug manufacturer or authorized distributor of record which makes distributions by mail or common carrier under this paragraph shall maintain, for a period of 3 years, the request forms submitted for such distributions and the receipts submitted for such distributions and shall maintain a record of distributions of drug samples which identifies the drugs distributed and the recipients of the distributions. Forms, receipts, and records required to be maintained under this subparagraph shall be made available by the drug manufacturer or distributor to Federal and State officials engaged in the regulation of drugs and in the enforcement of laws applicable to drugs.

(3) The manufacturer or distributor of a drug subject to subsection (b) of this section may, by means other than mail or common carrier, distribute drug samples only if the manufacturer or distributor makes the distributions in accordance with subparagraph (A) and carries out the activities described in subparagraphs (B) through (F) as follows:

(A) Drug samples may only be distributed—

(i) to practitioners licensed to prescribe such drugs if they make a written request for the drug samples, or

(ii) at the written request of such a licensed practitioner, to pharmacies of hospitals or other health care entities.

A written request for drug samples shall be made on a form which contains the practitioner's name, address, and professional designation, the identity of the drug sample requested, the quantity of drug samples requested, the name of the manufacturer or distributor of the drug sample, the date of the request and signature of the practitioner making the request.

(B) Drug manufacturers or authorized distributors of record shall store drug samples under conditions that will maintain their stability, integrity, and effectiveness and will assure that the drug samples will be free of contamination, deterioration, and adulteration.

(C) Drug manufacturers or authorized distributors of record shall conduct, at least annually, a complete and accurate inventory of all drug samples in the possession of representatives of the manufacturer or distributor. Drug manufacturers or authorized distributors of record shall maintain lists of the names and address of each of their representatives who distribute drug samples and of the sites where drug samples are stored. Drug manufacturers or authorized distributors of record shall maintain records for at least 3 years of all drug samples distributed, destroyed, or returned to the manufacturer or distributor, of all inventories maintained under this subparagraph, of all thefts or significant losses of drug samples, and of all requests made under subparagraph (A) for drug samples. Records and lists maintained under this subparagraph shall be made available by the drug manufacturer or distributor to the Secretary upon request.

(D) Drug manufacturers or authorized distributors of record shall notify the Secretary of any significant loss of drug samples and any known theft of drug samples.

(E) Drug manufacturers or authorized distributors of record shall report to the Secretary any conviction of their representatives for violations of subsection (c)(1) of this section or a State law because of the sale, purchase, or trade of a drug sample or the offer to sell, purchase, or trade a drug sample.

(F) Drug manufacturers or authorized distributors of record shall provide to the Secretary the name and telephone number of the individual responsible for responding to a request for information respecting drug samples.

(e) Wholesale distributors; guidelines for licensing; definitions

(1)(A) Each person who is engaged in the wholesale distribution of a drug subject to subsection (b) of this section and who is not the manufacturer or an authorized distributor of record of such drug shall, before each wholesale distribution of such drug (including each distribution to an authorized distributor of record or to a retail pharmacy), provide to the person who receives the drug a statement (in such form and containing such information as the Secretary may require) identifying each prior sale, purchase, or trade of such drug (including the date of the transaction and the names and addresses of all parties to the transaction).

(B) Each manufacturer of a drug subject to subsection (b) of this section shall maintain at its corporate offices a current list of the authorized distributors of record of such drug; and

(2)(A) No person may engage in the wholesale distribution in interstate commerce of drugs subject to subsection (b) of this section in a State unless such person is licensed by the State in accordance with the guidelines issued under subparagraph (B).

(B) The Secretary shall by regulation issue guidelines establishing minimum standards, terms, and conditions for the licensing of persons to make wholesale distributions in interstate commerce of drugs subject to subsection (b) of this section. Such guidelines shall prescribe requirements for the storage and handling of such drugs and for the establishment and maintenance of records of the distributions of such drugs.

(3) For the purposes of this subsection and subsection (d) of this section—

(A) the term "authorized distributors of record" means those distributors with whom a manufacturer has established an ongoing relationship to distribute such manufacturer's products, and

(B) the term "wholesale distribution" means distribution of drugs subject to subsection (b) of this section to other than the consumer or patient but does not include intracompany sales and does not include distributions of drugs described in subsection (c)(3)(B) of this section.

(f) Veterinary prescription drugs

(1)(A) A drug intended for use by animals other than man which—

(i) because of its toxicity or other potentiality for harmful effect, or the method of its use, or the collateral measures necessary for its use, is not safe for animal use except under the professional supervision of a licensed veterinarian, or

(ii) is limited by an approved application under subsection (b) of section 512 to use under the professional supervision of a licensed veterinarian,

shall be dispensed only by or upon the lawful written or oral order of a licensed veterinarian in the course of the veterinarian's professional practice.

(B) For purposes of subparagraph (A), an order is lawful if the order—

(i) is a prescription or other order authorized by law,

(ii) is, if an oral order, promptly reduced to writing by the person lawfully filling the order, and filed by that person, and

(iii) is refilled only if authorized in the original order or in a subsequent oral order promptly reduced to writing by the person lawfully filling the order, and filed by that person.

(C) The act of dispensing a drug contrary to the provisions, of this paragraph shall be deemed to be an act which results in the drug being misbranded while held for sale.

(2) Any drug when dispensed in accordance with paragraph (1) of this subsection—

    (A) shall be exempt from the requirements of section 352 of this title, except paragraphs (a), (g), (h), (i)(2), (i)(3), and (p) of such section, and

    (B) shall be exempt from the packaging requirements of paragraphs (g), (h), and (p) of such section, if—

        (i) when dispensed by a licensed veterinarian, the drug bears a label containing the name and address of the practitioner and any directions for use and cautionary statements specified by the practitioner, or

        (ii) when dispensed by filling the lawful order of a licensed veterinarian, the drug bears a label containing the name and address of the dispenser, the serial number and date of the order or of its filling, the name of the licensed veterinarian, and the directions for use and cautionary statements, if any, contained in such order.

The preceding sentence shall not apply to any drug dispensed in the course of the conduct of a business of dispensing drugs pursuant to diagnosis by mail.

(3) The Secretary may by regulation exempt drugs for animals other than man subject to section 512 from the requirements of paragraph (1) when such requirements are not necessary for the protection of the public health.

(4) A drug which is subject to paragraph (1) shall be deemed to be misbranded if at any time prior to dispensing its label fails to bear the statement "Caution: Federal law restricts this drug to use by or on the order of a licensed veterinarian.". A drug to which paragraph (1) does not apply shall be deemed to be misbranded if at any time prior to dispensing its label bears the statement specified in the preceding sentence.

(g) Combinations of drugs, devices, or biological products

(1) The Secretary shall designate a component of the Food and Drug Administration to regulate products that constitute a combination of a drug, device, or biological product. The Secretary shall determine the primary mode of action of the combination product. If the Secretary determines that the primary mode of action is that of—

    (A) a drug (other than a biological product), the persons charged with premarket review of drugs shall have primary jurisdiction,

(B) a device, the persons charged with premarket review of devices shall have primary jurisdiction, or

(C) a biological product, the persons charged with premarket review of biological products shall have primary jurisdiction.

(2) Nothing in this subsection shall prevent the Secretary from using any agency resources of the Food and Drug Administration necessary to ensure adequate review of the safety, effectiveness, or substantial equivalence of an article.

(3) The Secretary shall promulgate regulations to implement market clearance procedures in accordance with paragraphs (1) and (2) not later than 1 year after November 28, 1990.

(4) As used in this subsection:

(A) The term "biological product" has the meaning given the term in section 262(a) of Title 42.

(B) The term "market clearance" includes—

(i) approval of an application under section 355, 357, 360e, or 360j(g),

(ii) a finding of substantial equivalence under this subchapter, and

(iii) approval of a product or establishment license under subsection (a) or (d) of section 262 of Title 42.

§ 354. Repealed. Pub.L. 86–618, Title I, § 103(a)(2), July 12, 1960, 74 Stat. 398

§ 355. New drugs

(a) Necessity of effective approval of application

No person shall introduce or deliver for introduction into interstate commerce any new drug, unless an approval of an application filed pursuant to subsection (b) or (j) of this section is effective with respect to such drug.

(b) Filing application; contents

(1) Any person may file with the Secretary an application with respect to any drug subject to the provisions of subsection (a) of this section. Such person shall submit to the Secretary as a part of the application (A) full reports of investigations which have been made to show whether or not such drug is safe for use and whether such drug is effective in use; (B) a full list of the articles used as components of such drug; (C) a full statement of the composition of such drug; (D) a full description of the methods used in, and the facilities and controls used for, the manufacture, processing, and packing of such drug; (E) such samples of such drug and of the articles used as components thereof as the Secretary may require; and (F) specimens of the labeling proposed to

be used for such drug. The applicant shall file with the application the patent number and the expiration date of any patent which claims the drug for which the applicant submitted the application or which claims a method of using such drug and with respect to which a claim of patent infringement could reasonably be asserted if a person not licensed by the owner engaged in the manufacture, use, or sale of the drug. If an application is filed under this subsection for a drug and a patent which claims such drug or a method of using such drug is issued after the filing date but before approval of the application, the applicant shall amend the application to include the information required by the preceding sentence. Upon approval of the application, the Secretary shall publish information submitted under the two preceding sentences.

(2) An application submitted under paragraph (1) for a drug for which the investigations described in clause (A) of such paragraph and relied upon by the applicant for approval of the application were not conducted by or for the applicant and for which the applicant has not obtained a right of reference or use from the person by or for whom the investigations were conducted shall also include—

(A) a certification, in the opinion of the applicant and to the best of his knowledge, with respect to each patent which claims the drug for which such investigations were conducted or which claims a use for such drug for which the applicant is seeking approval under this subsection and for which information is required to be filed under paragraph (1) or subsection (c) of this section—

(i) that such patent information has not been filed,

(ii) that such patent has expired,

(iii) of the date on which such patent will expire, or

(iv) that such patent is invalid or will not be infringed by the manufacture use, or sale of the new drug for which the application is submitted; and

(B) if with respect to the drug for which investigations described in paragraph (1)(A) were conducted information was filed under paragraph (1) or subsection (c) of this section for a method of use patent which does not claim a use for which the applicant is seeking approval under this subsection, a statement that the method of use patent does not claim such a use.

(3)(A) An applicant who makes a certification described in paragraph (2)(A)(iv) shall include in the application a statement that the applicant will give the notice required by subparagraph (B) to—

(i) each owner of the patent which is the subject of the certification or the representative of such owner designated to receive such notice, and

(ii) the holder of the approved application under subsection (b) of this section for the drug which is claimed by the patent or a use of which is claimed by the patent or the representative of such holder designated to receive such notice.

(B) The notice referred to in subparagraph (A) shall state that an application has been submitted under this subsection for the drug with respect to which the certification is made to obtain approval to engage in the commercial manufacture, use, or sale of the drug before the expiration of the patent referred to in the certification. Such notice shall include a detailed statement of the factual and legal basis of the applicant's opinion that the patent is not valid or will not be infringed.

(C) If an application is amended to include a certification described in paragraph (2)(A)(iv), the notice required by subparagraph (B) shall be given when the amended application is submitted.

(c) Period for approval of application; period for, notice, and expedition of hearing; period for issuance of order

(1) Within one hundred and eighty days after the filing of an application under subsection (b) of this section, or such additional period as may be agreed upon by the Secretary and the applicant, the Secretary shall either—

(A) Approve the application if he then finds that none of the grounds for denying approval specified in subsection (d) of this section applies, or

(B) Give the applicant notice of an opportunity for a hearing before the Secretary under subsection (d) of this section on the question whether such application is approvable. If the applicant elects to accept the opportunity for hearing by written request within thirty days after such notice, such hearing shall commence not more than ninety days after the expiration of such thirty days unless the Secretary and the applicant otherwise agree. Any such hearing shall thereafter be conducted on an expedited basis and the Secretary's order thereon shall be issued within ninety days after the date fixed by the Secretary for filing final briefs.

(2) If the patent information described in subsection (b) of this section could not be filed with the submission of an application under subsection (b) of this section because the application was filed before the patent information was required under subsection (b) of this section or a patent was issued after the application was approved under such subsection, the holder of an approved application shall file with the Secretary the patent number and the expiration date of any patent which claims the drug for which the application was submitted or which claims a method of using such drug and with respect to which a claim of patent infringement could reasonably be asserted if a person not licensed by the owner engaged in the manufacture, use, or sale of the drug. If the holder of an approved application could not file patent information under subsection (b) of this section because it was not required at the time the application was approved, the holder shall file such information under

this subsection not later than thirty days after September 24, 1984, and if the holder of an approved application could not file patent information under subsection (b) of this section because no patent had been issued when an application was filed or approved, the holder shall file such information under this subsection not later than thirty days after the date the patent involved is issued. Upon the submission of patent information under this subsection, the Secretary shall publish it.

(3) The approval of an application filed under subsection (b) of this section which contains a certification required by paragraph (2) of such subsection shall be made effective on the last applicable date determined under the following:

(A) If the applicant only made a certification described in clause (i) or (ii) of subsection (b)(2)(A) of this section or in both such clauses, the approval may be made effective immediately.

(B) If the applicant made a certification described in clause (iii) of subsection (b)(2)(A) of this section, the approval may be made effective on the date certified under clause (iii).

(C) If the applicant made a certification described in clause (iv) of subsection (b)(2)(A) of this section, the approval shall be made effective immediately unless an action is brought for infringement of a patent which is the subject of the certification before the expiration of forty-five days from the date the notice provided under paragraph (3)(B) is received. If such an action is brought before the expiration of such days, the approval may be made effective upon the expiration of the thirty-month period beginning on the date of the receipt of the notice provided under paragraph (3)(B) or such shorter or longer period as the court may order because either party to the action failed to reasonably cooperate in expediting the action, except that—

(i) if before the expiration of such period the court decides that such patent is invalid or not infringed, the approval may be made effective on the date of the court decision,

(ii) if before the expiration of such period the court decides that such patent has been infringed, the approval may be made effective on such date as the court orders under section 271(e)(4)(A) of Title 35, or

(iii) if before the expiration of such period the court grants a preliminary injunction prohibiting the applicant from engaging in the commercial manufacture or sale of the drug until the court decides the issues of patent validity and infringement and if the court decides that such patent is invalid or not infringed, the approval shall be made effective on the date of such court decision.

In such an action, each of the parties shall reasonably cooperate in expediting the action. Until the expiration of forty-five days from the date the notice made under paragraph (3)(B) is received, no action may be brought under section 2201 of Title 28 for a declaratory judgment with respect to the patent. Any action brought under such section 2201 shall be brought in the judicial district where the defendant has its principal place of business or a regular and established place of business.

(D)(i) If an application (other than an abbreviated new drug application) submitted under subsection (b) of this section for a drug, no active ingredient (including any ester or salt of the active ingredient) of which has been approved in any other application under subsection (b) of this section, was approved during the period beginning January 1, 1982, and ending on September 24, 1984, the Secretary may not make the approval of another application for a drug for which the investigations described in clause (A) of subsection (b)(1) of this section and relied upon by the applicant for approval of the application were not conducted by or for the applicant and for which the applicant has not obtained a right of reference or use from the person by or for whom the investigations were conducted effective before the expiration of ten years from the date of the approval of the application previously approved under subsection (b) of this section.

(ii) If an application submitted under subsection (b) of this section for a drug, no active ingredient (including any ester or salt of the active ingredient) of which has been approved in any other application under subsection (b) of this section, is approved after September 24, 1984, no application which refers to the drug for which the subsection (b) application was submitted and for which the investigations described in clause (A) of subsection (b)(1) of this section and relied upon by the applicant for approval of the application were not conducted by or for the applicant and for which the applicant has not obtained a right of reference or use from the person by or for whom the investigations were conducted may be submitted under subsection (b) of this section before the expiration of five years from the date of the approval of the application under subsection (b) of this section, except that such an application may be submitted under subsection (b) of this section after the expiration of four years from the date of the approval of the subsection (b) application if it contains a certification of patent invalidity or noninfringement described in clause (iv) of subsection (b)(2)(A) of this section. The approval of such an application shall be made effective in accordance with this paragraph except that, if an action for patent infringement is commenced during the one-year period beginning forty-eight months after the date of the approval of the subsection (b) application, the thirty-month period referred to in subparagraph (C) shall be extended by such amount of time (if any) which is required for seven and one-half years to have elapsed from the date of approval of the subsection (b) application.

(iii) If an application submitted under subsection (b) of this section for a drug, which includes an active ingredient (including any ester or salt of the active ingredient) that has been approved in another application approved under subsection (b) of this section, is approved after September 24, 1984, and if such application contains reports of new clinical investigations (other than bioavailability studies) essential to the approval of the application and conducted or sponsored by the applicant, the Secretary may not make the approval of an application submitted under subsection (b) of this section for the conditions of approval of such drug in the approved subsection (b) application effective before the expiration of three years from the date of the approval of the application under subsection (b) of this section if the investigations described in clause (A) of subsection (b)(1) of this section and relied upon by the applicant for approval of the application were not conducted by or for the applicant and if the applicant has not obtained a right of reference or use from the person by or for whom the investigations were conducted.

(iv) If a supplement to an application approved under subsection (b) of this section is approved after September 24, 1984, and the supplement contains reports of new clinical investigations (other than bioavailability studies) essential to the approval of the supplement and conducted or sponsored by the person submitting the supplement, the Secretary may not make the approval of an application submitted under subsection (b) of this section for a change approved in the supplement effective before the expiration of three years from the date of the approval of the supplement under subsection (b) of this section if the investigations described in clause (A) of subsection (b)(1) of this section and relied upon by the applicant for approval of the application were not conducted by or for the applicant and if the applicant has not obtained a right of reference or use from the person by or for whom the investigations were conducted.

(v) If an application (or supplement to an application) submitted under subsection (b) of this section for a drug, which includes an active ingredient (including any ester or salt of the active ingredient) that has been approved in another application under subsection (b) of this section, was approved during the period beginning January 1, 1982, and ending on September 24, 1984, the Secretary may not make the approval of an application submitted under this subsection and for which the investigations described in clause (A) of subsection (b)(1) of this section and relied upon by the applicant for approval of the application were not conducted by or for the applicant and for which the applicant has not obtained a right of reference or use from the person by or for whom the investigations were conducted and which refers to the drug for which the subsection (b) application was submitted effective before the expiration of two years from September 24, 1984.

(d) Grounds for refusing application; approval of application; "substantial evidence" defined

If the Secretary finds, after due notice to the applicant in accordance with subsection (c) of this section and giving him an opportunity for a hearing, in accordance with said subsection, that (1) the investigations, reports of which are required to be submitted to the Secretary pursuant to subsection (b) of this section, do not include adequate tests by all methods reasonably applicable to show whether or not such drug is safe for use under the conditions prescribed, recommended, or suggested in the proposed labeling thereof; (2) the results of such tests show that such drug is unsafe for use under such conditions or do not show that such drug is safe for use under such conditions; (3) the methods used in, and the facilities and controls used for, the manufacture, processing, and packing of such drug are inadequate to preserve its identity, strength, quality, and purity; (4) upon the basis of the information submitted to him as part of the application, or upon the basis of any other information before him with respect to such drug, he has insufficient information to determine whether such drug is safe for use under such conditions; or (5) evaluated on the basis of the information submitted to him as part of the application and any other information before him with respect to such drug, there is a lack of substantial evidence that the drug will have the effect it purports or is represented to have under the conditions of use prescribed, recommended, or suggested in the proposed labeling thereof; or (6) the application failed to contain the patent information prescribed by subsection (b) of this section; or (7) based on a fair evaluation of all material facts, such labeling is false or misleading in any particular; he shall issue an order refusing to approve the application. If, after such notice and opportunity for hearing, the Secretary finds that clauses (1) through (6) do not apply, he shall issue an order approving the application. As used in this subsection and subsection (e) of this section, the term "substantial evidence" means evidence consisting of adequate and well- controlled investigations, including clinical investigations, by experts qualified by scientific training and experience to evaluate the effectiveness of the drug involved, on the basis of which it could fairly and responsibly be concluded by such experts that the drug will have the effect it purports or is represented to have under the conditions of use prescribed, recommended, or suggested in the labeling or proposed labeling thereof.

(e) Withdrawal of approval; grounds; immediate suspension upon finding imminent hazard to public health

The Secretary shall, after due notice and opportunity for hearing to the applicant, withdraw approval of an application with respect to any drug under this section if the Secretary finds (1) that clinical or other experience, tests, or other scientific data show that such drug is unsafe for use under the conditions of use upon the basis of which the application was approved; (2) that new evidence of clinical experience, not contained in such application or not available to the Secretary until after such application was approved, or tests by new methods, or tests by methods not deemed reasonably applicable when such application was approved, evaluated together with the evidence available to the Secretary when the application was approved, shows that such drug is not shown to be safe for use under the conditions of use upon the basis of which the application was approved; or (3) on the basis of new information before him with respect to such drug, evaluated together with the evidence available to him when the application was approved, that there is a lack of substantial evidence that the drug will have the effect it purports or is represented to have under the conditions of use prescribed, recommended, or suggested in the labeling thereof; or (4) the patent information prescribed by subsection (c) of this section was not filed within thirty days after the receipt of written notice from the Secretary specifying the failure to file such information; or (5) that the at the application contains any untrue statement of a material fact: Provided, That if the Secretary (or in his absence the officer acting as Secretary) finds that there is an imminent hazard to the public health, he may suspend the approval of such application immediately, and give the applicant prompt notice of his action and afford the applicant the opportunity for an expedited hearing under this subsection; but the authority conferred by this proviso to suspend the approval of an application shall not be delegated. The Secretary may also, after due notice and opportunity for hearing to the applicant, withdraw the approval of an application submitted under subsection (b) or (j) of this section with respect to any drug under this section if the Secretary finds (1) that the applicant has failed to establish a system for maintaining required records, or has repeatedly or deliberately failed to maintain such records or to make required reports, in accordance with a regulation or order under subsection (k) of this section or to comply with the notice requirements of section 360(k)(2) of this title, or the applicant has refused to permit access to, or copying or verification of, such records as required by paragraph (2) of such subsection; or (2) that on the basis of new information before him, evaluated together with the evidence before him when the application was approved, the methods used in, or the facilities and controls used for, the manufacture, processing, and packing of such drug are inadequate to assure and preserve its identity, strength, quality, and purity and were not made adequate within a reasonable time after receipt of written notice from the Secretary specifying the matter complained of; or (3) that on the basis of new information before him, evaluated together with the evidence before him when the application was approved, the labeling of such drug, based on a fair evaluation of all material facts, is false or misleading in any particular and was not corrected within a reasonable time after receipt of written notice from the Secretary specifying the matter complained of. Any order under this subsection shall state the findings upon which it is based.

(f) Revocation of order refusing, withdrawing or suspending approval of application

Whenever the Secretary finds that the facts so require, he shall revoke any previous order under subsection (d) or (e) of this section refusing, withdrawing, or suspending approval of an application and shall approve such application or reinstate such approval, as may be appropriate.

(g) Service of orders

Orders of the Secretary issued under this section shall be served (1) in person by any officer or employee of the Department designated by the Secretary or (2) by mailing the order by registered mail or by certified mail addressed to the applicant or respondent at his last-known address in the records of the Secretary.

(h) Appeal from order

An appeal may be taken by the applicant from an order of the Secretary refusing or withdrawing approval of an application under this section. Such appeal shall be taken by filing in the United States court of appeals for the circuit wherein such applicant resides or has his principal place of business, or in the United States Court of Appeals for the District of Columbia Circuit, within sixty days after the entry of such order, a written petition praying that the order of the Secretary be set aside. A copy of such petition shall be forthwith transmitted by the clerk of the court to the Secretary, or any officer designated by him for that purpose, and thereupon the Secretary shall certify and file in the court the record upon which the order complained of was entered, as provided in section 2112 of Title 28. Upon the filing of such petition such court shall have exclusive jurisdiction to affirm or set aside such order, except that until the filing of the record the Secretary may modify or set aside his order. No objection to the order of the Secretary shall be considered by the court unless such objection shall have been urged before the Secretary or unless there were reasonable grounds for failure so to do. The finding of the Secretary as to the facts, if supported by substantial evidence, shall be conclusive. If any person shall apply to the court for leave to adduce additional evidence, and shall show to the satisfaction of the court that such additional evidence is material and that there were reasonable grounds for failure to adduce such evidence in the proceeding before the Secretary, the court may order such additional evidence to be taken before the Secretary and to be adduced upon the hearing in such manner and upon such terms and conditions as to the court may seem proper. The Secretary may modify his findings as to the facts by reason of the additional evidence so taken, and he shall file with the court such modified findings which, if supported by substantial evidence, shall be conclusive, and his recommendation, if any, for the setting aside of the original order. The judgment of the court affirming or setting aside any such order of the Secretary shall be final, subject to review by the Supreme Court of the United States upon certiorari or certification as provided in section 1254 of Title 28. The commencement of proceedings under this subsection shall not, unless specifically ordered by the court to the contrary, operate as a stay of the Secretary's order.

(i) Exemptions of drugs for research; discretionary and mandatory conditions; direct reports to Secretary

The Secretary shall promulgate regulations for exempting from the operation of the foregoing subsections of this section drugs intended solely for investigational use by experts qualified by scientific training and experience to investigate the safety and effectiveness of drugs. Such regulations may, within the discretion of the Secretary, among other conditions relating to the protection of the public health, provide for conditioning such exemption upon—

(1) the submission to the Secretary, before any clinical testing of a new drug is undertaken, of reports, by the manufacturer or the sponsor of the investigation of such drug, of preclinical tests (including tests on animals) of such drug adequate to justify the proposed clinical testing;

(2) the manufacturer or the sponsor of the investigation of a new drug proposed to be distributed to investigators for clinical testing obtaining a signed agreement from each of such investigators that patients to whom the drug is administered will be under his personal supervision, or under the supervision of investigators responsible to him, and that he will not supply such drug to any other investigator, or to clinics, for administration to human beings; and

(3) the establishment and maintenance of such records, and the making of such reports to the Secretary, by the manufacturer or the sponsor of the investigation of such drug, of data (including but not limited to analytical reports by investigators) obtained as the result of such investigational use of such drug, as the Secretary finds will enable him to evaluate the safety and effectiveness of such drug in the event of the filing of an application pursuant to subsection (b) of this section.

Such regulations shall provide that such exemption shall be conditioned upon the manufacturer, or the sponsor of the investigation, requiring that experts using such drugs for investigational purposes certify to such manufacturer or sponsor that they will inform any human beings to whom such drugs, or any controls used in connection therewith, are being administered, or their representatives, that such drugs are being used for investigational purposes and will obtain the consent of such human beings or their representatives, except where they deem it not feasible or, in their professional judgment, contrary to the best interests of such human beings. Nothing in this subsection shall be construed to require any clinical investigator to submit directly to the Secretary reports on the investigational use of drugs.

(j) Abbreviated new drug applications

(1) Any person may file with the Secretary an abbreviated application for the approval of a new drug.

(2)(A) An abbreviated application for a new drug shall contain—

(i) information to show that the conditions of use prescribed, recommended, or suggested in the labeling proposed for the new drug have been previously approved for a drug listed under paragraph (6) (hereinafter in this subsection referred to as a "listed drug");

(ii)(I) if the listed drug referred to in clause (i) has only one active ingredient, information to show that the active ingredient of the new drug is the same as that of the listed drug;

(II) if the listed drug referred to in clause (i) has more than one active ingredient, information to show that the active ingredients of the new drug are the same as those of the listed drug, or

(III) if the listed drug referred to in clause (i) has more than one active ingredient and if one of the active ingredients of the new drug is different and the application is filed pursuant to the approval of a petition filed under subparagraph (C), information to show that the other active ingredients of the new drug are the same as the active ingredients of the listed drug, information to show that the different active ingredient is an active ingredient of a listed drug or of a drug which does not meet the requirements of section 321(p) of this title, and such other information respecting the different active ingredient with respect to which the petition was filed as the Secretary may require;

(iii) information to show that the route of administration, the dosage form, and the strength of the new drug are the same as those of the listed drug referred to in clause (i) or, if the route of administration, the dosage form, or the strength of the new drug is different and the application is filed pursuant to the approval of a petition filed under subparagraph (C), such information respecting the route of administration, dosage form, or strength with respect to which the petition was filed as the Secretary may require;

(iv) information to show that the new drug is bioequivalent to the listed drug referred to in clause (i), except that if the application is filed pursuant to the approval of a petition filed under subparagraph (C), information to show that the active ingredients of the new drug are of the same pharmacological or therapeutic class as those of the listed drug referred to in clause (i) and the new drug can be expected to have the same therapeutic effect as the listed drug when administered to patients for a condition of use referred to in clause (i);

(v) information to show that the labeling proposed for the new drug is the same as the labeling approved for the listed drug referred to in clause (i) except for changes required because of differences approved under a petition filed under subparagraph (C) or because the new drug and the listed drug are produced or distributed by different manufacturers;

(vi) the items specified in clauses (B) through (F) of subsection (b)(1) of this section;

(vii) a certification, in the opinion of the applicant and to the best of his knowledge, with respect to each patent which claims the listed drug referred to in clause (i) or which claims a use for such listed drug for which the applicant is seeking approval under this subsection and for which information is required to be filed under subsection (b) or (c) of this section—

(I) that such patent information has not been filed,

(II) that such patent has expired,

(III) of the date on which such patent will expire, or

(IV) that such patent is invalid or will not be infringed by the manufacture, use, or sale of the new drug for which the application is submitted; and

(viii) if with respect to the listed drug referred to in clause (i) information was filed under subsection (b) or (c) of this section for a method of use patent which does not claim a use for which the applicant is seeking approval under this subsection, a statement that the method of use patent does not claim such a use.

The Secretary may not require that an abbreviated application contain information in addition to that required by clauses (i) through (viii).

(B)(i) An applicant who makes a certification described in subparagraph (A)(vii)(IV) shall include in the application a statement that the applicant will give the notice required by clause (ii) to—

(I) each owner of the patent which is the subject of the certification or the representative of such owner designated to receive such notice, and

(II) the holder of the approved application under subsection (b) of this section for the drug which is claimed by the patent or a use of which is claimed by the patent or the representative of such holder designated to receive such notice.

(ii) The notice referred to in clause (i) shall state that an application, which contains data from bioavailability or bioequivalence studies, has been submitted under this subsection for the drug with respect to which the certification is made to obtain approval to engage in the commercial manufacture, use, or sale of such drug before the expiration of the patent referred to in the certification. Such notice shall include a detailed statement of the factual and legal basis of the applicant's opinion that the patent is not valid or will not be infringed.

(iii) If an application is amended to include a certification described in subparagraph (A)(vii)(IV), the notice required by clause (ii) shall be given when the amended application is submitted.

(C) If a person wants to submit an abbreviated application for a new drug which has a different active ingredient or whose route of adminis-tration, dosage form, or strength differ from that of a listed drug, such person shall submit a petition to the Secretary seeking permission to file such an application. The Secretary shall approve or disapprove a petition submitted under this subparagraph within ninety days of the date the petition is submitted. The Secretary shall approve such a petition unless the Secretary finds—

(i) that investigations must be conducted to show the safety and effectiveness of the drug or of any of its active ingredients, the route of administration, the dosage form, or strength which differ from the listed drug; or

(ii) that any drug with a different active ingredient may not be adequately evaluated for approval as safe and effective on the basis of the information required to be submitted in an abbreviated application.

(3) Subject to paragraph (4), the Secretary shall approve an applica-tion for a drug unless the Secretary finds—

(A) the methods used in, or the facilities and controls used for, the manufacture, processing, and packing of the drug are inadequate to assure and preserve its identity, strength, quality, and purity;

(B) information submitted with the application is insufficient to show that each of the proposed conditions of use have been previous-ly approved for the listed drug referred to in the application;

(C)(i) if the listed drug has only one active ingredient, informa-tion submitted with the application is insufficient to show that the active ingredient is the same as that of the listed drug;

(ii) if the listed drug has more than one active ingredient, information submitted with the application is insufficient to show that the active ingredients are the same as the active ingredients of the listed drug, or

(iii) if the listed drug has more than one active ingredient and if the application is for a drug which has an active ingredient different from the listed drug, information submitted with the application is insufficient to show—

(I) that the other active ingredients are the same as the active ingredients of the listed drug, or

(II) that the different active ingredient is an active ingredient of a listed drug or a drug which does not meet the requirements of section 321(p) of this title,

or no petition to file an application for the drug with the different ingredient was approved under paragraph (2)(C);

(D)(i) if the application is for a drug whose route of administration, dosage form, or strength of the drug is the same as the route of administration, dosage form, or strength of the listed drug referred to in the application, information submitted in the application is insufficient to show that the route of administration, dosage form, or strength is the same as that of the listed drug, or

(ii) if the application is for a drug whose route of administration, dosage form, or strength of the drug is different from that of the listed drug referred to in the application, no petition to file an application for the drug with the different route of administration, dosage form, or strength was approved under paragraph (2)(C);

(E) if the application was filed pursuant to the approval of a petition under paragraph (2)(C), the application did not contain the information required by the Secretary respecting the active ingredient, route of administration, dosage form, or strength which is not the same;

(F) information submitted in the application is insufficient to show that the drug is bioequivalent to the listed drug referred to in the application or, if the application was filed pursuant to a petition approved under paragraph (2)(C), information submitted in the application is insufficient to show that the active ingredients of the new drug are of the same pharmacological or therapeutic class as those of the listed drug referred to in paragraph (2)(A)(i) and that the new drug can be expected to have the same therapeutic effect as the listed drug when administered to patients for a condition of use referred to in such paragraph;

(G) information submitted in the application is insufficient to show that the labeling proposed for the drug is the same as the labeling approved for the listed drug referred to in the application except for changes required because of differences approved under a petition filed under paragraph (2)(C) or because the drug and the listed drug are produced or distributed by different manufacturers;

(H) information submitted in the application or any other information available to the Secretary shows that (i) the inactive ingredients of the drug are unsafe for use under the conditions prescribed, recommended, or suggested in the labeling proposed for the drug, or (ii) the composition of the drug is unsafe under such conditions because of the type or quantity of inactive ingredients included or the manner in which the inactive ingredients are included;

(I) the approval under subsection (c) of this section of the listed drug referred to in the application under this subsection has been withdrawn or suspended for grounds described in the first sentence of subsection (e) of this section, the Secretary has published a notice of opportunity for hearing to withdraw approval of the listed drug under subsection (c) of this section for grounds described in the first sentence of subsection (e) of this section, the approval under this subsection of the listed drug referred to in the application under this subsection has been withdrawn or suspended under paragraph (5), or the Secretary has determined that the listed drug has been withdrawn from sale for safety or effectiveness reasons;

(J) the application does not meet any other requirement of paragraph (2)(A); or

(K) the application contains an untrue statement of material fact.

(4)(A) Within one hundred and eighty days of the initial receipt of an application under paragraph (2) or within such additional period as may be agreed upon by the Secretary and the applicant, the Secretary shall approve or disapprove the application.

(B) The approval of an application submitted under paragraph (2) shall be made effective on the last applicable date determined under the following:

(i) If the applicant only made a certification described in subclause (I) or (II) of paragraph (2)(A)(vii) or in both such subclauses, the approval may be made effective immediately.

(ii) If the applicant made a certification described in subclause (III) of paragraph (2)(A)(vii), the approval may be made effective on the date certified under subclause (III).

(iii) If the applicant made a certification described in subclause (IV) of paragraph (2)(A)(vii), the approval shall be made effective immediately unless an action is brought for infringement of a patent which is the subject of the certification before the expiration of forty-five days from the date the notice provided under paragraph (2)(B)(i) is received. If such an action is brought before the expiration of such days, the approval shall be made effective upon the expiration of the thirty-month period beginning on the date of the receipt of the notice provided under paragraph (2)(B)(i) or such shorter or longer period as the court may order because either party to the action failed to reasonably cooperate in expediting the action, except that—

(I) if before the expiration of such period the court decides that such patent is invalid or not infringed, the approval shall be made effective on the date of the court decision,

(II) if before the expiration of such period the court decides that such patent has been infringed, the approval shall be made effective on such date as the court orders under section 271(e)(4)(A) of Title 35 or

(III) if before the expiration of such period the court grants a preliminary injunction prohibiting the applicant from engaging in the commercial manufacture or sale of the drug until the court decides the issues of patent validity and infringement and if the court decides that such patent is invalid or not infringed, the approval shall be made effective on the date of such court decision.

In such an action, each of the parties shall reasonably cooperate in expediting the action. Until the expiration of forty-five days from the date the notice made under paragraph (2)(B)(i) is received, no action may be brought under section 2201 of Title 28 for a declaratory judgment with respect to the patent. Any action brought under section 2201 shall be brought in the judicial district where the defendant has its principal place of business or a regular and established place of business.

(iv) If the application contains a certification described in subclause (IV) of paragraph (2)(A)(vii) and is for a drug for which a previous application has been submitted under this subsection continuing such a certification, the application shall be made effective not earlier than one hundred and eighty days after—

(I) the date the Secretary receives notice from the applicant under the previous application of the first commercial marketing of the drug under the previous application, or

(II) the date of a decision of a court in an action described in clause (iii) holding the patent which is the subject of the certification to be invalid or not infringed,

whichever is earlier.

(C) If the Secretary decides to disapprove an application, the Secretary shall give the applicant notice of an opportunity for a hearing before the Secretary on the question of whether such application is approvable. If the applicant elects to accept the opportunity for hearing by written request within thirty days after such notice, such hearing shall commence not more than ninety days after the expiration of such thirty days unless the Secretary and the applicant otherwise agree. Any such hearing shall thereafter be conducted on an expedited basis and the Secretary's order thereon shall be issued within ninety days after the date fixed by the Secretary for filing final briefs.

(D)(i) If an application (other than an abbreviated new drug application) submitted under subsection (b) of this section for a drug, no active ingredient (including any ester or salt of the active ingredient) of which has been approved in any other application under subsection (b) of this section, was approved during the period beginning January 1, 1982, and ending on September 24, 1984, the Secretary may not make the approval of an application submitted under this subsection which refers to the drug for which the subsection (b) application was submitted effective before the expiration of ten years from the date of the approval of the application under subsection (b) of this section.

(ii) If an application submitted under subsection (b) of this section for a drug, no active ingredient (including any ester or salt of the active ingredient) of which has been approved in any other application under subsection (b) of this section, is approved after September 24, 1984, no application may be submitted under this subsection which refers to the drug for which the subsection (b) application was submitted before the expiration of five years from the date of the approval of the application under subsection (b) of this section, except that such an application may be submitted under this subsection after the expiration of four years from the date of the approval of the subsection (b) application if it contains a certification of patent invalidity or noninfringement described in subclause (IV) of paragraph (2)(A)(vii). The approval of such an application shall be made effective in accordance with subparagraph (B) except that, if an action for patent infringement is commenced during the one-year period beginning forty-eight months after the date of the approval of the subsection (b) application, the thirty-month period referred to in subparagraph (B)(iii) shall be extended by such amount of time (if any) which is required for seven and one-half years to have elapsed from the date of approval of the subsection (b) application.

(iii) If an application submitted under subsection (b) of this section for a drug, which includes an active ingredient (including any ester or salt of the active ingredient) that has been approved in another application approved under subsection (b) of this section, is approved after September 24, 1984, and if such application contains reports of new clinical investigations (other than bioavailability studies) essential to the approval of the application and conducted or sponsored by the applicant, the Secretary may not make the approval of an application submitted under this subsection for the conditions of approval of such drug in the subsection (b) application effective before the expiration of three years from the date of the approval of the application under subsection (b) of this section for such drug.

(iv) If a supplement to an application approved under subsection (b) of this section is approved after September 24, 1984, and the supplement contains reports of new clinical investigations (other than bioavailability studies) essential to the approval of the supplement and conducted or sponsored by the person submitting the supplement, the Secretary may not make the approval of an application submitted under this subsection for a change approved in the supplement effective before the expiration of three years from the date of the approval of the supplement under subsection (b) of this section.

(v) If an application (or supplement to an application) submitted under subsection (b) of this section for a drug, which includes an active ingredient (including any ester or salt of the active ingredient) that has been approved in another application under subsection (b) of this section, was approved during the period beginning January 1, 1982, and ending on September 24, 1984, the Secretary may not make the approval of an application submitted under this subsection which refers to the drug for which the subsection (b) application was submitted or which refers to a change approved in a supplement to the subsection (b) application effective before the expiration of two years from September 24, 1984.

(5) If a drug approved under this subsection refers in its approved application to a drug the approval of which was withdrawn or suspended for grounds described in the first sentence of subsection (e) of this section or was withdrawn or suspended under this paragraph or which, as determined by the Secretary, has been withdrawn from sale for safety or effectiveness reasons, the approval of the drug under this subsection shall be withdrawn or suspended—

(A) for the same period as the withdrawal or suspension under subsection (e) of this section or this paragraph, or

(B) if the listed drug has been withdrawn from sale, for the period of withdrawal from sale or, if earlier, the period ending on the date the Secretary determines that the withdrawal from sale is not for safety or effectiveness reasons.

(6)(A)(i) Within sixty days of September 24, 1984, the Secretary shall publish and make available to the public—

(I) a list in alphabetical order of the official and proprietary name of each drug which has been approved for safety and effectiveness under subsection (c) of this section before September 24, 1984;

(II) the date of approval if the drug is approved after 1981 and the number of the application which was approved; and

(III) whether in vitro or in vivo bioequivalence studies, or both such studies, are required for applications filed under this subsection which will refer to the drug published.

(ii) Every thirty days after the publication of the first list under clause (i) the Secretary shall revise the list to include each drug which has been approved for safety and effectiveness under subsection (c) of this section or approved under this subsection during the thirty-day period.

(iii) When patent information submitted under subsection (b) or (c) of this section respecting a drug included on the list is to be published by the Secretary, the Secretary shall, in revisions made under clause (ii), include such information for such drug.

(B) A drug approved for safety and effectiveness under subsection (c) of this section or approved under this subsection shall, for purposes of this subsection, be considered to have been published under subparagraph (A) on the date of its approval or September 24, 1984, whichever is later.

(C) If the approval of a drug was withdrawn or suspended for grounds described in the first sentence of subsection (e) of this section or was withdrawn or suspended under paragraph (5) or if the Secretary determines that a drug has been withdrawn from sale for safety or effectiveness reasons, it may not be published in the list under subparagraph (A) or, if the withdrawal or suspension occurred after its publication in such list, it shall be immediately removed from such list—

(i) for the same period as the withdrawal or suspension under subsection (e) of this section or paragraph (5), or

(ii) if the listed drug has been withdrawn from sale, for the period of withdrawal from sale or, if earlier, the period ending on the date the Secretary determines that the withdrawal from sale is not for safety or effectiveness reasons.

A notice of the removal shall be published in the Federal Register.

(7) For purposes of this subsection:

(A) The term "bioavailability" means the rate and extent to which the active ingredient or therapeutic ingredient is absorbed from a drug and becomes available at the site of drug action.

(B) A drug shall be considered to be bioequivalent to a listed drug if—

(i) the rate and extent of absorption of the drug do not show a significant difference from the rate and extent of absorption of the listed drug when administered at the same molar dose of the therapeutic ingredient under similar experimental conditions in either a single dose or multiple doses; or

(ii) the extent of absorption of the drug does not show a significant difference from the extent of absorption of the listed drug when administered at the same molar dose of the therapeutic ingredient under similar experimental conditions in either a single dose or multiple doses and the difference from the listed drug in the rate of absorption of the drug is intentional, is reflected in its proposed labeling, is not essential to the attainment of effective body drug concentrations on chronic use, and is considered medically insignificant for the drug.

(8) The Secretary shall, with respect to each application submitted under this subsection, maintain a record of—

(A) the name of the applicant,

(B) the name of the drug covered by the application,

(C) the name of each person to whom the review of the chemistry of the application was assigned and the date of such assignment, and

(D) the name of each person to whom the bioequivalence review for such application was assigned and the date of such assignment.

The information the Secretary is required to maintain under this paragraph with respect to an application submitted under this subsection shall be made available to the public after the approval of such application.

(k) Records and reports; required information; regulations and orders; access to records

(1) In the case of any drug for which an approval of an application filed under subsection (b) or (j) of this section is in effect, the applicant shall establish and maintain such records, and make such reports to the Secretary, of data relating to clinical experience and other data or information, received or otherwise obtained by such applicant with respect to such drug, as the Secretary may by general regulation, or by order with respect to such application, prescribe on the basis of a finding that such records and reports are necessary in order to enable the Secretary to determine, or facilitate a determination, whether there is or may be ground for invoking subsection (e) of this section. Regulations and orders issued under this subsection and under subsection (i) of this section shall have due regard for the professional ethics of the medical profession and the interests of patients and shall provide, where the Secretary deems it to be appropriate, for the examination, upon request, by the persons to whom such regulations or orders are applicable, of similar information received or otherwise obtained by the Secretary.

(2) Every person required under this section to maintain records, and every person in charge or custody thereof, shall, upon request of an officer or employee designated by the Secretary, permit such officer or employee at all reasonable times to have access to and copy and verify such records.

(*l*) Public disclosure of safety and effectiveness data

Safety and effectiveness data and information which has been submitted in an application under subsection (b) of this section for a drug and which has not previously been disclosed to the public shall be made available to the public, upon request, unless extraordinary circumstances are shown—

(1) if no work is being or will be undertaken to have the application approved,

(2) if the Secretary has determined that the application is not approvable and all legal appeals have been exhausted,

(3) if approval of the application under subsection (c) of this section is withdrawn and all legal appeals have been exhausted,

(4) if the Secretary has determined that such drug is not a new drug, or

(5) upon the effective date of the approval of the first application under subsection (j) of this section which refers to such drug or upon the date upon which the approval of an application under subsection (j) of this section which refers to such drug could be made effective if such an application had been submitted.

(m) "Patent" defined

For purposes of this section, the term "patent" means a patent issued by the Patent and Trademark Office of the Department of Commerce.

§ 356. Certification of drugs containing insulin

(a) The Secretary, pursuant to regulations promulgated by him, shall provide for the certification of batches of drugs composed wholly or partly of insulin. A batch of any such drug shall be certified if such drug has such characteristics of identity and such batch has such characteristics of strength, quality, and purity, as the Secretary prescribes in such regulations as necessary to adequately insure safety and efficacy of use, but shall not otherwise be certified. Prior to the effective date of such regulations the Secretary, in lieu of certification, shall issue a release for any batch which, in his judgment, may be released without risk as to the safety and efficacy of its use. Such release shall prescribe the date of its expiration and other conditions under which it shall cease to be effective as to such batch and as to portions thereof.

(b) Regulations providing for such certification shall contain such provisions as are necessary to carry out the purposes of this section, including provisions prescribing (1) standards of identity and of strength, quality, and purity; (2) tests and methods of assay to determine compliance with such standards; (3) effective periods for certificates, and other conditions under which they shall cease to be effective as to certified batches and as to portions thereof; (4) administration and procedure; and (5) such fees, specified in such regulations, as are necessary to provide, equip, and maintain an adequate certification service. Such regulations shall prescribe no standard of identity or of strength, quality, or purity for any drug different from the standard of identity, strength, quality, or purity set forth for such drug in an official compendium.

(c) Such regulations, insofar as they prescribe tests or methods of assay to determine strength, quality, or purity of any drug, different from the tests or methods of assay set forth for such drug in an official compendium, shall be prescribed, after notice and opportunity for revision of such compendium, in the manner provided in the second sentence of section 351(b) of this title. The provisions of subsections (e), (f), and (g) of section 371 of this title shall be applicable to such portion of any regulation as prescribes any such different test or method, but shall not be applicable to any other portion of any such regulation.

§ 357. Certification of drugs containing penicillin, streptomycin, chlortetracycline, chloramphenicol, bacitracin or any other antibiotic drug

(a) Regulations prescribed by Secretary; release prior to certification; "antibiotic drug" defined

The Secretary, pursuant to regulations promulgated by him, shall provide for the certification of batches of drugs (except drugs for use in animals other than man) composed wholly or partly of any kind of penicillin, streptomycin, chlortetracycline, chloramphenicol, bacitracin, or any other antibiotic drug, or any derivative thereof. A batch of any such drug shall be certified if such drug has such characteristics of identity and such batch has such characteristics of strength, quality, and purity, as the Secretary prescribes in such regulations as necessary to adequately insure safety and efficacy of use, but shall not otherwise be certified. Prior to the effective date of such regulations the Secretary, in lieu of certification, shall issue a release for any batch which, in his judgment, may be released without risk as to the safety and efficacy of its use. Such release shall prescribe the date of its expiration and other conditions under which it shall cease to be effective as to such batch and as to portions thereof. For purposes of this section and of section 352(*l*) of this title, the term "antibiotic drug" means any drug intended for use by man containing any quantity of any chemical substance which is produced by a microorganism and which has the capacity to inhibit or destroy microorganisms in dilute solution (including the chemically synthesized equivalent of any such substance).

(b) Provisions of regulations

Regulations providing for such certifications shall contain such provisions as are necessary to carry out the purposes of this section, including provisions prescribing (1) standards of identity and of strength, quality, and purity; (2) tests and methods of assay to determine compliance with such standards; (3) effective periods for certificates, and other conditions under which they shall cease to be effective as to certified batches and as to portions thereof; (4) administration and procedure; and (5) such fees, specified in such regulations, as are necessary to provide, equip, and maintain an adequate certification service. Such regulations shall prescribe only such tests and methods of assay as will provide for certification or rejection within the shortest time consistent with the purposes of this section.

(c) Exemption of drugs not involving safety and efficacy of use; considerations; certification after exemption; labeling and advertising claims

Whenever in the judgment of the Secretary, the requirements of this section and of section 352(*l*) of this title with respect to any drug or class of drugs are not necessary to insure safety and efficacy of use, the Secretary shall promulgate regulations exempting such drug or class of drugs from such requirements. In deciding whether an antibiotic drug, or class of antibiotic drugs, is to be exempted from the requirement of certification the Secretary shall give consideration, among other relevant factors, to—

(1) whether such drug or class of drugs is manufactured by a person who has, or hereafter shall have, produced fifty consecutive batches of such drug or class of drugs in compliance with the regulations for the certification thereof within a period of not more than eighteen calendar months, upon the application by such person to the Secretary; or

(2) whether such drug or class of drugs is manufactured by any person who has otherwise demonstrated such consistency in the production of such drug or class of drugs, in compliance with the regulations for the certification thereof, as in the judgment of the Secretary is adequate to insure the safety and efficacy of use thereof.

When an antibiotic drug or a drug manufacturer has been exempted from the requirement of certification, the manufacturer may still obtain certification of a batch or batches of that drug if he applies for and meets the requirements for certification. Nothing in this chapter shall be deemed to prevent a manufacturer or distributor of an antibiotic drug from making a truthful statement in labeling or advertising of the product as to whether it has been certified or exempted from the requirement of certification.

(d) Exemption of drugs stored, processed, and labeled at plants other than manufacturer's, used in manufacture of other drugs or for investigational purposes; discretionary and mandatory condition; direct reports to Secretary

The Secretary shall promulgate regulations exempting from any requirement of this section and of section 352(*l*) of this title, (1) drugs which are to be stored, processed, labeled, or repacked at establishments other than those where manufactured, on condition that such drugs comply with all such requirements upon removal from such establishments; (2) drugs which conform to applicable standards of identity, strength, quality, and purity prescribed by these regulations and are intended for use in manufacturing other drugs; and (3) drugs which are intended solely for investigational use by experts qualified by scientific training and experience to investigate the safety and efficacy of drugs. Such regulations may, within the discretion of the Secretary, among other conditions relating to the protection of the public health, provide for conditioning the exemption under clause (3) of this subsection upon—

(1) the submission to the Secretary, before any clinical testing of a new drug is undertaken, of reports, by the manufacturer or the sponsor of the investigation of such drug, of preclinical tests (including tests on animals) of such drug adequate to justify the proposed clinical testing;

(2) the manufacturer or the sponsor of the investigation of a new drug proposed to be distributed to investigators for clinical testing obtaining a signed agreement from each of such investigators that patients to whom the drug is administered will be under his personal supervision, or under the supervision of investigators responsible to him, and that he will not supply such drug to any other investigator, or to clinics, for administration to human beings; and

(3) the establishment and maintenance of such records, and the making of such reports to the Secretary, by the manufacturer or the sponsor of the investigation of such drug, of data (including but not limited to analytical reports by investigators) obtained as the result of such investigational use of such drug, as the Secretary finds will enable him to evaluate the safety and effectiveness of such drug in the event of the filing of an application for certification or release pursuant to subsection (a) of this section.

Such regulations shall provide that such exemption shall be conditioned upon the manufacturer, or the sponsor of the investigation, requiring that experts using such drugs for investigational purposes certify to such manufacturer or sponsor that they will inform any human beings to whom such drugs, or any controls used in connection therewith, are being administered, or their representatives, that such drugs are being used for investigational purposes and will obtain the consent of such human beings or their representatives, except where they deem it not feasible or, in their professional judgment, contrary to the best interests of such human beings. Nothing in this subsection shall be construed to require any clinical investigator to submit directly to the Secretary reports on the investigational use of drugs.

(e) Exempted new drugs subject to section 355 of this title; request for certification of exempted drug; determination of compliance with sections 351(b) and 352(g) of this title

No drug which is subject to this section shall be deemed to be subject to any provision of section 355 of this title except a new drug exempted from the requirements of this section and of section 352(*l*) of this title pursuant to regulations promulgated by the Secretary. For purposes of section 355 of this title, the initial request for certification, as thereafter duly amended, pursuant to this section, of a new drug so exempted shall be considered a part of the application filed pursuant to section 355(b) of this title with respect to the person filing such request and to such drug as of the date of the exemption. Compliance of any drug subject to section 352(*l*) of this title or this section with sections 351(b) and 352(g) of this title shall be determined by the application of the standards of strength, quality, and purity, the tests and methods of assay, and the requirements of packaging and labeling, respectively, prescribed by regulations promulgated under this section.

(f) Filing of petitions; contents; notice; answer; public hearing; orders

Any interested person may file with the Secretary a petition proposing the issuance, amendment, or repeal of any regulation contemplated by this section. The petition shall set forth the proposal in general terms and shall state reasonable grounds therefor. The Secretary shall give public notice of the proposal and an opportunity for all interested persons to present their views thereon, orally or in writing, and as soon as practicable thereafter shall make public his action upon such proposal. At any time prior to the thirtieth day after such action is made public any interested person may file objections to such action, specifying with particularity the changes desired, stating reasonable grounds therefor, and requesting a public hearing upon such objections. The Secretary shall thereupon, after due notice, hold such public hearing. As soon as practicable after completion of the hearing, the Secretary shall by order make public his action on such objections. The Secretary shall base his order only on substantial evidence of record at the hearing and shall set forth as part of the order detailed findings of fact on which the order is based. The order shall be subject to the provisions of section 371(f) and (g) of this title.

(g) Records and reports; professional ethics and interests of patients; examination of data; access to records

(1) Every person engaged in manufacturing, compounding, or processing any drug within the purview of this section with respect to which a certificate or release has been issued pursuant to this section shall establish and maintain such records, and make such reports to the Secretary, of data relating to clinical experience and other data or information, received or otherwise obtained by such person with respect to such drug, as the Secretary may by general regulation, or by order with respect to such certification or release, prescribe on the basis of a finding that such records and reports are necessary in order to enable the Secretary to make, or to facilitate, a determination as to whether such certification or release should be rescinded or whether any regulation issued under this section should be amended or repealed. Regulations and orders issued under this subsection and under clause (3) of subsection (d) of this section shall have due regard for the professional ethics of the medical profession and the interests of patients and shall provide, where the Secretary deems it to be appropriate, for the examination, upon request, by the persons to whom such regulations or orders

are applicable, of similar information received or otherwise obtained by the Secretary.

(2) Every person required under this section to maintain records, and every person having charge or custody thereof, shall, upon request of an officer or employee designated by the Secretary, permit such officer or employee at all reasonable times to have access to and copy and verify such records.

(h) Issuance of regulations; conditions; amendment of repeal of regulations; effective date; procedure; lack of substantial evidence

In the case of a drug for which, on the day immediately preceding the effective date of this subsection, a prior approval of an application under section 355 of this title had not been withdrawn under section 355(e) of this title, the initial issuance of regulations providing for certification or exemption of such drug under this section shall, with respect to the conditions of use prescribed, recommended, or suggested in the labeling covered by such application, not be conditioned upon an affirmative finding of the efficacy of such drug. Any subsequent amendment or repeal of such regulations so as no longer to provide for such certification or exemption on the ground of a lack of efficacy of such drug for use under such conditions of use may be effected only on or after that effective date of clause (3) of the first sentence of section 355(e) of this title which would be applicable to such drug under such conditions of use if such drug were subject to section 355(e) of this title, and then only if (1) such amendment or repeal is made in accordance with the procedure specified in subsection (f) of this section (except that such amendment or repeal may be initiated either by a proposal of the Secretary or by a petition of any interested person) and (2) the Secretary finds, on the basis of new information with respect to such drug evaluated together with the information before him when the application under section 355 of this title became effective or was approved, that there is a lack of substantial evidence (as defined in section 355(d) of this title) that the drug has the effect it purports or is represented to have under such conditions of use.

§ 358. Authority to designate official names

(a) Necessity or desirability; use in official compendiums; infringement of trademarks

The Secretary may designate an official name for any drug or device if he determines that such action is necessary or desirable in the interest of usefulness and simplicity. Any official name designated under this section for any drug or device shall be the only official name of that drug or device used in any official compendium published after such name has been prescribed or for any other purpose of this chapter. In no event, however, shall the Secretary establish an official name so as to infringe a valid trademark.

(b) Review of names in official compendiums

Within a reasonable time after October 10, 1962, and at such other times as he may deem necessary, the Secretary shall cause a review to be made of the official names by which drugs are identified in the official United States Pharmacopoeia, the official Homeopathic Pharmacopoeia of the United States, and the official National Formulary, and all supplements thereto, and at such times as he may deem necessary shall cause a review to be made of the official names by which devices are identified in any official compendium (and all supplements thereto) to determine whether revision of any of those names is necessary or desirable in the interest of usefulness and simplicity.

(c) Determination of complexity, usefulness, multiplicity, or lack of name; designation by Secretary

Whenever he determines after any such review that (1) any such official name is unduly complex or is not useful for any other reason, (2) two or more official name have been applied to a single drug or device, or to two or more drugs which are identical in chemical structure and pharmacological action and which are substantially identical in strength, quality, and purity, or to two or more devices which are substantially equivalent in design and purpose or (3) no official name has been applied to a medically useful drug or device, he shall transmit in writing to the compiler of each official compendium in which that drug or drugs or device are identified and recognized his request for the recommendation of a single official name for such drug or drugs or device which will have usefulness and simplicity. Whenever such a single official name has not been recommended within one hundred and eighty days after such request, or the Secretary determines that any name so recommended is not useful for any reason, he shall designate a single official name for such drug or drugs or device. Whenever he determines that the name so recommended is useful, he shall designate that name as the official name of such drug or drugs or device. Such designation shall be made as a regulation upon public notice and in accordance with the procedure set forth in section 553 of Title 5.

(d) Revised official names; compilation, publication, and public distribution of listings

After each such review, and at such other times as the Secretary may determine to be necessary or desirable, the Secretary shall cause to be compiled, published, and publicly distributed a list which shall list all revised official names of drugs or devices designated under this section and shall contain such descriptive and explanatory matter as the Secretary may determine to be required for the effective use of those names.

(e) Request by compiler of official compendium for designation of name

Upon a request in writing by any compiler of an official compendium that the Secretary exercise the authority granted to him under subsection (a) of this section, he shall upon public notice and in accordance with the procedure set forth in section 553 of Title 5 designate the official name of the drug or device for which the request is made.

§ 359. Nonapplicability of subchapter to cosmetics

This subchapter, as amended by the Drug Amendments of 1962, shall not apply to any cosmetic unless such cosmetic is also a drug or device or component thereof.

§ 360. Registration of producers of drugs or devices

(a) Definitions

As used in this section—

(1) the term "manufacture, preparation, propagation, compounding, or processing" shall include repackaging or otherwise changing the container, wrapper, or labeling of any drug package or device package in furtherance of the distribution of the drug or device from the original place of manufacture to the person who makes final delivery or sale to the ultimate consumer or user; and

(2) the term "name" shall include in the case of a partnership the name of each partner and, in the case of a corporation, the name of each corporate officer and director, and the State of incorporation.

(b) Annual registration

On or before December 31 of each year every person who owns or operates any establishment in any State engaged in the manufacture, preparation, propagation, compounding, or processing of a drug or drugs or a device or devices shall register with the Secretary his name, places of business, and all such establishments.

(c) New producers

Every person upon first engaging in the manufacture, preparation, propagation, compounding, or processing of a drug or drugs or a device or devices in any establishment which he owns or operates in any State shall immediately register with the Secretary his name, place of business, and such establishment.

(d) Additional establishments

Every person duly registered in accordance with the foregoing subsections of this section shall immediately register with the Secretary any additional establishment which he owns or operates in any State and in which he begins the manufacture, preparation, propagation, compounding, or processing of a drug or drugs or a device or devices.

(e) Registration number; uniform system for identification of devices intended for human use

The Secretary may assign a registration number to any person or any establishment registered in accordance with this section. The

Secretary may also assign a listing number to each drug or class of drugs listed under subsection (j) of this section. Any number assigned pursuant to the preceding sentence shall be the same as that assigned pursuant to the National Drug Code. The Secretary may by regulation prescribe a uniform system for the identification of devices intended for human use and may require that persons who are required to list such devices pursuant to subsection (j) of this section shall list such devices in accordance with such system.

(f) Availability of registrations for inspection

The Secretary shall make available for inspection, to any person so requesting, any registration filed pursuant to this section; except that any list submitted pursuant to paragraph (3) of subsection (j) of this section and the information accompanying any list or notice filed under paragraph (1) or (2) of that subsection shall be exempt from such inspection unless the Secretary finds that such an exemption would be inconsistent with protection of the public health.

(g) Exclusions from application of section

The foregoing subsections of this section shall not apply to—

(1) pharmacies which maintain establishments in conformance with any applicable local laws regulating the practice of pharmacy and medicine and which are regularly engaged in dispensing prescription drugs or devices, upon prescriptions of practitioners licensed to administer such drugs or devices to patients under the care of such practitioners in the course of their professional practice, and which do not manufacture, prepare, propagate, compound, or process drugs or devices for sale other than in the regular course of their business of dispensing or selling drugs or devices at retail;

(2) practitioners licensed by law to prescribe or administer drugs or devices and who manufacture, prepare, propagate, compound, or process drugs or devices solely for use in the course of their professional practice;

(3) persons who manufacture, prepare, propagate, compound, or process drugs or devices solely for use in research, teaching, or chemical analysis and not for sale;

(4) such other classes of persons as the Secretary may by regulation exempt from the application of this section upon a finding that registration by such classes of persons in accordance with this section is not necessary for the protection of the public health.

(h) Inspection of premises

Every establishment in any State registered with the Secretary pursuant to this section shall be subject to inspection pursuant to section 374 of this title and every such establishment engaged in the manufacture, propagation, compounding, or processing of a drug or drugs or of a device or devices classified in class II or III shall be so inspected by one or more officers or employees duly designated by the Secretary at least once in the two-year period beginning with the date of registration of such establishment pursuant to this section and at least once in every successive two-year period thereafter.

(i) **Foreign establishments**

Any establishment within any foreign country engaged in the manufacture, preparation, propagation, compounding, or processing of a drug or drugs, or a device or devices, shall be permitted to register under this section pursuant to regulations promulgated by the Secretary. Such regulations shall require such establishment to provide the information required by subsection (j) of this section and shall require such establishment to provide the information required by subsection (j) of this section in the case of a device or devices and shall include provisions for registration of any such establishment upon condition that adequate and effective means are available, by arrangement with the government of such foreign country or otherwise, to enable the Secretary to determine from time to time whether drugs or devices manufactured, prepared, propagated, compounded, or processed in such establishment, if imported or offered for import into the United States, shall be refused admission on any of the grounds set forth in section 381(a) of this title.

(j) Filing of lists of drugs and devices manufactured, prepared, propagated and compounded by registrants; statements; accompanying disclosures

(1) Every person who registers with the Secretary under subsection (b), (c), or (d) of this section shall, at the time of registration under any such subsection, file with the Secretary a list of all drugs and a list of all devices and a brief statement of the basis for believing that each device included in the list is a device rather than a drug (with each drug and device in each list listed by its established name (as defined in section 352(e) of this title) and by any proprietary name) which are being manufactured, prepared, propagated, compounded, or processed by him for commercial distribution and which he has not included in any list of drugs or devices filed by him with the Secretary under this paragraph or paragraph (2) before such time of registration. Such list shall be prepared in such form and manner as the Secretary may prescribe and shall be accompanied by—

(A) in the case of a drug contained in the applicable list and subject to sections 355, 356, 357, or 360b of this title, or a device intended for human use contained in the applicable list with respect to which a performance standard has been established under section 360d of this title or which is subject to section 360e of this title, a reference to the authority for the marketing of such drug or device and a copy of all labeling for such drug or device;

(B) in the case of any other drug or device contained in an applicable list—

(i) which drug is subject to section 353(b)(1) of this title, or which device is a restricted device, a copy of all labeling for such drug or device, a representative sampling of advertisements for such drug or device, and, upon request made by the Secretary for good cause, a copy of all advertisements for a particular drug product or device, or

(ii) which drug is not subject to section 353(b)(1) of this title or which device is not a restricted device, the label and package insert for such drug or device and a representative sampling of any other labeling for such drug or device;

(C) in the case of any drug contained in an applicable list which is described in subparagraph (B), a quantitative listing of its active ingredient or ingredients, except that with respect to a particular drug product the Secretary may require the submission of a quantitative listing of all ingredients if he finds that such submission is necessary to carry out the purposes of this chapter; and

(D) if the registrant filing a list has determined that a particular drug product or device contained in such list is not subject to section 355, 356, 357, or 360b of this title, or the particular device contained in such list is not subject to a performance standard established under section 360d of this title or to section 360e of this title or is not a restricted device a brief statement of the basis upon which the registrant made such determination if the Secretary requests such a statement with respect to that particular drug product or device.

(2) Each person who registers with the Secretary under this section shall report to the Secretary once during the month of June of each year and once during the month of December of each year the following information:

(A) A list of each drug or device introduced by the registrant for commercial distribution which has not been included in any list previously filed by him with the Secretary under this subparagraph or paragraph (1) of this subsection. A list under this subparagraph shall list a drug or device by its established name (as defined in section 352(e) of this title) and by any proprietary name it may have and shall be accompanied by the other information required by paragraph (1).

(B) If since the date the registrant last made a report under this paragraph (or if he has not made a report under this paragraph, since February 1, 1973) he has discontinued the manufacture, preparation, propagation, compounding, or processing for commercial distribution of a drug or device included in a list filed by him under subparagraph (A) or paragraph (1); notice of such discontinuance, the date of such discontinuance, and the identity (by established name (as defined in section 352(e) of this title) and by any proprietary name) of such drug or device.

(C) If since the date the registrant reported pursuant to subparagraph (B) a notice of discontinuance he has resumed the manufacture, preparation, propagation, compounding, or processing for commercial distribution of the drug or device with respect to which such notice of discontinuance was reported; notice of such resumption, the date of such resumption, the identity of such drug or device (each by established name (as defined in section 352(e) of this title) and by any proprietary name), and the other information required by paragraph (1), unless the registrant has previously reported such resumption to the Secretary pursuant to this subparagraph.

(D) Any material change in any information previously submitted pursuant to this paragraph or paragraph (1).

(3) The Secretary may also require each registrant under this section to submit a list of each drug product which (A) the registrant is manufacturing, preparing, propagating, compounding, or processing for commercial distribution, and (B) contains a particular ingredient. The Secretary may not require the submission of such a list unless he has made a finding that the submission of such a list is necessary to carry out the purposes of this chapter.

(k) Report preceding introduction of devices into interstate commerce

Each person who is required to register under this section and who proposes to begin the introduction or delivery for introduction into interstate commerce for commercial distribution of a device intended for human use shall, at least ninety days before making such introduction or delivery, report to the Secretary (in such form and manner as the Secretary shall by regulation prescribe)—

(1) the class in which the device is classified under section 360c of this title or if such person determines that the device is not classified under such section, a statement of that determination and the basis for such person's determination that the device is or is not so classified, and

(2) action taken by such person to comply with requirements under section 360d or 360e of this title which are applicable to the device.

§ 360a.   Repealed. Pub.L. 91–513, Title II, § 701(a), Oct. 27, 1970, 84 Stat. 1281

§ 360b.   New animal drugs

(a) Unsafe new animal drugs and animal feed containing such drugs; conditions of safety; exemption of drugs for research

(1) A new animal drug shall, with respect to any particular use or intended use of such drug, be deemed unsafe for the purposes of section 351(a)(5) and section 342(a)(2)(D) of this title unless—

(A) there is in effect an approval of an application filed pursuant to subsection (b) of this section with respect to such use or intended use of such drug, and

(B) such drug, its labeling, and such use conform to such approved application.

A new animal drug shall also be deemed unsafe for such purposes in the event of removal from the establishment of a manufacturer, packer, or distributor of such drug for use in the manufacture of animal feed in any State unless at the time of such removal such manufacturer, packer, or distributor has an unrevoked written statement from the consignee of such drug, or notice from the Secretary, to the effect that, with respect to the use of such drug in animal feed, such consignee—

(i) is the holder of an approved application under subsection (m) of this section; or

(ii) will, if the consignee is not a user of the drug, ship such drug only to a holder of an approved application under subsection (m) of this section.

(2) An animal feed bearing or containing a new animal drug shall, with respect to any particular use or intended use of such animal feed, be deemed unsafe for the purposes of section 351(a)(6) of this title unless—

(A) there is in effect an approval of an application filed pursuant to subsection (b) of this section with respect to such drug, as used in such animal feed,

(B) there is in effect an approval of an application pursuant to subsection (m)(1) of this section with respect to such animal feed, and

(C) such animal feed, its labeling, and such use conform to the conditions and indications of use published pursuant to subsection (i) of this section and to the application with respect thereto approved under subsection (m) of this section.

(3) A new animal drug or an animal feed bearing or containing a new animal drug shall not be deemed unsafe for the purposes of section 351(a)(5) or (6) of this title if such article is for investigational use and conforms to the terms of an exemption in effect with respect thereto under subsection (j) of this section.

(4)(A) Except as provided in subparagraph (B), if an approval of an application filed under subsection (b) of this section is in effect with respect to a particular use or intended use of a new animal drug, the drug shall not be deemed unsafe for the purposes of paragraph (1) and shall be exempt from the requirements of section 352(f) of this title with respect to a different use or intended use of the drug, other than a use in or on animal feed, if such use or intended use—

131

(i) is by or on the lawful written or oral order of a licensed veterinarian within the context of a veterinarian-client-patient relationship, as defined by the Secretary; and

(ii) is in compliance with regulations promulgated by the Secretary that establish the conditions for such different use or intended use.

The regulations promulgated by the Secretary under clause (ii) may prohibit particular uses of an animal drug and shall not permit such different use of an animal drug if the labeling of another animal drug that contains the same active ingredient and which is in the same dosage form and concentration provides for such different use.

(B) If the Secretary finds that there is a reasonable probability that a use of an animal drug authorized under subparagraph (A) may present a risk to the public health, the Secretary may—

(i) establish a safe level for a residue of an animal drug when it is used for such different use authorized by subparagraph (A); and

(ii) require the development of a practical, analytical method for the detection of residues of such drug above the safe level established under clause (i).

The use of an animal drug that results in residues exceeding a safe level established under clause (i) shall be considered an unsafe use of such drug under paragraph (1). Safe levels may be established under clause (i) either by regulation or order.

(C) The Secretary may by general regulation provide access to the records of veterinarians to ascertain any use or intended use authorized under subparagraph (A) that the Secretary has determined may present a risk to the public health.

(D) If the Secretary finds, after affording an opportunity for public comment, that a use of an animal drug authorized under subparagraph (A) presents a risk to the public health or that an analytical method required under subparagraph (B) has not been developed and submitted to the Secretary, the Secretary may, by order, prohibit any such use.

(5) If the approval of an application filed under section 355 of this title is in effect, the drug under such application shall not be deemed unsafe for purposes of paragraph (1) and shall be exempt from the requirements of section 352(f) of this title with respect to a use or intended use of the drug in animals if such use or intended use—

(A) is by or on the lawful written or oral order of a licensed veterinarian within the context of a veterinarian-client-patient relationship, as defined by the Secretary; and

(B) is in compliance with regulations promulgated by the Secretary that establish the conditions for the use or intended use of the drug in animals.

(b) Filing application for uses of new animal drug; contents; patent information

(1) Any person may file with the Secretary an application with respect to any intended use or uses of a new animal drug. Such person shall submit to the Secretary as a part of the application (A) full reports of investigations which have been made to show whether or not such drug is safe and effective for use; (B) a full list of the articles used as components of such drug; (C) a full statement of the composition of such drug; (D) a full description of the methods used in, and the facilities and controls used for, the manufacture, processing, and packing of such drug; (E) such samples of such drug and of the articles used as components thereof, of any animal feed for use in or on which such drug is intended, and of the edible portions or products (before or after slaughter) of animals to which such drug (directly or in or on animal feed) is intended to be administered, as the Secretary may require; (F) specimens of the labeling proposed to be used for such drug, or in case such drug is intended for use in animal feed, proposed labeling appropriate for such use, and specimens of the labeling for the drug to be manufactured, packed, or distributed by the applicant; (G) a description of practicable methods for determining the quantity, if any, of such drug in or on food, and any substance formed in or on food, because of its use; and (H) the proposed tolerance or withdrawal period or other use restrictions for such drug if any tolerance or withdrawal period or other use restrictions are required in order to assure that the proposed use of such drug will be safe.The applicant shall file with the application the patent number and the expiration date of any patent which claims the new animal drug for which the applicant filed the application or which claims a method of using such drug and with respect to which a claim of patent infringement could reasonably be asserted if a person not licensed by the owner engaged in the manufacture, use, or sale of the drug. If an application is filed under this subsection for a drug and a patent which claims such drug or a method of using such drug is issued after the filing date but before approval of the application, the applicant shall amend the application to include the information required by the preceding sentence. Upon approval of the application, the Secretary shall publish information submitted under the two preceding sentences.

(2) Any person may file with the Secretary an abbreviated application for the approval of a new animal drug. An abbreviated application shall contain the information required by subsection (n) of this section.

(c) Period for submission and approval of application; period for notice, and expedition of hearing; period for issuance of order; abbreviated applications; withdrawal periods; effective date of approval; relationship to other applications; withdrawal or suspension of approval; bioequivalence; filing of additional patent information

(1) Within one hundred and eighty days after the filing of an application pursuant to subsection (b) of this section, or such additional

period as may be agreed upon by the Secretary and the applicant, the Secretary shall either (A) issue an order approving the application if he then finds that none of the grounds for denying approval specified in subsection (d) of this section applies, or (B) give the applicant notice of an opportunity for a hearing before the Secretary under subsection (d) of this section on the question whether such application is approvable. If the applicant elects to accept the opportunity for a hearing by written request within thirty days after such notice, such hearing shall commence not more than ninety days after the expiration of such thirty days unless the Secretary and the applicant otherwise agree. Any such hearing shall thereafter be conducted on an expedited basis and the Secretary's order thereon shall be issued within ninety days after the date fixed by the Secretary for filing final briefs.

(2)(A) Subject to subparagraph (C), the Secretary shall approve an abbreviated application for a drug unless the Secretary finds—

(i) the methods used in, or the facilities and controls used for, the manufacture, processing, and packing of the drug are inadequate to assure and preserve its identity, strength, quality, and purity;

(ii) the conditions of use prescribed, recommended, or suggested in the proposed labeling are not reasonably certain to be followed in practice or, except as provided in subparagraph (B), information submitted with the application is insufficient to show that each of the proposed conditions of use or similar limitations (whether in the labeling or published pursuant to subsection (i) of this section) have been previously approved for the approved new animal drug referred to in the application;

(iii) information submitted with the application is insufficient to show that the active ingredients are the same as those of the approved new animal drug referred to in the application;

(iv)(I) if the application is for a drug whose active ingredients, route of administration, dosage form, strength, or use with other animal drugs in animal feed is the same as the active ingredients, route of administration, dosage form, strength, or use with other animal drugs in animal feed of the approved new animal drug referred to in the application, information submitted in the application is insufficient to show that the active ingredients, route of administration, dosage form, strength, or use with other animal drugs in animal feed is the same as that of the approved new animal drug, or

(II) if the application is for a drug whose active ingredients, route of administration, dosage form, strength, or use with other animal drugs in animal feed is different from that of the approved new animal drug referred to in the application, no petition to file an application for the drug with the different active ingredients, route of administration, dosage form, strength, or use with other animal drugs in animal feed was approved under subsection (n)(3) of this section;

(v) if the application was filed pursuant to the approval of a petition under subsection (n)(3) of this section, the application did not contain the information required by the Secretary respecting the active ingredients, route of administration, dosage form, strength, or use with other animal drugs in animal feed which is not the same;

(vi) information submitted in the application is insufficient to show that the drug is bioequivalent to the approved new animal drug referred to in the application, or if the application is filed under a petition approved pursuant to subsection (n)(3) of this section, information submitted in the application is insufficient to show that the active ingredients of the new animal drug are of the same pharmacological or therapeutic class as the pharmacological or therapeutic class of the approved new animal drug and that the new animal drug can be expected to have the same therapeutic effect as the approved new animal drug when used in accordance with the labeling;

(vii) information submitted in the application is insufficient to show that the labeling proposed for the drug is the same as the labeling approved for the approved new animal drug referred to in the application except for changes required because of differences approved under a petition filed under subsection (n)(3) of this section, because of a different withdrawal period, or because the drug and the approved new animal drug are produced or distributed by different manufacturers;

(viii) information submitted in the application or any other information available to the Secretary shows that (I) the inactive ingredients of the drug are unsafe for use under the conditions prescribed, recommended, or suggested in the labeling proposed for the drug, (II) the composition of the drug is unsafe under such conditions because of the type or quantity of inactive ingredients included or the manner in which the inactive ingredients are included, or (III) in the case of a drug for food producing animals, the inactive ingredients of the drug or its composition may be unsafe with respect to human food safety;

(ix) the approval under subsection (b)(1) of this section of the approved new animal drug referred to in the application filed under subsection (b)(2) of this section has been withdrawn or suspended for grounds described in paragraph (1) of subsection (e) of this section, the Secretary has published a notice of a hearing to withdraw approval of the approved new animal drug for such grounds, the approval under this paragraph of the new animal drug for which the application under subsection (b)(2) of this section was filed has been withdrawn or suspended under subparagraph (G) for such

135

grounds, or the Secretary has determined that the approved new animal drug has been withdrawn from sale for safety or effectiveness reasons;

(x) the application does not meet any other requirement of subsection (n) of this section; or

(xi) the application contains an untrue statement of material fact.

(B) If the Secretary finds that a new animal drug for which an application is submitted under subsection (b)(2) of this section is bioequivalent to the approved new animal drug referred to in such application and that residues of the new animal drug are consistent with the tolerances established for such approved new animal drug but at a withdrawal period which is different than the withdrawal period approved for such approved new animal drug, the Secretary may establish, on the basis of information submitted, such different withdrawal period as the withdrawal period for the new animal drug for purposes of the approval of such application for such drug.

(C) Within 180 days of the initial receipt of an application under subsection (b)(2) of this section or within such additional period as may be agreed upon by the Secretary and the applicant, the Secretary shall approve or disapprove the application.

(D) The approval of an application filed under subsection (b)(2) of this section shall be made effective on the last applicable date determined under the following:

(i) If the applicant only made a certification described in clause (i) or (ii) of subsection (n)(1)(G) of this section or in both such clauses, the approval may be made effective immediately.

(ii) If the applicant made a certification described in clause (iii) of subsection (n)(1)(G) of this section, the approval may be made effective on the date certified under clause (iii).

(iii) If the applicant made a certification described in clause (iv) of subsection (n)(1)(G) of this section, the approval shall be made effective immediately unless an action is brought for infringement of a patent which is the subject of the certification before the expiration of 45 days from the date the notice provided under subsection (n)(2)(B)(i) of this section is received. If such an action is brought before the expiration of such days, the approval shall be made effective upon the expiration of the 30 month period beginning on the date of the receipt of the notice provided under subsection (n)(2)(B) of this section or such shorter or longer period as the court may order because either party to the action failed to reasonably cooperate in expediting the action, except that if before the expiration of such period—

(I) the court decides that such patent is invalid or not infringed, the approval shall be made effective on the date of the court decision,

(II) the court decides that such patent has been infringed, the approval shall be made effective on such date as the court orders under section 271(e)(4)(A) of Title 35, or

(III) the court grants a preliminary injunction prohibiting the applicant from engaging in the commercial manufacture or sale of the drug until the court decides the issues of patent validity and infringement and if the court decides that such patent is invalid or not infringed, the approval shall be made effective on the date of such court decision.

In such an action, each of the parties shall reasonably cooperate in expediting the action. Until the expiration of 45 days from the date the notice made under subsection (n)(2)(B) of this section is received, no action may be brought under section 2201 of Title 28, for a declaratory judgment with respect to the patent. Any action brought under section 2201 of Title 28 shall be brought in the the judicial district where the defendant has its principal place of business or a regular and established place of business.

(iv) If the application contains a certification described in clause (iv) of subsection (n)(1)(G) of this section and is for a drug for which a previous application has been filed under this subsection containing such a certification, the application shall be made effective not earlier than 180 days after—

(I) the date the Secretary receives notice from the applicant under the previous application of the first commercial marketing of the drug under the previous application, or

(II) the date of a decision of a court in an action described in subclause (III) holding the patent which is the subject of the certification to be invalid or not infringed, whichever is earlier.

(E) If the Secretary decides to disapprove an application, the Secretary shall give the applicant notice of an opportunity for a hearing before the Secretary on the question of whether such application is approvable. If the applicant elects to accept the opportunity for hearing by written request within 30 days after such notice, such hearing shall commence not more than 90 days after the expiration of such 30 days unless the Secretary and the applicant otherwise agree. Any such hearing shall thereafter be conducted on an expedited basis and the Secretary's order thereon shall be issued within 90 days after the date fixed by the Secretary for filing final briefs.

(F)(i) If an application submitted under subsection (b)(1) of this section for a drug, no active ingredient (including any ester or salt of the active ingredient) of which has been approved in any other application under subsection (b)(1) of this section, is approved November 16, 1988, no application may be submitted under subsection (b)(2) of this section which refers to the drug for which the subsection (b)(1) application was submitted before the expiration of 5 years from the date of the approval of the application under subsection (b)(1) of this section, except that such an application may be submitted under subsection (b)(2) of this section after the expiration of 4 years from the date of the approval of the subsection (b)(1) application if it contains a certification of patent invalidity or noninfringement described in clause (iv) of subsection (n)(1)(G) of this section. The approval of such an application shall be made effective in accordance with subparagraph (B) except that, if an action for patent infringement is commenced during the one-year period beginning 48 months after the date of the approval of the subsection (b) application, the 30 month period referred to in subparagraph (D)(iii) shall be extended by such amount of time (if any) which is required for seven and one-half years to have elapsed from the date of approval of the subsection (b) application.

(ii) If an application submitted under subsection (b)(1) of this section for a drug, which includes an active ingredient (including any ester or salt of the active ingredient) that has been approved in another application approved under such subsection, is approved after November 16, 1988 and if such application contains reports of new clinical or field investigations (other than bioequivalence or residue studies) and, in the case of food producing animals, human food safety studies (other than bioequivalence or residue studies) essential to the approval of the application and conducted or sponsored by the applicant, the Secretary may not make the approval of an application submitted under subsection (b)(2) of this section for the conditions of approval of such drug in the subsection (b)(1) application effective before the expiration of 3 years from the date of the approval of the application under subsection (b)(1) of this section for such drug.

(iii) If a supplement to an application approved under subsection (b)(1) of this section is approved after November 16, 1988 and the supplement contains reports of new clinical or field investigations (other than bioequivalence or residue studies) and, in the case of food producing animals, human food safety studies (other than bioequivalence or residue studies) essential to the approval of the supplement and conducted or sponsored by the person submitting the supplement, the Secretary may not make the approval of an application submitted under subsection (b)(2) of this section for a change approved in the supplement effective before the expiration of 3 years from the date of the approval of the supplement.

(iv) An applicant under subsection (b)(1) of this section who comes within the provisions of clause (i) of this subparagraph as a result of an application which seeks approval for a use solely in non-food producing animals, may elect, within 10 days of receiving such approval, to waive clause (i) of this subparagraph, in which event the limitation on approval of applications submitted under subsection (b)(2) of this section set forth in clause (ii) of this subparagraph shall be applicable to the subsection (b)(1) application.

(v) If an application (including any supplement to a new animal drug application) submitted under subsection (b)(1) of this section for a new animal drug for a food-producing animal use, which includes an active ingredient (including any ester or salt of the active ingredient) which has been the subject of a waiver under subparagraph (B)(iv) is approved after November 16, 1988 and if the application contains reports of clinical or field investigations or human food safety studies (other than bioequivalence or residue studies) essential to the new approval of the application and conducted or sponsored by the applicant, the Secretary may not make the approval of an application (including any supplement to such application) submitted under subsection (b)(2) of this section for the new conditions of approval of such drug in the subsection (b)(1) application effective before the expiration of five years from the date of approval of the application under subsection (b)(1) of this section for such drug. The provisions of this paragraph shall apply only to the first approval for a food-producing animal use for the same applicant after the waiver under subparagraph (B)(iv).

(G) If an approved application submitted under subsection (b)(2) of this section for a new animal drug refers to a drug the approval of which was withdrawn or suspended for grounds described in paragraph (1) or (2) of subsection (e) of this section or was withdrawn or suspended under this subparagraph or which, as determined by the Secretary, has been withdrawn from sale for safety or effectiveness reasons, the approval of the drug under this paragraph shall be withdrawn or suspended—

(i) for the same period as the withdrawal or suspension under subsection (e) of this section or this subparagraph, or

(ii) if the approved new animal drug has been withdrawn from sale, for the period of withdrawal from sale or, if earlier, the period ending on the date the Secretary determines that the withdrawal from sale is not for safety or effectiveness reasons.

(H) For purposes of this paragraph:

(i) The term "bioequivalence" means the rate and extent to which the active ingredient or therapeutic ingredient is absorbed from a new animal drug and becomes available at the site of drug action.

(ii) A new animal drug shall be considered to be bioequivalent to the approved new animal drug referred to in its application under subsection (n) of this section if—

(I) the rate and extent of absorption of the drug do not show a significant difference from the rate and extent of absorption of the approved new animal drug referred to in the application when administered at the same dose of the active ingredient under similar experimental conditions in either a single dose or multiple doses;

(II) the extent of absorption of the drug does not show a significant difference from the extent of absorption of the approved new animal drug referred to in the application when administered at the same dose of the active ingredient under similar experimental conditions in either a single dose or multiple doses and the difference from the approved new animal drug in the rate of absorption of the drug is intentional, is reflected in its proposed labeling, is not essential to the attainment of effective drug concentrations in use, and is considered scientifically insignificant for the drug in attaining the intended purposes of its use and preserving human food safety; or

(III) in any case in which the Secretary determines that the measurement of the rate and extent of absorption or excretion of the new animal drug in biological fluids is inappropriate or impractical, an appropriate acute pharmacological effects test or other test of the new animal drug and, when deemed scientifically necessary, of the approved new animal drug referred to in the application in the species to be tested or in an appropriate animal model does not show a significant difference between the new animal drug and such approved new animal drug when administered at the same dose under similar experimental conditions.

If the approved new animal drug referred to in the application for a new animal drug under subsection (n) of this section is approved for use in more than one animal species, the bioequivalency information described in subclauses (I), (II), and (III) shall be obtained for one species, or if the Secretary deems appropriate based on scientific principles, shall be obtained for more than one species. The Secretary may prescribe the dose to be used in determining bioequivalency under subclause (I), (II), or (III). To assure that the residues of the new animal drug will be consistent with the established tolerances for the approved new animal drug referred to in the application under subsection (b)(2) of this section upon the expiration of the withdrawal period contained in the application for the new animal drug, the Secretary shall require bioequivalency data or residue depletion studies of the new animal drug or such other data or studies as the Secretary considers appropriate based on scientific principles. If the Secretary requires one or more residue studies under the preceding sentence, the Secretary may not require that the assay methodology used to determine the withdrawal period of the new animal drug be more rigorous than the methodology used to determine the withdrawal period for the approved new animal drug referred to in the application. If such studies are required and if the approved new animal drug, referred to in the application for the new animal drug for which such studies are required, is approved for use in more than one animal species, such studies shall be conducted for one species, or if the Secretary deems appropriate based on scientific principles, shall be conducted for more than one species.

(3) If the patent information described in subsection (b)(1) of this section could not be filed with the submission of an application under subsection (b)(1) of this section because the application was filed before the patent information was required under subsection (b)(1) of this section or a patent was issued after the application was approved under such subsection, the holder of an approved application shall file with the Secretary the patent number and the expiration date of any patent which claims the new animal drug for which the application was filed or which claims a method of using such drug and with respect to which a claim of patent infringement could reasonably be asserted if a person not licensed by the owner engaged in the manufacture, use, or sale of the drug.   If the holder of an approved application could not file patent information under subsection (b)(1) of this section because it was not required at the time the application was approved, the holder shall file such information under this subsection not later than 30 days after November 16, 1988 and if the holder of an approved application could not file patent information under subsection (b)(1) of this section because no patent had been issued when an application was filed or approved, the holder shall file such information under this subsection not later than 30 days after the date the patent involved is issued.   Upon the submission of patent information under this subsection, the Secretary shall publish it.

(d) Grounds for refusing application; approval of application; factors; "substantial evidence" defined

(1) If the Secretary finds, after due notice to the applicant in accordance with subsection (c) of this section and giving him an opportunity for a hearing, in accordance with said subsection, that—

(A) the investigations, reports of which are required to be submitted to the Secretary pursuant to subsection (b) of this section, do not include adequate tests by all methods reasonably applicable to show whether or not such drug is safe for use under the conditions prescribed, recommended, or suggested in the proposed labeling thereof;

(B) the results of such tests show that such drug is unsafe for use under such conditions or do not show that such drug is safe for use under such conditions;

(C) the methods used in, and the facilities and controls used for, the manufacture, processing, and packing of such drug are inadequate to preserve its identity, strength, quality, and purity;

(D) upon the basis of the information submitted to him as part of the application, or upon the basis of any other information before him with respect to such drug, he has insufficient information to determine whether such drug is safe for use under such conditions;

(E) evaluated on the basis of the information submitted to him as part of the application and any other information before him with respect to such drug, there is a lack of substantial evidence that the drug will have the effect it purports or is represented to have under the conditions of use prescribed, recommended, or suggested in the proposed labeling thereof;

(F) upon the basis of the information submitted to him as part of the application or any other information before him with respect to such drug, the tolerance limitation proposed, if any, exceeds that reasonably required to accomplish the physical or other technical effect for which the drug is intended;

(G) the application failed to contain the patent information prescribed by subsection (b)(1) of this section;

(H) based on a fair evaluation of all material facts, such labeling is false or misleading in any particular; or

(I) such drug induces cancer when ingested by man or animal or, after tests which are appropriate for the evaluation of the safety of such drug, induces cancer in man or animal, except that the foregoing provisions of this subparagraph shall not apply with respect to such drug if the Secretary finds that, under the conditions of use specified in proposed labeling and reasonably certain to be followed in practice (i) such drug will not adversely affect the animals for which it is intended, and (ii) no residue of such drug will be found (by methods of examination prescribed or approved by the Secretary by regulations, which regulations shall not be subject to subsection (c), (d), and (h) of this section), in any edible portion of such animals after slaughter or in any food yielded by or derived from the living animals;

he shall issue an order refusing to approve the application. If, after such notice and opportunity for hearing, the Secretary finds that subparagraphs (A) through (I) do not apply, he shall issue an order approving the application.

(2) In determining whether such drug is safe for use under the conditions prescribed, recommended, or suggested in the proposed labeling thereof, the Secretary shall consider, among other relevant factors, (A) the probable consumption of such drug and of any substance formed in or on food because of the use of such drug, (B) the cumulative effect on man or animal of such drug, taking into account any chemically or pharmacologically related substance, (C) safety factors which in the opinion of experts, qualified by scientific training and experience to evaluate the safety of such drugs, are appropriate for the use of animal

experimentation data, and (D) whether the conditions of use prescribed, recommended, or suggested in the proposed labeling are reasonably certain to be followed in practice. Any order issued under this subsection refusing to approve an application shall state the findings upon which it is based.

(3) As used in this subsection and subsection (e) of this section, the term "substantial evidence" means evidence consisting of adequate and well- controlled investigations, including field investigation, by experts qualified by scientific training and experience to evaluate the effectiveness of the drug involved, on the basis of which it could fairly and reasonably be concluded by such experts that the drug will have the effect it purports or is represented to have under the conditions of use prescribed, recommended, or suggested in the labeling or proposed labeling thereof.

(e) Withdrawal of approval; grounds; immediate suspension upon finding imminent hazard to health of man or animals

(1) The Secretary shall, after due notice and opportunity for hearing to the applicant, issue an order withdrawing approval of an application filed pursuant to subsection (b) of this section with respect to any new animal drug if the Secretary finds—

(A) that experience or scientific data show that such drug is unsafe for use under the conditions of use upon the basis of which the application was approved or the condition of use authorized under subsection (a)(4)(A);

(B) that new evidence not contained in such application or not available to the Secretary until after such application was approved, or tests by new methods, or tests by methods not deemed reasonably applicable when such application was approved, evaluated together with the evidence available to the Secretary when the application was approved, shows that such drug is not shown to be safe for use under the conditions of use upon the basis of which the application was approved or that subparagraph (I) of paragraph (1) of subsection (d) of this section applies to such drug;

(C) on the basis of new information before him with respect to such drug, evaluated together with the evidence available to him when the application was approved, that there is a lack of substantial evidence that such drug will have the effect it purports or is represented to have under the conditions of use prescribed, recommended, or suggested in the labeling thereof;

(D) the patent information prescribed by subsection (c)(3) of this section was not filed within 30 days after the receipt of written notice from the Secretary specifying the failure to file such information;

(E) that the application contains any untrue statement of a material fact; or

(F) that the applicant has made any changes from the standpoint of safety or effectiveness beyond the variations provided for in the application unless he has supplemented the application by filing with the Secretary adequate information respecting all such changes and unless there is in effect an approval of the supplemental application. The supplemental application shall be treated in the same manner as the original application.

If the Secretary (or in his absence the officer acting as Secretary) finds that there is an imminent hazard to the health of man or of the animals for which such drug is intended, he may suspend the approval of such application immediately, and give the applicant prompt notice of his action and afford the applicant the opportunity for an expedited hearing under this subsection; but the authority conferred by this sentence to suspend the approval of an application shall not be delegated.

(2) The Secretary may also, after due notice and opportunity for hearing to the applicant, issue an order withdrawing the approval of an application with respect to any new animal drug under this section if the Secretary finds—

(A) that the applicant has failed to establish a system for maintaining required records, or has repeatedly or deliberately failed to maintain such records or to make required reports in accordance with a regulation or order under subsection (1) of this section, or the applicant has refused to permit access to, or copying or verification of, such records as required by paragraph (2) of such subsection;

(B) that on the basis of new information before him, evaluated together with the evidence before him when the application was approved, the methods used in, or the facilities and controls used for, the manufacture, processing, and packing of such drug are inadequate to assure and preserve its identity, strength, quality, and purity and were not made adequate within a reasonable time after receipt of written notice from the Secretary specifying the matter complained of; or

(C) that on the basis of new information before him, evaluated together with the evidence before him when the application was approved, the labeling of such drug, based on a fair evaluation of all material facts, is false or misleading in any particular and was not corrected within a reasonable time after receipt of written notice from the Secretary specifying the matter complained of.

(3) Any order under this subsection shall state the findings upon which it is based.

(f) Revocation of order refusing, withdrawing or suspending approval of application

Whenever the Secretary finds that the facts so require, he shall revoke any previous order under subsection (d), (e), or (m) of this section refusing, withdrawing, or suspending approval of an application and shall approve such application or reinstate such approval, as may be appropriate.

(g) Service of orders

Orders of the Secretary issued under this section (other than orders issuing, amending, or repealing regulations) shall be served (1) in person by any officer or employee of the department designated by the Secretary or (2) by mailing the order by registered mail or by certified mail addressed to the applicant or respondent at his last known address in the records of the Secretary.

(h) Appeal from order

An appeal may be taken by the applicant from an order of the Secretary refusing or withdrawing approval of an application filed under subsection (b) or (m) of this section. The provisions of subsection (h) of section 355 of this title shall govern any such appeal.

(i) Publication in Federal Register; effective date and revocation or suspension of regulation

When a new animal drug application filed pursuant to subsection (b) of this section is approved, the Secretary shall by notice, which upon publication shall be effective as a regulation, publish in the Federal Register the name and address of the applicant and the conditions and indications of use of the new animal drug covered by such application, including any tolerance and withdrawal period or other use restrictions and, if such new animal drug is intended for use in animal feed, appropriate purposes and conditions of use (including special labeling requirements) applicable to any animal feed for use in which such drug is approved, and such other information, upon the basis of which such application was approved, as the Secretary deems necessary to assure the safe and effective use of such drug. Upon withdrawal of approval of such new animal drug application or upon its suspension, the Secretary shall forthwith revoke or suspend, as the case may be, the regulation published pursuant to this subsection (i) insofar as it is based on the approval of such application.

(j) Exemption of drugs for research; discretionary and mandatory conditions

To the extent consistent with the public health, the Secretary shall promulgate regulations for exempting from the operation of this section new animal drugs, and animal feeds bearing or containing new animal drugs, intended solely for investigational use by experts qualified by scientific training and experience to investigate the safety and effectiveness of animal drugs. Such regulations may, in the discretion of the Secretary, among other conditions relating to the protection of the public health, provide for conditioning such exemption upon the establishment and maintenance of such records, and the making of such reports to the Secretary, by the manufacturer or the sponsor of the investigation of such article, of data (including but not limited to analytical reports by investigators) obtained as a result of such investigational use of such article, as the Secretary finds will enable him to evaluate the safety and effectiveness of such article in the event of the filing of an application pursuant to this section. Such regulations, among other things, shall set forth the conditions (if any) upon which animals treated with such articles, and any products of such animals (before or after slaughter), may be marketed for food use.

(k) Food containing new animal drug considered unadulterated while approval of application for such drug is effective

While approval of an application for a new animal drug is effective, a food shall not, by reason of bearing or containing such drug or any substance formed in or on the food because of its use in accordance with such application (including the conditions and indications of use prescribed pursuant to subsection (i) of this section), be considered adulterated within the meaning of clause (1) of section 342(a) of this title.

(*l*) Records and reports; required information; regulations and orders; examination of data; access to records

(1) In the case of any new animal drug for which an approval of an application filed pursuant to subsection (b) of this section is in effect, the applicant shall establish and maintain such records, and make such reports to the Secretary, of data relating to experience, including experience with uses authorized under subsection (a)(4)(A) of this section, and other data or information, received or otherwise obtained by such applicant with respect to such drug, or with respect to animal feeds bearing or containing such drug, as the Secretary may by general regulation, or by order with respect to such application, prescribe on the basis of a finding that such records and reports are necessary in order to enable the Secretary to determine, or facilitate a determination, whether there is or may be ground for invoking subsection (e) or subsection (m)(4) of this section. Such regulation or order shall provide, where the Secretary deems it to be appropriate, for the examination, upon request, by the persons to whom such regulation or order is applicable, of similar information received or otherwise obtained by the Secretary.

(2) Every person required under this subsection to maintain records, and every person in charge or custody thereof, shall, upon request of an officer or employee designated by the Secretary, permit such officer or employee at all reasonable times to have access to and copy and verify such records.

(m) Filing application for uses of animal feed containing new animal drug; contents

(1) Any person may file with the Secretary an application with respect to any intended use or uses of an animal feed bearing or containing a new animal drug. Such person shall submit to the Secretary as part of the application (A) a full statement of the composition of such animal feed, (B) an identification of the regulation or regulations (relating to the new animal drug or drugs to be used in such feed), published pursuant to subsection (i) of this section, on which he relies as a basis for approval of his application with respect to the use of such drug in such feed, (C) a full description of the methods used in, and the facilities and controls used for, the manufacture, processing, and packing of such animal feed, (D) specimens of the labeling proposed to be used for such animal feed, and (E) if so requested by the Secretary, samples of such animal feed or components thereof.

(2) Same; period for approval of application; period for, notice, and expedition of hearing; period for issuance of order

Within ninety days after the filing of an application pursuant to paragraph (1) of this subsection, or such additional period as may be agreed upon by the Secretary and the applicant, the Secretary shall either (A) issue an order approving the application if he then finds that none of the grounds for denying approval specified in paragraph (3) applies, or (B) give the applicant notice of an opportunity for a hearing before the Secretary under paragraph (3) on the question whether such application is approvable. The procedure governing such a hearing shall be the procedure set forth in the last two sentences of subsection (c) of this section.

(3) Same; grounds for refusing application; approval of application; approval effective during existence of subsection (i) regulation

If the Secretary, after due notice to the applicant in accordance with paragraph (2) and giving him an opportunity for a hearing in accordance with such paragraph, finds, on the basis of information submitted to him as part of the application or on the basis of any other information before him—

(A) that there is not in effect a regulation under subsection (i) of this section (identified in such application) on the basis of which such application may be approved;

(B) that such animal feed (including the proposed use of any new animal drug therein or thereon) does not conform to an applicable regulation published pursuant to subsection (i) of this section referred to in the application, or that the purposes and conditions or indications of use prescribed, recommended, or suggested in the labeling of such feed do not conform to the applicable purposes and conditions or indications of use (including warnings) published pursuant to subsection (i) of this section or such labeling omits or fails to conform to other applicable information published pursuant to subsection (i) of this section;

(C) that the methods used in, and the facilities and controls used for, the manufacture, processing, and packing of such animal feed are inadequate to preserve the identity, strength, quality, and purity of the new animal drug therein; or

(D) that, based on a fair evaluation of all material facts, such labeling is false or misleading in any particular;

he shall issue an order refusing to approve the application. If, after such notice and opportunity for hearing, the Secretary finds that subparagraphs (A) through (D) do not apply, he shall issue an order approving the application. An order under this subsection approving an application with respect to an animal feed bearing or containing a new animal drug shall be effective only while there is in effect a regulation pursuant to subsection (i) of this section, on the basis of which such application (or a supplement thereto) was approved, relating to the use of such drug in or on such feed.

(4) Same; withdrawal of approval; grounds; immediate suspension upon finding imminent hazard to health of man or animals

(A) The Secretary shall, after due notice and opportunity for hearing to the applicant, issue an order withdrawing approval of an application with respect to any animal feed under this subsection if the Secretary finds—

(i) that the application contains any untrue statement of a material fact; or

(ii) that the applicant has made any changes from the standpoint of safety or effectiveness beyond the variations provided for in the application unless he has supplemented the application by filing with the Secretary adequate information respecting all such changes and unless there is in effect an approval of the supplemental application. The supplemental application shall be treated in the same manner as the original application.

If the Secretary (or in his absence the officer acting as Secretary) finds that there is an imminent hazard to the health of man or of the animals for which such animal feed is intended, he may suspend the approval of such application immediately, and give the applicant prompt notice of his action and afford the applicant the opportunity for an expedited hearing under this subsection; but the authority conferred by this sentence shall not be delegated.

(B) The Secretary may also, after due notice and opportunity for hearing to the applicant, issue an order withdrawing the approval of an application with respect to any animal feed under this subsection if the Secretary finds—

(i) that the applicant has failed to establish a system for maintaining required records, or has repeatedly or deliberately failed to maintain such records or to make required reports in accordance with a regulation or order under paragraph (5)(A) of this subsection, or the applicant has refused to permit access to, or copying or verification of, such records as required by subparagraph (B) of such paragraph;

(ii) that on the basis of new information before him, evaluated together with the evidence before him when such application was approved, the methods used in, or the facilities and controls used for, the manufacture, processing, and packing of such animal feed are inadequate to assure and preserve the identity, strength, quality, and purity of the new animal drug therein, and were not made adequate within a reasonable time after receipt of written notice from the Secretary, specifying the matter complained of; or

(iii) that on the basis of new information before him, evaluated together with the evidence before him when the application was approved, the labeling of such animal feed, based on a fair evaluation of all material facts, is false or misleading in any particular and was not corrected within a reasonable time after receipt of written notice from the Secretary specifying the matter complained of.

(C) Any order under paragraph (4) of this subsection shall state the findings upon which it is based.

(5) Same; records and reports; regulations and orders; access to records

In the case of any animal feed for which an approval of an application filed pursuant to this subsection is in effect—

(A) the applicant shall establish and maintain such records, and make such reports to the Secretary, or (at the option of the Secretary) to the appropriate person or persons holding an approved application filed under subsection (b) of this section, as the Secretary may by general regulation, or by order with respect to such application, prescribe on the basis of a finding that such records and reports are necessary in order to enable the Secretary to determine, or facilitate a determination, whether there is or may be ground for invoking subsection (e) of this section or paragraph (4) of this subsection.

(B) every person required under this subsection to maintain records, and every person in charge or custody thereof, shall, upon request of an officer or employee designated by the Secretary, permit such officer or employee at all reasonable times to have access to and copy and verify such records.

(n) Abbreviated applications for new animal drugs; contents, filing, etc.; lists of approved drugs

(1) An abbreviated application for a new animal drug shall contain—

(A)(i) except as provided in clause (ii), information to show that the conditions of use or similar limitations (whether in the labeling or published pursuant to subsection (i) of this section) prescribed, recommended, or suggested in the labeling proposed for the new animal drug have been previously approved for a new animal drug listed under paragraph (4)(hereinafter in this subsection referred to as an "approved new animal drug"), and

(ii) information to show that the withdrawal period at which residues of the new animal drug will be consistent with the tolerances established for the approved new animal drug is the same as the withdrawal period previously established for the approved new animal drug or, if the withdrawal period is proposed to be different, information showing that the residues of the new animal drug at the proposed different withdrawal period will be consistent with the tolerances established for the approved new animal drug;

(B)(i) information to show that the active ingredients of the new animal drug are the same as those of the approved new animal drug, and

(ii) if the approved new animal drug has more than one active ingredient, and if one of the active ingredients of the new animal drug is different from one of the active ingredients of the approved new animal drug and the application is filed pursuant to the approval of a petition filed under paragraph (3)—

(I) information to show that the other active ingredients of the new animal drug are the same as the active ingredients of the approved new animal drug,

(II) information to show either that the different active ingredient is an active ingredient of another approved new animal drug or of an animal drug which does not meet the requirements of section 321(v) of this title, and

(III) such other information respecting the different active ingredients as the Secretary may require;

(C)(i) if the approved new animal drug is permitted to be used with one or more animal drugs in animal feed, information to show that the proposed uses of the new animal drug with other animal drugs in animal feed are the same as the uses of the approved new animal drug, and

(ii) if the approved new animal drug is permitted to be used with one or more other animal drugs in animal feed, and one of the other animal drugs proposed for use with the new animal drug in animal feed is different from one of the other animal drugs permitted to be used in animal feed with the approved new animal drug, and the application is filed pursuant to the approval of a petition filed under paragraph (3)—

(I) information to show either that the different animal drug proposed for use with the approved new animal drug in animal feed is an approved new animal drug permitted to be used in animal feed or does not meet the requirements of section 321(v) of this title when used with another animal drug in animal feed,

(II) information to show that other animal drugs proposed for use with the new animal drug in animal feed are the same as the other animal drugs permitted to be used with the approved new animal drug, and

(III) such other information respecting the different animal drug or combination with respect to which the petition was filed as the Secretary may require,

(D) information to show that the route of administration, the dosage form, and the strength of the new animal drug are the same as those of the approved new animal drug or, if the route of administration, the dosage form, or the strength of the new animal drug is different and the application is filed pursuant to the approval of a petition filed under paragraph (3), such information respecting the route of administration, dosage form, or strength with respect to which the petition was filed as the Secretary may require;

(E) information to show that the new animal drug is bioequivalent to the approved new animal drug, except that if the application is filed pursuant to the approval of a petition filed under paragraph (3) for the purposes described in subparagraph (B) or (C), information to show that the active ingredients of the new animal drug are of the same pharmacological or therapeutic class as the pharmacological or therapeutic class of the approved new animal drug and that the new animal drug can be expected to have the same therapeutic effect as the approved new animal drug when used in accordance with the labeling;

(F) information to show that the labeling proposed for the new animal drug is the same as the labeling approved for the approved new animal drug except for changes required because of differences approved under a petition filed under paragraph (3), because of a different withdrawal period, or because the new animal drug and the approved new animal drug are produced or distributed by different manufacturers;

(G) the items specified in clauses (B) through (F) of subsection (b)(1) of this section;

(H) a certification, in the opinion of the applicant and to the best of his knowledge, with respect to each patent which claims the approved new animal drug or which claims a use for such approved new animal drug for which the applicant is seeking approval under this subsection and for which information is required to be filed under subsection (b)(1) or (c)(3) of this section

    (i) that such patent information has not been filed,

    (ii) that such patent has expired,

    (iii) of the date on which such patent will expire, or

    (iv) that such patent is invalid or will not be infringed by the manufacture, use, or sale of the new animal drug for which the application is filed; and

(I) if with respect to the approved new animal drug information was filed under subsection (b)(1) or (c)(3) of this section for a method of use patent which does not claim a use for which the applicant is seeking approval of an application under subsection (c)(2) of this section, a statement that the method of use patent does not claim such a use.

The Secretary may not require that an abbreviated application contain information in addition to that required by subparagraphs (A) through (I).

(2)(A) An applicant who makes a certification described in paragraph (1)(G)(iv) shall include in the application a statement that the applicant will give the notice required by subparagraph (B) to—

    (i) each owner of the patent which is the subject of the certification or the representative of such owner designated to receive such notice, and

    (ii) the holder of the approved application under subsection (c)(1) of this section for the drug which is claimed by the patent or a use of which is claimed by the patent or the representative of such holder designated to receive such notice.

(B) The notice referred to in subparagraph (A) shall state that an application, which contains data from bioequivalence studies, has been filed under this subsection for the drug with respect to which the certification is made to obtain approval to engage in the commercial manufacture, use, or sale of such drug before the expiration of the patent referred to in the certification. Such notice shall include a detailed statement of the factual and legal basis of the applicant's opinion that the patent is not valid or will not be infringed.

(C) If an application is amended to include a certification described in paragraph (1)(G)(iv), the notice required by subparagraph (B) shall be given when the amended application is filed.

(3) If a person wants to submit an abbreviated application for a new animal drug—

(A) whose active ingredients, route of administration, dosage form, or strength differ from that of an approved new animal drug, or

(B) whose use with other animal drugs in animal feed differs from that of an approved new animal drug,

such person shall submit a petition to the Secretary seeking permission to file such an application. The Secretary shall approve a petition for a new animal drug unless the Secretary finds that—

(C) investigations must be conducted to show the safety and effectiveness, in animals to be treated with the drug, of the active ingredients, route of administration, dosage form, strength, or use with other animal drugs in animal feed which differ from the approved new animal drug, or

(D) investigations must be conducted to show the safety for human consumption of any residues in food resulting from the proposed active ingredients, route of administration, dosage form, strength, or use with other animal drugs in animal feed for the new animal drug which is different from the active ingredients, route of administration, dosage form, strength, or use with other animal drugs in animal feed of the approved new animal drug.

The Secretary shall approve or disapprove a petition submitted under this paragraph within 90 days of the date the petition is submitted.

(4)(A)(i) Within 60 days of November 16, 1988, the Secretary shall publish and make available to the public a list in alphabetical order of the official and proprietary name of each new animal drug which has been approved for safety and effectiveness before November 16, 1988.

(ii) Every 30 days after the publication of the first list under clause (i) the Secretary shall revise the list to include each new animal drug which has been approved for safety and effectiveness under subsection (c) of this section during the 30 day period.

(iii) When patent information submitted under subsection (b)(1) or (c)(3) of this section respecting a new animal drug included on the list is to be published by the Secretary, the Secretary shall, in revisions made under clause (ii), include such information for such drug.

(B) A new animal drug approved for safety and effectiveness before November 16, 1988 or approved for safety and effectiveness under subsection (c) of this section shall, for purposes of this subsection, be considered to have been published under subparagraph (A) on the date of its approval or November 16, 1988, whichever is later.

(C) If the approval of a new animal drug was withdrawn or suspended under subsection (c)(2)(G) of this section or for grounds described in subsection (e) of this section or if the Secretary determines that a drug has been withdrawn from sale for safety or effectiveness reasons, it may not be published in the list under subparagraph (A) or, if the withdrawal or suspension occurred after its publication in such list, it shall be immediately removed from such list—

(i) for the same period as the withdrawal or suspension under subsection (c)(2)(G) or (e) of this section, or

(ii) if the listed drug has been withdrawn from sale, for the period of withdrawal from sale or, if earlier, the period ending on the date the Secretary determines that the withdrawal from sale is not for safety or effectiveness reasons.

A notice of the removal shall be published in the Federal Register.

(5) If an application contains the information required by clauses (A), (G), and (H) of subsection (b)(1) of this section and such information—

(A) is relied on by the applicant for the approval of the application, and

(B) is not information derived either from investigations, studies, or tests conducted by or for the applicant or for which the applicant had obtained a right of reference or use from the person by or for whom the investigations, studies, or tests were conducted,

such application shall be considered to be an application filed under subsection (b)(2) of this section.

(o) "Patent" defined

For purposes of this section, the term "patent" means a patent issued by the Patent and Trademark Office of the Department of Commerce.

(p) Safety and effectiveness data

(1) Safety and effectiveness data and information which has been submitted in an application filed under subsection (b)(1) of this section for a drug and which has not previously been disclosed to the public shall be made available to the public, upon request, unless extraordinary circumstances are shown—

(A) if no work is being or will be undertaken to have the application approved,

(B) if the Secretary has determined that the application is not approvable and all legal appeals have been exhausted,

(C) if approval of the application under subsection (c) of this section is withdrawn and all legal appeals have been exhausted,

(D) if the Secretary has determined that such drug is not a new drug, or

(E) upon the effective date of the approval of the first application filed under subsection (b)(2) of this section which refers to such drug or upon the date upon which the approval of an application filed under subsection (b)(2) of this section which refers to such drug could be made effective if such an application had been filed.

(2) Any request for data and information pursuant to paragraph (1) shall include a verified statement by the person making the request that any data or information received under such paragraph shall not be disclosed by such person to any other person—

(A) for the purpose of, or as part of a plan, scheme, or device for, obtaining the right to make, use, or market, or making, using, or marketing, outside the United States, the drug identified in the application filed under subsection (b)(1) of this section, and

(B) without obtaining from any person to whom the data and information are disclosed an identical verified statement, a copy of which is to be provided by such person to the Secretary, which meets the requirements of this paragraph.

§ 360c. Classification of devices intended for human use

(a) Classes of devices

(1) There are established the following classes of devices intended for human use:

(A) Class I, General Controls

(i) A device for which the controls authorized by or under section 351, 352, 360, 360f, 360h, 360i, or 360j of this title or any combination of such sections are sufficient to provide reasonable assurance of the safety and effectiveness of the device.

(ii) A device for which insufficient information exists to determine that the controls referred to in clause (i) are sufficient to provide reasonable assurance of the safety and effectiveness of the device or to establish special controls to provide such assurance, but because it—

(I) is not purported or represented to be for a use in supporting or sustaining human life or for a use which is of substantial importance in preventing impairment of human health, and

(II) does not present a potential unreasonable risk of illness or injury,

is to be regulated by the controls referred to in clause (i).

(B) Class II, Special Controls

A device which cannot be classified as a class I device because the general controls by themselves are insufficient to provide reasonable assurance of the safety and effectiveness of the device, and for which there is sufficient information to establish special controls to provide such assurance, including the promulgation of performance standards, postmarket surveillance, patient registries, development and dissemination of guidelines (including guidelines for the submission of clinical data in premarket notification submissions in accordance with section 360(k) of this title), recommendations, and other appropriate actions as the Secretary deems necessary to provide such assurance. For a device that is purported or represented to be for a use in supporting or sustaining human life, the Secretary shall examine and identify the special controls, if any, that are necessary to provide adequate assurance of safety and effectiveness and describe how such controls provide such assurance.

(C) Class III, Premarket Approval

A device which because—

(i) it (I) cannot be classified as a class I device because insufficient information exists to determine that the application of general controls are sufficient to provide reasonable assurance of the safety and effectiveness of the device, and (II) cannot be classified as a class II device because insufficient information exists to determine that the special controls described in subparagraph (B) would provide reasonable assurance of its safety and effectiveness, and

(ii)(I) is purported or represented to be for a use in supporting or sustaining human life or for a use which is of substantial importance in preventing impairment of human health, or

(II) presents a potential unreasonable risk of illness or injury,

is to be subject, in accordance with section 360e of this title, to premarket approval to provide reasonable assurance of its safety and effectiveness.

If there is not sufficient information to establish a performance standard for a device to provide reasonable assurance of its safety and effectiveness, the Secretary may conduct such activities as may be necessary to develop or obtain such information.

(2) For purposes of this section and sections 360d and 360e of this title, the safety and effectiveness of a device are to be determined—

(A) with respect to the persons for whose use the device is represented or intended,

(B) with respect to the conditions of use prescribed, recommended, or suggested in the labeling of the device, and

(C) weighing any probable benefit to health from the use of the device against any probable risk of injury or illness from such use.

(3)(A) Except as authorized by subparagraph (B), the effectiveness of a device is, for purposes of this section and sections 360d and 360e of this title, to be determined, in accordance with regulations promulgated by the Secretary, on the basis of well-controlled investigations, including clinical investigations where appropriate, by experts qualified by training and experience to evaluate the effectiveness of the device, from which investigations it can fairly and responsibly be concluded by qualified experts that the device will have the effect it purports or is represented to have under the conditions of use prescribed, recommended, or suggested in the labeling of the device.

(B) If the Secretary determines that there exists valid scientific evidence (other than evidence derived from investigations described in subparagraph (A))—

(i) which is sufficient to determine the effectiveness of a device, and

(ii) from which it can fairly and responsibly be concluded by qualified experts that the device will have the effect it purports or is represented to have under the conditions of use prescribed, recommended, or suggested in the labeling of the device,

then, for purposes of this section and sections 360d and 360e of this title, the Secretary may authorize the effectiveness of the device to be determined on the basis of such evidence.

(b) Classification panels

(1) For purposes of—

(A) determining which devices intended for human use should be subject to the requirements of general controls, performance standards, or premarket approval, and

(B) providing notice to the manufacturers and importers of such devices to enable them to prepare for the application of such requirements to devices manufactured or imported by them,

the Secretary shall classify all such devices (other than devices classified by subsection (f) of this section) into the classes established by subsection (a) of this section. For the purpose of securing recommendations with respect to the classification of devices, the Secretary shall establish panels of experts or use panels of experts established before May 28, 1976, or both. Section 14 of the Federal Advisory Committee Act shall not apply to the duration of a panel established under this paragraph.

(2) The Secretary shall appoint to each panel established under paragraph (1) persons who are qualified by training and experience to evaluate the safety and effectiveness of the devices to be referred to the panel and who, to the extent feasible, possess skill in the use of, or experience in the development, manufacture, or utilization of, such devices. The Secretary shall make appointments to each panel so that each panel shall consist of members with adequately diversified expertise in such fields as clinical and administrative medicine, engineering, biological and physical sciences, and other related professions. In addi-

tion, each panel shall include as nonvoting members a representative of consumer interests and a representative of interests of the device manufacturing industry. Scientific, trade, and consumer organizations shall be afforded an opportunity to nominate individuals for appointment to the panels. No individual who is in the regular full-time employ of the United States and engaged in the administration of this chapter may be a member of any panel. The Secretary shall designate one of the members of each panel to serve as chairman thereof.

(3) Panel members (other than officers or employees of the United States), while attending meetings or conferences of a panel or otherwise engaged in its business, shall be entitled to receive compensation at rates to be fixed by the Secretary, but not at rates exceeding the daily equivalent of the rate in effect for grade GS–18 of the General Schedule, for each day so engaged, including traveltime; and while so serving away from their homes or regular places of business each member may be allowed travel expenses (including per diem in lieu of subsistence) as authorized by section 5703 of Title 5, for persons in the Government service employed intermittently.

(4) The Secretary shall furnish each panel with adequate clerical and other necessary assistance.

(c) Classification panel organization and operation

(1) The Secretary shall organize the panels according to the various fields of clinical medicine and fundamental sciences in which devices intended for human use are used. The Secretary shall refer a device to be classified under this section to an appropriate panel established or authorized to be used under subsection (b) of this section for its review and for its recommendation respecting the classification of the device. The Secretary shall by regulation prescribe the procedure to be followed by the panels in making their reviews and recommendations. In making their reviews of devices, the panels, to the maximum extent practicable, shall provide an opportunity for interested persons to submit data and views on the classification of the devices.

(2)(A) Upon completion of a panel's review of a device referred to it under paragraph (1), the panel shall, subject to subparagraphs (B) and (C), submit to the Secretary its recommendation for the classification of the device. Any such recommendation shall (i) contain (I) a summary of the reasons for the recommendation, (II) a summary of the data upon which the recommendation is based, and (III) an identification of the risks to health (if any) presented by the device with respect to which the recommendation is made, and (ii) to the extent practicable, include a recommendation for the assignment of a priority for the application of the requirements of section 360d or 360e of this title to a device recommended to be classified in class II or class III.

(B) A recommendation of a panel for the classification of a device in class I shall include a recommendation as to whether the device should be exempted from the requirements of section 360, 360i, or 360j(f) of this title.

(C) In the case of a device which has been referred under paragraph (1) to a panel, and which—

(i) is intended to be implanted in the human body or is purported or represented to be for a use in supporting or sustaining human life, and

(ii)(I) has been introduced or delivered for introduction into interstate commerce for commercial distribution before May 28, 1976, or

(II) is within a type of device which was so introduced or delivered before such date and is substantially equivalent to another device within that type,

such panel shall recommend to the Secretary that the device be classified in class III unless the panel determines that classification of the device in such class is not necessary to provide reasonable assurance of its safety and effectiveness. If a panel does not recommend that such a device be classified in class III, it shall in its recommendation to the Secretary for the classification of the device set forth the reasons for not recommending classification of the device in such class.

(3) The panels shall submit to the Secretary within one year of the date funds are first appropriated for the implementation of this section their recommendations respecting all devices of a type introduced or delivered for introduction into interstate commerce for commercial distribution before May 28, 1976.

(d) Panel recommendation; publication; priorities

(1) Upon receipt of a recommendation from a panel respecting a device, the Secretary shall publish in the Federal Register the panel's recommendation and a proposed regulation classifying such device and shall provide interested persons an opportunity to submit comments on such recommendation and the proposed regulation. After reviewing such comments, the Secretary shall, subject to paragraph (2), by regulation classify such device.

(2)(A) A regulation under paragraph (1) classifying a device in class I shall prescribe which, if any, of the requirements of section 360, 360i, or 360j(f) of this title shall not apply to the device. A regulation which makes a requirement of section 360, 360i, or 360j(f) of this title inapplicable to a device shall be accompanied by a statement of the reasons of the Secretary for making such requirement inapplicable.

(B) A device described in subsection (c)(2)(C) of this section shall be classified in class III unless the Secretary determines that classification of the device in such class is not necessary to provide reasonable assurance of its safety and effectiveness. A proposed regulation under paragraph (1) classifying such a device in a class other than class III shall be accompanied by a full statement of the reasons of the Secretary (and supporting documentation and data) for not classifying such device in such class and an identification of the risks to health (if any) presented by such device.

(3) In the case of devices classified in class II and devices classified under this subsection in class III and described in section 360e(b)(1) of this title the Secretary may establish priorities which, in his discretion, shall be used in applying sections 360d and 360e of this title, as appropriate, to such devices.

(e) Classification changes

(1) Based on new information respecting a device, the Secretary may, upon his own initiative or upon petition of an interested person, by regulation (A) change such device's classification, and (B) revoke, because of the change in classification, any regulation or requirement in effect under section 360d or 360e of this title with respect to such device. In the promulgation of such a regulation respecting a device's classification, the Secretary may secure from the panel to which the device was last referred pursuant to subsection (c) of this section a recommendation respecting the proposed change in the device's classification and shall publish in the Federal Register any recommendation submitted to the Secretary by the panel respecting such change. A regulation under this subsection changing the classification of a device from class III to class II may provide that such classification shall not take effect until the effective date of a performance standard established under section 360d of this title for such device.

(2) By regulation promulgated under paragraph (1), the Secretary may change the classification of a device from class III—

(A) to class II if the Secretary determines that special controls would provide reasonable assurance of the safety and effectiveness of the device and that general controls would not provide reasonable assurance of the safety and effectiveness of the device, or

(B) to class I if the Secretary determines that general controls would provide reasonable assurance of the safety and effectiveness of the device.

(f) Initial classification and reclassification of certain devices

(1) Any device intended for human use which was not introduced or delivered for introduction into interstate commerce for commercial distribution before May 28, 1976, is classified in class III unless—

(A) the device—

(i) is within a type of device (I) which was introduced or delivered for introduction into interstate commerce for commercial distribution before such date and which is to be classified pursuant to subsection (b) of this section, or (II) which was not so introduced or delivered before such date and has been classified in class I or II, and

(ii) is substantially equivalent to another device within such type, or

(B) the Secretary in response to a petition submitted under paragraph (2) has classified such device in class I or II.

A device classified in class III under this paragraph shall be classified in that class until the effective date of an order of the Secretary under paragraph (2) classifying the device in class I or II.

(2)(A) The Secretary may initiate the reclassification of a device classified into class III under paragraph (1) of this subsection or the manufacturer or importer of a device classified under paragraph (1) may petition the Secretary (in such form and manner as he shall prescribe) for the issuance of an order classifying the device in class I or class II. Within thirty days of the filing of such a petition, the Secretary shall notify the petitioner of any deficiencies in the petition which prevent the Secretary from making a decision on the petition.

(B)(i) Upon determining that a petition does not contain any deficiency which prevents the Secretary from making a decision on the petition, the Secretary may for good cause shown refer the petition to an appropriate panel established or authorized to be used under subsection (b) of this section. A panel to which such a petition has been referred shall not later than ninety days after the referral of the petition make a recommendation to the Secretary respecting approval or denial of the petition. Any such recommendation shall contain (I) a summary of the reasons for the recommendation, (II) a summary of the data upon which the recommendation is based, and (III) an identification of the risks to health (if any) presented by the device with respect to which the petition was filed. In the case of a petition for a device which is intended to be implanted in the human body or which is purported or represented to be for a use in supporting or sustaining human life, the panel shall recommend that the petition be denied unless the panel determines that the classification in class III of the device is not necessary to provide reasonable assurance of its safety and effectiveness. If the panel recommends that such petition be approved, it shall in its recommendation to the Secretary set forth its reasons for such recommendation.

(ii) The requirements of paragraphs (1) and (2) of subsection (c) of this section (relating to opportunities for submission of data and views and recommendations respecting priorities and exemptions from sections 360, 360i, and 360j(f) of this title) shall apply with respect to consideration by panels of petitions submitted under subparagraph (A).

(C)(i) Within ninety days from the date the Secretary receives the recommendation of a panel respecting a petition (but not later than 210 days after the filing of such petition) the Secretary shall by order deny or approve the petition. If the Secretary approves the petition, the Secretary shall order the classification of the device into class I or class II in accordance with the criteria prescribed by subsection (a)(1) (A) or (a)(1)(B) of this section. In the case of a petition for a device which is intended to be implanted in the human body or which is purported or represented to be for a use in supporting or sustaining human life, the Secretary shall deny the petition unless the Secretary determines that the classification in class III of the device is not necessary to provide reasonable assurance of its safety and effectiveness. An order approving such petition shall be accompanied by a full statement of the reasons of the Secretary (and supporting documentation and data) for approving the petition and an identification of the risks to health (if any) presented by the device to which such order applies.

(ii) The requirements of paragraphs (1) and (2)(A) of subsection (d) of this section (relating to publication of recommendations, opportunity for submission of comments, and exemption from sections 360, 360i, and 360j(f) of this title) shall apply with respect to action by the Secretary on petitions submitted under subparagraph (A).

(3) If a manufacturer reports to the Secretary under section 360(k) of this title that a device is substantially equivalent to another device—

(A) which the Secretary has classified as a class III device under subsection (b) of this section,

(B) which was introduced or delivered for introduction into interstate commerce for commercial distribution before December 1, 1990, and

(C) for which no final regulation requiring premarket approval has been promulgated under section 360e(b) of this title,

the manufacturer shall certify to the Secretary that the manufacturer has conducted a reasonable search of all information known or otherwise available to the manufacturer respecting such other device and has included in the report under section 360(k) of this title a summary of and a citation to all adverse safety and effectiveness data respecting such other device and respecting the device for which the section 360(k) report is being made and which has not been submitted to the Secretary under section 360i of this title. The Secretary may require the manufacturer to submit the adverse safety and effectiveness data described in the report.

(g) Information

Within sixty days of the receipt of a written request of any person for information respecting the class in which a device has been classified or the requirements applicable to a device under this chapter, the Secretary shall provide such person a written statement of the classification (if any) of such device and the requirements of this chapter applicable to the device.

(h) Definitions

For purposes of this section and sections 351, 360, 360d, 360e, 360f, 360i, and 360j of this title

(1) a reference to "general controls" is a reference to the controls authorized by or under sections 351, 352, 360, 360f, 360h, 360i, and 360j of this title,

(2) a reference to "class I", "class II", or "class III" is a reference to a class of medical devices described in subparagraph (A), (B), or (C) of subsection (a)(1) of this section, and

(3) a reference to a "panel under section 360c of this title" is a reference to a panel established or authorized to be used under this section.

(i) Substantial equivalence

(1)(A) For purposes of determinations of substantial equivalence under subsection (f) of this section and section 360j(*l*) of this title, the term "substantially equivalent" or "substantial equivalence" means, with respect to a device being compared to a predicate device, that the device has the same intended use as the predicate device and that the Secretary by order has found that the device—

(i) has the same technological characteristics as the predicate device, or

(ii)(I) has different technological characteristics and the information submitted that the device is substantially equivalent to the predicate device contains information, including clinical data if deemed necessary by the Secretary, that demonstrates that the device is as safe and effective as a legally marketed device, and (II) does not raise different questions of safety and efficacy than the predicate device.

(B) For purposes of subparagraph (A), the term "different technological characteristics" means, with respect to a device being compared to a predicate device, that there is a significant change in the materials, design, energy source, or other features of the device from those of the predicate device.

(2) A device may not be found to be substantially equivalent to a predicate device that has been removed from the market at the initiative of the Secretary or that has been determined to be misbranded or adulterated by a judicial order.

(3)(A) As part of a submission under section 360(k) of this title respecting a device, the person required to file a premarket notification under such section shall provide an adequate summary of any information respecting safety and effectiveness or state that such information will be made available upon request by any person.

(B) Any summary under subparagraph (A) respecting a device shall contain detailed information regarding data concerning adverse health effects and shall be made available to the public by the Secretary within 30 days of the issuance of a determination that such device is substantially equivalent to another device.

§ 360d. Performance standards

(a) Reasonable assurance of safe and effective performance; periodic evaluation

(1) The special controls required by section 360c(a)(1)(B) of this title shall include performance standards for a class II device if the Secretary determines that a performance standard is necessary to provide reasonable assurance of the safety and effectiveness of the device. A class III device may also be considered a class II device for purposes of establishing a standard for the device under this section if the device has been reclassified as a class II device under a regulation under section 360c(e) of this title but such regulation provides that the reclassification is not to take effect until the effective date of such a standard for the device.

(2) A performance standard established under this section for a device—

(A) shall include provisions to provide reasonable assurance of its safe and effective performance;

(B) shall, where necessary to provide reasonable assurance of its safe and effective performance, include—

(i) provisions respecting the construction, components, ingredients, and properties of the device and its compatibility with power systems and connections to such systems,

(ii) provisions for the testing (on a sample basis or, if necessary, on an individual basis) of the device or, if it is determined that no other more practicable means are available to the Secretary to assure the conformity of the device to the standard, provisions for the testing (on a sample basis or, if necessary, on an individual basis) by the Secretary or by another person at the direction of the Secretary,

(iii) provisions for the measurement of the performance characteristics of the device,

(iv) provisions requiring that the results of each or of certain of the tests of the device required to be made under clause (ii) show that the device is in conformity with the portions of the standard for which the test or tests were required, and

(v) a provision requiring that the sale and distribution of the device be restricted but only to the extent that the sale and distribution of a device may be restricted under a regulation under section 360j(e) of this title; and

(C) shall, where appropriate, require the use and prescribe the form and content of labeling for the proper installation, maintenance, operation, and use of the device.

(3) The Secretary shall provide for periodic evaluation of performance standards established under this section to determine if such standards should be changed to reflect new medical, scientific, or other technological data.

(4) In carrying out his duties under this section, the Secretary shall, to the maximum extent practicable—

(A) use personnel, facilities, and other technical support available in other Federal agencies,

(B) consult with other Federal agencies concerned with standard-setting and other nationally or internationally recognized standard-setting entities, and

(C) invite appropriate participation, through joint or other conferences, workshops, or other means, by informed persons representative of scientific, professional, industry, or consumer organizations who in his judgment can make a significant contribution.

(b) Notice of proposed rulemaking for performance standards; request for change of classification; regulations establishing, amending, or revoking performance standards; advisory committee

(1)(A) The Secretary shall publish in the Federal Register a notice of proposed rulemaking for the establishment, amendment, or revocation of any performance standard for a device.

(B) A notice of proposed rulemaking for the establishment or amendment of a performance standard for a device shall—

(i) set forth a finding with supporting justification that the performance standard is appropriate and necessary to provide reasonable assurance of the safety and effectiveness of the device.

(ii) set forth proposed findings with respect to the risk of illness or injury that the performance standard is intended to reduce or eliminate.

(iii) invite interested persons to submit to the Secretary, within 30 days of the publication of the notice, requests for changes in the classification of the device pursuant to section 360c(e) of this title based on new information relevant to the classification, and

(iv) invite interested persons to submit an existing performance standard for the device, including a draft or proposed performance standard, for consideration by the Secretary.

(C) A notice of proposed rulemaking for the revocation of a performance standard shall set forth a finding with supporting justification that the performance standard is no longer necessary to provide reasonable assurance of the safety and effectiveness of a device.

(D) The Secretary shall provide for a comment period of not less than 60 days.

(2) If, after publication of a notice in accordance with paragraph (1), the Secretary receives a request for a change in the classification of the device, the Secretary shall, within 60 days of the publication of the notice, after consultation with the appropriate panel under section 360c of this title, either deny the request or give notice of an intent to initiate such change under section 360c(e) of this title.

(3)(A) After the expiration of the period for comment on a notice of proposed rulemaking published under paragraph (1) respecting a performance standard and after consideration of such comments and any report from an advisory committee under paragraph (5), the Secretary shall (i) promulgate a regulation establishing a performance standard and publish in the Federal Register findings on the matters referred to in paragraph (1), or (ii) publish a notice terminating the proceeding for the development of the standard together with the reasons for such termination. If a notice of termination is published, the Secretary shall (unless such notice is issued because the device is a banned device under section 360f of this title) initiate a proceeding under section 360c(e) of this title to reclassify the device subject to the proceeding terminated by such notice.

(B) A regulation establishing a performance standard shall set forth the date of dates upon which the standard shall take effect, but no such regulation may take effect before one year after the date of its publication unless (i) the Secretary determines that an earlier effective date is necessary for the protection of the public health and safety, or (ii) such standard has been established for a device which, effective upon the effective date of the standard, has been reclassified from class III to class II. Such date or dates shall be established so as to minimize, consistent with the public health and safety, economic loss to, and disruption or dislocation of, domestic and international trade.

(4)(A) The Secretary, upon his own initiative or upon petition of an interested person may by regulation, promulgated in accordance with the requirements of paragraphs (1), (2), and (3)(B) of this subsection, amend or revoke a performance standard.

(B) The Secretary may declare a proposed amendment of a performance standard to be effective on and after its publication in the Federal Register and until the effective date of any final action taken on such amendment if he determines that making it so effective is in the public interest. A proposed amendment of a performance standard made so effective under the preceding sentence may not prohibit, during the period in which it is so effective, the introduction or delivery for introduction into interstate commerce of a device which conforms to such standard without the change or changes provided by such proposed amendment.

(5)(A) The Secretary—

(i) may on his own initiative refer a proposed regulation for the establishment, amendment, or revocation of a performance standard, or

(ii) shall, upon the request of an interested person which demonstrates good cause for referral and which is made before the expiration of the period for submission of comments on such proposed regulation refer such proposed regulation,

to an advisory committee of experts, established pursuant to subparagraph (B), for a report and recommendation with respect to any matter involved in the proposed regulation which requires the exercise of scientific judgment. If a proposed regulation is referred under this subparagraph to an advisory committee, the Secretary shall provide the advisory committee with the data and information on which such proposed regulation is based. The advisory committee shall, within sixty days of the referral of a proposed regulation and after independent study of the data and information furnished to it by the Secretary and other data and information before it, submit to the Secretary a report and recommendation respecting such regulation, together with all underlying data and information and a statement of the reason or basis for the recommendation. A copy of such report and recommendation shall be made public by the Secretary.

(B) The Secretary shall establish advisory committees (which may not be panels under section 360c of this title) to receive referrals under subparagraph (A). The Secretary shall appoint as members of any such advisory committee persons qualified in the subject matter to be referred to the committee and of appropriately diversified professional background, except that the Secretary may not appoint to such a committee any individual who is in the regular full- time employ of the United States and engaged in the administration of this chapter. Each such committee shall include as nonvoting members a representative of consumer interests and a representative of interests of the device manufacturing industry. Members of an advisory committee who are not officers or employees of the United States, while attending conferences or meetings of their committee or otherwise serving at the request of the Secretary, shall be entitled to receive compensation at rates to be fixed by the Secretary, which rates may not exceed the daily equivalent of the rate in effect for grade GS–18 of the General Schedule, for each day (including traveltime) they are so engaged; and while so serving away from their homes or regular places of business each member may be allowed travel expenses, including per diem in lieu of subsistence, as authorized by section 5703 of Title 5 for persons in the Government service employed intermittently. The Secretary shall designate one of the members of each advisory committee to serve as chairman thereof. The Secretary shall furnish each advisory committee with clerical and other assistance, and shall by regulation prescribe the procedures to be followed by each such committee in acting on referrals made under subparagraph (A).

(c) to (f) Repealed.

(g) Redesignated (b)

§ 360e. Premarket approval

(a) General requirement

A class III device—

(1) which is subject to a regulation promulgated under subsection (b) of this section; or

(2) which is a class III device because of section 360c(f) of this title,

is required to have, unless exempt under section 360j(g) of this title, an approval under this section of an application for premarket approval.

(b) Regulation to require premarket approval

(1) In the case of a class III device which—

(A) was introduced or delivered for introduction into interstate commerce for commercial distribution before May 28, 1976; or

(B) is (i) of a type so introduced or delivered, and (ii) is substantially equivalent to another device within that type,

the Secretary shall by regulation, promulgated in accordance with this subsection, require that such device have an approval under this section of an application for premarket approval.

(2)(A) A proceeding for the promulgation of a regulation under paragraph (1) respecting a device shall be initiated by the publication in the Federal Register of a notice of proposed rulemaking. Such notice shall contain—

(i) the proposed regulation;

(ii) proposed findings with respect to the degree of risk of illness or injury designed to be eliminated or reduced by requiring the device to have an approved application for premarket approval and the benefit to the public from use of the device;

(iii) opportunity for the submission of comments on the proposed regulation and the proposed findings; and

(iv) opportunity to request a change in the classification of the device based on new information relevant to the classification of the device.

(B) If, within fifteen days after publication of a notice under subparagraph (A), the Secretary receives a request for a change in the classification of a device, he shall, within sixty days of the publication of such notice and after consultation with the appropriate panel under section 360c of this title, by order published in the Federal Register, either deny the request for change in classification or give notice of his intent to initiate such a change under section 360c(e) of this title.

(3) After the expiration of the period for comment on a proposed regulation and proposed findings published under paragraph (2) and after consideration of comments submitted on such proposed regulation and findings, the Secretary shall (A) promulgate such regulation and publish in the Federal Register findings on the matters referred to in paragraph (2)(A)(ii), or (B) publish a notice terminating the proceeding for the promulgation of the regulation together with the reasons for such termination. If a notice of termination is published, the Secretary shall (unless such notice is issued because the device is a banned device under section 360f of this title) initiate a proceeding under section 360c(e) of this title to reclassify the device subject to the proceeding terminated by such notice.

(4) The Secretary, upon his own initiative or upon petition of an interested person, may by regulation amend or revoke any regulation promulgated under this subsection. A regulation to amend or revoke a regulation under this subsection shall be promulgated in accordance with the requirements prescribed by this subsection for the promulgation of the regulation to be amended or revoked.

(c) Application for premarket approval

(1) Any person may file with the Secretary an application for premarket approval for a class III device. Such an application for a device shall contain—

(A) full reports of all information, published or known to or which should reasonably be known to the applicant, concerning investigations which have been made to show whether or not such device is safe and effective;

(B) a full statement of the components, ingredients, and properties and of the principle or principles of operation, of such device;

(C) a full description of the methods used in, and the facilities and controls used for, the manufacture, processing, and, when relevant, packing and installation of, such device;

(D) an identifying reference to any performance standard under section 360d of this title which would be applicable to any aspect of such device if it were a class II device, and either adequate information to show that such aspect of such device fully meets such performance standard or adequate information to justify any deviation from such standard;

(E) such samples of such device and of components thereof as the Secretary may reasonably require, except that where the submission of such samples is impracticable or unduly burdensome, the requirement of this subparagraph may be met by the submission of complete information concerning the location of one or more such devices readily available for examination and testing;

(F) specimens of the labeling proposed to be used for such device; and

(G) such other information relevant to the subject matter of the application as the Secretary, with the concurrence of the appropriate panel under section 360c of this title, may require.

(2) Upon receipt of an application meeting the requirements set forth in paragraph (1), the Secretary—

(A) may on the Secretary's own initiative, or

(B) shall, upon the request of an applicant unless the Secretary finds that the information in the application which would be reviewed by a panel substantially duplicates information which has previously been reviewed by a panel appointed under section 360c of this title,

refer such application to the appropriate panel under section 360c of this title for study and for submission (within such period as he may establish) of a report and recommendation respecting approval of the application, together with all underlying data and the reasons or basis for the recommendation.

(d) Action on application for premarket approval

(1)(A) As promptly as possible, but in no event later than one hundred and eighty days after the receipt of an application under subsection (c) of this section (except as provided in section 360j(*l*)(3)(D)(ii) of this title or unless, in accordance with subparagraph (B)(i), an additional period as agreed upon by the Secretary and the applicant), the Secretary, after considering the report and recommendation submitted under paragraph (2) of such subsection, shall—

(i) issue an order approving the application if he finds that none of the grounds for denying approval specified in paragraph (2) of this subsection applies; or

(ii) deny approval of the application if he finds (and sets forth the basis for such finding as part of or accompanying such denial) that one or more grounds for denial specified in paragraph (2) of this subsection apply.

(B)(i) The Secretary may not enter into an agreement to extend the period in which to take action with respect to an application submitted for a device subject to a regulation promulgated under subsection (b) of this section unless he finds that the continued availability of the device is necessary for the public health.

(ii) An order approving an application for a device may require as a condition to such approval that the sale and distribution of the device be restricted but only to the extent that the sale and distribution of a device may be restricted under a regulation under section 360j(e) of this title.

(2) The Secretary shall deny approval of an application for a device if, upon the basis of the information submitted to the Secretary as part of the application and any other information before him with respect to such device, the Secretary finds that—

(A) there is a lack of a showing of reasonable assurance that such device is safe under the conditions of use prescribed, recommended, or suggested in the proposed labeling thereof;

(B) there is a lack of a showing of reasonable assurance that the device is effective under the conditions of use prescribed, recommended, or suggested in the proposed labeling thereof;

(C) the methods used in, or the facilities or controls used for, the manufacture, processing, packing, or installation of such device do not conform to the requirements of section 360j(f) of this title;

(D) based on a fair evaluation of all material facts, the proposed labeling is false or misleading in any particular; or

(E) such device is not shown to conform in all respects to a performance standard in effect under section 360d of this title compliance with which is a condition to approval of the application and there is a lack of adequate information to justify the deviation from such standard.

Any denial of an application shall, insofar as the Secretary determines to be practicable, be accompanied by a statement informing the applicant of the measures required to place such application in approvable form (which measures may include further research by the applicant in accordance with one or more protocols prescribed by the Secretary).

(3) An applicant whose application has been denied approval may, by petition filed on or before the thirtieth day after the date upon which he receives notice of such denial, obtain review thereof in accordance with either paragraph (1) or (2) of subsection (g) of this section, and any interested person may obtain review, in accordance with paragraph (1) or (2) of subsection (g) of this section, of an order of the Secretary approving an application.

(e) Withdrawal and temporary suspension of approval of application for premarket approval

(1) The Secretary shall, upon obtaining, where appropriate, advice on scientific matters from a panel or panels under section 360c of this

title, and after due notice and opportunity for informal hearing to the holder of an approved application for a device, issue an order withdrawing approval of the application if the Secretary finds—

(A) that such device is unsafe or ineffective under the conditions of use prescribed, recommended, or suggested in the labeling thereof;

(B) on the basis of new information before him with respect to such device, evaluated together with the evidence available to him when the application was approved, that there is a lack of a showing of reasonable assurance that the device is safe or effective under the conditions of use prescribed, recommended, or suggested in the labeling thereof;

(C) that the application contained or was accompanied by an untrue statement of a material fact;

(D) that the applicant (i) has failed to establish a system for maintaining records, or has repeatedly or deliberately failed to maintain records or to make reports, required by an applicable regulation under section 360i(a) of this title, (ii) has refused to permit access to, or copying or verification of, such records as required by section 374 of this title, or (iii) has not complied with the requirements of section 360 of this title;

(E) on the basis of new information before him with respect to such device, evaluated together with the evidence before him when the application was approved, that the methods used in, or the facilities and controls used for, the manufacture, processing, packing, or installation of such device do not conform with the requirements of section 360j(f) of this title and were not brought into conformity with such requirements within a reasonable time after receipt of written notice from the Secretary of nonconformity;

(F) on the basis of new information before him, evaluated together with the evidence before him when the application was approved, that the labeling of such device, based on a fair evaluation of all material facts, is false or misleading in any particular and was not corrected within a reasonable time after receipt of written notice from the Secretary of such fact; or

(G) on the basis of new information before him, evaluated together with the evidence before him when the application was approved, that such device is not shown to conform in all respects to a performance standard which is in effect under section 360d of this title compliance with which was a condition to approval of the application and that there is a lack of adequate information to justify the deviation from such standard.

(2) The holder of an application subject to an order issued under paragraph (1) withdrawing approval of the application may, by petition

filed on or before the thirtieth day after the date upon which he receives notice of such withdrawal, obtain review thereof in accordance with either paragraph (1) or (2) of subsection (g) of this section.

(3) If, after providing an opportunity for an informal hearing, the Secretary determines there is reasonable probability that the continuation of distribution of a device under an approved application would cause serious, adverse health consequences or death, the Secretary shall by order temporarily suspend the approval of the application approved under this section. If the Secretary issues such an order, the Secretary shall proceed expeditiously under paragraph (1) to withdraw such application.

(f) Product development protocol

(1) In the case of a class III device which is required to have an approval of an application submitted under subsection (c) of this section, such device shall be considered as having such an approval if a notice of completion of testing conducted in accordance with a product development protocol approved under paragraph (4) has been declared completed under paragraph (6).

(2) Any person may submit to the Secretary a proposed product development protocol with respect to a device. Such a protocol shall be accompanied by data supporting it. If, within thirty days of the receipt of such a protocol, the Secretary determines that it appears to be appropriate to apply the requirements of this subsection to the device with respect to which the protocol is submitted, he shall refer the proposed protocol to the appropriate panel under section 360c of this title for its recommendation respecting approval of the protocol.

(3) A proposed product development protocol for a device may be approved only if—

(A) the Secretary determines that it is appropriate to apply the requirements of this subsection to the device in lieu of the requirement of approval of an application submitted under subsection (c) of this section; and

(B) the Secretary determines that the proposed protocol provides—

(i) a description of the device and the changes which may be made in the device,

(ii) a description of the preclinical trials (if any) of the device and a specification of (I) the results from such trials to be required before the commencement of clinical trials of the device, and (II) any permissible variations in preclinical trials and the results therefrom,

(iii) a description of the clinical trials (if any) of the device and a specification of (I) the results from such trials to be required before the filing of a notice of completion of the requirements of the protocol, and (II) any permissible variations in such trials and the results therefrom,

(iv) a description of the methods to be used in, and the facilities and controls to be used for, the manufacture, processing, and, when relevant, packing and installation of the device,

(v) an identifying reference to any performance standard under section 360d of this title to be applicable to any aspect of such device,

(vi) if appropriate, specimens of the labeling proposed to be used for such device,

(vii) such other information relevant to the subject matter of the protocol as the Secretary, with the concurrence of the appropriate panel or panels under section 360c of this title, may require, and

(viii) a requirement for submission of progress reports and, when completed, records of the trials conducted under the protocol which records are adequate to show compliance with the protocol.

(4) The Secretary shall approve or disapprove a proposed product development protocol submitted under paragraph (2) within one hundred and twenty days of its receipt unless an additional period is agreed upon by the Secretary and the person who submitted the protocol. Approval of a protocol or denial of approval of a protocol is final agency action subject to judicial review under chapter 7 of Title 5.

(5) At any time after a product development protocol for a device has been approved pursuant to paragraph (4), the person for whom the protocol was approved may submit a notice of completion—

(A) stating (i) his determination that the requirements of the protocol have been fulfilled and that, to the best of his knowledge, there is no reason bearing on safety or effectiveness why the notice of completion should not become effective, and (ii) the data and other information upon which such determination was made, and

(B) setting forth the results of the trials required by the protocol and all the information required by subsection (c)(1) of this section.

(6)(A) The Secretary may, after providing the person who has an approved protocol an opportunity for an informal hearing and at any time prior to receipt of notice of completion of such protocol, issue a final order to revoke such protocol if he finds that—

(i) such person has failed substantially to comply with the requirements of the protocol,

(ii) the results of the trials obtained under the protocol differ so substantially from the results required by the protocol that further trials cannot be justified, or

(iii) the results of the trials conducted under the protocol or available new information do not demonstrate that the device tested under the protocol does not present an unreasonable risk to health and safety.

(B) After the receipt of a notice of completion of an approved protocol the Secretary shall, within the ninety-day period beginning on the date such notice is received, by order either declare the protocol completed or declare it not completed. An order declaring a protocol not completed may take effect only after the Secretary has provided the person who has the protocol opportunity for an informal hearing on the order. Such an order may be issued only if the Secretary finds—

(i) such person has failed substantially to comply with the requirements of the protocol,

(ii) the results of the trials obtained under the protocol differ substantially from the results required by the protocol, or

(iii) there is a lack of a showing of reasonable assurance of the safety and effectiveness of the device under the conditions of use prescribed, recommended, or suggested in the proposed labeling thereof.

(C) A final order issued under subparagraph (A) or (B) shall be in writing and shall contain the reasons to support the conclusions thereof.

(7) At any time after a notice of completion has become effective, the Secretary may issue an order (after due notice and opportunity for an informal hearing to the person for whom the notice is effective) revoking the approval of a device provided by a notice of completion which has become effective as provided in subparagraph (B) if he finds that any of the grounds listed in subparagraphs (A) through (G) of subsection (e)(1) of this section apply. Each reference in such subparagraphs to an application shall be considered for purposes of this paragraph as a reference to a protocol and the notice of completion of such protocol, and each reference to the time when an application was approved shall be considered for purposes of this paragraph as a reference to the time when a notice of completion took effect.

(8) A person who has an approved protocol subject to an order issued under paragraph (6)(A) revoking such protocol, a person who has an approved protocol with respect to which an order under paragraph (6)(B) was issued declaring that the protocol had not been completed, or a person subject to an order issued under paragraph (7) revoking the approval of a device may, by petition filed on or before the thirtieth day after the date upon which he receives notice of such order, obtain review

thereof in accordance with either paragraph (1) or (2) of subsection (g) of this section.

(g) Review

(1) Upon petition for review of—

(A) an order under subsection (d) of this section approving or denying approval of an application or an order under subsection (e) of this section withdrawing approval of an application, or

(B) an order under subsection (f)(6)(A) of this section revoking an approved protocol, under subsection (f)(6)(B) of this section declaring that an approved protocol has not been completed, or under subsection (f) (7) of this section revoking the approval of a device,

the Secretary shall, unless he finds the petition to be without good cause or unless a petition for review of such order has been submitted under paragraph (2), hold a hearing, in accordance with section 554 of Title 5, on the order. The panel or panels which considered the application, protocol, or device subject to such order shall designate a member to appear and testify at any such hearing upon request of the Secretary, the petitioner, or the officer conducting the hearing, but this requirement does not preclude any other member of the panel or panels from appearing and testifying at any such hearing. Upon completion of such hearing and after considering the record established in such hearing, the Secretary shall issue an order either affirming the order subject to the hearing or reversing such order and, as appropriate, approving or denying approval of the application, reinstating the application's approval, approving the protocol, or placing in effect a notice of completion.

(2)(A) Upon petition for review of—

(i) an order under subsection (d) of this section approving or denying approval of an application or an order under subsection (e) of this section withdrawing approval of an application, or

(ii) an order under subsection (f)(6)(A) of this section revoking an approved protocol, under subsection (f)(6)(B) of this section declaring that an approved protocol has not been completed, or under subsection (f) (7) of this section revoking the approval of a device,

the Secretary shall refer the application or protocol subject to the order and the basis for the order to an advisory committee of experts established pursuant to subparagraph (B) for a report and recommendation with respect to the order. The advisory committee shall, after independent study of the data and information furnished to it by the Secretary and other data and information before it, submit to the Secretary a report and recommendation, together with all underlying data and information and a statement of the reasons or basis for the recommendation. A copy of such report shall be promptly supplied by the Secretary to any person who petitioned for such referral to the advisory committee.

(B) The Secretary shall establish advisory committees (which may not be panels under section 360c of this title) to receive referrals under subparagraph (A). The Secretary shall appoint as members of any such advisory committee persons qualified in the subject matter to be referred to the committee and of appropriately diversified professional backgrounds, except that the Secretary may not appoint to such a committee any individual who is in the regular full-time employ of the United States and engaged in the administration of this chapter. Members of an advisory committee (other than officers or employees of the United States), while attending conferences or meetings of their committee or otherwise serving at the request of the Secretary, shall be entitled to receive compensation at rates to be fixed by the Secretary, which rates may not exceed the daily equivalent for grade GS–18 of the General Schedule for each day (including traveltime) they are so engaged; and while so serving away from their homes or regular places of business each member may be allowed travel expenses, including per diem in lieu of subsistence, as authorized by section 5703 of Title 5 for persons in the Government service employed intermittently. The Secretary shall designate the chairman of an advisory committee from its members. The Secretary shall furnish each advisory committee with clerical and other assistance, and shall by regulation prescribe the procedures to be followed by each such committee in acting on referrals made under subparagraph (A).

(C) The Secretary shall make public the report and recommendation made by an advisory committee with respect to an application and shall by order, stating the reasons therefor, either affirm the order referred to the advisory committee or reverse such order and, if appropriate, approve or deny approval of the application, reinstate the application's approval, approve the protocol, or place in effect a notice of completion.

(h) Service of orders

Orders of the Secretary under this section shall be served (1) in person by any officer or employee of the department designated by the Secretary, or (2) by mailing the order by registered mail or certified mail addressed to the applicant at his last known address in the records of the Secretary.

(i) Revision

(1) Before December 1, 1995, the Secretary shall by order require manufacturers of devices, which were introduced or delivered for introduction into interstate commerce for commercial distribution before May 28, 1976, and which are subject to revision of classification under paragraph (2), to submit to the Secretary a summary of and citation to any information known or otherwise available to the manufacturer respecting such devices, including adverse safety or effectiveness infor-

mation which has not been submitted under section 360i of this title. The Secretary may require the manufacturer to submit the adverse safety or effectiveness data for which a summary and citation were submitted, if such data are available to the manufacturer.

(2) After the issuance of an order under paragraph (1) but before December 1, 1995, the Secretary shall publish a regulation in the Federal Register for each device—

(A) which the Secretary has classified as a class III device, and

(B) for which no final regulation has been promulgated under subsection (b) of this section,

revising the classification of the device so that the device is classified into class I or class II, unless the regulation requires the device to remain in class III. In determining whether to revise the classification of a device or to require a device to remain in class III, the Secretary shall apply the criteria set forth in section 360c(a) of this title. Before the publication of a regulation requiring a device to remain in class III or revising its classification, the Secretary shall publish a proposed regulation respecting the classification of a device under this paragraph and provide reasonable opportunity for the submission of comments on any such regulation. No regulation requiring a device to remain in class III or revising its classification may take effect before the expiration of 90 days from the date of its publication in the Federal Register as a proposed regulation.

(3) The Secretary shall, as promptly as is reasonably achievable, but not later than 12 months after the effective date of the regulation requiring a device to remain in class III, establish a schedule for the promulgation of a regulation under subsection (b) of this section for each device which is subject to the regulation requiring the device to remain in class III.

§ 360f. Banned devices

(a) General rule

Whenever the Secretary finds, on the basis of all available data and information that—

(1) a device intended for human use presents substantial deception or an unreasonable and substantial risk of illness or injury; and

(2) in the case of substantial deception or an unreasonable and substantial risk of illness or injury which the Secretary determined could be corrected or eliminated by labeling or change in labeling and with respect to which the Secretary provided written notice to the manufacturer specifying the deception or risk of illness or injury, the labeling or change in labeling to correct the deception or eliminate or reduce such risk, and the period within which such

labeling or change in labeling was to be done, such labeling or change in labeling was not done within such period;

he may initiate a proceeding to promulgate a regulation to make such device a banned device.

(b) Special effective date

The Secretary may declare a proposed regulation under subsection (a) of this section to be effective upon its publication in the Federal Register and until the effective date of any final action taken respecting such regulation if (1) he determines, on the basis of all available data and information, that the deception or risk of illness or injury associated with the use of the device which is subject to the regulation presents an unreasonable, direct, and substantial danger to the health of individuals, and (2) before the date of the publication of such regulation, the Secretary notifies the manufacturer of such device that such regulation is to be made so effective. If the Secretary makes a proposed regulation so effective, he shall, as expeditiously as possible, give interested persons prompt notice of his action under this subsection, provide reasonable opportunity for an informal hearing on the proposed regulation, and either affirm, modify, or revoke such proposed regulation.

§ 360g. Judicial review

(a) Petition; record

Not later than thirty days after—

(1) the promulgation of a regulation under section 360c of this title classifying a device in class I or changing the classification of a device to class I or an order under subsection (f)(2) of such section reclassifying a device or denying a petition for reclassification of a device,

(2) the promulgation of a regulation under section 360d of this title establishing, amending, or revoking a performance standard for a device,

(3) the issuance of an order under section 360d(b)(2) or 360e(b)(2)(B) of this title denying a request for reclassification of a device,

(4) the promulgation of a regulation under paragraph (3) of section 360e(b) of this title requiring a device to have an approval of a premarket application, a regulation under paragraph (4) of that section amending or revoking a regulation under paragraph (3), or an order pursuant to section 360e(g)(1) or 360e(g)(2)(C) of this title,

(5) the promulgation of a regulation under section 360f of this title (other than a proposed regulation made effective under subsection (b) of such section upon the regulation's publication) making a device a banned device,

179

(6) the issuance of an order under section 360j(f)(2) of this title,

(7) an order under section 360j(g)(4) of this title disapproving an application for an exemption of a device for investigational use or an order under section 360j(g)(5) of this title withdrawing such an exemption for a device,

(8) an order pursuant to section 360c(i) of this title,

(9) a regulation under section 360e(i)(2) or 360j(*l*)(5)(B) of this title, or

(10) an order under section 360j(h)(4)(B) of this title,

any person adversely affected by such regulation or order may file a petition with the United States Court of Appeals for the District of Columbia or for the circuit wherein such person resides or has his principal place of business for judicial review of such regulation or order. A copy of the petition shall be transmitted by the clerk of the court to the Secretary or other officer designated by him for that purpose. The Secretary shall file in the court the record of the proceedings on which the Secretary based his regulation or order as provided in section 2112 of Title 28. For purposes of this section, the term "record" means all notices and other matter published in the Federal Register with respect to the regulation or order reviewed, all information submitted to the Secretary with respect to such regulation or order, proceedings of any panel or advisory committee with respect to such regulation or order, any hearing held with respect to such regulation or order, and any other information identified by the Secretary, in the administrative proceeding held with respect to such regulation or order, as being relevant to such regulation or order.

(b) Additional data, views, and arguments

If the petitioner applies to the court for leave to adduce additional data, views, or arguments respecting the regulation or order being reviewed and shows to the satisfaction of the court that such additional data, views, or arguments are material and that there were reasonable grounds for the petitioner's failure to adduce such data, views, or arguments in the proceedings before the Secretary, the court may order the Secretary to provide additional opportunity for the oral presentation of data, views, or arguments and for written submissions. The Secretary may modify his findings, or make new findings by reason of the additional data, views, or arguments so taken and shall file with the court such modified or new findings, and his recommendation, if any, for the modification or setting aside of the regulation or order being reviewed, with the return of such additional data, views, or arguments.

(c) Standard for review

Upon the filing of the petition under subsection (a) of this section for judicial review of a regulation or order, the court shall have jurisdiction to review the regulation or order in accordance with chapter 7 of Title 5 and to grant appropriate relief, including interim relief, as provided in such chapter. A regulation described in paragraph (2) or (5) of subsection (a) of this section and an order issued after the review provided by section 360e(g) of this title shall not be affirmed if it is found to be unsupported by substantial evidence on the record taken as a whole.

(d) Finality of judgments

The judgment of the court affirming or setting aside, in whole or in part, any regulation or order shall be final, subject to review by the Supreme Court of the United States upon certiorari or certification, as provided in section 1254 of Title 28.

(e) Remedies

The remedies provided for in this section shall be in addition to and not in lieu of any other remedies provided by law.

(f) Statement of reasons

To facilitate judicial review under this section or under any other provision of law of a regulation or order issued under section 360c, 360d, 360e, 360f, 360h, 360i, 360j, or 360k of this title each such regulation or order shall contain a statement of the reasons for its issuance and the basis, in the record of the proceedings held in connection with its issuance, for its issuance.

§ 360h. Notification and other remedies

(a) Notification

If the Secretary determines that—

(1) a device intended for human use which is introduced or delivered for introduction into interstate commerce for commercial distribution presents an unreasonable risk of substantial harm to the public health, and

(2) notification under this subsection is necessary to eliminate the unreasonable risk of such harm and no more practicable means is available under the provisions of this chapter (other than this section) to eliminate such risk,

the Secretary may issue such order as may be necessary to assure that adequate notification is provided in an appropriate form, by the persons and means best suited under the circumstances involved, to all health professionals who prescribe or use the device and to any other person (including manufacturers, importers, distributors, retailers, and device users) who should properly receive such notification in order to eliminate such risk. An order under this subsection shall require that the individuals subject to the risk with respect to which the order is to be issued be included in the persons to be notified of the risk unless the Secretary

determines that notice to such individuals would present a greater
danger to the health of such individuals than no such notification. If
the Secretary makes such a determination with respect to such individuals, the order shall require that the health professionals who prescribe or
use the device provide for the notification of the individuals whom the
health professionals treated with the device of the risk presented by the
device and of any action which may be taken by or on behalf of such
individuals to eliminate or reduce such risk. Before issuing an order
under this subsection, the Secretary shall consult with the persons who
are to give notice under the order.

(b) Repair, replacement, or refund

(1)(A) If, after affording opportunity for an informal hearing, the
Secretary determines that—

(i) a device intended for human use which is introduced or
delivered for introduction into interstate commerce for commercial
distribution presents an unreasonable risk of substantial harm to
the public health,

(ii) there are reasonable grounds to believe that the device was
not properly designed or manufactured with reference to the state of
the art as it existed at the time of its design or manufacture,

(iii) there are reasonable grounds to believe that the unreasonable risk was not caused by failure of a person other than a
manufacturer, importer, distributor, or retailer of the device to
exercise due care in the installation, maintenance, repair, or use of
the device, and

(iv) the notification authorized by subsection (a) of this section
would not by itself be sufficient to eliminate the unreasonable risk
and action described in paragraph (2) of this subsection is necessary
to eliminate such risk,

the Secretary may order the manufacturer, improper, or any distributor
of such device, or any combination of such persons, to submit to him
within a reasonable time a plan for taking one or more of the actions
described in paragraph (2). An order issued under the preceding sentence which is directed to more than one person shall specify which
person may decide which action shall be taken under such plan and the
person specified shall be the person who the Secretary determines bears
the principal, ultimate financial responsibility for action taken under the
plan unless the Secretary cannot determine who bears such responsibility or the Secretary determines that the protection of the public health
requires that such decision be made by a person (including a device user
or health professional) other than the person he determines bears such
responsibility.

(B) The Secretary shall approve a plan submitted pursuant to an
order issued under subparagraph (A) unless he determines (after afford-

ing opportunity for an informal hearing) that the action or actions to be taken under the plan or the manner in which such action or actions are to be taken under the plan will not assure that the unreasonable risk with respect to which such order was issued will be eliminated. If the Secretary disapproves a plan, he shall order a revised plan to be submitted to him within a reasonable time. If the Secretary determines (after affording opportunity for an informal hearing) that the revised plan is unsatisfactory or if no revised plan or no initial plan has been submitted to the Secretary within the prescribed time, the Secretary shall (i) prescribe a plan to be carried out by the person or persons to whom the order issued under subparagraph (A) was directed, or (ii) after affording an opportunity for an informal hearing, by order prescribe a plan to be carried out by a person who is a manufacturer, importer, distributor, or retailer of the device with respect to which the order was issued but to whom the order under subparagraph (A) was not directed.

(2) The actions which may be taken under a plan submitted under an order issued under paragraph (1) are as follows:

(A) To repair the device so that it does not present the unreasonable risk of substantial harm with respect to which the order under paragraph (1) was issued.

(B) To replace the device with a like or equivalent device which is in conformity with all applicable requirements of this chapter.

(C) To refund the purchase price of the device (less a reasonable allowance for use if such device has been in the possession of the device user for one year or more—

(i) at the time of notification ordered under subsection (a) of this section, or

(ii) at the time the device user receives actual notice of the unreasonable risk with respect to which the order was issued under paragraph (1).

whichever first occurs).

(3) No charge shall be made to any person (other than a manufacturer, importer, distributor or retailer) for availing himself of any remedy, described in paragraph (2) and provided under an order issued under paragraph (1), and the person subject to the order shall reimburse each person (other than a manufacturer, importer, distributor, or retailer) who is entitled to such a remedy for any reasonable and foreseeable expenses actually incurred by such person in availing himself of such remedy.

(c) Reimbursement

An order issued under subsection (b) of this section with respect to a device may require any person who is a manufacturer, importer, distributor, or retailer of the device to reimburse any other person who is a manufacturer, importer, distributor, or retailer of such device for such other person's expenses actually incurred in connection with carrying out the order if the Secretary determines such reimbursement is required for the protection of the public health. Any such requirement shall not affect any rights or obligations under any contract to which the person receiving reimbursement or the person making such reimbursement is a party.

(d) Effect on other liability

Compliance with an order issued under this section shall not relieve any person from liability under Federal or State law. In awarding damages for economic loss in an action brought for the enforcement of any such liability, the value to the plaintiff in such action of any remedy provided him under such order shall be taken into account.

(e) Recall authority

(1) If the Secretary finds that there is a reasonable probability that a device intended for human use would cause serious, adverse health consequences or death, the Secretary shall issue an order requiring the appropriate person (including the manufacturers, importers, distributors, or retailers of the device)—

    (A) to immediately cease distribution of such device, and

    (B) to immediately notify health professionals and device user facilities of the order and to instruct such professionals and facilities to cease use of such device.

The order shall provide the person subject to the order with an opportunity for an informal hearing, to be held not later than 10 days after the date of the issuance of the order, on the actions required by the order and on whether the order should be amended to require a recall of such device. If, after providing an opportunity for such a hearing, the Secretary determines that inadequate grounds exist to support the actions required by the order, the Secretary shall vacate the order.

(2)(A) If, after providing an opportunity for an informal hearing under paragraph (1), the Secretary determines that the order should be amended to include a recall of the device with respect to which the order was issued, the Secretary shall, except as provided in subparagraphs (B) and (C), amend the order to require a recall. The Secretary shall specify a timetable in which the device recall will occur and shall require periodic reports to the Secretary describing the progress of the recall.

    (B) An amended order under subparagraph (A)—

        (i) shall—

            (I) not include recall of a device from individuals, and

            (II) not include recall of a device from device user facilities if the Secretary determines that the risk of recalling such device from the facilities presents a greater health risk than the health risk of not recalling the device from use, and

(ii) shall provide for notice to individuals subject to the risks associated with the use of such device.

In providing the notice required by clause (ii), the Secretary may use the assistance of health professionals who prescribed or used such a device for individuals. If a significant number of such individuals cannot be identified, the Secretary shall notify such individuals pursuant to section 375(b) of this title.

(3) The remedy provided by this subsection shall be in addition to remedies provided by subsections (a), (b), and (c) of this section.

§ 360i. Records and reports on devices

(a) General rule

Every person who is a manufacturer, importer, or distributor of a device intended for human use shall establish and maintain such records, make such reports, and provide such information, as the Secretary may by regulation reasonably require to assure that such device is not adulterated or misbranded and to otherwise assure its safety and effectiveness. Regulations prescribed under the preceding sentence—

(1) shall require a device manufacturer or importer to report to the Secretary whenever the manufacturer or importer receives or otherwise becomes aware of information that reasonably suggests that one of its marketed devices—

(A) may have caused or contributed to a death or serious injury, or

(B) has malfunctioned and that such device or a similar device marketed by the manufacturer or importer would be likely to cause or contribute to a death or serious injury if the malfunction were to recur;

(2) shall define the term "serious injury" to mean an injury that—

(A) is life threatening,

(B) results in permanent impairment of a body function or permanent damage to a body structure, or

(C) necessitates medical or surgical intervention to preclude permanent impairment of a body function or permanent damage to a body structure;

(3) shall require reporting of other significant adverse device experiences as determined by the Secretary to be necessary to be reported;

(4) shall not impose requirements unduly burdensome to a device manufacturer, importer, or distributor taking into account his cost of complying with such requirements and the need for the

protection of the public health and the implementation of this chapter;

(5) which prescribe the procedure for making requests for reports or information shall require that each request made under such regulations for submission of a report or information to the Secretary state the reason or purpose for such request and identify to the fullest extent practicable such report or information;

(6) which require submission of a report or information to the Secretary shall state the reason or purpose for the submission of such report or information and identify to the fullest extent practicable such report or information;

(7) may not require that the identity of any patient be disclosed in records, reports, or information required under this subsection unless required for the medical welfare of an individual, to determine the safety or effectiveness of a device, or to verify a record, report, or information submitted under this chapter;

(8) may not require a manufacturer, importer, or distributor of a class I device to—

(A) maintain for such a device records respecting information not in the possession of the manufacturer, importer, or distributor, or

(B) to submit for such a device to the Secretary any report or information—

(i) not in the possession of the manufacturer, importer, or distributor, or

(ii) on a periodic basis,

unless such report or information is necessary to determine if the device should be reclassified or if the device is adulterated or misbranded; and

(9) shall require distributors who submit such reports to submit copies of the reports to the manufacturer of the device for which the report was made.

In prescribing such regulations, the Secretary shall have due regard for the professional ethics of the medical profession and the interests of patients. The prohibitions of paragraph (7) of this subsection continue to apply to records, reports, and information concerning any individual who has been a patient, irrespective of whether or when he ceases to be a patient.

(b) User reports

(1)(A) Whenever a device user facility receives or otherwise becomes aware of information that reasonably suggests that a device has or may have caused or contributed to the death of a patient of the facility, the facility shall, as soon as practicable but not later than 10 working days after becoming aware of the information, report the information to the Secretary and, if the identity of the manufacturer is known, to the manufacturer of the device. In the case of deaths, the Secretary may by regulation prescribe a shorter period for the reporting of such information.

(B) Whenever a device user facility receives or otherwise becomes aware of—

(i) information that reasonably suggests that a device has or may have caused or contributed to the serious illness of, or serious injury to, a patient of the facility, or

(ii) other significant adverse device experiences as determined by the Secretary by regulation to be necessary to be reported,

the facility shall, as soon as practicable but not later than 10 working days after becoming aware of the information, report the information to the manufacturer of the device or to the Secretary if the identity of the manufacturer is not known.

(C) Each device user facility shall submit to the Secretary on a semiannual basis a summary of the reports made under subparagraphs (A) and (B). Such summary shall be submitted on January 1 and July 1 of each year. The summary shall be in such form and contain such information from such reports as the Secretary may require and shall include—

(i) sufficient information to identify the facility which made the reports for which the summary is submitted,

(ii) in the case of any product which was the subject of a report, the product name, serial number, and model number,

(iii) the name and the address of the manufacturer of such device, and

(iv) a brief description of the event reported to the manufacturer.

The Secretary may by regulation alter the frequency and timing of reports required by this subparagraph.

(D) For purposes of subparagraphs (A), (B), and (C), a device user facility shall be treated as having received or otherwise become aware of information with respect to a device of that facility when medical personnel who are employed by or otherwise formally affiliated with the facility receive or otherwise become aware of information with respect to that device in the course of their duties.

(2) The Secretary may not disclose the identity of a device user facility which makes a report under paragraph (1) except in connection with—

(A) an action brought to enforce section 331(q) of this title,

(B) a communication to a manufacturer of a device which is the subject of a report under paragraph (1), or

(C) a disclosure required under subsection (a) of this section,

This paragraph does not prohibit the Secretary from disclosing the identity of a device user facility making a report under paragraph (1) or any information in such a report to employees of the Department of Health and Human Services, to the Department of Justice, or to the duly authorized committees and subcommittees of the Congress.

(3) No report made under paragraph (1) by—

(A) a device user facility,

(B) an individual who is employed by or otherwise formally affiliated with such a facility, or

(C) a physician who is not required to make such a report,

shall be admissible into evidence or otherwise used in any civil action involving private parties unless the facility, individual, or physician who made the report had knowledge of the falsity of the information contained in the report.

(4) A report made under paragraph (1) does not affect any obligation of a manufacturer who receives the report to file a report as required under subsection (a) of this section,

(5) For purposes of this subsection:

(A) The term "device user facility" means a hospital, ambulatory surgical facility, nursing home, or outpatient treatment facility which is not a physician's office. The Secretary may by regulation include an outpatient diagnostic facility which is not a physician's office in such term.

(B) The terms "serious illness" and "serious injury" mean illness or injury, respectively, that—

(i) is life threatening,

(ii) results in permanent impairment of a body function or permanent damage to a body structure, or

(iii) necessitates medical or surgical intervention to preclude permanent impairment of a body function or permanent damage to a body structure.

(c) Persons exempt

Subsection (a) of this section shall not apply to—

(1) any practitioner who is licensed by law to prescribe or administer devices intended for use in humans and who manufactures or imports devices solely for use in the course of his professional practice;

(2) any person who manufactures or imports devices intended for use in humans solely for such person's use in research or teaching and not for sale (including any person who uses a device under an exemption granted under section 360j(g) of this title); and

(3) any other class of persons as the Secretary may be regulation exempt from subsection (a) of this section upon a finding that compliance with the requirements of such subsection by such class with respect to a device is not necessary to (A) assure that a device is not adulterated or misbranded or (B) otherwise to assure its safety and effectiveness.

(d) Certification

Each manufacturer, importer, and distributor required to make reports under subsection (a) of this section shall submit to the Secretary annually a statement certifying that—

(1) the manufacturer, importer, or distributor did file a certain number of such reports, or

(2) the manufacturer, importer, or distributor did not file any report under subsection (a) of this section.

(e) Device tracking

Every person who registers under section 360 of this title and is engaged in the manufacture of—

(1) a device the failure of which would be reasonably likely to have serious adverse health consequences and which is (A) a permanently implantable device, or (B) a life sustaining or life supporting device used outside a device user facility, or

(2) any other device which the Secretary may designate,

shall adopt a method of device tracking.

(f) Reports of removals and corrections

(1) Except as provided in paragraph (2), the Secretary shall by regulation require a manufacturer, importer, or distributor of a device to report promptly to the Secretary any correction or removal of a device undertaken by such manufacturer, importer, or distributor if the removal or correction was undertaken—

(A) to reduce a risk to health posed by the device, or

(B) to remedy a violation of this chapter caused by the device which may present a risk to health.

A manufacturer, importer, or distributor of a device who undertakes a correction or removal of a device which is not required to be reported under this paragraph shall keep a record of such correction or removal.

(2) No report of the corrective action or removal of a device may be required under paragraph (1) if a report of the corrective action or removal is required and has been submitted under subsection (a) of this section.

(3) For purposes of paragraphs (1) and (2), the terms "correction" and "removal" do not include routine servicing.

§ 360j. General provisions respecting control of devices intended for human use

(a) General rule

Any requirement authorized by or under section 351, 352, 360, or 360i of this title applicable to a device intended for human use shall apply to such device until the applicability of the requirement to the device has been changed by action taken under section 360c, 360d, or 360e of this title or under subsection (g) of this section, and any requirement established by or under section 351, 352, 360, or 360i of this title which is inconsistent with a requirement imposed on such device under section 360d or 360e of this title or under subsection (g) of this section shall not apply to such device.

(b) Custom devices

Sections 360d and 360e of this title do not apply to any device which, in order to comply with the order of an individual physician or dentist (or any other specially qualified person designated under regulations promulgated by the Secretary after an opportunity for an oral hearing) necessarily deviates from an otherwise applicable performance standard or requirement prescribed by or under section 360e of this title if (1) the device is not generally available in finished form for purchase or for dispensing upon prescription and is not offered through labeling or advertising by the manufacturer, importer, or distributor thereof for commercial distribution, and (2) such device—

(A)(i) is intended for use by an individual patient named in such order of such physician or dentist (or other specially qualified person so designated) and is to be made is a specific form for such patient, or

(ii) is intended to meet the special needs of such physician or dentist (or other specially qualified person so designated) in the course of the professional practice of such physician or dentist (or other specially qualified person so designated), and

(B) is not generally available to or generally used by other physicians or dentists (or other specially qualified persons so designated).

(c) Trade secrets

Any information reported to or otherwise obtained by the Secretary or his representative under section 360c, 360d, 360e, 360f, 360h, 360i, or

374 of this title or under subsection (f) or (g) of this section which is exempt from disclosure pursuant to subsection (a) of section 552 of Title 5 by reason of subsection (b)(4) of such section shall be considered confidential and shall not be disclosed and may not be used by the Secretary as the basis for the reclassification of a device from class III to class II or class I or as the basis for the establishment or amendment of a performance standard under section 360d of this title for a device reclassified from class III to class II, except (1) in accordance with subsection (h) of this section, and (2) that such information may be disclosed to other officers or employees concerned with carrying out this chapter or when relevant in any proceeding under this chapter (other than section 360c or 360d of this title).

(d) Notices and findings

Each notice of proposed rulemaking under section 360c, 360d, 360e, 360f, 360h, or 360i of this title, or under this section, any other notice which is published in the Federal Register with respect to any other action taken under any such section and which states the reasons for such action, and each publication of findings required to be made in connection with rulemaking under any such section shall set forth—

(1) the manner in which interested persons may examine data and other information on which the notice or findings is based, and

(2) the period within which interested persons may present their comments on the notice or findings (including the need therefor) orally or in writing, which period shall be at least sixty days but may not exceed ninety days unless the time is extended by the Secretary by a notice published in the Federal Register stating good cause therefor.

(e) Restricted devices

(1) The Secretary may by regulation require that a device be restricted to sale, distribution, or use—

(A) only upon the written or oral authorization of a practitioner licensed by law to administer or use such device, or

(B) upon such other conditions as the Secretary may prescribe in such regulation,

if, because of its potentiality for harmful effect or the collateral measures necessary to its use, the Secretary determines that there cannot otherwise be reasonable assurance of its safety and effectiveness. No condition prescribed under subparagraph (B) may restrict the use of a device to persons with specific training or experience in its use or to persons for use in certain facilities unless the Secretary determines that such a restriction is required for the safe and effective use of the device. No such condition may exclude a person from using a device solely because the person does not have the training or experience to make him eligible for certification by a certifying board recognized by the American Board of Medical Specialties or has not been certified by such a Board. A device subject to a regulation under this subsection is a restricted device.

(2) The label of a restricted device shall bear such appropriate statements of the restrictions required by a regulation under paragraph (1) as the Secretary may in such regulation prescribe.

(f) Good manufacturing practice requirements

(1)(A) The Secretary may, in accordance with subparagraph (B), prescribe regulations requiring that the methods used in, and the facilities and controls used for, the manufacture, pre-production design validation (including a process to access the performance of a device but not including an evaluation of the safety or effectiveness of a device), packing, storage, and installation of a device conform to current good manufacturing practice, as prescribed in such regulations, to assure that the device will be safe and effective and otherwise in compliance with this chapter.

(B) Before the Secretary may promulgate any regulation under subparagraph (A) he shall—

(i) afford the advisory committee established under paragraph (3) an opportunity to submit recommendations to him with respect to the regulation proposed to be promulgated, and

(ii) afford opportunity for an oral hearing.

The Secretary shall provide the advisory committee a reasonable time to make its recommendation with respect to proposed regulations under subparagraph (A).

(2)(A) Any person subject to any requirement prescribed by regulations under paragraph (1) may petition the Secretary for an exemption or variance from such requirement. Such a petition shall be submitted to the Secretary in such form and manner as he shall prescribe and shall—

(i) in the case of a petition for an exemption from a requirement, set forth the basis for the petitioner's determination that compliance with the requirement is not required to assure that the device will be safe and effective and otherwise in compliance with this chapter,

(ii) in the case of a petition for a variance from a requirement, set forth the methods proposed to be used in, and the facilities and controls proposed to be used for, the manufacture, packing, storage, and installation of the device in lieu of the methods, facilities, and controls prescribed by the requirement, and

(iii) contain such other information as the Secretary shall prescribe.

(B) The Secretary may refer to the advisory committee established under paragraph (3) any petition submitted under subparagraph (A). The advisory committee shall report its recommendations to the Secretary with respect to a petition referred to it within sixty days of the date of the petition's referral. Within sixty days after—

(i) the date the petition was submitted to the Secretary under subparagraph (A), or

(ii) if the petition was referred to an advisory committee, the expiration of the sixty-day period beginning on the date the petition was referred to the advisory committee,

whichever occurs later, the Secretary shall by order either deny the petition or approve it.

(C) The Secretary may approve—

(i) a petition for an exemption for a device from a requirement if he determines that compliance with such requirement is not required to assure that the device will be safe and effective and otherwise in compliance with this chapter, and

(ii) a petition for a variance for a device from a requirement if he determines that the methods to be used in, and the facilities and controls to be used for, the manufacture, packing, storage, and installation of the device in lieu of the methods, controls, and facilities prescribed by the requirement are sufficient to assure that the device will be safe and effective and otherwise in compliance with this chapter.

An order of the Secretary approving a petition for a variance shall prescribe such conditions respecting the methods used in, and the facilities and controls used for, the manufacture, packing, storage, and installation of the device to be granted the variance under the petition as may be necessary to assure that the device will be safe and effective and otherwise in compliance with this chapter.

(D) After the issuance of an order under subparagraph (B) respecting a petition, the petitioner shall have an opportunity for an informal hearing on such order.

(3) The Secretary shall establish an advisory committee for the purpose of advising and making recommendations to him with respect to regulations proposed to be promulgated under paragraph (1)(A) and the approval or disapproval of petitions submitted under paragraph (2). The advisory committee shall be composed of nine members as follows:

(A) Three of the members shall be appointed from persons who are officers or employees of any State or local government or of the Federal Government.

(B) Two of the members shall be appointed from persons who are representative of interests of the device manufacturing industry;

two of the members shall be appointed from persons who are representative of the interests of physicians and other health professionals; and two of the members shall be representative of the interests of the general public.

Members of the advisory committee who are not officers or employees of the United States, while attending conferences or meetings of the committee or otherwise engaged in its business, shall be entitled to receive compensation at rates to be fixed by the Secretary, which rates may not exceed the daily equivalent of the rate in effect for grade GS–18 of the General Schedule, for each day (including traveltime) they are so engaged; and while so serving away from their homes or regular places of business each member may be allowed travel expenses, including per diem in lieu of subsistence, as authorized by section 5703 of Title 5 for persons in the Government service employed intermittently. The Secretary shall designate one of the members of the advisory committee to serve as its chairman. The Secretary shall furnish the advisory committee with clerical and other assistance. Section 14 of the Federal Advisory Committee Act shall not apply with respect to the duration of the advisory committee established under this paragraph.

(g) Exemption for devices for investigational use

(1) It is the purpose of this subsection to encourage, to the extent consistent with the protection of the public health and safety and with ethical standards, the discovery and development of useful devices intended for human use and to that end to maintain optimum freedom for scientific investigators in their pursuit of that purpose.

(2)(A) The Secretary shall, within the one hundred and twenty-day period beginning on May 28, 1976, by regulation prescribe procedures and conditions under which devices intended for human use may upon application be granted an exemption from the requirements of section 352, 360, 360d, 360e, 360f, 360i, or 379e of this title or subsection (e) or (f) of this section or from any combination of such requirements to permit the investigational use of such devices by experts qualified by scientific training and experience to investigate the safety and effectiveness of such devices.

(B) The conditions prescribed pursuant to subparagraph (A) shall include the following:

(i) A requirement that an application be submitted to the Secretary before an exemption may be granted and that the application be submitted in such from and manner as the Secretary shall specify.

(ii) A requirement that the person applying for an exemption for a device assure the establishment and maintenance of such records, and the making of such reports to the Secretary of data obtained as a result of the investigational use of the device during the exemption, as the Secretary determines will enable him to assure compliance with such conditions, review the progress of the investigation, and evaluate the safety and effectiveness of the device.

(iii) Such other requirements as the Secretary may determine to be necessary for the protection of the public health and safety.

(C) Procedures and conditions prescribed pursuant to subparagraph (A) for an exemption may appropriately vary depending on (i) the scope and duration of clinical testing to be conducted under such exemption, (ii) the number of human subjects that are to be involved in such testing, (iii) the need to permit changes to be made in the device subject to the exemption during testing conducted in accordance with a clinical testing plan required under paragraph (3)(A), and (iv) whether the clinical testing of such device is for the purpose of developing data to obtain approval for the commercial distribution of such device.

(3) Procedures and conditions prescribed pursuant to paragraph (2)(A) shall require, as a condition to the exemption of any device to be the subject of testing involving human subjects, that the person applying for the exemption—

(A) submit a plan for any proposed clinical testing of the device and a report of prior investigations of the device (including, where appropriate, tests on animals) adequate to justify the proposed clinical testing—

(i) to the local institutional review committee which has been established in accordance with regulations of the Secretary to supervise clinical testing of devices in the facilities where the proposed clinical testing is to be conducted, or

(ii) to the Secretary, if—

(I) no such committee exists, or

(II) the Secretary finds that the process of review by such committee is inadequate (whether or not the plan for such testing has been approved by such committee),

for review for adequacy to justify the commencement of such testing; and, unless the plan and report are submitted to the Secretary, submit to the Secretary a summary of the plan and a report of prior investigations of the device (including, where appropriate, tests on animals);

(B) promptly notify the Secretary (under such circumstances and in such manner as the Secretary prescribes) of approval by a local institutional review committee of any clinical testing plan submitted to it in accordance with subparagraph (A);

(C) in the case of a device to be distributed to investigators for testing, obtain signed agreements from each of such investigators that any testing of the device involving human subjects will be under such investigator's supervision and in accordance with subparagraph (D) and submit such agreements to the Secretary; and

(D) assure that informed consent will be obtained from each human subject (or his representative) of proposed clinical testing involving such device, except where subject to such conditions as the Secretary may prescribe, the investigator conducting or supervising the proposed clinical testing of the device determines in writing that there exists a life threatening situation involving the human subject of such testing which necessitates the use of such device and it is not feasible to obtain informed consent from the subject and there is not sufficient time to obtain such consent from his representative.

The determination required by subparagraph (D) shall be concurred in by a licensed physician who is not involved in the testing of the human subject with respect to which such determination is made unless immediate use of the device is required to save the life of the human subject of such testing and there is not sufficient time to obtain such concurrence.

(4)(A) An application, submitted in accordance with the procedures prescribed by regulations under paragraph (2), for an exemption for a device (other than an exemption from section 360f of this title) shall be deemed approved on the thirtieth day after the submission of the application to the Secretary unless on or before such day the Secretary by order disapproves the application and notifies the applicant of the disapproval of the application.

(B) The Secretary may disapprove an application only if he finds that the investigation with respect to which the application is submitted does not conform to procedures and conditions prescribed under regulations under paragraph (2). Such a notification shall contain the order of disapproval and a complete statement of the reasons for the Secretary's disapproval of the application and afford the applicant opportunity for an informal hearing on the disapproval order.

(5) The Secretary may by order withdraw an exemption granted under this subsection for a device if the Secretary determines that the conditions applicable to the device under this subsection for such exemption are not met. Such an order may be issued only after opportunity for an informal hearing, except that such an order may be issued before the provision of an opportunity for an informal hearing if the Secretary determines that the continuation of testing under the exemption with respect to which the order is to be issued will result in an unreasonable risk to the public health.

(h) Release of information respecting safety and effectiveness

(1) The Secretary shall promulgate regulations under which a detailed summary of information respecting the safety and effectiveness of a device which information was submitted to the Secretary and which was the basis for—

(A) an order under section 360e(d)(1)(A) of this title approving an application for premarket approval for the device or denying approval of such an application or an order under section 360e(e) of this title withdrawing approval of such an application for the device,

(B) an order under section 360e(f)(6)(A) of this title revoking an approved protocol for the device, an order under section 360e(f)(6)(B) of this title declaring a protocol for the device completed or not completed, or an order under section 360e(f)(7) of this title revoking the approval of the device, or

(C) an order approving an application under subsection (g) of this section for an exemption for the device from section 360f of this title or an order disapproving, or withdrawing approval of, an application for an exemption under such subsection for the device,

shall be made available to the public upon issuance of the order. Summaries of information made available pursuant to this paragraph respecting a device shall include information respecting any adverse effects on health of the device.

(2) The Secretary shall promulgate regulations under which each advisory committee established under section 360e(g)(2)(B) of this title shall make available to the public a detailed summary of information respecting the safety and effectiveness of a device which information was submitted to the advisory committee and which was the basis for its recommendation to the Secretary made pursuant to section 360e(g)(2)(A) of this title. A summary of information upon which such a recommendation is based shall be made available pursuant to this paragraph only after the issuance of the order with respect to which the recommendation was made and each summary shall include information respecting any adverse effect on health of the device subject to such order.

(3) Except as provided in paragraph (4), any information respecting a device which is made available pursuant to paragraph (1) or (2) of this subsection (A) may not be used to establish the safety or effectiveness of another device for purposes of this chapter by any person other than the person who submitted the information so made available, and (B) shall be made available subject to subsection (c) of this section.

(4)(A) Any information contained in an application for premarket approval filed with the Secretary pursuant to section 360e(c) of this title, including clinical and preclinical tests or studies, but excluding descriptions of methods of manufacture and product composition, that demonstrates the safety and effectiveness of a device shall be available 1 year after the original application for the fourth device of a kind has been approved by the Secretary, for use by the Secretary in approving devices, or determining whether a product development protocol has been completed, under section 360e of this title, establishing a performance standard under section 360d of this title, and reclassifying devices under subsections (e) and (f) of section 360c of this title, and subsection (1)(2) of this section. The Secretary shall deem devices that incorporate the same technologies, have the same principles of operation, and are intended for the same use or uses to be within a kind of device.

(B) The Secretary, contemporaneously with the approval of the fourth device of a kind, shall publish an order in the Federal Register identifying the four devices of a kind that have been approved under section 360e of this title and the date on which the data contained in premarket approval applications for the devices will be available to the Secretary for use, as described in subparagraph (A).

(C) The publicly available detailed summaries of information respecting the safety and effectiveness of devices required by paragraph (1)(A) shall be available for use by the Secretary as the evidentiary basis for the regulatory action described in subparagraph (A).

(D)(i) This paragraph shall become effective—

(I) on November 15, 1990, for devices for which four devices of a kind were approved on or before December 31, 1987, and

(II) on November 15, 1991, for devices not described in subclause (I).

(ii) For each device described in clause (i)(I), the Secretary shall publish a notice in the Federal Register setting forth the date, which shall be not earlier than 1 year after the date of the notice, that data identified in subparagraph (A) shall be available for the use of the Secretary.

(E)(i) Except as provided in clause (ii), the approval date of a device, for purposes of this paragraph, shall be the date of the letter of the Secretary to the applicant approving a device under section 360e of this title and permitting the applicant to commercially distribute the device.

(ii) For each device described in subparagraph (D)(i)(II) for which the original application for a fourth device of a kind is approved by the Secretary before November 1, 1991, the approval date of the fourth device of a kind shall be deemed to be November 15, 1991.

(F) Any challenge to an order under subparagraph (B) shall be made not later than 30 days after the date of the Federal Register notice referred to in such subparagraph.

(i) Proceedings of advisory panels and committees

Each panel under section 360c of this title and each advisory committee established under section 360d(b)(5)(B) or 360e(g) of this title or under subsection (f) of this section shall make and maintain a transcript of any proceeding of the panel or committee. Each such panel and committee shall delete from any transcript made pursuant to this subsection information which under subsection (c) of this section is to be considered confidential.

198

(j) Traceability

Except as provided in section 360i(e) of this title, no regulation under this chapter may impose on a type or class of device requirements for the traceability of such type or class of device unless such requirements are necessary to assure the protection of the public health.

(k) Research and development

The Secretary may enter into contracts for research, testing, and demonstrations respecting devices and may obtain devices for research, testing, and demonstration purposes without regard to section 3324(a) and (b) of Title 31 and section 5 of Title 41.

(*l*) Transitional provisions for devices considered as new drugs or antibiotic drugs

(1) Any device intended for human use—

(A) for which on May 28, 1976 (hereinafter in this subsection referred to as the "enactment date") an approval of an application submitted under section 355(b) of this Title was in effect;

(B) for which such an application was filed on or before the enactment date and with respect to which application no order of approval or refusing to approve had been issued on such date under subsection (c) or (d) of such section;

(C) for which on the enactment date an exemption under subsection (i) of such section was in effect;

(D) which is within a type of device described in subparagraph (A), (B), or (C) and is substantially equivalent to another device within that type;

(E) which the Secretary in a notice published in the Federal Register before the enactment date has declared to be a new drug subject to section 355 of this title; or

(F) with respect to which on the enactment date an action is pending in a United States court under section 332, 333, or 334 of this title for an alleged violation of a provision of section 331 of this title which enforces a requirement of section 355 of this title or for an alleged violation of section 355(a) of this title,

is classified in class III unless the Secretary in response to a petition submitted under paragraph (2) has classified such device in class I or II.

(2) The Secretary may initiate the reclassification of a device classified into class III under paragraph (1) of this subsection or the manufacturer or importer of a device classified under paragraph (1) may petition the Secretary (in such form and manner as he shall prescribe) for the issuance of an order classifying the device in class I or class II. Within thirty days of the filing of such a petition, the Secretary shall notify the petitioner of any deficiencies in the petition which prevent the Secretary from making a decision on the petition. Except as provided in para-

graph (3)(D)(ii), within one hundred and eighty days after the filing of a petition under this paragraph, the Secretary shall, after consultation with the appropriate panel under section 360c of this title, by order either deny the petition or order the classification, in accordance with the criteria prescribed by section 360c(a)(1)(A) of this title or 360c(a)(1)(B) of this title, of the device in class I or class II.

(3)(A) In the case of a device which is described in paragraph (1)(A) and which is in class III—

　　(i) such device shall on the enactment date be considered a device with an approved application under section 360e of this title, and

　　(ii) the requirements applicable to such device before the enactment date under section 355 of this title shall continue to apply to such device until changed by the Secretary as authorized by this chapter.

(B) In the case of a device which is described in paragraph (1)(B) and which is in class III, an application for such device shall be considered as having been filed under section 360e of this title on the enactment date. The period in which the Secretary shall act on such application in accordance with section 360e(d)(1) of this title shall be one hundred and eighty days from the enactment date (or such greater period as the Secretary and the applicant may agree upon after the Secretary has made the finding required by section 360e(d)(1)(B)(i) of this title) less the number of days in the period beginning on the date an application for such device was filed under section 355 of this title and ending on the enactment date. After the expiration of such period such device is required, unless exempt under subsection (g) of this section, to have in effect an approved application under section 360e of this title.

(C) A device which is described in paragraph (1)(C) and which is in class III shall be considered a new drug until the expiration of the ninety-day period beginning on the date of the promulgation of regulations under subsection (g) of this section. After the expiration of such period such device is required, unless exempt under subsection (g) of this section, to have in effect an approved application under section 360e of this title.

(D)(i) Except as provided in clauses (ii) and (iii), a device which is described in subparagraph (D), (E), or (F) of paragraph (1) and which is in class III is required, unless exempt under subsection (g) of this section, to have on and after sixty days after the enactment date in effect an approved application under section 360e of this title.

　　(ii) If—

　　　　(I) a petition is filed under paragraph (2) for a device described in subparagraph (D), (E), or (F) of paragraph (1), or

(II) an application for premarket approval is filed under section 360e of this title for such a device,

within the sixty-day period beginning on the enactment date (or within such greater period as the Secretary, after making the finding required under section 360e(d)(1)(B) of this title, and the petitioner or applicant may agree upon), the Secretary shall act on such petition or application in accordance with paragraph (2) or section 360e of this title except that the period within which the Secretary must act on the petition or application shall be within the one hundred and twenty-day period beginning on the date the petition or application is filed. If such a petition or application is filed within such sixty-day (or greater) period, clause (i) of this subparagraph shall not apply to such device before the expiration of such one hundred and twenty-day period, or if such petition is denied or such application is denied approval, before the date of such denial, whichever occurs first.

(iii) In the case of a device which is described in subparagraph (E) of paragraph (1), which the Secretary in a notice published in the Federal Register after March 31, 1976, declared to be a new drug subject to section 355 of this title, and which is in class III—

(I) the device shall, after eighteen months after the enactment date, have in effect an approved application under section 360e of this title unless exempt under subsection (g) of this section, and

(II) the Secretary may, during the period beginning one hundred and eighty days after the enactment date and ending eighteen months after such date, restrict the use of the device to investigational use by experts qualified by scientific training and experience to investigate the safety and effectiveness of such device, and to investigational use in accordance with the requirements applicable under regulations under subsection (g) of this section to investigational use of devices granted an exemption under such subsection.

If the requirements under subsection (g) of this section are made applicable to the investigational use of such a device, they shall be made applicable in such a manner that the device shall be made reasonably available to physicians meeting appropriate qualifications prescribed by the Secretary.

(4) Any device intended for human use which on the enactment date was subject to the requirements of section 357 of this title shall be subject to such requirements as follows:

(A) In the case of such a device which is classified into class I, such requirements shall apply to such device until the effective date of the regulation classifying the device into such class.

(B) In the case of such a device which is classified into class II, such requirements shall apply to such device until the effective date of a performance standard applicable to the device under section 360d of this title.

(C) In the case of such a device which is classified into class III, such requirements shall apply to such device until the date on which the device is required to have in effect an approved application under section 360e of this title.

(5)(A) Before December 1, 1991, the Secretary shall by order require manufacturers of devices described in paragraph (1), which are subject to revision of classification under subparagraph (B), to submit to the Secretary a summary of and citation to any information known or otherwise available to the manufacturers respecting the devices, including adverse safety or effectiveness information which has not been submitted under section 360i of this title. The Secretary may require a manufacturer to submit the adverse safety or effectiveness data for which a summary and citation were submitted, if such data are available to the manufacturer.

(B) Except as provided in subparagraph (C), after the issuance of an order under subparagraph (A) but before December 1, 1992, the Secretary shall publish a regulation in the Federal Register for each device which is classified in class III under paragraph (1) revising the classification of the device so that the device is classified into class I or class II, unless the regulation requires the device to remain in class III. In determining whether to revise the classification of a device or to require a device to remain in class III, the Secretary shall apply the criteria set forth in section 360c(a) of this title. Before the publication of a regulation requiring a device to remain in class III or revising its classification, the Secretary shall publish a proposed regulation respecting the classification of a device under this subparagraph and provide an opportunity for the submission of comments on any such regulation. No regulation under this subparagraph requiring a device to remain in class III or revising its classification may take effect before the expiration of 90 days from the date of the publication in the Federal Register of the proposed regulation.

(C) The Secretary may by notice published in the Federal Register extend the period prescribed by subparagraph (B) for a device for an additional period not to exceed 1 year.

(m) Humanitarian device exemption

(1) to the extent consistent with the protection of the public health and safety and with ethical standards, it is the purpose of this subsection to encourage the discovery and use of devices intended to benefit patients in the treatment and diagnosis of diseases or conditions that affect fewer than 4,000 individuals in the United States.

(2) The Secretary may grant a request for an exemption from the effectiveness requirements of sections 360d and 360e of this title for a device for which the Secretary finds that—

(A) the device is designed to treat or diagnose a disease or condition that affects fewer than 4,000 individuals in the United States,

(B) the device would not be available to a person with a disease or condition referred to in subparagraph (A) unless the Secretary grants such an exemption and there is no comparable device, other than under this exemption, available to treat or diagnose such disease or condition, and

(C) the device will not expose patients to an unreasonable or significant risk of illness or injury and the probable benefit to health from the use of the device outweighs the risk of injury or illness from its use, taking into account the probable risks and benefits of currently available devices or alternative forms of treatment.

(3) No person granted an exemption under paragraph (2) with respect to a device may sell the device for an amount that exceeds the costs of research and development, fabrication, and distribution of the device.

(4) Devices granted an exemption under paragraph (2) may only be used—

(A) in facilities that have established, in accordance with regulations of the Secretary, a local institutional review committee to supervise clinical testing of devices in the facilities, and

(B) if, before the use of a device, an institutional review committee approves the use in the treatment or diagnosis of a disease or condition referred to in paragraph (2)(A).

(5) An exemption under paragraph (2) shall be for a term of 18 months and may only be initially granted in the 5–year period beginning on the date regulations under paragraph (6) take effect. The Secretary may extend such an exemption for a period of 18 months if the Secretary is able to make the findings set forth in paragraph (2) and if the applicant supplies information demonstrating compliance with paragraph (3). An exemption may be extended more than once and may be extended after the expiration of such 5–year period.

(6) Within one year of November 28, 1990, the Secretary shall issue regulations to implement this subsection.

§ 360k. State and local requirements respecting devices

(a) General rule

Except as provided in subsection (b) of this section, no State or political subdivision of a State may establish or continue in effect with respect to a device intended for human use any requirement—

(1) which is different from, or in addition to, any requirement applicable under this chapter to the device, and

(2) which relates to the safety or effectiveness of the device or to any other matter included in a requirement applicable to the device under this chapter.

(b) Exempt requirements

Upon application of a State or a political subdivision thereof, the Secretary may, by regulation promulgated after notice and opportunity for an oral hearing, exempt from subsection (a) of this section, under such conditions as may be prescribed in such regulation, a requirement of such State or political subdivision applicable to a device intended for human use if—

(1) the requirement is more stringent than a requirement under this chapter which would be applicable to the device if an exemption were not in effect under this subsection; or

(2) the requirement—

(A) is required by compelling local conditions, and

(B) compliance with the requirement would not cause the device to be in violation of any applicable requirement under this chapter.

§ 360*l*. Postmarket surveillance

(a) In general

(1) Required surveillance

The Secretary shall require a manufacturer to conduct postmarket surveillance for any device of the manufacturer first introduced or delivered for introduction into interstate commerce after January 1, 1991, that—

(A) is a permanent implant the failure of which may cause serious, adverse health consequences or death,

(B) is intended for a use in supporting or sustaining human life, or

(C) potentially presents a serious risk to human health.

(2) Discretionary surveillance

The Secretary may require a manufacturer to conduct postmarket surveillance for a device of the manufacturer if the Secretary determines that postmarket surveillance of the device is necessary to protect the public health or to provide safety or effectiveness data for the device.

(b) Surveillance approval

Each manufacturer required to conduct a surveillance of a device under subsection (a)(1) of this section shall, within 30 days of the first introduction or delivery for introduction of such device into interstate commerce, submit, for the approval of the Secretary, a protocol for the required surveillance. Each manufacturer required to conduct a surveillance of a device under subsection (a)(2) of this section shall, within 30 days after receiving notice that the manufacturer is required to conduct such surveillance, submit, for the approval of the Secretary, a protocol for the required surveillance. The Secretary, within 60 days of the receipt of such protocol, shall determine if the principal investigator proposed to be used in the surveillance has sufficient qualifications and experience to conduct such surveillance and if such protocol will result in collection of useful data or other information necessary to protect the public health and to provide safety and effectiveness information for the device. The Secretary may not approve such a protocol until it has been reviewed by an appropriately qualified scientific and technical review committee established by the Secretary.

PART B—DRUGS FOR RARE DISEASES OR CONDITIONS

§ 360aa. Recommendation for investigations of drugs for rare diseases or conditions

(a) Request by sponsor; response by Secretary

The sponsor of a drug for a disease or condition which is rare in the States may request the Secretary to provide written recommendations for the non-clinical and clinical investigations which must be conducted with the drug before—

(1) it may be approved for such disease or condition under section 355 of this title,

(2) if the drug is an antibiotic, it may be certified for such disease or condition under section 357 of this title, or

(3) if the drug is a biological product, it may be licensed for such disease or condition under section 262 of Title 42.

If the Secretary has reason to believe that a drug for which a request is made under this section is a drug for a disease or condition which is rare in the States, the Secretary shall provide the person making the request written recommendations for the non-clinical and clinical investigations which the Secretary believes, on the basis of information available to the Secretary at the time of the request under this section, would be necessary for approval of such drug for such disease or condition under section 355 of this title, certification of such drug for such disease or condition under section 357 of this title, or licensing of such drug for such disease or condition under section 262 of Title 42.

(b) Regulations

The Secretary shall by regulation promulgate procedures for the implementation of subsection (a) of this section.

205

§ 360bb. Designation of Drugs for Rare Diseases or Conditions

(a) Request by sponsor; preconditions; definition

(1) The manufacturer or the sponsor of a drug may request the Secretary to designate the drug as a drug for a rare disease or condition. A request for designation of a drug shall be made before the submission of an application under section 355(b) of this title for the drug, the submission of an application for certification of the drug under section 357 of this title, or the submission of an application for licensing of the drug under section 262 of Title 42. If the Secretary finds that a drug for which a request is submitted under this subsection is being or will be investigated for a rare disease or condition and—

(A) if an application for such drug is approved under section 355 of this title,

(B) if a certification for such drug is issued under section 357 of this title, or

(C) if a license for such drug is issued under section 262 of Title 42,

the approval, certification, or license would be for use for such disease or condition, the Secretary shall designate the drug as a drug for such disease or condition. A request for a designation of a drug under this subsection shall contain the consent of the applicant to notice being given by the Secretary under subsection (b) of this section respecting the designation of the drug.

(2) For purposes of paragraph (1), the term "rare disease or condition" means any disease or condition which (A) affects less than 200,000 persons in the United States, or (B) affects more than 200,000 in the United States and for which there is no reasonable expectation that the cost of developing and making available in the United States a drug for such disease or condition will be recovered from sales in the United States of such drug. Determinations under the preceding sentence with respect to any drug shall be made on the basis of the facts and circumstances as of the date the request for designation of the drug under this subsection is made.

(b) Notification of discontinuance of drug or application as condition

. A designation of a drug under subsection (a) of this section shall be subject to the condition that—

(1) if an application was approved for the drug under section 355(b) of this title, a certificate was issued for the drug under section 357 of this title, or a license was issued for the drug under section 262 of Title 42, the manufacturer of the drug will notify the Secretary of any discontinuance of the production of the drug at least one year before discontinuance, and

(2) if an application has not been approved for the drug under section 355(b) of this title, a certificate has not been issued for the drug under section 357 of this title, or a license has not been issued for the drug under section 262 of Title 42, and if preclinical investigations or investigations under section 355(i) of this title are being conducted with the drug, the manufacturer or sponsor of the drug will notify the Secretary of any decision to discontinue active pursuit of approval of an application under section 355(b) of this title, approval of an application for certification under section 357 of this title, or approval of a license under section 262 of Title 42.

(c) Notice to public

Notice respecting the designation of a drug under subsection (a) of this section shall be made available to the public.

(d) Regulations

The Secretary shall by regulation promulgate procedures for the implementation of subsection (a) of this section.

§ 360cc. Protection for Drugs for Rare Diseases or conditions

(a) Exclusive approval, certification, or license

Except as provided in subsection (b) of this section, if the Secretary—

(1) approves an application filed pursuant to section 355 of this title, or

(2) issues a certification under section 357 of this title, or

(3) issues a license under section 262 of Title 42

for a drug designated under section 360bb of this title for a rare disease or condition, the Secretary may not approve another application under section 355 of this title, issue another certification under section 357 of this title, or issue another license under section 262 of Title 42 for such drug for such disease or condition for a person who is not the holder of such approved application, of such certification, or of such license until the expiration of seven years from the date of the approval of the approved application, the issuance of the certification, or the issuance of the license. Section 355(c)(2) of this title does not apply to the refusal to approve an application under the preceding sentence.

(b) Exceptions

If an application filed pursuant to section 355 of this title is approved for a drug designated under section 360bb of this title for a rare disease or condition, if a certification is issued under section 357 of this title for such a drug, or if a license is issued under section 262 of Title 42 for such a drug, the Secretary may, during the seven-year period beginning on the date of the application approval, of the issuance of the certification under section 357 of this title, or of the issuance of the license, approve another application under section 355 of this title, issue another certification under section 357 of this title, or issue a license under section 262 of Title 42, for such drug for such disease or condition for a person who is not the holder of such approved application, of such certification, or of such license if—

(1) the Secretary finds, after providing the holder notice and opportunity for the submission of views, that in such period the holder of the approved application, of the certification, or of the license cannot assure the availability of sufficient quantities of the drug to meet the needs of persons with the disease or condition for which the drug was designated; or

(2) such holder provides the Secretary in writing the consent of such holder for the approval of other applications, issuance of other certifications, or the issuance of other licenses before the expiration of such seven-year period.

§ 360dd. Open protocols for investigations of Drugs for Rare Diseases or conditions

If a drug is designated under section 360bb of this title as a drug for a rare disease or condition and if notice of a claimed exemption under section 355(i) of this title or regulations issued thereunder is filed for such drug, the Secretary shall encourage the sponsor of such drug to design protocols for clinical investigations of the drug which may be conducted under the exemption to permit the addition to the investigations of persons with the disease or condition who need the drug to treat the disease or condition and who cannot be satisfactorily treated by available alternative drugs.

§ 360ee. Grants and contracts for development of drugs for rare diseases and conditions

(a) Authority of Secretary

The Secretary may make grants to and enter into contracts with public and private entities and individuals to assist in (1) defraying the costs of qualified testing expenses incurred in connection with the development of drugs for rare diseases and conditions, (2) defraying the costs of developing medical devices for rare diseases or conditions, and (3) defraying the costs of developing medical foods for rare diseases or conditions.

(b) Definitions

For purposes of subsection (a) of this section:

(1) The term "qualified testing" means—

(A) human clinical testing—

(i) which is carried out under an exemption for a drug for a rare disease or condition under section 355(i) of this title (or regulations issued under such section); and

(ii) which occurs after the date such drug is designated under section 360bb of this title and before the date on which an application with respect to such drug is submitted under section 355(b) or 357 of this title or under section 262 of Title 42; and

(B) preclinical testing involving a drug for a rare disease or condition which occurs after the date such drug is designated under section 360bb of this title and before the date on which an application with respect to such drug is submitted under section 355(b) or 357 of this title or under section 262 of Title 42.

(2) The term "rare disease or condition" means (1) in the case of a drug, any disease or condition which (A) affects less than 200,000 persons in the United States, or (B) affects more than 200,000 in the United States and for which there is no reasonable expectation that the cost of developing and making available in the United States a drug for such disease or condition will be recovered from sales in the United States of such drug, (2) in the case of a medical device, any disease or condition that occurs so infrequently in the United States that there is no reasonable expectation that a medical device for such disease or condition will be developed without assistance under subsection (a) of this section, and (3) in the case of a medical food, any disease or condition that occurs so infrequently in the United States that there is no reasonable expectation that a medical food for such disease or condition will be developed without assistance under subsection (a) of this section. Determinations under the preceding sentence with respect to any drug shall be made on the basis of the facts and circumstances as of the date the request for designation of the drug under section 360bb of this title is made.

(3) The term "medical food" means a food which is formulated to be consumed or administered enterally under the supervision of a physician and which is intended for the specific dietary management of a disease or condition for which distinctive nutritional requirements, based on recognized scientific principles, are established by medical evaluation.

(c) Appropriations

For grants and contracts under subsection (a) of this section there are authorized to be appropriated $10,000,000 for fiscal year 1988, $12,000,000 for fiscal year 1989, $14,000,000 for fiscal year 1990.

PART C—ELECTRONIC PRODUCT RADIATION CONTROL

§ 360ii. Program of control

(a) Establishment

The Secretary shall establish and carry out an electronic product radiation control program designed to protect the public health and safety from electronic product radiation. As a part of such program, he shall—

(1) pursuant to section 360kk of this title, develop and administer performance standards for electronic products;

(2) plan, conduct, coordinate, and support research, development, training, and operational activities to minimize the emissions of and the exposure of people to, unnecessary electronic product radiation;

(3) maintain liaison with and receive information from other Federal and State departments and agencies with related interests, professional organizations, industry, industry and labor associations, and other organizations on present and future potential electronic product radiation;

(4) study and evaluation emissions of, and conditions of exposure to, electronic product radiation and intense magnetic fields;

(5) develop, test, and evaluate the effectiveness of procedures and techniques for minimizing exposure to electronic product radiation; and

(6) consult and maintain liaison with the Secretary of Commerce, the Secretary of Defense, the Secretary of Labor, the Atomic Energy Commission, and other appropriate Federal departments and agencies on (A) techniques, equipment, and programs for testing and evaluating electronic product radiation, and (B) the development of performance standards pursuant to section 360kk of this title to control such radiation emissions.

(b) Powers of Secretary

In carrying out the purposes of subsection (a) of this section, the Secretary is authorized to—

(1)(A) collect and make available, through publications and other appropriate means, the results of, and other information concerning, research and studies relating to the nature and extent of the hazards and control of electronic product radiation; and (B) make such recommendations relating to such hazards and control as he considers appropriate;

(2) make grants to public and private agencies, organizations, and institutions, and to individuals for the purposes stated in paragraphs (2), (4), and (5) of subsection (a) of this section;

(3) contract with public or private agencies, institutions, and organizations, and with individuals, without regard to section 3324 of Title 31 and section 5 of Title 41; and

(4) procure (by negotiation otherwise) electronic products for research and testing purposes, and sell or otherwise dispose of such products.

(c) Record keeping

(1) Each recipient of assistance under this part pursuant to grants or contracts entered into under other than competitive bidding procedures shall keep such records as the Secretary shall prescribe including records which fully disclose the amount and disposition by such recipient of the proceeds of such assistance, the total cost of the project or undertaking in connection with which such assistance is given or used, and the amount of that portion of the cost of the project or undertaking supplied by other sources, and such other records as will facilitate an effective audit.

(2) The Secretary and the Comptroller General of the United States, or any of their duly authorized representatives, shall have access for the purpose of audit and examination to any books, documents, papers, and records of the recipients that are pertinent to the grants or contracts entered into under this part under other than competitive bidding procedures.

§ 360jj. Studies by Secretary

(a) Report to Congress

The Secretary shall conduct the following studies, and shall make a report or reports of the results of such studies to the Congress on or before January 1, 1970, and from time to time thereafter as he may find necessary, together with such recommendations for legislation as he may deem appropriate:

(1) A study of present State and Federal control of health hazards from electronic product radiation and other types of ionizing radiation, which study shall include, but not be limited to—

(A) control of health hazards from radioactive materials other than materials regulated under the Atomic Energy Act of 1954;

(B) any gaps and inconsistencies in present controls;

(C) the need for controlling the sale of certain used electronic products, particularly antiquated X-ray equipment, without upgrading such products to meet the standards for new products or separate standards for used products;

(D) measures to assure consistent and effective control of the aforementioned health hazards;

(E) measures to strengthen radiological health programs of State governments; and

(F) the feasibility of authorizing the Secretary to enter into arrangements with individual States or groups of States to define their respective functions and responsibilities for the control of electronic product radiation and other ionizing radiation;

(2) A study to determine the necessity for the development of standards for the use of nonmedical electronic products for commercial and industrial purposes; and

(3) A study of the development of practicable procedures for the detection and measurement of electronic product radiation which may be emitted from electronic products manufactured or imported prior to the effective date of any applicable standard established pursuant to this part.

(b) Participation of other Federal agencies

In carrying out these studies, the Secretary shall invite the participation of other Federal departments and agencies having related responsibilities and interests, State governments—particularly those of States which regulate radioactive materials under section 2021 of Title 42 and interested professional, labor, and industrial organizations. Upon request from congressional committees interested in these studies, the Secretary shall keep these committees currently informed as to the progress of the studies and shall permit the committees to send observers to meetings of the study groups.

(c) Organization of studies and participation

The Secretary or his designee shall organize the studies and the participation of the invited participants as he deems best. Any dissent from the findings and recommendations of the Secretary shall be included in the report if so requested by the dissenter.

§ 360kk. Performance standards for electronic products

(a) Promulgation of regulations

(1) The Secretary shall by regulation prescribe performance standards for electronic products to control the emission of electronic product radiation from such products if he determines that such standards are necessary for the protection of the public health and safety. Such standards may include provisions for the testing of such products and the measurement of their electronic product radiation emissions, may require the attachment of warning signs and labels, and may require the provision of instructions for the installation, operation, and use of such products. Such standards may be prescribed from time to time whenever such determinations are made, but the first of such standards shall be prescribed prior to January 1, 1970. In the development of such standards, the Secretary shall consult with Federal and State depart-

ments and agencies having related responsibilities or interests and with appropriate professional organizations and interested persons, including representatives of industries and labor organizations which would be affected by such standards, and shall give consideration to—

(A) the latest available scientific and medical data in the field of electronic product radiation;

(B) the standards currently recommended by (i) other Federal agencies having responsibilities relating to the control and measurement of electronic product radiation, and (ii) public or private groups having an expertise in the field of electronic product radiation;

(C) the reasonableness and technical feasibility of such standards as applied to a particular electronic product;

(D) the adaptability of such standards to the the need for uniformity and reliability of testing and measuring procedures and equipment; and

(E) in the case of a component, or accessory described in paragraph (2)(B) of section 360hh of this title, the performance of such article in the manufactured or assembled product for which it is designed.

(2) The Secretary may prescribe different and individual performance standards, to the extent appropriate and feasible, for different electronic products so as to recognize their different operating characteristics and uses.

(3) The performance standards prescribed under this section shall not apply to any electronic product which is intended solely for export if (A) such product and the outside of any shipping container used in the export of such product are labeled or tagged to show that such product is intended for export, and (B) such product meets all the applicable requirements of the country to which such product is intended for export.

(4) The Secretary may by regulation amend or revoke any performance standard prescribed under this section.

(5) The Secretary may exempt from the provisions of this section any electronic product intended for use by departments or agencies of the United States provided such department or agency has prescribed procurement specifications governing emissions of electronic product radiation and provided further that such product is a type used solely or predominantly by departments or agencies of the United States.

(b) Administrative procedure

The provisions of subchapter II of chapter 5 of Title 5 (relating to the administrative procedure for rulemaking), and of chapter 7 of Title 5 (relating to judicial review), shall apply with respect to any regulation prescribing, amending, or revoking any standard prescribed under this section.

(c) Publication in Federal Register

Each regulation prescribing, amending, or revoking a standard shall specify the date on which it shall take effect which, in the case of any regulation prescribing, or amending any standard, may not be sooner than one year or not later than two years after the date on which such regulation is issued, unless the Secretary finds, for good cause shown, that an earlier or later effective date is in the public interest and publishes in the Federal Register his reason for such finding, in which case such earlier or later date shall apply.

(d) Judicial review

(1) In a case of actual controversy as to the validity of any regulation issued under this section prescribing, amending, or revoking a performance standard, any person who will be adversely affected by such regulation when it is effective may at any time prior to the sixtieth day after such regulation is issued file a petition with the United States court of appeals for the circuit wherein such person resides or has his principal place of business, for a judicial review of such regulation. A copy of the petition shall be forthwith transmitted by the clerk of the court to the Secretary or other officer designated by him for that purpose. The Secretary thereupon shall file in the court the record of the proceedings on which the Secretary based the regulation, as provided in section 2112 of Title 28.

(2) If the petitioner applies to the court for leave to adduce additional evidence, and shows to the satisfaction of the court that such additional evidence is material and that there were reasonable grounds for the failure to adduce such evidence in the proceeding before the Secretary, the court may order such additional evidence (and evidence in rebuttal thereof) to be taken before the Secretary, and to be adduced upon the hearing, in such manner and upon such terms and conditions as to the court may seem proper. The Secretary may modify his findings, or make new findings, by reason of the additional evidence so taken, and he shall file such modified or new findings, and his recommendations, if any, for the modification or setting aside of his original regulation, with the return of such additional evidence.

(3) Upon the filing of the petition referred to in paragraph (1) of this subsection, the court shall have jurisdiction to review the regulation in accordance with chapter 7 of Title 5 and to grant appropriate relief as provided in such chapter.

(4) The judgment of the court affirming or setting aside, in whole or in part, any such regulation of the Secretary shall be final, subject to review by the Supreme Court of the United States upon certiorari or certification as provided in section 1254 of Title 28.

(5) Any action instituted under this subsection shall survive, notwithstanding any change in the person occupying the office of Secretary or any vacancy in such office.

(6) The remedies provided for in this subsection shall be in addition to and not in substitution for any other remedies provided by law.

(e) Availability of record

A certified copy of the transcript of the record and administrative proceedings under this section shall be furnished by the Secretary to any interested party at his request, and payment of the costs thereof, and shall be admissible in any criminal, exclusion of imports, or other proceeding arising under or in respect of this part irrespective of whether proceedings with respect to the regulation have previously been initiated or become final under this section.

(f) Technical Electronic Product Radiation Safety Standards Committee

(1)(A) The Secretary shall establish a Technical Electronic Product Radiation Safety Standards Committee (hereafter in this part referred to as the "Committee") which he shall consult before prescribing any standard under this section. The Committee shall be appointed by the Secretary, after consultation with public and private agencies concerned with the technical aspect of electronic product radiation safety, and shall be composed of fifteen members each of whom shall be technically qualified by training and experience in one or more fields of science or engineering applicable to electronic product radiation safety, as follows:

(i) Five members shall be selected from governmental agencies, including State and Federal Governments;

(ii) Five members shall be selected from the affected industries after consultation with industry representatives; and

(iii) Five members shall be selected from the general public, of which at least one shall be a representative of organized labor.

(B) The Committee may propose electronic product radiation safety standards to the Secretary for his consideration. All proceedings of the Committee shall be recorded and the record of each such proceeding shall be available for public inspection.

(2) Payments to members of the Committee who are not officers or employees of the United States pursuant to section 210(c) of Title 42 shall not render members of the Committee officers or employees of the United States for any purpose.

(g) Review and evaluation

The Secretary shall review and evaluate on a continuing basis testing programs carried out by industry to assure the adequacy of safeguards against hazardous electronic product radiation and to assure that electronic products comply with standards prescribed under this section.

(h) Product certification

Every manufacturer of an electronic product to which is applicable a standard in effect under this section shall furnish to the distributor or dealer at the time of delivery of such product, in the form of a label or tag permanently affixed to such product or in such manner as approved by the Secretary, the certification that such product conforms to all applicable standards under this section. Such certification shall be based upon a test, in accordance with such standard, of the individual article to which it is attached or upon a testing program which is in accord with good manufacturing practice and which has not been disapproved by the Secretary (in such manner as he shall prescribe by regulation) on the grounds that it does not assure the adequacy of safeguards against hazardous electronic product radiation or that it does not assure that electronic products comply with the standards prescribed under this section.

§ 360*ll*. Notification of defects in and repair or replacement of electronic products

(a) Notification; exemption

(1) Every manufacturer of electronic products who discovers that an electronic product produced, assembled, or imported by him has a defect which relates to the safety of use of such product by reason of the emission of electronic product radiation, or that an electronic product produced, assembled, or imported by him on or after the effective date of an applicable standard prescribed pursuant to section 360kk of this title fails to comply with such standard, shall immediately notify the Secretary of such defect or failure to comply if such product has left the place of manufacture and shall (except as authorized by paragraph (2)) with reasonable promptness furnish notification of such defect or failure to the persons (where known to the manufacturer) specified in subsection (b) of this section.

(2) If, in the opinion of such manufacturer, the defect or failure to comply is not such as to create a significant risk of injury, including genetic injury, to any person, he may, at the time of giving notice to the Secretary of such defect or failure to comply, apply to the Secretary for an exemption from the requirement of notice to the persons specified in subsection (b) of this section. If such application states reasonable grounds for such exemption, the Secretary shall afford such manufacturer an opportunity to present his views and evidence in support of the application, the burden of proof being on the manufacturer. If, after such presentation, the Secretary is satisfied that such defect or failure to comply is not such as to create a significant risk of injury, including genetic injury, to any person, he shall exempt such manufacturer from the requirement of notice to the persons specified in subsection (b) of

this section and from the requirements of repair or replacement imposed by subsection (f) of this section.

(b) Method of notification

The notification (other than to the Secretary) required by paragraph (1) of subsection (a) of this section shall be accomplished—

(1) by certified mail to the first purchaser of such product for purposes other than resale, and to any subsequent transferee of such product; and

(2) by certified mail or other more expeditious means to the dealers or distributors of such manufacturer to whom such product was delivered.

(c) Requisite elements of notification

The notifications required by paragraph (1) of subsection (a) of this section shall contain a clear description of such defect or failure to comply with an applicable standard, an evaluation of the hazard reasonably related to such defect or failure to comply, and a statement of the measures to be taken to repair such defect. In the case of a notification to a person referred to in subsection (b) of this section, the notification shall also advise the person of his rights under subsection (f) of this section.

(d) Copies to Secretary of communications by manufacturers to dealers or distributors regarding defects

Every manufacturer of electronic products shall furnish to the Secretary a true or representative copy of all notices, bulletins, and other communications to the dealers or distributors of such manufacturer or to purchasers (or subsequent transferees) of electronic products of such manufacturer regarding any such defect in such product or any such failure to comply with a standard applicable to such product. The Secretary shall disclose to the public so much of the information contained in such notice or other information obtained under section 360nn of this title as he deems will assist in carrying out the purposes of this part, but he shall not disclose any information which contains or relates to a trade secret or other matter referred to in section 1905 of Title 18 unless he determines that it is necessary to carry out the purposes of this part.

(e) Notice from Secretary to manufacturer of defects or failure to comply with standards

If through testing, inspection, investigation, or research carried out pursuant to this part, or examination of reports submitted pursuant to section 360nn of this title, or otherwise, the Secretary determines that any electronic product—

(1) does not comply with an applicable standard prescribed pursuant to section 360kk of this title; or

(2) contains a defect which relates to the safety of use of such product by reason of the emission of electronic product radiation;

he shall immediately notify the manufacturer of such product of such defect or failure to comply. The notice shall contain the findings of the Secretary and shall include all information upon which the findings are based. The Secretary shall afford such manufacturer an opportunity to present his views and evidence in support thereof, to establish that there is no failure of compliance or that the alleged defect does not exist or does not relate to safety of use of the product by reason of the emission of such radiation hazard. If after such presentation by the manufacturer the Secretary determines that such product does not comply with an applicable standard prescribed pursuant to section 360kk of this title, or that it contains a defect which relates to the safety of use of such product by reason of the emission of electronic product radiation, the Secretary shall direct the manufacturer to furnish the notification specified in subsection (c) of this section to the persons specified in paragraphs (1) and (2) of subsection (b) of this section (where known to the manufacturer), unless the manufacturer has applied for an exemption from the requirement of such notification on the ground specified in paragraph (2) of subsection (a) of this section and the Secretary is satisfied that such noncompliance or defect is not such as to create a significant risk of injury, including genetic injury, to any person.

(f) Correction of defects

If any electronic product is found under subsection (a) or (e) of this section to fail to comply with an applicable standard prescribed under this part or to have a defect which relates to the safety of use of such product, and the notification specified in subsection (c) of this section is required to be furnished on account of such failure or defect, the manufacturer of such product shall (1) without charge, bring such product into conformity with such standard or remedy such defect and provide reimbursement for any expenses for transportation of such product incurred in connection with having such product brought into conformity or having such defect remedied, (2) replace such product with a like or equivalent product which complies with each applicable standard prescribed under this part and which has no defect relating to the safety of its use, or (3) make a refund of the cost of such product. The manufacturer shall take the action required by this subsection in such manner, and with respect to such persons, as the Secretary by regulations shall prescribe.

(g) Effective date

This section shall not apply to any electronic product that was manufactured before October 18, 1968.

§ 360mm. Imports

(a) Refusal of admission to noncomplying electronic products

Any electronic product offered for importation into the United States which fails to comply with an applicable standard prescribed under this part, or to which is not affixed a certification in the form of a label or tag in conformity with section 360kk(h) of this title shall be refused admission into the United States. The Secretary of the Treasury shall deliver to the Secretary of Health and Human Services, upon the latter's request, samples of electronic products which are being imported or offered for import into the United States, giving notice thereof to the owner or consignee, who may have a hearing before the Secretary of Health and Human Services. If it appears from an examination of such samples or otherwise that any electronic product fails to comply with applicable standards prescribed pursuant to section 360kk of this title, then, unless subsection (b) of this section applies and is complied with, (1) such electronic product shall be refused admission, and (2) the Secretary of the Treasury shall cause destruction of such electronic product unless such article is exported, under regulations prescribed by the Secretary of the Treasury, within 90 days after the date of notice of refusal of admission or within such additional time as may be permitted by such regulations.

(b) Bond

If it appears to the Secretary of Health and Human Services that any electronic product refused admission pursuant to subsection (a) of this section can be brought into compliance with applicable standards prescribed pursuant to section 360kk of this title, final determination as to admission of such electronic product may be deferred upon filing of timely written application by the owner or consignee and the execution by him of a good and sufficient bond providing for the payment of such liquidated damages in the event of default as the Secretary of Health and Human Services may by regulation prescribe. If such application is filed and such bond is executed the Secretary of Health and Human Services may, in accordance with rules prescribed by him, permit the applicant to perform such operations with respect to such electronic product as may be specified in the notice of permission.

(c) Liability of owner or consignee for expenses connected with refusal of admission

All expenses (including travel, per diem or subsistence, and salaries of officers or employees of the United States) in connection with the destruction provided for in subsection (a) of this section and the supervision of operations provided for in subsection (b) of this section, and all expenses in connection with the storage, cartage, or labor with respect to any electronic product refused admission pursuant to subsection (a) of this section, shall be paid by the owner or consignee, and, in event of default, shall constitute a lien against any future importations made by such owner or consignee.

(d) Designation of agent for purposes of service

It shall be the duty of every manufacturer offering an electronic product for importation into the United States to designate in writing an agent upon whom service of all administrative and judicial processes, notices, orders, decisions, and requirements may be made for and on behalf of said manufacturer, and to file such designation with the Secretary, which designation may from time to time be changed by like writing, similarly filed. Service of all administrative and judicial processes, notices, orders, decisions, and requirements may be made upon said manufacturer by service upon such designated agent at his office or usual place of residence with like effect as if made personally upon said manufacturer, and in default of such designation of such agent, service of process, notice, order, requirement, or decision in any proceeding before the Secretary or in any judicial proceeding for enforcement of this part or any standards prescribed pursuant to this part may be made by posting such process, notice, order, requirement, or decision in the Office of the Secretary or in a place designated by him by regulation.

§ 360nn.   Inspection, records, and reports

(a) Inspection of premises

If the Secretary finds for good cause that the methods, tests, or programs related to electronic product radiation safety in a particular factory, warehouse, or establishment in which electronic products are manufactured or held, may not be adequate or reliable, officers or employees duly designated by the Secretary, upon presenting appropriate credentials and a written notice to the owner, operator, or agent in charge, are thereafter authorized (1) to enter, at reasonable times, any area in such factory, warehouse, or establishment in which the manufacturer's tests (or testing programs) required by section 360kk(h) of this title are carried out, and (2) to inspect, at reasonable times and within reasonable limits and in a reasonable manner, the facilities and procedures within such area which are related to electronic product radiation safety. Each such inspection shall be commenced and completed with reasonable promptness. In addition to other grounds upon which good cause may be found for purposes of this subsection, good cause will be considered to exist in any case where the manufacturer has introduced into commerce any electronic product which does not comply with an applicable standard prescribed under this part and with respect to which no exemption from the notification requirements has been granted by the Secretary under section 360ll(a)(2) or 360ll(e) of this title.

(b) Record keeping

Every manufacturer of electronic products shall establish and maintain such records (including testing records), make such reports, and provide such information, as the Secretary may reasonably require to enable him to determine whether such manufacturer has acted or is acting in compliance with this part and standards prescribed pursuant to this part and shall, upon request of an officer or employee duly designated by the Secretary, permit such officer or employee to inspect appropriate books, papers, records, and documents relevant to determining whether such manufacturer has acted or is acting in compliance with standards prescribed pursuant to this part.

(c) Disclosure of technical data

Every manufacturer of electronic products shall provide to the Secretary such performance data and other technical data related to safety as may be required to carry out the purposes of this part. The Secretary is authorized to require the manufacturer to give such notification of such performance and technical data at the time of original purchase to the ultimate purchaser of the electronic product, as he determines necessary to carry out the purposes of this part after consulting with the affected industry.

(d) Public nature of reports

Accident and investigation reports made under this part by any officer, employee, or agent of the Secretary shall be available for use in any civil, criminal, or other judicial proceeding arising out of such accident. Any such officer, employee, or agent may be required to testify in such proceedings as to the facts developed in such investigations. Any such report shall be made available to the public in a manner which need not identify individuals. All reports on research projects, demonstration projects, and other related activities shall be public information.

(e) Trade secrets

The Secretary or his representative shall not disclose any information reported to or otherwise obtained by him, pursuant to subsection (a) or (b) of this section, which concerns any information which contains or relates to a trade secret or other matter referred to in section 1905 of Title 18, except that such information may be disclosed to other officers or employees of the Department and of other agencies concerned with carrying out this part or when relevant in any proceeding under this part. Nothing in this section shall authorize the withholding of information by the Secretary, or by any officers or employees under his control, from the duly authorized committees of the Congress.

(f) Information required to identify and locate first purchasers of electronic products

The Secretary may by regulation (1) require dealers and distributors of electronic products, to which there are applicable standards prescribed under this part and the retail prices of which is not less than $50, to furnish manufacturers of such products such information as may be necessary to identify and locate, for purposes of section 360ll of this title, the first purchasers of such products for purposes other than resale, and (2) require manufacturers to preserve such information. Any regulation establishing a requirement pursuant to clause (1) of the preceding sentence shall (A) authorize such dealers and distributors to elect, in lieu of immediately furnishing such information to the manufacturer, to hold and preserve such information until advised by the manufacturer or Secretary that such information is needed by the manufacturer for purposes of section 360ll of this title, and (B) provide that the dealer or distributor shall, upon making such election, give prompt notice of such election (together with information identifying the notifier and the product) to the manufacturer and shall, when advised by the manufacturer or Secretary, of the need therefor for the purposes of section 360ll of this title, immediately furnish the manufacturer with the required information. If a dealer or distributor discontinues the dealing in or distribution of electronic products, he shall turn the information over to the manufacturer. Any manufacturer receiving information pursuant to this subsection concerning first purchasers of products for purposes other than resale shall treat it as confidential and may use it only if necessary for the purpose of notifying persons pursuant to section 360ll(a) of this title.

§ 360oo. Prohibited acts

(a) It shall be unlawful—

(1) for any manufacturer to introduce, or to deliver for introduction, into commerce, or to import into the United States, any electronic product which does not comply with an applicable standard prescribed pursuant to section 360kk of this title;

(2) for any person to fail to furnish any notification or other material or information required by section 360ll or 360nn of this title; or to fail to comply with the requirements of section 360ll (f) of this title;

(3) for any person to fail or to refuse to establish or maintain records required by this part or to permit access by the Secretary or any of his duly authorized representatives to, or the copying of, such records, or to permit entry or inspection, as required by or pursuant to section 360nn of this title;

(4) for any person to fail or to refuse to make any report required pursuant to section 360nn(b) of this title or to furnish or preserve any information required pursuant to section 360nn(f) of this title; or

(5) for any person (A) to fail to issue a certification as required by section 360kk(h) of this title, or (B) to issue such a certification when such certification is not based upon a test or testing program meeting the requirements of section 360kk(h) of this title or when the issuer, in the exercise of due care, would have reason to know that such certification is false or misleading in a material respect.

(b) The Secretary may exempt any electronic product, or class thereof, from all or part of subsection (a) of this section, upon such conditions as he may find necessary to protect the public health or welfare, for the purpose of research, investigations, studies, demonstrations, or training, or for reasons of national security.

§ 360pp. Enforcement

(a) Jurisdiction of courts

The district courts of the United States shall have jurisdiction, for cause shown, to restrain violations of section 360oo of this title and to restrain dealers and distributors of electronic products from selling or otherwise disposing of electronic products which do not conform to an applicable standard prescribed pursuant to section 360kk of this title except when such products are disposed of by returning them to the distributor or manufacturer from whom they were obtained. The district courts of the United States shall also have jurisdiction in accordance with section 1355 of Title 28 to enforce the provisions of subsection (b) of this section.

(b) Penalties

(1) Any person who violates section 360oo of this title shall be subject to a civil penalty of not more than $1,000. For purposes of this subsection, any such violation shall with respect to each electronic product involved, or with respect to each act or omission made unlawful by section 360oo of this title, constitute a separate violation, except that the maximum civil penalty imposed on any person under this subsection for any related series of violations shall not exceed $300,000.

(2) Any such civil penalty may on application be remitted or mitigated by the Secretary. In determining the amount of such penalty, or whether it should be remitted or mitigated and in what amount, the appropriateness of such penalty to the size of the business of the person charged and the gravity of the violation shall be considered. The amount of such penalty, when finally determined, may be deducted from any sums owing by the United States to the person charged.

(c) Venue; process

Actions under subsections (a) and (b) of this section may be brought in the district court of the United States for the district wherein any act or omission or transaction constituting the violation occurred, or in such court for the district where the defendant is found or transacts business, and process in such cases may be served in any other district of which the defendant is an inhabitant or wherever the defendant may be found.

(d) Warnings

Nothing in this part shall be construed as requiring the Secretary to report for the institution of proceedings minor violations of this part whenever he believes that the public interest will be adequately served by a suitable written notice or warning.

(e) Compliance with regulations

Except as provided in the first sentence of section 360ss of this title, compliance with this part or any regulations issued thereunder shall not relieve any person from liability at common law or under statutory law.

(f) Additional remedies

The remedies provided for in this part shall be in addition to and not in substitution for any other remedies provided by law.

§ 360qq. Annual report

(a) The Secretary shall prepare and submit to the President for transmittal to the Congress on or before April 1 of each year a comprehensive report on the administration of this part for the preceding calendar year. Such report shall include—

(1) a thorough appraisal (including statistical analyses, estimates, and long-term projections) of the incidence of biological injury and effects, including genetic effects, to the population resulting from exposure to electronic product radiation, with a breakdown, insofar as practicable, among the various sources of such radiation;

(2) a list of Federal electronic product radiation control standards prescribed or in effect in such year, with identification of standards newly prescribed during such year;

(3) an evaluation of the degree of observance of applicable standards, including a list of enforcement actions, court decisions, and compromises of alleged violations by location and company name;

(4) a summary of outstanding problems confronting the administration of this part in order of priority;

(5) an analysis and evaluation of research activities completed as a result of Government and private sponsorship, and technological progress for safety achieved during such year;

(6) a list, with a brief statement of the issues, of completed or pending judicial actions under this part;

(7) the extent to which technical information was disseminated to the scientific, commercial, and labor community and consumer-oriented information was made available to the public; and

(8) the extent of cooperation between Government officials and representatives of industry and other interested parties in the implementation of this subpart including a log or summary of meetings held between Government officials and representatives of industry and other interested parties.

(b) The report required by subsection (a) of this section shall contain such recommendations for additional legislation as the Secretary deems necessary to promote cooperation among the several States in the improvement of electronic product radiation control and to strengthen the national electronic product radiation control program.

§ 360rr. Federal–State cooperation

The Secretary is authorized (1) to accept from State and local authorities engaged in activities related to health or safety or consumer protection, on a reimbursable basis or otherwise, any assistance in the administration and enforcement of this part which he may request and which they may be able and willing to provide and, if so agreed, may pay in advance or otherwise for the reasonable cost of such assistance, and (2) he may, for the purpose of conducting examinations, investigations, and inspections, commission any officer or employee of any such authority as an officer of the Department.

§ 360ss. State standards

Whenever any standard prescribed pursuant to section 360kk of this title with respect to an aspect of performance of an electronic product is in effect, no State or political subdivision of a State shall have any authority either to establish, or to continue in effect, any standard which is applicable to the same aspect of performance of such product and which is not identical to the Federal Standard. Nothing in this part shall be construed to prevent the Federal Government or the government of any State or political subdivision thereof from establishing a requirement with respect to emission of radiation from electronic products procured for its own use if such requirement imposes a more restrictive standard than that required to comply with the otherwise applicable Federal standard.

SUBCHAPTER VI—COSMETICS

§ 361. Adulterated cosmetics

A cosmetic shall be deemed to be adulterated—

(a) If it bears or contains any poisonous or deleterious substance which may render it injurious to users under the conditions of use prescribed in the labeling thereof, or under such conditions of use as are customary or usual, except that this provision shall not apply to coal-tar hair dye, the label of which bears the following legend conspicuously displayed thereon: "Caution—This product contains ingredients which may cause skin irritation on certain individuals and a preliminary test according to accompanying directions should first be made. This product must not be used for dyeing the eyelashes or eyebrows; to do so may cause blindness.", and the labeling of which bears adequate directions for such preliminary testing. For the purposes of this paragraph and paragraph (e) the term "hair dye" shall not include eyelash dyes or eyebrow dyes.

(b) If it consists in whole or in part of any filthy, putrid, or decomposed substance.

(c) If it has been prepared, packed, or held under insanitary conditions whereby it may have become contaminated with filth, or whereby it may have been rendered injurious to health.

(d) If its container is composed, in whole or in part, of any poisonous or deleterious substance which may render the contents injurious to health.

(e) If it is not a hair dye and it is, or it bears or contains, a color additive which is unsafe within the meaning of section 379e of this title.

§ 362. Misbranded cosmetics

A cosmetic shall be deemed to be misbranded—

(a) If its labeling is false or misleading in any particular.

(b) If in package form unless it bears a label containing (1) the name and place of business of the manufacturer, packer, or distributor; and (2) an accurate statement of the quantity of the contents in terms of weight, measure, or numerical count: Provided, That under clause (2) of this paragraph reasonable variations shall be permitted, and exemptions as to small packages shall be established, by regulations prescribed by the Secretary.

(c) If any word, statement, or other information required by or under authority of this chapter to appear on the label or labeling is not prominently placed thereon with such conspicuousness (as compared with other words, statements, designs, or devices, in the labeling) and in such terms as to render it likely to be read and understood by the ordinary individual under customary conditions of purchase and use.

(d) If its container is so made, formed, or filled as to be misleading.

(e) If it is a color additive, unless its packaging and labeling are in conformity with such packaging and labeling requirements, applicable to such color additive, as may be contained in regulations issued under section 379e of this title. This paragraph shall not apply to packages of color additives which, with respect to their use for cosmetics, are marketed and intended for use only in or on hair dyes (as defined in the last sentence of section 361(a) of this title).

(f) If its packaging or labeling is in violation of an applicable regulation issued pursuant to section 1472 or 1473 of Title 15.

§ 363. Regulations making exemptions

The Secretary shall promulgate regulations exempting from any labeling requirement of this chapter cosmetics which are, in accordance with the practice of the trade, to be processed, labeled, or repacked in substantial quantities at establishments other than those where originally processed or packed, on condition that such cosmetics are not adulterated or misbranded under the provisions of this chapter upon removal from such processing, labeling, or repacking establishment.

SUBCHAPTER VII—GENERAL AUTHORITY

PART A—GENERAL ADMINISTRATIVE PROVISIONS

§ 371. Regulations and hearings   701e

(a) Authority to promulgate regulations

The authority to promulgate regulations for the efficient enforcement of this chapter, except as otherwise provided in this section, is vested in the Secretary.

(b) Regulations for imports and exports

The Secretary of the Treasury and the Secretary of Health and Human Services shall jointly prescribe regulations for the efficient enforcement of the provisions of section 381 of this title, except as otherwise provided therein. Such regulations shall be promulgated in such manner and take effect at such time, after due notice, as the Secretary of Health and Human Services shall determine.

(c) Conduct of hearings

Hearings authorized or required by this chapter shall be conducted by the Secretary of Health and Human Services or such officer or employee as he may designate for the purpose.

(d) Effectiveness of definitions and standards of identity

The definitions and standards of identity promulgated in accordance with the provisions of this chapter shall be effective for the purposes of the enforcement of this chapter, notwithstanding such definitions and standards as may be contained in other laws of the United States and regulations promulgated thereunder.

(e) Procedure for establishment

(1) Any action for the issuance, amendment, or repeal of any regulation under section 343(j), 344(a), 346, 351(b), or 352(d) or (h) of this title, and any action for the amendment or repeal of any definition and standard of identity under section 341 of this title for any dairy product (including products regulated under parts 131, 133 and 135 of title 21, Code of Federal Regulations) shall be begun by a proposal made (A) by the Secretary on his own initiative, or (B) by petition of any interested person, showing reasonable works grounds therefor, filed with the Secretary. The Secretary shall publish such proposal and shall afford all interested persons an opportunity to present their views thereon, orally or in writing. As soon as practicable thereafter, the Secretary shall by order act upon such proposal and shall make such order public. Except as provided in paragraph (2) of this subsection, the order shall become

(A) promulgate a regulation
(B) publish it, allow people to read & make comment

effective at such time as may be specified therein, but not prior to the day following the last day on which objections may be filed under such paragraph.

(2) On or before the thirtieth day after the date on which an order entered under paragraph (1) of this subsection is made public, any person who will be adversely affected by such order if placed in effect may file objections thereto with the Secretary, specifying with particularity the provisions of the order deemed objectionable, stating the grounds therefor, and requesting a public hearing upon such objections. Until final action upon such objections is taken by the Secretary under paragraph (3) of this subsection, the filing of such objections shall operate to stay the effectiveness of those provisions of the order to which the objections are made. As soon as practicable after the time for filing objections has expired the Secretary shall publish a notice in the Federal Register specifying those parts of the order which have been stayed by the filing of objections and, if no objections have been filed, stating that fact.

(3) As soon as practicable after such request for a public hearing, the Secretary, after due notice, shall hold such a public hearing for the purpose of receiving evidence relevant and material to the issues raised by such objections. At the hearing, any interested person may be heard in person or by representative. As soon as practicable after completion of the hearing, the Secretary shall by order act upon such objections and make such order public. Such order shall be based only on substantial evidence of record at such hearing and shall set forth, as part of the order, detailed findings of fact on which the order is based. The Secretary shall specify in the order the date on which it shall take effect, except that it shall not be made to take effect prior to the ninetieth day after its publication unless the Secretary finds that emergency conditions exist necessitating an earlier effective date, in which event the Secretary shall specify in the order his findings as to such conditions.

(f) Review of order

(1) In a case of actual controversy as to the validity of any order under subsection (e) of this section, any person who will be adversely affected by such order if placed in effect may at any time prior to the ninetieth day after such order is issued file a petition with the United States court of appeals for the circuit wherein such person resides or has his principal place of business, for a judicial review of such order. A copy of the petition shall be forthwith transmitted by the clerk of the court to the Secretary or other officer designated by him for that purpose. The Secretary thereupon shall file in the court the record of the proceedings on which the Secretary based his order, as provided in section 2112 of Title 28.

(2) If the petitioner applies to the court for leave to adduce additional evidence, and shows to the satisfaction of the court that such addition-

al evidence is material and that there were reasonable grounds for the failure to adduce such evidence in the proceeding before the Secretary, the court may order such additional evidence (and evidence in rebuttal thereof) to be taken before the Secretary, and to be adduced upon the hearing, in such manner and upon such terms and conditions as to the court may seem proper. The Secretary may modify his findings as to the facts, or make new findings, by reason of the additional evidence so taken, and he shall file such modified or new findings, and his recommendation, if any, for the modification or setting aside of his original order, with the return of such additional evidence.

(3) Upon the filing of the petition referred to in paragraph (1) of this subsection, the court shall have jurisdiction to affirm the order, or to set it aside in whole or in part, temporarily or permanently. If the order of the Secretary refuses to issue, amend, or repeal a regulation and such order is not in accordance with law the court shall by its judgment order the Secretary to take action, with respect to such regulation, in accordance with law. The findings of the Secretary as to the facts, if supported by substantial evidence, shall be conclusive.

(4) The judgment of the court affirming or setting aside, in whole or in part, any such order of the Secretary shall be final, subject to review by the Supreme Court of the United States upon certiorari or certification as provided in section 1254 of Title 28.

(5) Any action instituted under this subsection shall survive notwithstanding any change in the person occupying the office of Secretary or any vacancy in such office.

(6) The remedies provided for in this subsection shall be in addition to and not in substitution for any other remedies provided by law.

(g) Copies of records of hearings

A certified copy of the transcript of the record and proceedings under subsection (e) of this section shall be furnished by the Secretary to any interested party at his request, and payment of the costs thereof, and shall be admissible in any criminal, libel for condemnation, exclusion of imports, or other proceeding arising under or in respect to this chapter, irrespective of whether proceedings with respect to the order have previously been instituted or become final under subsection (f) of this section.

§ 372. Examinations and investigations

(a) Authority to conduct

The Secretary is authorized to conduct examinations and investigations for the purposes of this chapter through officers and employees of the Department or through any health, food, or drug officer or employee of any State, Territory, or political subdivision thereof, duly commissioned by the Secretary as an officer of the Department. In the case of food packed in the Commonwealth of Puerto Rico or a Territory the Secretary shall attempt to make inspection of such food at the first point of entry within the United States when, in his opinion and with due regard to the enforcement of all the provisions of this chapter, the facilities at his disposal will permit of such inspection. For the purposes of this subsection the term "United States" means the States and the District of Columbia.

(b) Availability to owner of part of analysis samples

Where a sample of a food, drug, or cosmetic is collected for analysis under this chapter the Secretary shall, upon request, provide a part of such official sample for examination or analysis by any person named on the label of the article, or the owner thereof, or his attorney or agent; except that the Secretary is authorized, by regulations, to make such reasonable exceptions from, and impose such reasonable terms and conditions relating to, the operation of this subsection as he finds necessary for the proper administration of the provisions of this chapter.

(c) Records of other departments and agencies

For purposes of enforcement of this chapter, records of any department or independent establishment in the executive branch of the Government shall be open to inspection by any official of the Department duly authorized by the Secretary to make such inspection.

(d) Information on patents for drugs

The Secretary is authorized and directed, upon request from the Commissioner of Patents, to furnish full and complete information with respect to such questions relating to drugs as the Commissioner may submit concerning any patent application. The Secretary is further authorized, upon receipt of any such request, to conduct or cause to be conducted, such research as may be required.

(e) Powers of enforcement personnel

Any officer or employee of the Department designated by the Secretary to conduct examinations, investigations, or inspections under this chapter relating to counterfeit drugs may, when so authorized by the Secretary—

(1) carry firearms;

(2) execute and serve search warrants and arrest warrants;

(3) execute seizure by process issued pursuant to libel under section 334 of this title;

(4) make arrests without warrant for offenses under this chapter with respect to such drugs if the offense is committed in his presence or, in the case of a felony, if he has probable cause to believe that the person so arrested has committed, or is committing, such offense; and

(5) make, prior to the institution of libel proceedings under section 334(a)(2) of this title, seizures of drugs or containers or of equipment,

punches, dies, plates, stones, labeling, or other things, if they are, or he has reasonable grounds to believe that they are, subject to seizure and condemnation under such section 334(a)(2). In the event of seizure pursuant to this paragraph (5), libel proceedings under section 334(a)(2) of this title shall be instituted promptly and the property seized be placed under the jurisdiction of the court.

§ 372a. Transferred

§ 373. Records of interstate shipment

For the purpose of enforcing the provisions of this chapter, carriers engaged in interstate commerce, and persons receiving food, drugs, devices, or cosmetics in interstate commerce or holding such articles so received, shall, upon the request of an officer or employee duly designated by the Secretary, permit such officer or employee, at reasonable times, to have access to and to copy all records showing the movement in interstate commerce of any food, drug, device, or cosmetic, or the holding thereof during or after such movement, and the quantity, shipper, and consignee thereof; and it shall be unlawful for any such carrier or person to fail to permit such access to and copying of any such record so requested when such request is accompanied by a statement in writing specifying the nature or kind of food, drug, device, or cosmetic to which such request relates, except that evidence obtained under this section, or any evidence which is directly or indirectly derived from such evidence, shall not be used in a criminal prosecution of the person from whom obtained, and except that carriers shall not be subject to the other provisions of this chapter by reason of their receipt, carriage, holding, or delivery of food, drugs, devices, or cosmetics in the usual course of business as carriers.

§ 374. Inspection

(a) Right of agents to enter; scope of inspection; notice; promptness; exclusions

(1) For purposes of enforcement of this chapter, officers or employees duly designated by the Secretary, upon presenting appropriate credentials and a written notice to the owner, operator, or agent in charge, are authorized (A) to enter, at reasonable times, any factory, warehouse, or establishment in which food, drugs, devices, or cosmetics are manufactured, processed, packed, or held, for introduction into interstate commerce or after such introduction, or to enter any vehicle being used to transport or hold such food, drugs, devices, or cosmetics in interstate commerce; and (B) to inspect, at reasonable times and within reasonable limits and in a reasonable manner, such factory, warehouse, establishment, or vehicle and all pertinent equipment, finished and unfinished materials, containers, and labeling therein. In the case of any factory, warehouse, establishment, or consulting laboratory in which prescription

drugs or restricted devices are manufactured, processed, packed, or held, the inspection shall extend to all things therein (including records, files, papers, processes, controls, and facilities) bearing on whether prescription drugs or restricted devices which are adulterated or misbranded within the meaning of this chapter, or which may not be manufactured, introduced into interstate commerce, or sold, or offered for sale by reason of any provision of this chapter, have been or are being manufactured, processed, packed, transported, or held in any such place, or otherwise bearing on violation of this chapter. No inspection authorized by the preceding sentence or by paragraph (3) shall extend to financial data, sales data other than shipment data, pricing data, personnel data (other than data as to qualifications of technical and professional personnel performing functions subject to this chapter), and research data (other than data relating to new drugs, antibiotic drugs, and devices and subject to reporting and inspection under regulations lawfully issued pursuant to section 355(i) or (k), section 357(d) or (g), section 360i, or 360j(g) of this title, and data relating to other drugs or devices which in the case of a new drug would be subject to reporting or inspection under lawful regulations issued pursuant to section 355(j) of this title). A separate notice shall be given for each such inspection, but a notice shall not be required for each entry made during the period covered by the inspection. Each such inspection shall be commenced and completed with reasonable promptness.

(2) The provisions of the second sentence of paragraph (1) shall not apply to—

(A) pharmacies which maintain establishments in conformance with any applicable local laws regulating the practice of pharmacy and medicine and which are regularly engaged in dispensing prescription drugs or devices, upon prescriptions of practitioners licensed to administer such drugs or devices to patients under the care of such practitioners in the course of their professional practice, and which do not, either through a subsidiary or otherwise, manufacture, prepare, propagate, compound, or process drugs or devices for sale other than in the regular course of their business of dispensing or selling drugs or devices at retail;

(B) practitioners licensed by law to prescribe or administer drugs, or prescribe or use devices, as the case may be, and who manufacture, prepare, propagate, compound, or process drugs, or manufacture or process devices, solely for use in the course of their professional practice;

(C) persons who manufacture, prepare, propagate, compound, or process drugs or manufacture or process devices, solely for use in research, teaching, or chemical analysis and not for sale;

(D) such other classes of persons as the Secretary may by regulation exempt from the application of this section upon a finding that inspection as applied to such classes of persons in accordance with this section is not necessary for the protection of the public health.

(3) An officer or employee making an inspection under paragraph (1) for purposes of enforcing the requirements of section 350a of this title applicable to infant formulas shall be permitted, at all reasonable times, to have access to and to copy and verify any records—

> (A) bearing on whether the infant formula manufactured or held in the facility inspected meets the requirements of section 350a of this title, or

> (B) required to be maintained under section 350a of this title.

(b) Written report to owner; copy to Secretary

Upon completion of any such inspection of a factory, warehouse, consulting laboratory, or other establishment, and prior to leaving the premises, the officer or employee making the inspection shall give to the owner, operator, or agent in charge a report in writing setting forth any conditions or practices observed by him which, in his judgment, indicate that any food, drug, device, or cosmetic in such establishment (1) consists in whole or in part of any filthy, putrid, or decomposed substance, or (2) has been prepared, packed, or held under insanitary conditions whereby it may have become contaminated with filth, or whereby it may have been rendered injurious to health. A copy of such report shall be sent promptly to the Secretary.

(c) Receipt for samples taken

If the officer or employee making any such inspection of a factory, warehouse, or other establishment has obtained any sample in the course of the inspection, upon completion of the inspection and prior to leaving the premises he shall give to the owner, operator, or agent in charge a receipt describing the samples obtained.

(d) Analysis of samples furnished owner

Whenever in the course of any such inspection of a factory or other establishment where food is manufactured, processed, or packed, the officer or employee making the inspection obtains a sample of any such food, and an analysis is made of such sample for the purpose of ascertaining whether such food consists in whole or in part of any filthy, putrid, or decomposed substance, or is otherwise unfit for food, a copy of the results of such analysis shall be furnished promptly to the owner, operator, or agent in charge.

(e) Accessibility of records

Every person required under section 360i or 360j(g) of this title to maintain records and every person who is in charge or custody of such records shall, upon request of an officer or employee designated by the

Secretary, permit such officer or employee at all reasonable times to have access to, and to copy and verify, such records.

§ 375.　Publicity

(a) Reports

The Secretary shall cause to be published from time to time reports summarizing all judgments, decrees, and court orders which have been rendered under this chapter, including the nature of the charge and the disposition thereof.

(b) Information regarding certain goods

The Secretary may also cause to be disseminated information regarding food, drugs, devices, or cosmetics in situations involving, in the opinion of the Secretary, imminent danger to health or gross deception of the consumer. Nothing in this section shall be construed to prohibit the Secretary from collecting, reporting, and illustrating the results of the investigations of the Department.

§ 376.　Examination of seafood on request of packer; marking food with results; fees; penalties

The Secretary, upon application of any packer of any seafood for shipment or sale within the jurisdiction of this chapter, may, at his discretion, designate inspectors to examine and inspect such food and the production, packing, and labeling thereof. If on such examination and inspection compliance is found with the provisions of this chapter and regulations promulgated thereunder, the applicant shall be authorized or required to mark the food as provided by regulation to show such compliance. Services under this section shall be rendered only upon payment by the applicant of fees fixed by regulation in such amounts as may be necessary to provide, equip, and maintain an adequate and efficient inspection service. Receipts from such fees shall be covered into the Treasury and shall be available to the Secretary for expenditures incurred in carrying out the purposes of this section, including expenditures for salaries of additional inspectors when necessary to supplement the number of inspectors for whose salaries Congress has appropriated. The Secretary is authorized to promulgate regulations governing the sanitary and other conditions under which the service herein provided shall be granted and maintained, and for otherwise carrying out the purposes of this section. Any person who forges, counterfeits, simulates, or falsely represents, or without proper authority uses any mark, stamp, tag, label, or other identification devices authorized or required by the provisions of this section or regulations thereunder, shall be guilty of a misdemeanor, and shall on conviction thereof be subject to imprisonment for not more than one year or a fine of not less than $1,000 nor more than $5,000, or both such imprisonment and fine.

§ 377. Revision of United States Pharmacopoeia; development of analysis and mechanical and physical tests

The Secretary, in carrying into effect the provisions of this chapter, is authorized on and after July 12, 1943, to cooperate with associations and scientific societies in the revision of the United States Pharmacopoeia and in the development of methods of analysis and mechanical and physical tests necessary to carry out the work of the Food and Drug Administration.

§ 378. Advertising of foods

(a) Determination of misbranding; notification of Federal Trade Commission by Secretary; contents

(1) Except as provided in subsection (c) of this section, before the Secretary may initiate any action under subchapter III of this chapter—

(A) with respect to any food which the Secretary determines is misbranded under section 343(a)(2) of this title because of its advertising, or

(B) with respect to a food's advertising which the Secretary determines causes the food to be so misbranded,

the Secretary shall, in accordance with paragraph (2), notify in writing the Federal Trade Commission of the action the Secretary proposes to take respecting such food or advertising.

(2) The notice required by paragraph (1) shall—

(A) contain (i) a description of the action the Secretary proposes to take and of the advertising which the Secretary has determined causes a food to be misbranded, (ii) a statement of the reasons for the Secretary's determination that such advertising has caused such food to be misbranded, and

(B) be accompanied by the records, documents, and other written materials which the Secretary determines supports his determination that such food is misbranded because of such advertising.

(b) Action by Federal Trade Commission precluding action by Secretary; exception

(1) If the Secretary notifies the Federal Trade Commission under subsection (a) of this section of action proposed to be taken under subchapter III of this chapter with respect to a food or food advertising and the Commission notifies the Secretary in writing, within the 30–day period beginning on the date of the receipt of such notice, that—

(A) it has initiated under the Federal Trade Commission Act [15 U.S.C.A. § 41 et seq.] an investigation of such advertising to determine if it is prohibited by such Act or any order or rule under such Act,

(B) it has commenced (or intends to commence) a civil action under section 5, 13, or 19 [15 U.S.C.A. §§ 45, 53, or 57b] with respect to such advertising or the Attorney General has commenced (or intends to commence) a civil action under section 5 [15 U.S.C.A. § 45] with respect to such advertising,

(C) it has issued and served (or intends to issue and serve) a complaint under section 5(b) of such Act [15 U.S.C.A. § 45(b)]respecting such advertising, or

(D) pursuant to section 16(b) of such Act [15 U.S.C.A. § 56(b)]it has made a certification to the Attorney General respecting such advertising,

the Secretary may not, except as provided by paragraph (2), initiate the action described in the Secretary's notice to the Federal Trade Commission.

(2) If, before the expiration of the 60-day period beginning on the date the Secretary receives a notice described in paragraph (1) from the Federal Trade Commission in response to a notice of the Secretary under subsection (a) of this section—

(A) the Commission or the Attorney General does not commence a civil action described in subparagraph (B) of paragraph (1) of this subsection respecting the advertising described in the Secretary's notice,

(B) the Commission does not issue and serve a complaint described in subparagraph (C) of such paragraph respecting such advertising, or

(C) the Commission does not (as described in subparagraph (D) of such paragraph) make a certification to the Attorney General respecting such advertising, or, if the Commission does make such a certification to the Attorney General respecting such advertising, the Attorney General, before the expiration of such period, does not cause appropriate criminal proceedings to be brought against such advertising,

the Secretary may, after the expiration of such period, initiate the action described in the notice to the Commission pursuant to subsection (a) of this section. The Commission shall promptly notify the Secretary of the commencement by the Commission of such a civil action, the issuance and service by it of such a complaint, or the causing by the Attorney General of criminal proceedings to be brought against such advertising.

(c) Secretary's determination of imminent hazard to health as suspending applicability of provisions

The requirements of subsections (a) and (b) of this section do not apply with respect to action under subchapter III of this chapter with respect to any food or food advertising if the Secretary determines that such action is required to eliminate an imminent hazard to health.

(d) Coordination of action by Secretary with Federal Trade Commission

For the purpose of avoiding unnecessary duplication, the Secretary shall coordinate any action taken under subchapter III of this chapter because of advertising which the Secretary determines causes a food to be misbranded with any action of the Federal Trade Commission under the Federal Trade Commission Act [15 U.S.C.A. § 41 et seq.] with respect to such advertising.

§ 379. Confidential information

The Secretary may provide any information which is exempt from disclosure pursuant to subsection (a) of section 552 of Title 5 by reason of subsection (b)(4) of such section to a person other than an officer or employee of the Department if the Secretary determines such other person requires the information in connection with an activity which is undertaken under contract with the Secretary, which relates to the administration of this chapter, and with respect to which the Secretary (or an officer or employee of the Department) is not prohibited from using such information. The Secretary shall require as a condition to the provision of information under this section that the person receiving it take such security precautions respecting the information as the Secretary may by regulation prescribe.

§ 379a. Presumption of existence of jurisdiction

In any action to enforce the requirements of this chapter respecting a device the connection with interstate commerce required for jurisdiction in such action shall be presumed to exist.

§ 379b. Consolidated administrative and laboratory facility

(a) Authority

The Secretary, in consultation with the Administrator of the General Services Administration, shall enter into contracts for the design, construction, and operation of a consolidated Food and Drug Administration administrative and laboratory facility.

(b) Awarding of contract

The Secretary shall solicit contract proposals under subsection (a) of this section from interested parties. In awarding contracts under such subsection, the Secretary shall review such proposals and give priority to those alternatives that are the most cost effective for the Federal Government and that allow for the use of donated land, federally owned property, or lease-purchase arrangements. A contract under this subsection shall not be entered into unless such contract results in a net cost savings to the Federal Government over the duration of the contract, as compared to the Government purchase price including borrowing by the Secretary of the Treasury.

(c) Donations

In carrying out this section, the Secretary shall have the power, in connection with real property, buildings, and facilities, to accept on behalf of the Food and Drug Administration gifts or donations of services or property, real or personal, as the Secretary determines to be necessary.

(d) Authorization of appropriations

There are authorized to be appropriated to carry out this section $100,000,000 for fiscal year 1991, and such sums as may be necessary for each of the subsequent fiscal years, to remain available until expended.

§ 379c. Transferred

§ 379d. Automation of Food and Drug Administration

(a) In general

The Secretary, acting through the Commissioner of Food and Drugs, shall automate appropriate activities of the Food and Drug Administration to ensure timely review of activities regulated under this chapter.

(b) Authorization of appropriations

There are authorized to be appropriated each fiscal year such sums as are necessary to carry out this section.

§ 379e. Listing and certification of color additives for foods, drugs, devices, and cosmetics

(a) Unsafe color additives

A color additive shall, with respect to any particular use (for which it is being used or intended to be used or is represented as suitable) in or on food or drugs or devices or cosmetics, be deemed unsafe for the purposes of the application of section 342(c), 351(a)(4), or 361(e) of this title, as the case may be, unless—

(1)(A) there is in effect, and such additive and such use are in conformity with, a regulation issued under subsection (b) of this section listing such additive for such use, including any provision of such regulation prescribing the conditions under which such additive may be safely used, and (B) such additive either (i) is from a batch certified, in accordance with regulations issued pursuant to subsection (c) of this section, for such use, or (ii) has, with respect to such use, been exempted by the Secretary from the requirement of certification; or

(2) such additive and such use thereof conform to the terms of an exemption which is in effect pursuant to subsection (f) of this section.

While there are in effect regulations under subsections (b) and (c) of this section relating to a color additive or an exemption pursuant to subsection (f) of this section with respect to such additive, an article shall not, by reason of bearing or containing such additive in all respects in accordance with such regulations or such exemption, be considered adulterated within the meaning of clause (1) of section 342(a) of this title if such article is a food, or within the meaning of section 361(a) of this title if such article is a cosmetic other than a hair dye (as defined in the last sentence of section 361(a) of this title). A color additive for use in or on a device shall be subject to this section only if the color additive comes in direct contact with the body of man or other animals for a significant period of time. The Secretary may by regulation designate the uses of color additives in or on devices which are subject to this section.

(b) Listing of colors; regulations; issuance, amendment or repeal; referral to advisory committee; report and recommendations; appointment and compensation of advisory committee

(1) The Secretary shall, by regulation, provide for separately listing color additives for use in or on food, color additives for use in or on drugs, or devices, and color additives for use in or on cosmetics, if and to the extent that such additives are suitable and safe for any such use when employed in accordance with such regulations.

(2)(A) Such regulations may list any color additive for use generally in or on food, or in or on drugs or devices, or in or on cosmetics, if the Secretary finds that such additive is suitable and may safely be employed for such general use.

(B) If the data before the Secretary do not establish that the additive satisfies the requirements for listing such additive on the applicable list pursuant to subparagraph (A) of this paragraph, or if the proposal is for listing such additive for a more limited use or uses, such regulations may list such additive only for any more limited use or uses for which it is suitable and may safely be employed.

(3) Such regulations shall, to the extent deemed necessary by the Secretary to assure the safety of the use or uses for which a particular color additive is listed, prescribe the conditions under which such additive may be safely employed for such use or uses (including, but not limited to, specifications, hereafter in this section referred to as tolerance limitations, as to the maximum quantity or quantities which may be used or permitted to remain in or on the article or articles in or on which it is used; specifications as to the manner in which such additive may be added to or used in or on such article or articles; and directions or other labeling or packaging requirements for such additive).

(4) The Secretary shall not list a color additive under this section for a proposed use unless the data before him establish that such use, under the conditions of use specified in the regulations, will be safe:

Provided, however, That a color additive shall be deemed to be suitable and safe for the purpose of listing under this subsection for use generally in or on food, while there is in effect a published finding of the Secretary declaring such substance exempt from the term "food additive" because of its being generally recognized by qualified experts as safe for its intended use, as provided in section 321(s) of this title.

(5)(A) In determining, for the purposes of this section, whether a proposed use of a color additive is safe, the Secretary shall consider, among other relevant factors—

(i) the probable consumption of, or other relevant exposure from, the additive and of any substance formed in or on food, drugs or devices, or cosmetics because of the use of the additive;

(ii) the cumulative effect, if any, of such additive in the diet of man or animals, taking into account the same or any chemically or pharmacologically related substance or substances in such diet,

(iii) safety factors which, in the opinion of experts qualified by scientific training and experience to evaluate the safety of color additives for the use or uses for which the additive is proposed to be listed, are generally recognized as appropriate for the use of animal experimentation data, and

(iv) the availability of any needed practicable methods of analysis for determining the identity and quantity of (I) the pure dye and all intermediates and other impurities contained in such color additive, (II) such additive in or on any article of food, drug or device, or cosmetic, and (III) any substance formed in or on such article because of the use of such additive.

(B) A color additive (i) shall be deemed unsafe, and shall not be listed, for any use which will or may result in ingestion of all or part of such additive, if the additive is found by the Secretary to induce cancer when ingested by man or animal, or if it is found by the Secretary, after tests which are appropriate for the evaluation of the safety of additives for use in food, to induce cancer in man or animal, and (ii) shall be deemed unsafe, and shall not be listed, for any use which will not result in ingestion of any part of such additive, if, after tests which are appropriate for the evaluation of the safety of additives for such use, or after other relevant exposure of man or animal to such additive, it is found by the Secretary to induce cancer in man or animal: Provided, That clause (i) of this subparagraph (B) shall not apply with respect to the use of a color additive as an ingredient of feed for animals which are raised for food production, if the Secretary finds that, under the conditions of use and feeding specified in proposed labeling and reasonably certain to be followed in practice, such additive will not adversely affect the animals for which such feed is intended, and that no residue of the additive will be found (by methods of examination prescribed or approved by the Secretary by regulations, which regulations shall not be subject to subsection (d) of this section) in any edible portion of such animals after slaughter or in any food yielded by or derived from the living animal.

(C)(i) In any proceeding for the issuance, amendment, or repeal of a regulation listing a color additive, whether commenced by a proposal of the Secretary on his own initiative or by a proposal contained in a petition, the petitioner, or any other person who will be adversely affected by such proposal or by the Secretary's order issued in accordance with paragraph (1) of section 371(e) of this title if placed in effect, may request, within the time specified in this subparagraph, that the petition or order thereon, or the Secretary's proposal, be referred to an advisory committee for a report and recommendations with respect to any matter arising under subparagraph (B) of this paragraph, which is involved in such proposal or order and which requires the exercise of scientific judgment. Upon such request, or if the Secretary within such time deems such a referral necessary, the Secretary shall forthwith appoint an advisory committee under subparagraph (D) of this paragraph and shall refer to it, together with all the data before him, such matter arising under subparagraph (B) for study thereof and for a report and recommendations on such matter. A person who has filed a petition or who has requested the referral of a matter to an advisory committee pursuant to this subparagraph (C), as well as representatives of the Department, shall have the right to consult with such advisory committee in connection with the matter referred to it. The request for referral under this subparagraph, or the Secretary's referral on his own initiative, may be made at any time before, or within thirty days after, publication of an order of the Secretary acting upon the petition or proposal.

(ii) Within sixty days after the date of such referral, or within an additional thirty days if the committee deems such additional time necessary, the committee shall, after independent study of the data furnished to it by the Secretary and other data before it, certify to the Secretary a report and recommendations, together with all underlying data and a statement of the reasons or basis for the recommendations. A copy of the foregoing shall be promptly supplied by the Secretary to any person who has filed a petition, or who has requested such referral to the advisory committee. Within thirty days after such certification, and after giving due consideration to all data then before him, including such report, recommendations, underlying data, and statement, and to any prior order issued by him in connection with such matter, the Secretary shall by order confirm or modify any order theretofore issued or, if no such prior order has been issued, shall by order act upon the petition or other proposal.

(iii) Where—

(I) by reason of subparagraph (B) of this paragraph, the Secretary has initiated a proposal to remove from listing a color additive previously listed pursuant to this section; and

(II) a request has been made for referral of such proposal to an advisory committee;

the Secretary may not act by order on such proposal until the advisory committee has made a report and recommendations to him under clause (ii) of this subparagraph and he has considered such recommendations, unless the Secretary finds that emergency conditions exist necessitating the issuance of an order notwithstanding this clause.

(D) The advisory committee referred to in subparagraph (C) of this paragraph shall be composed of experts selected by the National Academy of Sciences, qualified in the subject matter referred to the committee and of adequately diversified professional background, except that in the event of the inability or refusal of the National Academy of Sciences to act, the Secretary shall select the members of the committee. The size of the committee shall be determined by the Secretary. Members of any advisory committee established under this chapter, while attending conferences or meetings of their committees or otherwise serving at the request of the Secretary, shall be entitled to receive compensation at rates to be fixed by the Secretary but at rates not exceeding the daily equivalent of the rate specified at the time of such service for grade GS–18 of the General Schedule, including travel time, and while away from their homes or regular places of business they may be allowed travel expenses, including per diem in lieu of subsistence, as authorized by section 5703 of Title 5 for persons in the Government service employed intermittently. The members shall not be subject to any other provisions of law regarding the appointment and compensation of employees of the United States. The Secretary shall furnish the committee with adequate clerical and other assistance, and shall by rules and regulations prescribe the procedure to be followed by the committee.

(6) The Secretary shall not list a color additive under this subsection for a proposed use if the data before him show that such proposed use would promote deception of the consumer in violation of this chapter or would otherwise result in misbranding or adulteration within the meaning of this chapter.

(7) If, in the judgment of the Secretary, a tolerance limitation is required in order to assure that a proposed use of a color additive will be safe, the Secretary—

(A) shall not list the additive for such use if he finds that the data before him do not establish that such additive, if used within a safe tolerance limitation, would achieve the intended physical or other technical effect; and

(B) shall not fix such tolerance limitation at a level higher than he finds to be reasonably required to accomplish the intended physical or other technical effect.

(8) If, having regard to the aggregate quantity of color additive likely to be consumed in the diet or to be applied to the human body, the Secretary finds that the data before him fail to show that it would be safe and otherwise permissible to list a color additive (or pharmacologically related color additives) for all the uses proposed therefor and at the levels of concentration proposed, the Secretary shall, in determining for which use or uses such additive (or such related additives) shall be or remain listed, or how the aggregate allowable safe tolerance for such additive or additives shall be allocated by him among the uses under consideration, take into account, among other relevant factors (and subject to the paramount criterion of safety), (A) the relative marketability of the articles involved as affected by the proposed uses of the color additive (or of such related additives) in or on such articles, and the relative dependence of the industries concerned on such uses; (B) the relative aggregate amounts of such color additive which he estimates would be consumed in the diet or applied to the human body by reason of the various uses and levels of concentration proposed; and (C) the availability, if any, of other color additives suitable and safe for one or more of the uses proposed.

(c) Certification of colors

The Secretary shall further, by regulation, provide (1) for the certification, with safe diluents or without diluents, of batches of color additives listed pursuant to subsection (b) of this section and conforming to the requirements for such additives established by regulations under such subsection and this subsection, and (2) for exemption from the requirement of certification in the case of any such additive, or any listing or use thereof, for which he finds such requirement not to be necessary in the interest of the protection of the public health: Provided, That, with respect to any use in or on food for which a listed color additive is deemed to be safe by reason of the proviso to paragraph (4) of subsection (b), the requirement of certification shall be deemed not to be necessary in the interest of public health protection.

(d) Procedure for issuance, amendment, or repeal of regulations

The provisions of section 371(e), (f), and (g) of this title shall, subject to the provisions of subparagraph (C) of subsection (b)(5) of this section, apply to and in all respects govern proceedings for the issuance, amendment, or repeal of regulations under subsection (b) or (c) of this section (including judicial review of the Secretary's action in such proceedings) and the admissibility of transcripts of the record of such proceedings in other proceedings, except that—

(1) if the proceeding is commenced by the filing of a petition, notice of the proposal made by the petition shall be published in general terms

by the Secretary within thirty days after such filing, and the Secretary's order (required by paragraph (1) of section 371(e) of this title) acting upon such proposal shall, in the absence of prior referral (or request for referral) to an advisory committee, be issued within ninety days after the date of such filing, except that the Secretary may (prior to such ninetieth day), by written notice to the petitioner, extend such ninety-day period to such time (not more than one hundred and eighty days after the date of filing of the petition) as the Secretary deems necessary to enable him to study and investigate the petition;

(2) any report, recommendations, underlying data, and reasons certified to the Secretary by an advisory committee appointed pursuant to subparagraph (D) of subsection (b)(5) of this section, shall be made a part of the record of any hearing if relevant and material, subject to the provisions of section 1006(c) of Title 5. The advisory committee shall designate a member to appear and testify at any such hearing with respect to the report and recommendations of such committee upon request of the Secretary, the petitioner, or the officer conducting the hearing, but this shall not preclude any other member of the advisory committee from appearing and testifying at such hearing;

(3) the Secretary's order after public hearing (acting upon objections filed to an order made prior to hearing) shall be subject to the requirements of section 348(f)(2) of this title; and

(4) the scope of judicial review of such order shall be in accordance with the fourth sentence of paragraph (2), and with the provisions of paragraph (3), of section 348(g) of this title.

(e) Fees

The admitting to listing and certification of color additives, in accordance with regulations prescribed under this chapter, shall be performed only upon payment of such fees, which shall be specified in such regulations, as may be necessary to provide, maintain, and equip an adequate service for such purposes.

(f) Exemptions

The Secretary shall by regulations (issued without regard to subsection (d) of this section) provide for exempting from the requirements of this section any color additive or any specific type of use thereof, and any article of food, drug or device, or cosmetic bearing or containing such additive, intended solely for investigational use by qualified experts when in his opinion such exemption is consistent with the public health.

§ 379f. Recovery and retention of fees for freedom of information requests

(a) In general

The Secretary, acting through the Commissioner of Food and Drugs may—

(1) set and charge fees, in accordance with section 552(a)(4)(A) of Title 5, to recover all reasonable costs incurred in processing requests made under section 552 of Title 5, for records obtained or created under this chapter or any other Federal law for which responsibility for administration has been delegated to the Commissioner by the Secretary;

(2) retain all fees charged for such requests; and

(3) establish an accounting system and procedures to control receipts and expenditures of fees received under this section.

(b) Use of fees

The Secretary and the Commissioner of Food and Drugs shall not use fees received under this section for any purpose other than funding the processing of requests described in subsection (a)(1) of this section. Such fees shall not be used to reduce the amount of funds made to carry out other provisions of this chapter.

(c) Waiver of fees

Nothing in this section shall supersede the right of a requester to obtain a waiver of fees pursuant to section 552(a)(4)(A) of Title 5.

§ 379g. Definitions

For purposes of this part:

(1) The term "human drug application" means an application for—

(A) approval of a new drug submitted under section 355(b)(1) of this title,

(B) approval of a new drug submitted under section 355(b)(2) of this title after September 30, 1992, which requests approval of—

(i) a molecular entity which is an active ingredient (including any salt or ester of an active ingredient), or

(ii) an indication for a use,

that had not been approved under an application submitted under section 355(b) of this title,

(C) initial certification or initial approval of an antibiotic drug under section 357 of this title, or

(D) licensure of a biological product under section 262 of Title 42.

Such term does not include a supplement to such an application, does not include an application with respect to whole blood or a blood component for transfusion, does not include an application with respect to a bovine blood product for topical application licensed before September 1, 1992, an allergenic extract product, or an in vitro diagnostic biologic product licensed under section 262 of Title 42, and does not include an application with respect to a large volume parenteral drug product approved before September 1, 1992.

(2) The term "supplement" means a request to the Secretary to approve a change in a human drug application which has been approved.

(3) The term "prescription drug product" means a specific strength or potency of a drug in final dosage form—

    (A) for which a human drug application has been approved, and

    (B) which may be dispensed only under prescription pursuant to section 353(b) of this title.

Such term does not include whole blood or a blood component for transfusion, does not include a bovine blood product for topical application licensed before September 1, 1992, an allergenic extract product, or an in vitro diagnostic biologic product licensed under section 262 of Title 42, and does not include a large volume parenteral drug product approved before September 1, 1992.

(4) The term "final dosage form" means, with respect to a prescription drug product, a finished dosage form which is approved for administration to a patient without further manufacturing.

(5) The term "prescription drug establishment" means a foreign or domestic place of business which is—

    (A) at one general physical location consisting of one or more buildings all of which are within 5 miles of each other, at which one or more prescription drug products are manufactured in final dosage form, and

    (B) under the management of a person that is listed as the applicant in a human drug application for a prescription drug product with respect to at least one such product.

For purposes of this paragraph, the term "manufactured" does not include packaging.

(6) The term "process for the review of human drug applications" means the following activities of the Secretary with respect to the review of human drug applications and supplements:

    (A) The activities necessary for the review of human drug applications and supplements.

    (B) The issuance of action letters which approve human drug applications or which set forth in detail the specific deficiencies in such applications and, where appropriate, the actions necessary to place such applications in condition for approval.

    (C) The inspection of prescription drug establishments and other facilities undertaken as part of the Secretary's review of pending human drug applications and supplements.

(D) Activities necessary for the review of applications for licensure of establishments subject to section 262 of Title 42 and for the release of lots of biologics under such section.

(E) Monitoring of research conducted in connection with the review of human drug applications.

(7) The term "costs of resources allocated for the process for the review of human drug applications" means the expenses incurred in connection with the process for the review of human drug applications for—

(A) officers and employees of the Food and Drug Administration, employees under contract with the Food and Drug Administration who work in facilities owned or leased for the Food and Drug Administration, advisory committees, and costs related to such officers, employees, and committees,

(B) management of information, and the acquisition, maintenance, and repair of computer resources,

(C) leasing, maintenance, renovation, and repair of facilities and acquisition, maintenance, and repair of fixtures, furniture, scientific equipment, and other necessary materials and supplies, and

(D) collecting fees under section 379h of this title and accounting for resources allocated for the review of human drug applications and supplements.

(8) The term "adjustment factor" applicable to a fiscal year is the lower of—

(A) the Consumer Price Index for all urban consumers (all items; United States city average) for August of the preceding fiscal year divided by such Index for August 1992, or

(B) the total of discretionary budget authority provided for programs in the domestic category for the immediately preceding fiscal year (as reported in the Office of Management and Budget sequestration preview report, if available, required under section 254(d) of the Balanced Budget and Emergency Deficit Control Act of 1985 [2 U.S.C.A. § 904(d)]) divided by such budget authority for fiscal year 1992 (as reported in the Office of Management and Budget final sequestration report submitted after the end of the 102d Congress, 2d Session).

The terms "budget authority" and "category" in subparagraph (B) are as defined in the Balanced Budget and Emergency Deficit Control Act of 1985, as in effect as of September 1, 1992.[13]

13. Pub.L. 102–571, Title I, § 105, Oct. 29, 1992, 106 Stat. 4498, provided that: "The amendments made by section 103 [enacting this subpart] shall not be in effect after October 1, 1997 and section 104 [set

§ 379h. Authority to assess and use drug fees

(a) Types of fees

Beginning in fiscal year 1993, the Secretary shall assess and collect fees in accordance with this section as follows:

(1) Human drug application and supplement fee

(A) In general

Each person that submits, on or after September 1, 1992, a human drug application or a supplement shall be subject to a fee as follows:

(i) A fee established in subsection (b) of this section for a human drug application for which clinical data (other than bioavailability or bioequivalence studies) with respect to safety or effectiveness are required for approval.

(ii) A fee established in subsection (b) of this section for a human drug application for which clinical data with respect to safety or effectiveness are not required or a supplement for which clinical data (other than bioavailability or bioequivalence studies) with respect to safety or effectiveness are required.

(B) Payment schedule

(i) First payment

50 percent of the fee required by subparagraph (A) shall be due upon submission of the application or supplement.

(ii) Final payment

The remaining 50 percent of the fee required by subparagraph (A) shall be due upon—

(I) the expiration of 30 days from the date the Secretary sends to the applicant a letter designated by the Secretary as an action letter described in section 379g(6)(B) of this title, or

(II) the withdrawal of the application or supplement after it is filed unless the Secretary waives the fee or a portion of the fee because no substantial work was performed on such application or supplement after it was filed.

The designation under subclause (I) or the waiver under subclause (II) shall be solely in the discretion of the Secretary and shall not be reviewable.

(C) Exception for previously filed application or supplement

If a human drug application or supplement was submitted by a person that paid the fee for such application or supplement, was

out as a note under this section] shall not be in effect after 120 days after such date.''

accepted for filing, and was not approved or was withdrawn (without a waiver), the submission of a human drug application or a supplement for the same product by the same person (or the person's licensee, assignee, or successor) shall not be subject to a fee under subparagraph (A).

(D) Refund of fee if application not accepted for filing

The Secretary shall refund 50 percent of the fee paid under subparagraph (B)(i) for any application or supplement which is not accepted for filing.

(2) Prescription drug establishment fee

Each person that—

(A) owns a prescription drug establishment, at which is manufactured at least 1 prescription drug product which is not the, or not the same as a, product approved under an application filed under section 355(b)(2) or 355(j) of this title, and

(B) after September 1, 1992, had pending before the Secretary a human drug application or supplement,

shall be subject to the annual fee established in subsection (b) of this section for each such establishment, payable on or before January 31 of each year.

(3) Prescription drug product fee

(A) In general

Except as provided in subparagraph (B), each person—

(i) who is named as the applicant in a human drug application for a prescription drug product which is listed under section 360 of this title, and

(ii) who, after September 1, 1992, had pending before the Secretary a human drug application or supplement,

shall pay for each such prescription drug product the annual fee established in subsection (b) of this section. Such fee shall be payable at the time of the first such listing of such product in each calendar year. Such fee shall be paid only once each year for each listed prescription drug product irrespective of the number of times such product is listed under section 360 of this title.

(B) Exception

The listing of a prescription drug product under section 360 of this title shall not require the person who listed such product to pay the fee prescribed by subparagraph (A) if such product is the same product as a product approved under an application filed under section 355(b)(2) or 355(j) of this title.

(b) Fee amounts

(1) Schedule

Except as provided in paragraph (2) and subsections (c), (d), (f), and (g) of this section, the fees required under subsection (a) of this section shall be paid in accordance with the following schedule:

	Fiscal Year 1993	Fiscal Year 1994	Fiscal Year 1995	Fiscal Year 1996	Fiscal Year 1997
Drug application fee:					
Subsection (a)(1)(A)(i) fee	$ 100,000	$ 150,000	$ 208,000	$ 217,000	$ 233,000
Subsection (a)(1)(A)(ii) fee	$ 50,000	$ 75,000	$ 104,000	$ 108,000	$ 116,000
Fee revenue	$12,000,000	$18,000,000	$25,000,000	$26,000,000	$28,000,000
Annual establishment fee:					
Fee per establishment	$ 60,000	$ 88,000	$ 126,000	$ 131,000	$ 138,000
Fee revenue	$12,000,000	$18,000,000	$25,000,000	$26,000,000	$28,000,000
Annual product fee:					
Fee per product	$ 6,000	$ 9,000	$ 12,500	$ 13,000	$ 14,000
Fee revenue	$12,000,000	$18,000,000	$25,000,000	$26,000,000	$28,000,000
Total fee revenues	$36,000,000	$54,000,000	$75,000,000	$78,000,000	$84,000,000

(2) Small business exception

Any business which has fewer than 500 employees, including employees of affiliates, and which does not have a prescription drug product introduced or delivered for introduction into interstate commerce shall pay one-half the amount of the fee for human drug applications it submits and shall pay the entire amount of the fee for supplements it submits. Such a business shall not be required to pay any portion of any fee required under subsection (a)(1)(A) of this section until 1 year after the date of the submission of the application involved. For purposes of this paragraph, one business is an affiliate of another business when, directly or indirectly, one business controls, or has the power to control, the other business or a third party controls, or has the power to control, both businesses.

(c) Increases and adjustments

(1) Revenue increase

The total fee revenues established by the schedule in subsection (b)(1) of this section shall be increased by the Secretary by notice, published in the Federal Register, for a fiscal year to reflect the greater of—

> (A) the total percentage increase that occurred during the preceding fiscal year in the Consumer Price Index for all urban consumers (all items; U.S. city average), or

> (B) the total percentage increase for such fiscal year in basic pay under the General Schedule in accordance with section 5332 of Title 5, as adjusted by any locality-based comparability payment pursuant to section 5304 of such title for Federal employees stationed in the District of Columbia.

(2) Annual fee adjustment

Subject to the amount appropriated for a fiscal year under subsection (g) of this section, the Secretary shall, within 60 days after the end of each fiscal year beginning after October 1, 1992, adjust the fees established by the schedule in subsection (b)(1) of this section for the following fiscal year to achieve the total fee revenues, as may be increased under paragraph (1). Such fees shall be adjusted under this paragraph to maintain the proportions established in such schedule.

(3) Limit

The total amount of fees charged, as adjusted under paragraph (2), for a fiscal year may not exceed the total costs for such fiscal year for the resources allocated for the process for the review of human drug applications.

(d) Fee waiver or reduction

The Secretary shall grant a waiver from or a reduction of 1 or more fees under subsection (a) of this section where the Secretary finds that—

(1) such waiver or reduction is necessary to protect the public health,

(2) the assessment of the fee would present a significant barrier to innovation because of limited resources available to such person or other circumstances,

(3) the fees to be paid by such person will exceed the anticipated present and future costs incurred by the Secretary in conducting the process for the review of human drug applications for such person, or

(4) assessment of the fee for an application or a supplement filed under section 355(b)(1) of this title pertaining to a drug containing an active ingredient would be inequitable because an application for a product containing the same active ingredient filed by another person under section 355(b)(2) of this title could not be assessed fees under subsection (a)(1) of this section.

In making the finding in paragraph (3), the Secretary may use standard costs.

(e) Effect of failure to pay fees

A human drug application or supplement submitted by a person subject to fees under subsection (a) of this section shall be considered incomplete and shall not be accepted for filing by the Secretary until all fees owed by such person have been paid.

(f) Assessment of fees

(1) Limitation

Fees may not be assessed under subsection (a) of this section for a fiscal year beginning after fiscal year 1993 unless appropriations for salaries and expenses of the Food and Drug Administration for such fiscal year (excluding the amount of fees appropriated for such fiscal year) are equal to or greater than the amount of appropriations for the salaries and expenses of the Food and Drug Administration for the fiscal year 1992 multiplied by the adjustment factor applicable to the fiscal year involved.

(2) Authority

If the Secretary does not assess fees under subsection (a) of this section during any portion of a fiscal year because of paragraph (1) and if at a later date in such fiscal year the Secretary may assess such fees, the Secretary may assess and collect such fees, without any modification in the rate, for human drug applications and supplements, prescription drug establishments, and prescription drug products at any time in such fiscal year notwithstanding the provisions of subsection (a) of this section relating to the date fees are to be paid.

(g) Crediting and availability of fees

(1) In general

Fees collected for a fiscal year pursuant to subsection (a) of this section shall be credited to the appropriation account for salaries and expenses of the Food and Drug Administration and shall be available in accordance with appropriation Acts until expended without fiscal year limitation.

(2) Collections and appropriation acts

The fees authorized by this section—

(A) shall be collected in each fiscal year in an amount equal to the amount specified in appropriation Acts for such fiscal year, and

(B) shall only be collected and available to defray increases in the costs of the resources allocated for the process for the review of human drug applications (including increases in such costs for an additional number of full-time equivalent positions in the Department of Health and Human Services to be engaged in such process) over such costs for fiscal year 1992 multiplied by the adjustment factor.

(3) Authorization of appropriations

There are authorized to be appropriated for fees under this section—

(A) $36,000,000 for fiscal year 1993,

(B) $54,000,000 for fiscal year 1994,

(C) $75,000,000 for fiscal year 1995,

(D) $78,000,000 for fiscal year 1996, and

(E) $84,000,000 for fiscal year 1997,

as adjusted to reflect increases in the total fee revenues made under subsection (c)(1) of this section.

(h) Collection of unpaid fees

In any case where the Secretary does not receive payment of a fee assessed under subsection (a) of this section within 30 days after it is due, such fee shall be treated as a claim of the United States Government subject to subchapter II of chapter 37 of Title 31.

(i) Construction

This section may not be construed to require that the number of full-time equivalent positions in the Department of Health and Human Services, for officers, employers, and advisory committees not engaged in the process of the review of human drug applications, be reduced to offset the number of officers, employees, and advisory committees so engaged.

SUBCHAPTER VIII—IMPORTS AND EXPORTS

§ 381. Imports and exports

(a) Imports; list of registered foreign establishments; samples from unregistered foreign establishments; examination and refusal of admission

The Secretary of the Treasury shall deliver to the Secretary of Health and Human Services, upon his request, samples of food, drugs, devices, and cosmetics which are being imported or offered for import into the United States, giving notice thereof to the owner or consignee, who may appear before the Secretary of Health and Human Services and have the right to introduce testimony. The Secretary of Health and Human Services Welfare shall furnish to the Secretary of the Treasury a list of establishments registered pursuant to section 360(i) of this title and shall request that if any drugs or devices manufactured, prepared, propagated, compounded, or processed in an establishment not so registered are imported or offered for import into the United States, samples of such drugs or devices be delivered to the Secretary of Health and Human Services, with notice of such delivery to the owner or consignee, who may appear before the Secretary of Health and Human Services and have the right to introduce testimony. If it appears from the examination of such samples or otherwise that (1) such article has been manufactured, processed, or packed under insanitary conditions or, in the case of a device, the methods used in, or the facilities or controls used for, the manufacture, packing, storage, or installation of the device do not conform to the requirements of section 360j(f) of this title, or (2) such article is forbidden or restricted in sale in the country in which it was produced or from which it was exported, or (3) such article is adulterated, misbranded, or in violation of section 355 of this title, then such article shall be refused admission, except as provided in subsection (b) of this section. The Secretary of the Treasury shall cause the destruction of any such article refused admission unless such article is exported, under regulations prescribed by the Secretary of the Treasury, within ninety days of the date of notice of such refusal or within such additional time as may be permitted pursuant to such regulations. Clause (2) of the third sentence of this subsection shall not be construed to prohibit the admission of narcotic drugs the importation of which is permitted under the Controlled Substances Import and Export Act [21 U.S.C.A. § 951 et seq.].

(b) Same; disposition of refused articles

Pending decision as to the admission of an article being imported or offered for import, the Secretary of the Treasury may authorize delivery of such article to the owner or consignee upon the execution by him of a good and sufficient bond providing for the payment of such liquidated damages in the event of default as may be required pursuant to regulations of the Secretary of the Treasury. If it appears to the Secretary of Health and Human Services that an article included within the provisions of clause (3) of subsection (a) of this section can, by relabeling or other action, be brought into compliance with this chapter or rendered other than a food, drug, device, or cosmetic, final determination as to admission of such article may be deferred and, upon filing of timely written application by the owner or consignee and the execution by him of a bond as provided in the preceding provisions of this subsection, the Secretary may, in accordance with regulations, authorize the applicant to perform such relabeling or other action specified in such authorization (including destruction or export of rejected articles or portions thereof, as may be specified in the Secretary's authorization). All such relabeling or other action pursuant to such authorization shall in accordance with regulations be under the supervision of an officer or employee of the Department of Health and Human Services designated by the Secretary, or an officer or employee of the Department of the Treasury designated by the Secretary of the Treasury.

(c) Same; charges concerning refused articles

All expenses (including travel, per diem or subsistence, and salaries of officers or employees of the United States) in connection with the destruction provided for in subsection (a) of this section and the supervision of the relabeling or other action authorized under the provisions of subsection (b) of this section, the amount of such expenses to be determined in accordance with regulations, and all expenses in connection with the storage, cartage, or labor with respect to any article refused admission under subsection (a) of this section, shall be paid by the owner or consignee and, in default of such payment, shall constitute a lien against any future importations made by such owner or consignee.

(d) Reimportation

(1) Except as provided in paragraph (2), no drug subject to section 353(b) of this title which is manufactured in a State and exported may be imported into the United States unless the drug is imported by the manufacturer of the drug.

(2) The Secretary may authorize the importation of a drug the importation of which is prohibited by paragraph (1) if the drug is required for emergency medical care.

(e) Exports

(1) A food, drug, device, or cosmetic intended for export shall not be deemed to be adulterated or misbranded under this chapter if it—

(A) accords to the specifications of the foreign purchaser,

(B) is not in conflict with the laws of the country to which it is intended for export,

(C) is labeled on the outside of the shipping package that it is intended for export, and

(D) is not sold or offered for sale in domestic commerce.

This paragraph does not authorize the exportation of any new animal drug, or an animal feed bearing or containing a new animal drug, which is unsafe within the meaning of section 360b of this title.

(2) Paragraph (1) does not apply to any device—

(A) which does not comply with an applicable requirement of section 360d or 360e of this title,

(B) which under section 360j(g) of this title is exempt from either such section, or

(C) which is a banned device under section 360f of this title,

unless, in addition to the requirements of paragraph (1), the Secretary has determined that the exportation of the device is not contrary to public health and safety and has the approval of the country to which it is intended for export.

§ 382. Exports of certain unapproved products

(a) Drugs intended for human or animal use which require approval or licensing

A drug (including a biological product) intended for human or animal use—

(1) which—

(A) requires approval by the Secretary under section 355 or section 360b of this title, or

(B) requires licensing by the Secretary under section 262 of Title 42 or by the Secretary of Agriculture under the Act of March 4, 1913 (known as the Virus Serum Toxin Act [21 U.S.C.A. § 151 et seq.]),

before it may be introduced or delivered for introduction into interstate commerce to a country, and

(2) which does not have such approval or license, which is not exempt from such sections or Act, and which is introduced or delivered for introduction into interstate commerce to a country,

is adulterated, misbranded, and in violation of such sections or Act unless the export of the drug is authorized under subsection (b) of this section.

(b) Conditions for export; active pursuit of drug approval or licensing; application for export, contents, approval or disapproval; list of eligible countries for export; criteria for list change

(1) A drug (including a biological product) may, upon approval of an application submitted under paragraph (3), be exported if—

(A) the drug contains the same active ingredient as a—

(i) new drug—

(I) which has an exemption under section 355(i) of this title, and

(II) for which approval is actively being pursued by the person who has the exemption,

(ii) biological product for human use—

(I) which has an exemption under section 355(i) of this title, and

(II) for which licensing of the biological product under section 262 of Title 42 is actively being pursued by the person who has the exemption,

(iii) biological product for animal use—

(I) for which authority has been granted under the Virus–Serum Toxin Act [21 U.S.C.A. § 151 et seq.] for the preparation of an experimental drug product, and

(II) for which the licensing of the biological product under such Act is actively being pursued by the person who has the authority, or

(iv) new animal drug—

(I) which has an exemption under section 360b(j) of this title, and

(II) for which approval is actively being pursued by the person who has the exemption,

(B) except as provided in paragraph (2), the drug is exported to a country which is listed under paragraph (4) and in which the drug is approved and has not been withdrawn from sale,

(C) an application for the drug under section 355 or 360b of this title, section 262 of Title 42, or the Virus–Serum Toxin Act [21 U.S.C.A. § 151 et seq.] has not been disapproved by an order of the Secretary under section 355(d) or 360b(d) of this title or section 262 of Title 42 or by the Secretary of Agriculture in the case of an application under the Virus–Serum Toxin Act [21 U.S.C.A. § 151 et seq.],

(D) the drug is manufactured, processed, packaged, and held in conformity with current good manufacturing practice and is not adulterated under paragraph (a)(1), (a)(2)(A), (a)(3), (c), or (d) of section 351 of this title,

(E) the outside of the shipping package is labeled with the following statement: "This drug may be sold or offered for sale only in the following countries: ", the blank space being filled with a list of the countries to which export of the drug is authorized under this subsection,

(F) the drug is not the subject of a notice by the Secretary or the Secretary of Agriculture of a determination that the manufacture of the drug in the United States for export to a country is contrary to the public health and safety of the United States,

(G) the requirements of subparagraphs (A) through (D) of section 381(d)(1) of this title have been met.

The Secretary shall determine that an applicant is actively pursuing the approval or licensing of a drug if the applicant has demonstrated that degree of attention and continuous directed effort as may reasonably be expected from, and are ordinarily exercised by, a person before approval or licensing of a drug, such as the preparation for and the conduct of preclinical or clinical investigations, the analysis of the results of such investigations, conferences on such investigations with government officials, and the preparation of an application of approval or licensing for the drug.

(2) The Secretary may permit the export of a drug under paragraph (1) to a country which is listed under paragraph (4) and in which the drug is not approved if the drug is exported to such country solely for the purpose of further export to a country listed in paragraph (4) in which the drug is approved.

(3)(A) Any person may apply to have a drug exported under paragraph (1). Such an application shall be filed at least 90 days before the date the applicant proposes to export the drug for which the application is submitted. Before the expiration of 10 days from the date of the submission of such an application, the Secretary shall publish a notice in the Federal Register which identifies the applicant under such application, the drug proposed to be exported under such application, and the country to which the drug is proposed to be exported.

(B) An application for the export of a drug shall—

(i) identify the drug to be exported,

(ii) list each country to which the drug is to be exported and list the persons in each such country to which the drug is to be exported,

(iii) contain a certification by the applicant that—

(I) the applicant will export the drug only to a country which is listed in paragraph (4) and in which the drug is approved unless the drug is authorized to be exported under paragraph (2) and will export only those quantities of the drug which may reasonably be sold in each country to which it is to be exported,

(II) the drug is approved by each country to which it is to be exported unless the drug is authorized to be exported under paragraph (2) and the drug has not been withdrawn from sale in such country,

(III) the drug meets the requirements of paragraph (1)(D),

(IV) the drug will be labeled in accordance with paragraph (1)(E), and

(V) the drug meets the requirements of paragraph (1)(C) and (1)(G),

(iv) contain a certification by the holder of the exemption or authority for such drug described in paragraph (1)(A) that the holder will actively pursue the approval or licensing of the drug,

(v) identify the exemption or authority for an experimental drug product in effect for such drug under the laws referred to in paragraph (1)(A),

(vi) identify the establishments in which the drug is manufactured, and

(vii) include a written agreement from each importer to whom the drug is to be exported from the United States that such importer will not export the drug to a country which is not listed under paragraph (4) and will provide notice to the applicant of any knowledge of an export of the drug to such a country by any person and will maintain records of the drug wholesale distributors to which the drug is sold.

(C)(i) Before the expiration of 30 days after the date an application is submitted to the Secretary, the Secretary shall review the application to determine if the application meets the requirements of clauses (i), (ii), (iv), (v), (vi), and (vii) of subparagraph (B) and contains the certifications described in clauses (iii)(other than the certification required by clause (iii)(II)) and (iv). If the Secretary determines that the application meets such requirements and contains such certifications the Secretary shall conditionally approve the application. An application which is so conditionally approved shall be finally approved within 5 days of the submission of the certification required by clause (iii)(II).

(ii) If the Secretary proposes to disapprove an application, the Secretary shall provide the applicant with a written statement specifying—

(I) the deficiencies which the applicant must correct in order to enable the Secretary to approve the application, and

(II) that the applicant has 60 days after receiving the statement to correct such deficiencies.

(D) If the holder of an application approved under subparagraph (C) for the export of a drug intends to export such drug to a country listed in paragraph (4) which is not listed in such application, such holder shall submit an amendment to such application to the Secretary not later than 30 days before the date of the proposed export to such country identifying the country to which the holder intends to export such drug and containing information sufficient to show that the drug is approved by such country and has not been withdrawn from sale in such country. The Secretary shall approve or disapprove the export of such drug to such country within 15 days of the receipt of the notice required by this subparagraph.

(4)(A) The countries to which a drug may be exported under paragraph (1) are—

(i) Australia,

(ii) Austria,

(iii) Belgium,

(iv) Canada,

(v) Denmark,

(vi) Federal Republic of Germany,

(vii) Finland,

(viii) France,

(ix) Iceland,

(x) Ireland,

(xi) Italy,

(xii) Japan,

(xiii) Luxembourg,

(xiv) The Netherlands,

(xv) New Zealand,

(xvi) Norway,

(xvii) Portugal,

(xviii) Spain,

(xix) Sweden,

(xx) Switzerland, and

(xxi) The United Kingdom,

(B) Changes in the list contained in subparagraph (A) shall be based on the following criteria:

(i) Statutory or regulatory requirements which require the review of drugs for safety and effectiveness by an entity of the government of such country and which authorize the approval of only those drugs which have been determined to be safe and effective by experts employed by or acting on behalf of such entity and qualified by scientific training and experience to evaluate the safety and effectiveness of drugs on the basis of adequate and well-controlled investigations, including clinical investigations, conducted by experts qualified by scientific training and experience to evaluate the safety and effectiveness of drugs.

(ii) Statutory or regulatory requirements that the methods used in, and the facilities and controls used for, the manufacture, processing, and packing of drugs in the country are adequate to preserve their identity, quality, purity, and strength.

(iii) Statutory or regulatory requirements for the reporting of adverse reactions to drugs and procedures to withdraw approval and remove drugs found not to be safe or effective.

(iv) Statutory or regulatory requirements that the labeling and promotion of drugs must be in accordance with the approval of the drug.

(c) Report to Secretary by holder of approved application; events requiring report; annual report to Secretary on pursuit of approval of drug

(1) The holder of an approved application under subsection (b) of this section authorizing the export of a drug shall report to the Secretary—

(A) any withdrawal of an approval of the drug by any country to which it has been exported,

(B) any withdrawal of the drug from sale in any such country,

(C) the withdrawal of an application by the holder under section 355 or 360 of this title, section 262 of Title 42, or the Virus–Serum Toxin Act [21 U.S.C.A. § 151 et seq.], and

(D) the receipt of any credible information indicating that the drug is being or may have been exported from a country listed under subsection (b)(4) of this section to a country which is not listed under such subsection.

The reporting of an event described in subparagraph (A), (B), or (C) shall be made within 15 days of the occurrence of the event and the reporting of the receipt of information under subparagraph (D) shall be made within 15 days of the receipt of such information.

(2) The holder of an approved application under subsection (b) of this section authorizing the export of a drug shall report annually to the Secretary after the date of the approval of the application of the actions taken by the holder in pursuit of the approval of such drug during the year reported on. Not later than 90 days from the date of the receipt of a report under this paragraph the Secretary shall determine if the holder is actively pursuing the approval of such drug.

(d) Export of drug under approved application prohibited

A drug authorized to be exported to a country under an application approved under subsection (b) of this section may not be exported to such country if—

(1) an approval of such drug is withdrawn by such country,

(2) the drug is withdrawn from sale in such country,

(3) the Secretary issues an order refusing to approve an application of the holder of such application under section 355 or 360b of this title, section 262 of Title 42, or the Virus–Serum Toxin Act [21 U.S.C.A. § 151 et seq.], or

(4) an application for such drug under such section or Act is withdrawn or if an exemption for such drug under section 355(i) or 360b(j) of this title or the authority granted for such drug to prepare an experimental drug product under the Virus–Serum Toxin Act [21 U.S.C.A. § 151 et seq.] is withdrawn and no application for approval of such drug has been submitted under section 355 or 360b of this title, section 262 of Title 42, or the Virus–Serum Toxin Act [21 U.S.C.A. § 151 et seq.].

(e) Determination by Secretary of noncompliance, failure of active pursuit of drug approval, imminent hazard of drug to public health, or exportation of drug to noneligible country; notices and hearings; prohibition on exportation of drug

(1) If the Secretary determines that—

(A) a drug for which an application was approved under subsection (b) of this section no longer complies with subparagraphs (A), (D), (E), and (G) of paragraph (1) of such subsection or with paragraph (2) of such subsection or the holder of such application has not made the reports required by subsection (c) of this section, or

(B) the manufacture of a drug in the United States for export is contrary to the public health and safety of the United States and an application for the export of such drug has been approved under subsection (b) of this section,

then before taking action against the holder of an application for which a determination was made under subparagraph (A) or (B), the Secretary shall notify the holder in writing of the determination and provide the holder 30 days to take such action as may be required so that the Secretary would be unable to make such determination. When the Secretary takes action against such holder because of such a determination, the Secretary shall provide the holder a written statement specifying the reasons for such determination and provide the person, on request, an opportunity for an informal hearing with respect to such determination.

(2) If the Secretary determines that the approval of a drug is not being actively pursued as required by subsection (b)(1)(A) of this section, the Secretary shall give the holder of the application authorizing the export of such drug 60 days to assure that actions are taken to actively pursue such approval. During the 60–day period the Secretary shall give the holder an opportunity for an informal hearing on the determination of the Secretary. If upon the expiration of such 60–day period the Secretary determines that approval of such drug is not being actively pursued, the Secretary shall prohibit the export of such drug.

(3)(A) If at any time the Secretary, or in the absence of the Secretary the individual acting as the Secretary, determines that—

(i) the holder of an approved application under subsection (b) of this section is exporting a drug from the United States to an importer,

(ii) such importer is exporting the drug to a country which is not listed under subsection (b)(4) of this section, and

(iii) such export presents an imminent hazard to the public health in such country,

the Secretary shall immediately prohibit the export of the drug to such importer, give the person exporting the drug from the United States prompt notice of the determination, and afford such person an opportunity for an expedited hearing.

(B) The authority conferred by subparagraph (A) shall not be delegated by the Secretary. A determination by the Secretary under subparagraph (A) may not be stayed pending final action by a reviewing court.

(4)(A) If the Secretary, or in the absence of the Secretary the individual acting as the Secretary, determines that the holder of an approved application under subsection (b) of this section is exporting a drug to a country which is not listed under subsection (b)(4) of this section and that the export of the drug presents an imminent hazard, the Secretary shall immediately prohibit the export of the drug to such country, give the holder prompt notice of the determination, and afford the holder an opportunity for an expedited hearing.

(B) The authority conferred by subparagraph (A) shall not be delegated by the Secretary. A determination by the Secretary under subparagraph (A) may not be stayed pending final action by a reviewing court.

(5) If the Secretary receives credible evidence that the holder of an application approved under subsection (b) of this section is exporting a drug to a country which is not listed under subsection (b)(4) of this section, the Secretary shall give the holder 60 days to provide information to the Secretary respecting such evidence and shall provide the holder an opportunity for an informal hearing on such evidence. Upon the expiration of such 60 days the Secretary shall prohibit the export of such drug to such country if the Secretary determines that the holder of the application is exporting the drug to a country which is not listed under subsection (b)(4) of this section.

(6) If the Secretary receives credible evidence that an importer is exporting a drug to a country which is not listed under subsection (b)(4) of this section, the Secretary shall notify the holder of the application authorizing the export of such drug of such evidence and shall require the holder to investigate the export by such importer and to report to the Secretary within 14 days of the receipt of such notice the findings of the holder. If the Secretary determines that the importer has exported a drug to such a country, the Secretary shall prohibit such holder from exporting such drug to the importer unless the Secretary determines that the export by the importer was unintentional.

(f) Drugs used in prevention or treatment of tropical disease

(1) A drug (including a biological product) which is to be used in the prevention or treatment of a tropical disease may, upon approval of an application submitted under paragraph (2), be exported if—

(A) the Secretary finds, based on credible scientific evidence, including clinical investigations, that the drug is safe and effective in the country to which it is to be exported in the prevention or treatment of a tropical disease in such country,

(B) the drug is manufactured, processed, packaged, and held in conformity with current good manufacturing practice and is not adulterated under paragraph [14](a)(1), (a)(2)(A), (a)(3), (c), or (d) of section 351 of this title,

(C) the outside of the shipping package is labeled with the following statement: "This drug may be sold or offered for sale only in the following countries: ", the blank space being filled with a list of the countries to which export of the drug is authorized under this subsection,

(D) the drug is not the subject of a notice by the Secretary or the Secretary of Agriculture of a determination that the manufacture of the drug in the United States for export to a country is contrary to the public health and safety of the United States, and

(E) the requirements of subparagraphs (A) through (D) of section 381(d)(1) of this title have been met.

(2) Any person may apply to have a drug exported under paragraph (1). The application shall—

(A) describe the drug to be exported,

(B) list each country to which the drug is to be exported,

(C) contain a certification by the applicant that the drug will not be exported to a country for which the Secretary cannot make a finding described in paragraph (1)(A),

(D) identify the establishments in which the drug is manufactured, and

(E) demonstrate to the Secretary that the drug meets the requirements of paragraph (1).

(3) The holder of an approved application for the export of a drug under this subsection shall report to the Secretary—

(A) the receipt of any information indicating that the drug is being or may have been exported from a country for which the Secretary made a finding under paragraph (1)(A) to a country for which the Secretary cannot make such a finding, and

(B) the receipt of any information indicating any adverse reactions to such drug.

(4)(A) If the Secretary determines that—

(i) a drug for which an application is approved under paragraph (2) does not continue to meet the requirements of paragraph (1),

(ii) the holder of such application has not made the report required by paragraph (3), or

(iii) the manufacture of such drug in the United States for export is contrary to the public health and safety of the United

---

14. So in original. Probably should be "subsection".

States and an application for the export of such drug has been approved under paragraph (2),

then before taking action against the holder of an application for which a determination was made under clause (i), (ii), or (iii), the Secretary shall notify the holder in writing of the determination and provide the holder 30 days to take such action as may be required so that the Secretary would be unable to make such determination. When the Secretary takes action against such holder because of such a determination, the Secretary shall provide the holder a written statement specifying the reasons for such determination and provide the person, on request, an opportunity for an informal hearing with respect to such determination.

(B) If at any time the Secretary, or in the absence of the Secretary the individual acting as the Secretary, determines that—

(i) the holder of an approved application under paragraph (2) is exporting a drug from the United States to an importer,

(ii) such importer is exporting the drug to a country for which the Secretary cannot make a finding under paragraph (1)(A), and

(iii) such export presents an imminent hazard to the public health in such country,

the Secretary shall immediately prohibit the export of the drug to such importer, give the person exporting the drug from the United States prompt notice of the determination, and afford such person an opportunity for an expedited hearing. A determination by the Secretary under this subparagraph may not be stayed pending final action by a reviewing court. The authority conferred by this subparagraph shall not be delegated by the Secretary.

(C) If the Secretary, or in the absence of the Secretary the individual acting as the Secretary, determines that the holder of an approved application under paragraph (2) is exporting a drug to a country for which the Secretary cannot make a finding under paragraph (1)(A), and that the export of the drug presents an imminent hazard, the Secretary shall immediately prohibit the export of the drug to such country, give the holder prompt notice of the determination, and afford the holder an opportunity for an expedited hearing. A determination by the Secretary under this subparagraph may not be stayed pending final action by a reviewing court. The authority conferred by this subparagraph shall not be delegated by the Secretary.

(D) If the Secretary receives credible evidence that the holder of an application approved under paragraph (2) is exporting a drug to a country for which the Secretary cannot make a finding under paragraph (1)(A), the Secretary shall give the holder 60 days to provide information to the Secretary respecting such evidence and shall provide the holder an opportunity for an informal hearing on such evidence. Upon the expiration of such 60 days the Secretary shall prohibit the export of such drug to such country if the Secretary determines the holder is exporting the drug to a country for which the Secretary cannot make a finding under paragraph (1)(A).

(E) If the Secretary receives credible evidence that an importer is exporting a drug to a country for which the Secretary cannot make a finding under paragraph (1)(A), the Secretary shall notify the holder of the application authorizing the export of such drug of such evidence and shall require the holder to investigate the export by such importer and to report to the Secretary within 14 days of the receipt of such notice the findings of the holder. If the Secretary determines that the importer has exported a drug to such a country, the Secretary shall prohibit such holder from exporting such drug to the importer unless the Secretary determines that the export by the importer was unintentional.

(g) Reference to Secretary and holder of application

For purposes of this section—

(1) a reference to the Secretary shall in the case of a biological product which is required to be licensed under the Virus–Serum Toxin Act [21 U.S.C.A. § 151 et seq.] be considered to be a reference to the Secretary of Agriculture, and

(2) a reference in paragraph (3), (4), (5), or (6) of subsection (e) of this section and in subparagraph (B), (C), (D), or (E) of subsection (f)(4) of this section to the holder of an application shall be considered a reference to any person which is under common control with holder, is controlled by the holder, controls the holder, is owned by the holder, or owns the holder.

§ 383.   Office of International Relations

(a) There is established in the Department of Health and Human Services an Office of International Relations.

(b) In carrying out the functions of the office under subsection (a) of this section, the Secretary may enter into agreements with foreign countries to facilitate commerce in devices between the United States and such countries consistent with the requirements of this chapter. In such agreements, the Secretary shall encourage the mutual recognition of—

(1) good manufacturing practice regulations promulgated under section 360j(f) of this title, and

(2) other regulations and testing protocols as the Secretary determines to be appropriate.

SUBCHAPTER IX—MISCELLANEOUS

§ 391.   Separability clause

If any provision of this chapter is declared unconstitutional, or the applicability thereof to any person or circumstances is held invalid, the constitutionality of the remainder of the chapter and the applicability thereof to other persons and circumstances shall not be affected thereby.

§ 392. Exemption of meats and meat food products; laws unaffected

(a) Meats and meat food products shall be exempt from the provisions of this chapter to the extent of the application or the extension thereto of the Meat Inspection Act, approved March 4, 1907, as amended.

(b) Nothing contained in this chapter shall be construed as in any way affecting, modifying, repealing, or superseding the provisions of section 262 of Title 42 (relating to viruses, serums, toxins, and analogous products applicable to man); the virus, serum, toxin, and analogous products provisions, applicable to domestic animals, of the Act of Congress approved March 4, 1913; the Filled Cheese Act of June 6, 1896, the Filled Milk Act of March 4, 1923; or the Import Milk Act of February 15, 1927.

§ 393. Food and Drug Administration

(a) In general

There is established in the Department of Health and Human Services the Food and Drug Administration (hereinafter in this section referred to as the "Administration").

(b) Commissioner

(1) Appointment

There shall be in the Administration a Commissioner of Food and Drugs (hereinafter in this section referred to as the "Commissioner") who shall be appointed by the President by and with the advice and consent of the Senate.

(2) General powers

The Secretary, through the Commissioner, shall be responsible for executing this chapter and for—

(A) providing overall direction to the Food and Drug Administration and establishing and implementing general policies respecting the management and operation of programs and activities of the Food and Drug Administration;

(B) coordinating and overseeing the operation of all administrative entities within the Administration;

(C) research relating to foods, drugs, cosmetics, and devices in carrying out this chapter;

(D) conducting educational and public information programs relating to the responsibilities of the Food and Drug Administration; and

(E) performing such other functions as the Secretary may prescribe.

(c) Technical and scientific review groups

The Secretary through the Commissioner of Food and Drugs may, without regard to the provisions of Title 5 governing appointments in the competitive service and without regard to the provisions of chapter 51 and subchapter III of chapter 53 of Title 5 relating to classification and General Schedule pay rates, establish such technical and scientific review groups as are needed to carry out the functions of the Administration, including functions under this chapter, and appoint and pay the members of such groups, except that officers and employees of the United States shall not receive additional compensation for service as members of such groups.

§ 394. Scientific review groups

Without regard to the provisions of Title 5, governing appointments in the competitive service and without regard to the provisions of chapter 51 and subchapter III of chapter 53 of Title 5 relating to classification and General Schedule pay rates, the Commissioner of Food and Drugs may—

(1) establish such technical and scientific review groups as are needed to carry out the functions of the Food and Drug Administration (including functions prescribed under this chapter); and

(2) appoint and pay the members of such groups, except that officers and employees of the United States shall not receive additional compensation for service as members of such groups.

§ 395. Loan repayment program

(a) In general

(1) Authority for program

Subject to paragraph (2), the Secretary shall carry out a program of entering into contracts with appropriately qualified health professionals under which such health professionals agree to conduct research, as employees of the Food and Drug Administration, in consideration of the Federal Government agreeing to repay, for each year of such service, not more than $20,000 of the principal and interest of the educational loans of such health professionals.

(2) Limitation

The Secretary may not enter into an agreement with a health professional pursuant to paragraph (1) unless such professional—

(A) has a substantial amount of educational loans relative to income; and

(B) agrees to serve as an employee of the Food and Drug Administration for purposes of paragraph (1) for a period of not less than 3 years.

(b) Applicability of certain provisions

With respect to the National Health Service Corps Loan Repayment Program established in subpart III of part D of title III of the Public Health Service Act [42 U.S.C.A. § 254*l* et seq.], the provisions of such subpart shall, except as inconsistent with subsection (a) of this section, apply to the program established in such subsection in the same manner and to the same extent as such provisions apply to the National Health Service Corps Loan Repayment Program.

(c) Authorization of appropriations

For the purpose of carrying out this section, there are authorized to be appropriated such sums as may be necessary for each of the fiscal years 1994 through 1996.

PUBLIC HEALTH SERVICE ACT

TITLE 42, U.S.C.A.

PART F—LICENSING OF BIOLOGICAL PRODUCTS AND CLINICAL LABORATORIES

SUBPART 1—BIOLOGICAL PRODUCTS

§ 262. Regulation of biological products

(a) Intrastate and interstate traffic; suspension or revocation of license as affecting prior sales

No person shall sell, barter, or exchange, or offer for sale, barter, or exchange in the District of Columbia, or send, carry, or bring for sale, barter, or exchange from any State or possession into any other State or possession or into any foreign county, or from any foreign country into any State or possession, any virus, therapeutic serum, toxin, antitoxin, vaccine, blood, blood component or derivative, allergenic product, or analogous product, or arsphenamine or its derivatives (or any other trivalent organic arsenic compound), applicable to the prevention, treatment, or cure of diseases or injuries of man, unless (1) such virus, serum, toxin, antitoxin, vaccine, blood, blood component or derivative, allergenic product, or other product has been propagated or manufactured and prepared at an establishment holding an unsuspended and unrevoked license, issued by the Secretary as hereinafter authorized, to propagate or manufacture, and prepare such virus, serum, toxin, antitoxin, vaccine, blood, blood component or derivative, allergenic product, or other product for sale in the District of Columbia, or for sending, bringing, or carrying from place to place aforesaid; and (2) each package of such virus, serum, toxin, antitoxin, vaccine, blood, blood component or derivative, allergenic product, or other product is plainly marked with the proper name of the article contained therein, the name, address, and license number of the manufacturer, and the date beyond which the contents cannot be expected beyond reasonable doubt to yield their specific results. The suspension or revocation of any license shall not prevent the sale, barter, or exchange of any virus, serum, toxin, antitoxin, vaccine, blood, blood component or derivative, allergenic product, or other product aforesaid which has been sold and delivered by the licensee prior to such suspension or revocation, unless the owner or custodian of such virus, serum, toxin, antitoxin, vaccine, blood, blood component or derivative, allergenic product, or other product aforesaid has been notified by the Secretary not to sell, barter, or exchange the same.

(b) Falsely labeling or marking package or container; altering label or mark

No person shall falsely label or mark any package or container of any virus, serum, toxin, antitoxin, vaccine, blood, blood component or derivative, allergenic product, or other product aforesaid; nor alter any label or mark on any package or container of any virus, serum, toxin, antitoxin, vaccine, blood, blood component or derivative, allergenic product, or other product aforesaid so as to falsify such label or mark.

(c) Inspection of establishment for propagation and preparation

Any officer, agent, or employee of the Department of Health and Human Services, authorized by the Secretary for the purpose, may during all reasonable hours enter and inspect any establishment for the propagation or manufacture and preparation of any virus, serum, toxin, antitoxin, vaccine, blood, blood component or derivative, allergenic product, or other product aforesaid for sale, barter, or exchange in the District of Columbia, or to be sent, carried, or brought from any State or possession into any other State or possession or into any foreign country, or from any foreign country into any State or possession.

(d) Regulations governing licenses; recall of product presenting imminent hazard; violations

(1) Licenses for the maintenance of establishments for the propagation or manufacture and preparation of products described in subsection (a) of this section may be issued only upon a showing that the establishment and the products for which a license is desired meet standards, designed to insure the continued safety, purity, and potency of such products, prescribed in regulations, and licenses for new products may be issued only upon a showing that they meet such standards. All such licenses shall be issued, suspended, and revoked as prescribed by regulations and all licenses issued for the maintenance of establishments for the propagation or manufacture and preparation, in any foreign country, of any such products for sale, barter, or exchange in any State or possession shall be issued upon condition that the licensees will permit the inspection of their establishments in accordance with subsection (c) of this section.

(2)(A) Upon a determination that a batch, lot, or other quantity of a product licensed under this section presents an imminent or substantial hazard to the public health, the Secretary shall issue an order immediately ordering the recall of such batch, lot, or other quantity of such product. An order under this paragraph shall be issued in accordance with section 554 of Title 5.

(B) Any violation of subparagraph (A) shall subject the violator to a civil penalty of up to $100,000 per day of violation. The amount of a civil penalty under this subparagraph shall, effective December 1 of each year beginning 1 year after the effective date of this subparagraph, be increased by the percent change in the Consumer Price Index for the base quarter of such year over the Consumer Price Index for the base quarter of the preceding year, adjusted to the nearest $\frac{1}{10}$ of 1 percent. For purposes of this subparagraph, the term "base quarter", as used with respect to a year, means the calendar quarter ending on September 30 of such year and the price index for a base quarter is the arithmetical mean of such index for the 3 months comprising such quarter.

(e) Interference with officers

No person shall interfere with any officer, agent, or employee of the Service in the performance of any duty imposed upon him by this section or by regulations made by authority thereof.

(f) Penalties for offenses

Any person who shall violate, or aid or abet in violating, any of the provisions of this section shall be punished upon conviction by a fine not exceeding $500 or by imprisonment not exceeding one year, or by both such fine and imprisonment, in the discretion of the court.

(g) Construction with other laws

Nothing contained in this chapter shall be construed as in any way affecting, modifying, repealing, or superseding the provisions of the Federal Food, Drug, and Cosmetic Act [21 U.S.C.A. § 301 et seq.].

(h) Exportation of partially processed biological products

(1)(A) A partially processed biological product which is not in a form applicable to the prevention, treatment, or cure of diseases or injuries of man, which is not intended for sale in the United States, and which is intended for further manufacture into final dosage form outside the United States in a country listed under section 802(b)(A) of the Federal Food, Drug, and Cosmetic Act [21 U.S.C.A. § 382(b)(4)(A)] may, upon approval of an application meeting the requirements of subparagraph (B), be exported to a country listed under section 802(b)(4) of the Federal Food, Drug, and Cosmetic Act [21 U.S.C.A. § 382(b)(4)]. The Secretary may not approve an application to export such a product unless the Secretary determines that the product is manufactured, processed, packaged, and held in conformity with current good manufacturing practice and the outside of the shipping package is labeled with the following statement: "This product may be sold or offered for sale only in the following countries: _____", the blank space being filled with a list of the countries to which export of the drug is authorized.

(B) An application for the export of a partially processed biological product shall—

(i) describe the partially processed biological product to be exported,

(ii) list each country to which the product is to be exported,

(iii) contain a certification by the applicant that the product will not be exported to a country not listed under clause (ii),

(iv) identify the establishments in which the product is manufactured, and

(v) contain a certification by the applicant that the final product to be developed from the partially processed product is approved in the country to which it is to be exported or approval of the final product is being sought in such country.

(2) A product described in paragraph (1) is not subject to licensure under this section.

(3) If the Secretary determines that prohibiting the export of a product described in paragraph (1) is necessary for protection of the public health in the United States or the country to which it is to be exported, the Secretary may not approve an application under paragraph (1) for the export of such product.

PART G—QUARANTINE AND INSPECTION

§ 264. Regulations to control communicable diseases

(a) Promulgation and enforcement by Surgeon General

The Surgeon General, with the approval of the Secretary, is authorized to make and enforce such regulations as in his judgment are necessary to prevent the introduction, transmission, or spread of communicable diseases from foreign countries into the States or possessions, or from one State or possession into any other State or possession. For purposes of carrying out and enforcing such regulations, the Surgeon General may provide for such inspection, fumigation, disinfection, sanitation, pest extermination, destruction of animals or articles found to be so infected or contaminated as to be sources of dangerous infection to human beings, and other measures, as in his judgment may be necessary.

(b) Apprehension, detention, or conditional release of individuals

Regulations prescribed under this section shall not provide for the apprehension, detention, or conditional release of individuals except for the purpose of preventing the introduction, transmission, or spread of such communicable diseases as may be specified from time to time in Executive orders of the President upon the recommendation of the National Advisory Health Council and the Surgeon General.

(c) Application of regulations to persons entering from foreign countries

Except as provided in subsection (d) of this section, regulations prescribed under this section, insofar as they provide for the apprehension, detention, examination, or conditional release of individuals, shall be applicable only to individuals coming into a State or possession from a foreign country or a possession.

(d) Apprehension and examination of persons reasonably believed to be
    infected

On recommendation of the National Advisory Health Council, regulations prescribed under this section may provide for the apprehension and examination of any individual reasonably believed to be infected with a communicable disease in a communicable stage and (1) to be moving or about to move from a State to another State; or (2) to be a probable source of infection to individuals who, while infected with such disease in a communicable stage, will be moving from a State to another State. Such regulations may provide that if upon examination any such individual is found to be infected, he may be detained for such time and in such manner as may be reasonably necessary. For purposes of this subsection, the term "State" includes, in addition to the several States, only the District of Columbia.

§ 679. Federal Food, Drug and Cosmetic Act Applications

(a) Authorities under food, drug, and cosmetic provisions unaffected

Notwithstanding any other provisions of law, including section 392(a) of this title, the provisions of this chapter shall not derogate from any authority conferred by the Federal Food, Drug, and Cosmetic Act prior to December 15, 1967.

(b) Enforcement proceedings; detainer authority of representatives of Secretary of Health, Education, and Welfare

The detainer authority conferred by section 672 of this title shall apply to any authorized representative of the Secretary of Health, Education, and Welfare for purposes of the enforcement of the Federal Food, Drug, and Cosmetic Act with respect to any carcass, part thereof, meat, or meat food product of cattle, sheep, swine, goats, or equines that is outside any premises at which inspection is being maintained under this chapter, and for such purposes the first reference to the Secretary in section 672 of this title shall be deemed to refer to the Secretary of Health, Education, and Welfare.

FILLED MILK ACT

TITLE 21, U.S.C.A.

§ 61. Definitions

Whenever used in this chapter—

(a) The term "person" includes an individual, partnership, corporation, or association;

(b) The term "interstate or foreign commerce" means commerce (1) between any State, Territory, or possession, or the District of Columbia, and any place outside thereof; (2) between points within the same State, Territory, or possession, or within the District of Columbia, but through any place outside thereof; or (3) within any Territory or possession, or within the District of Columbia; and

(c) The term "filled milk" means any milk, cream, or skimmed milk, whether or not condensed, evaporated, concentrated, powdered, dried, or desiccated, to which has been added, or which has been blended or compounded with, any fat or oil other than milk fat, so that the resulting product is in limitation or semblance of milk, cream, or skimmed milk, whether or not condensed, evaporated, concentrated, powdered, dried, or desiccated. This definition shall not include any distinctive proprietary food compound not readily mistaken in taste for milk or cream or for evaporated, condensed, or powdered milk, or cream where such compound (1) is prepared and designed for feeding infants and young children and customarily used on the order of a physician; (2) is packed in individual cans containing not more than sixteen and one-half ounces and bearing a label in bold type that the content is to be used only for said purpose; (3) is shipped in interstate or foreign commerce exclusively to physicians, wholesale and retail druggists, orphan asylums, child-welfare associations, hospitals, and similar institutions and generally disposed of by them.

§ 62. Manufacture, shipment, or delivery for shipment in interstate or foreign commerce prohibited

It is hereby declared that filled milk, as defined in section 61 of this title, is an adulterated article of food, injurious to the public health, and its sale constitutes a fraud upon the public. It shall be unlawful for any person to manufacture within any Territory or possession, or within the District of Columbia, or to ship or deliver for shipment in interstate or foreign commerce, any filled milk.

§ 63. Penalty for violations of law; acts, omissions, and so forth, of agents

Any person violating any provision of this chapter shall upon conviction thereof be subject to a fine of not more than $1,000 or imprisonment of not more than one year, or both. When construing and enforcing the provisions of this chapter, the act, omission, or failure of any person acting for or employed by any individual, partnership, corporation, or association, within the scope of his employment or office, shall in every case be deemed the act, omission, or failure, of such individual, partnership, corporation, or association, as well as of such person.

§ 64. Regulations for enforcement

The Secretary of Health, Education, and Welfare is hereby authorized and directed to make and enforce such regulations as may in his judgment be necessary to carry out the purposes of this chapter.

1906 FEDERAL FOOD AND DRUGS ACT *

Be it enacted by the Senate and House of Representatives of the United States of America in Congress assembled. [1] That it shall be unlawful for any person to manufacture within any Territory or the District of Columbia any article of food or drug which is adulterated or misbranded, within the meaning of this act; and any person who shall violate any of the provisions of this section shall be guilty of a misdemeanor, and for each offense shall, upon conviction thereof, be fined not to exceed five hundred dollars or shall be sentenced to one year's imprisonment, or both such fine and imprisonment, in the discretion of the court, and for each subsequent offense and conviction thereof shall be fined not less than one thousand dollars or sentenced to one year's imprisonment, or both such fine and imprisonment, in the discretion of the court.

Sec. 2[2]. That the introduction into any State or Territory or the District of Columbia from any other State or Territory or the District of Columbia, or from any foreign country, or shipment to any foreign country of any article of food or drugs which is adulterated or misbranded, within the meaning of this act, is hereby prohibited; and any person who shall ship or deliver for shipment from any State or Territory or the District of Columbia to any other State or Territory or the District of Columbia, or to a foreign country, or who shall receive in any State or Territory or the District of Columbia from any other State or Territory or the District of Columbia, or foreign country, and having so received, shall deliver, in original unbroken packages, for pay or otherwise, or offer to deliver to any other person, any such articles so adulterated or misbranded within the meaning of this act, or any person who shall sell or offer for sale in the District of Columbia or the Territories of the United States any such adulterated or misbranded foods or drugs, or export or offer to export the same to any foreign country, shall be guilty of a misdemeanor, and for such offense be fined not exceeding two hundred dollars for the first offense, and upon conviction for each subsequent offense not exceeding three hundred dollars or be imprisoned not exceeding one year, or both, in the discretion of the court: *Provided,* That no article shall be deemed misbranded or adulterated within the provisions of this act when intended for export to any foreign country and prepared or packed according to the specifications or directions of the foreign purchaser when no substance is used in the preparation or packing thereof in conflict with the laws of the foreign country to which

---

* [Pub.L. No. 59–384, 34 Stat. 768 (1906), as amended. The 1906 Act was repealed by Section 902(a) of the 1938 Act. The 1906 Act is reproduced in the form in which it was enacted, as amended as of 1938. The numbers in brackets refer to the corresponding sections in title 21 of the U.S.Code at that time.]

said article is intended to be shipped; but if said article shall be in fact sold or offered for sale for domestic use or consumption, then this proviso shall not exempt said article from the operation of any of the other provisions of this act.

SEC. 3[3]. That the Secretary of the Treasury, the Secretary of Agriculture and the Secretary of Commerce ... shall make uniform rules and regulations for carrying out the provisions of this act, including the collection and examination of specimens of foods and drugs manufactured or offered for sale in the District of Columbia, or in any Territory of the United States, or which shall be offered for sale in unbroken packages in any State other than that in which they shall have been respectively manufactured or produced, or which shall be received from any foreign country, or intended for shipment to any foreign country, or which may be submitted for examination by the chief health, food, or drug officer of any State, Territory, or the District of Columbia, or at any domestic or foreign port through which such product is offered for interstate commerce, or for export or import between the United States and any foreign port or country.

SEC. 4[11]. That the examinations of specimens of foods and drugs shall be made in the [Food and Drug Administration] of the Department of Agriculture, or under the direction and supervision of such bureau, for the purpose of determining from such examinations whether such articles are adulterated or misbranded within the meaning of this act; and if it shall appear from any such examination that any of such specimens is adulterated or misbranded within the meaning of this act, the Secretary of Agriculture shall cause notice thereof to be given to the party from whom such sample was obtained. Any party so notified shall be given an opportunity to be heard, under such rules and regulations as may be prescribed as aforesaid, and if it appears that any of the provisions of this act have been violated by such party, then the Secretary of Agriculture shall at once certify the facts to the proper United States district attorney, with a copy of the results of the analysis or the examination of such article duly authenticated by the analyst or officer making such examination, under the oath of such officer. After judgment of the court, notice shall be given by publication in such manner as may be prescribed by the rules and regulations aforesaid.

SEC. 5[12]. That it shall be the duty of each district attorney to whom the Secretary of Agriculture shall report any violation of this act, or to whom any health or food or drug officer or agent of any State, Territory, or the District of Columbia shall present satisfactory evidence of any such violation, to cause appropriate proceedings to be commenced and prosecuted in the proper courts of the United States, without delay, for the enforcement of the penalties as in such case herein provided.

SEC. 6[7]. That the term "drug," as used in this act, shall include all medicines and preparations recognized in the United States Pharmacopoeia or National Formulary for internal or external use, and any substance or mixture of substances intended to be used for the cure, mitigation, or prevention of disease of either man or other animals. The term "food," as used herein, shall include all articles used for food, drink, confectionery, or condiment by man or other animals, whether simple, mixed, or compound.

SEC. 7[8]. That for the purposes of this act an article shall be deemed to be adulterated:

In case of drugs:

First. If, when a drug is sold under or by a name recognized in the United States Pharmacopoeia or National Formulary, it differs from the standard of strength, quality, or purity, as determined by the test laid down in the United States Pharmacopoeia or National Formulary official at the time of investigation: *Provided,* That no drug defined in the United States Pharmacopoeia or National Formulary shall be deemed to be adulterated under this provision if the standard of strength, quality, or purity be plainly stated upon the bottle, box, or other container thereof, although the standard may differ from that determined by the test laid down in the United States Pharmacopoeia or National Formulary.

Second. If its strength or purity fall below the professed standard or quality under which it is sold.

In the case of confectionery:

If it contain terra alba, barytes, talc, chrome yellow, or other mineral substance or poisonous color or flavor, or other ingredient deleterious or detrimental to health, or any vinous, malt, or spirituous liquor or compound or narcotic drug.

In the case of food:

First. If any substance has been mixed and packed with it so as to reduce or lower or injuriously affect its quality or strength.

Second. If any substance has been substituted wholly or in part for the article.

Third. If any valuable constituent of the article has been wholly or in part abstracted.

Fourth. If it be mixed, colored, powdered, coated, or stained in a manner whereby damage or inferiority is concealed.

Fifth. If it contain any added poisonous or other added deleterious ingredient which may render such article injurious to health: *Provided,* That when in the preparation of food products for shipment they are preserved by any external application applied in such manner that the preservative is necessarily removed mechanically, or by maceration in water, or otherwise, and directions for the removal of said preservative shall be printed on the covering or the package, the provisions of this act shall be construed as applying only when said products are ready for consumption.

Sixth. If it consist in whole or in part of a filthy, decomposed, or putrid animal or vegetable substance, or any portion of an animal unfit for food, whether manufactured or not, or if it is the product of a diseased animal, or one that has died otherwise than by slaughter.

SEC. 8[9]. That the term "misbranded," as used herein, shall apply to all drugs, or articles of food, or articles which enter into the composition of food, the package or label of which shall bear any statement, design, or device regarding such article, or the ingredients or substances contained therein which shall be false or misleading in any particular, and to any food or drug product which is falsely branded as to the State, Territory, or country in which it is manufactured or produced.

That for the purposes of this act an article shall also be deemed to be misbranded:

In case of drugs:

First. If it be an imitation of or offered for sale under the name of another article.

Second. If the contents of the package as originally put up shall have been removed, in whole or in part, and other contents shall have been placed in such package, or if the package fail to bear a statement on the label of the quantity or proportion of any alcohol, morphine, opium, cocaine, heroine, alpha or beta eucaine, chloroform, cannabis indica, chloral hydrate, or acetanilid, or any derivative or preparation of any such substances contained therein.

Third. If its package or label shall bear or contain any statement, design, or device regarding the curative or therapeutic effect of such article or any of the ingredients or substances contained therein, which is false and fraudulent.

In the case of food:

First. If it be an imitation of or offered for sale under the distinctive name of another article.

Second. If it be labeled or branded so as to deceive or mislead the purchaser, or purport to be a foreign product when not so, or if the contents of the package as originally put up shall have been removed in whole or in part and other contents shall have been placed in such package, or if it fail to bear a statement on the label of the quantity or proportion of any morphine, opium, cocaine, heroine, alpha or beta eucaine, chloroform, cannabis indica, chloral hydrate, or acetanilid, or any derivative or preparation of any such substances contained therein.

Third. If in package form, the quantity of the contents be not plainly and conspicuously marked on the outside of the package in terms of weight, measure, or numerical count: *Provided, however,* That reasonable variations shall be permitted, and tolerances and also exemptions as to small packages shall be established by rules and regulations made in accordance with the provisions of section three of this act.*

Fourth. If the package containing it or its label shall bear any statement, design, or device regarding the ingredients or the substances contained therein, which statement, design, or device shall be false or misleading in any particular: *Provided,* That an article of food which does not contain any added poisonous or deleterious ingredients shall not be deemed to be adulterated or misbranded in the following cases:

First. In the case of mixtures or compounds which may be now or from time to time hereafter known as articles of food, under their own distinctive names, and not an imitation of or offered for sale under the distinctive name of another article, if the name be accompanied on the same label or brand with a statement of the place where said article has been manufactured or produced.

Second. In the case of articles labeled, branded, or tagged so as to plainly indicate that they are compounds, imitations, or blends, and the word "compound," "imitation," or "blend," as the case may be, is plainly stated on the package in which it is offered for sale: *Provided,* That the term blend as used herein shall be construed to mean a mixture of like substances, not excluding harmless coloring or flavoring ingredients used for the purpose of coloring and flavoring only: *And provided further,* That nothing in this act shall be construed as requiring or compelling proprietors or manufacturers of proprietary foods which contain no unwholesome added ingredient to disclose their trade formulas, except in so far as the provisions of this act may require to secure freedom from adulteration or misbranding.

Fifth. If it be canned food and falls below the standard of quality, condition, and/or fill of container, promulgated by the Secretary of Agriculture for such canned food and its package or label does not bear a plain and conspicuous statement prescribed by the Secretary of Agriculture indicating that such canned food falls below such standard. For the purposes of this paragraph the words canned food mean all food which is in hermetically sealed containers and is sterilized by heat, except meat and meat food products which are subject to the provisions of the meat inspection act of March 4, 1907 (Thirty-fourth Statutes, page 1260), as amended, and except canned milk; the word class means and is limited to a generic product for which a standard is to be established and does not mean a grade, variety, or species of a generic product. The Secretary of Agriculture is authorized to determine, establish, and promulgate, from time to time, a reasonable standard of quality, condition, and/or fill of container for each class of canned food as will, in his judgment, promote honesty and fair dealing in the interest of the

---

* [The Kenyon amendment (41 Stat. 271) states that the word "package" shall include and shall be construed to include wrapped meats inclosed in papers or other materials as prepared by the manufacturers thereof for sale.]

consumer; and he is authorized to alter or modify such standard from time to time as, in his judgment, honesty and fair dealing in the interest of the consumer may require. The Secretary of Agriculture is further authorized to prescribe and promulgate from time to time the form of statement which must appear in a plain and conspicuous manner on each package or label of canned food which falls below the standard promulgated by him, and which will indicate that such canned food falls below such standard, and he is authorized to alter or modify such form of statement, from time to time, as in his judgment may be necessary. In promulgating such standards and forms of statements and any alteration or modification thereof, the Secretary of Agriculture shall specify the date or dates when such standards shall become effective, or after which such statements shall be used, and shall give public notice not less than ninety days in advance of the date or dates on which such standards shall become effective or such statements shall be used. Nothing in this paragraph shall be construed to authorize the manufacture, sale, shipment, or transportation of adulterated or misbranded foods.

SEC. 9[13]. That no dealer shall be prosecuted under the provisions of this act when he can establish a guaranty signed by the wholesaler, jobber, manufacturer, or other party residing in the United States, from whom he purchases such articles, to the effect that the same is not adulterated or misbranded within the meaning of this act, designating it. Said guaranty, to afford protection, shall contain the name and address of the party or parties making the sale of such articles to such dealer, and in such cases said party or parties shall be amenable to the prosecutions, fines, and other penalties, which would attach, in due course, to the dealer under the provisions of this act.

SEC. 10[14]. That any article of food, drug, or liquor that is adulterated or misbranded within the meaning of this act, and is being transported from one State, Territory, District, or insular possession to another for sale, or, having been transported, remains unloaded, unsold, or in original unbroken packages, or if it be sold or offered for sale in the District of Columbia or the Territories, or insular possessions of the United States, or if it be imported from a foreign country for sale, or if it is intended for export to a foreign country, shall be liable to be proceeded against in any district court of the United States within the district where the same is found, and seized for confiscation by a process of libel for condemnation. And if such article is condemned as being adulterated or misbranded, or of a poisonous or deleterious character, within the meaning of this act, the same shall be disposed of by destruction or sale, as the said court may direct, and the proceeds thereof, if sold, less the legal costs and charges, shall be paid into the Treasury of the United States, but such goods shall not be sold in any jurisdiction contrary to the provisions of this act, or the laws of that jurisdiction: *Provided, however,* That upon the payment of the costs of such libel proceedings and the execution and delivery of a good and sufficient bond to the effect that such articles shall not be sold or otherwise disposed of contrary to the provisions of this act, or the laws of any State, Territory, District, or insular possession, the court may by order direct that such articles be delivered to the owner thereof. The proceedings of such libel cases shall conform, as near as may be, to the proceedings in admiralty, except, that either party may demand trial by jury of any issue of fact joined in any such case, and all such proceedings shall be at the suit of and in the name of the United States.

SEC. 10A[14a]. The Secretary of Agriculture, upon application of any packer of any sea food for shipment or sale within the jurisdiction of this Act, may, at his discretion, designate inspectors to examine and inspect such food and the production, packing, and labeling thereof. If on such examination and inspection compliance is found with the provisions of this Act and regulations promulgated thereunder, the applicant shall be authorized or required to mark the food as provided by regulation to show such compliance. Services under this section shall be rendered only upon payment by the applicant of fees fixed by regulation in such amounts as may be necessary to provide, equip, and maintain an adequate and efficient inspection service. Receipts from such fees shall be covered into the Treasury and shall be available to the Secretary of Agriculture for expenditures incurred in carrying out the purposes of this section, including expenditures for salaries of additional inspectors when necessary to supplement the number of inspectors for whose salaries Congress has appropriated. The Secretary is hereby authorized to promulgate regulations governing the sanitary and other conditions under which the service herein provided shall be granted and maintained, and for otherwise carrying out the purposes of this section. Any person who forges, counterfeits, simulates, or falsely represents, or without proper authority uses any mark, stamp, tag, label, or other identification devices authorized or required by the provisions of this section or regulations thereunder, shall be guilty of a misdemeanor, and shall on conviction thereof be subject to imprisonment for not more than one year or a fine of not less than $1,000 nor more than $5,000, or both such imprisonment and fine.

SEC. 11[15]. The Secretary of the Treasury shall deliver to the Secretary of Agriculture, upon his request from time to time, samples of foods and drugs which are being imported into the United States or offered for import, giving notice thereof to the owner or consignee, who may appear before the Secretary of Agriculture, and have the right to introduce testimony, and if it appear from the examination of such samples that any article of food or drug offered to be imported into the United States is adulterated or misbranded within the meaning of this act, or is otherwise dangerous to the health of the people of the United States, or is of a kind forbidden entry into, or forbidden to be sold or restricted in sale in the country in which it is made or from which it is exported or is otherwise falsely labeled in any respect, the said article shall be refused admission, and the Secretary of the Treasury shall refuse delivery to the consignee and shall cause the destruction of any goods refused delivery which shall not be exported by the consignee within three months from the date of notice of such refusal under such regulations as the Secretary of the Treasury may prescribe: *Provided,* That the Secretary of the Treasury may deliver to the consignee such goods pending examination and decision in the matter on execution of a penal bond for the amount of the full invoice value of such goods, together with the duty thereon, and on refusal to return such goods for any cause to the custody of the Secretary of the Treasury, when demanded, for the purpose of excluding them from the country, or for any other purpose, said consignee shall forfeit the full amount of the bond: *And provided further,* That all charges for storage, cartage, and labor on goods which are refused admission or delivery shall be paid by the owner or consignee, and in default of such payment shall constitute a lien against any future importation made by such owner or consignee.

Sec. 12[5]. That the term "Territory" as used in this act shall include the insular possessions of the United States. The word "person" as used in this act shall be construed to import both the plural and the singular, as the case demands, and shall include corporations, companies, societies, and associations. [4] When construing and enforcing the provisions of this act, the act, omission, or failure of any officer, agent, or other person acting for or employed by any corporation, company, society, or association, within the scope of his employment or office, shall in every case be also deemed to be the act, omission, or failure of such corporation, company, society, or association as well as that of the person.

Sec. 13. That this act shall be in force and effect from and after the first day of January, nineteen hundred and seven.

FAIR PACKAGING AND LABELING ACT

TITLE 15, U.S.C.A.

§ 1451. Congressional declaration of policy

Informed consumers are essential to the fair and efficient functioning of a free market economy. Packages and their labels should enable consumers to obtain accurate information as to the quantity of the contents and should facilitate value comparisons. Therefore, it is hereby declared to be the policy of the Congress to assist consumers and manufacturers in reaching these goals in the marketing of consumer goods.

§ 1452. Unfair and deceptive packaging and labeling; scope of prohibition

(a) It shall be unlawful for any person engaged in the packaging or labeling of any consumer commodity (as defined in this chapter) for distribution in commerce, or for any person (other than a common carrier for hire, a contract carrier for hire, or a freight forwarder for hire) engaged in the distribution in commerce of any packaged or labeled consumer commodity, to distribute or to cause to be distributed in commerce any such commodity if such commodity is contained in a package, or if there is affixed to that commodity a label, which does not conform to the provisions of this chapter and of regulations promulgated under the authority of this chapter.

(b) The prohibition contained in subsection (a) of this section shall not apply to persons engaged in business as wholesale or retail distributors of consumer commodities except to the extent that such persons (1) are engaged in the packaging or labeling of such commodities, or (2) prescribe or specify by any means the manner in which such commodities are packaged or labeled.

§ 1453. Requirements of labeling; placement, form, and contents of statement of quantity; supplemental statement of quantity

(a) No person subject to the prohibition contained in section 1452 of this title shall distribute or cause to be distributed in commerce any packaged consumer commodity unless in conformity with regulations which shall be established by the promulgating authority pursuant to section 1455 of this title which shall provide that—

(1) The commodity shall bear a label specifying the identity of the commodity and the name and place of business of the manufacturer, packer, or distributor;

286

(2) The net quantity of contents (in terms of weight or mass, measure, or numerical count) shall be separately and accurately stated in a uniform location upon the principal display panel of that label, using the most appropriate units of both the customary inch/pound system of measure, as provided in paragraph (3) of this subsection, and, except as provided in paragraph (3)(A)(ii) or paragraph (6) of this subsection, the SI metric system;

(3) The separate label statement of net quantity of contents appearing upon or affixed to any package—

(A)(i) if on a package labeled in terms of weight, shall be expressed in pounds, with any remainder in terms of ounces or common or decimal fractions of the pound; or in the case of liquid measure, in the largest whole unit (quarts, quarts and pints, or pints, as appropriate) with any remainder in terms of fluid ounces or common or decimal fractions of the pint or quart;

(ii) if on a random package, may be expressed in terms of pounds and decimal fractions of the pound carried out to not more than three decimal places and is not required to, but may, include a statement in terms of the SI metric system carried out to not more than three decimal places;

(iii) if on a package labeled in terms of linear measure, shall be expressed in terms of the largest whole unit (yards, yards and feet, or feet, as appropriate) with any remainder in terms of inches or common or decimal fractions of the foot or yard;

(iv) if on a package labeled in terms of measure of area, shall be expressed in terms of the largest whole square unit (square yards, square yards and square feet, or square feet, as appropriate) with any remainder in terms of square inches or common or decimal fractions of the square foot or square yard;

(B) shall appear in conspicuous and easily legible type in distinct contrast (by typography, layout, color, embossing, or molding) with other matter on the package;

(C) shall contain letters or numerals in a type size which shall be (i) established in relationship to the area of the principal display panel of the package, and (ii) uniform for all packages of substantially the same size; and

(D) shall be so placed that the lines of printed matter included in that statement are generally parallel to the base on which the package rests as it is designed to be displayed.

(4) The label of any package of a consumer commodity which bears a representation as to the number of servings of such commodity contained in such package shall bear a statement of the net

quantity (in terms of weight or mass, measure, or numerical count) of each such serving.

(5) For purposes of paragraph (3)(A)(ii) of this subsection the term "random package" means a package which is one of a lot, shipment, or delivery of packages of the same consumer commodity with varying weights or masses, that is, packages with no fixed weight or mass pattern.

(6) The requirement of paragraph (2) that the statement of net quantity of contents include a statement in terms of the SI metric system shall not apply to foods that are packaged at the retail store level.

(b) No person subject to the prohibition contained in section 1452 of this title shall distribute or cause to be distributed in commerce any packaged consumer commodity if any qualifying words or phrases appear in conjunction with the separate statement of the net quantity of contents required by subsection (a) of this section, but nothing in this subsection or in paragraph (2) of subsection (a) of this section shall prohibit supplemental statements, at other places on the package, describing in nondeceptive terms the net quantity of contents: Provided, That such supplemental statements of net quantity of contents shall not include any term qualifying a unit of weight or mass, measure, or count that tends to exaggerate the amount of the commodity contained in the package.

§ 1454. Rules and regulations

(a) Promulgating authority

The authority to promulgate regulations under this chapter is vested in (A) the Secretary of Health and Human Services (referred to hereinafter as the "Secretary") with respect to any consumer commodity which is a food, drug, device, or cosmetic, as each such term is defined by section 321 of Title 21; and (B) the Federal Trade Commission (referred to hereinafter as the "Commission") with respect to any other consumer commodity.

(b) Exemption of commodities from regulations

If the promulgating authority specified in this section finds that, because of the nature, form, or quantity of a particular consumer commodity, or for other good and sufficient reasons, full compliance with all the requirements otherwise applicable under section 1453 of this title is impracticable or is not necessary for the adequate protection of consumers, the Secretary or the Commission (whichever the case may be) shall promulgate regulations exempting such commodity from those requirements to the extent and under such conditions as the promulgating authority determines to be consistent with section 1451 of this title.

(c) Scope of additional regulations

Whenever the promulgating authority determines that regulations containing prohibitions or requirements other than those prescribed by section 1453 of this title are necessary to prevent the deception of consumers or to facilitate value comparisons as to any consumer commodity, such authority shall promulgate with respect to that commodity regulations effective to—

(1) establish and define standards for characterization of the size of a package enclosing any consumer commodity, which may be used to supplement the label statement of net quantity of contents of packages containing such commodity, but this paragraph shall not be construed as authorizing any limitation on the size, shape, weight or mass, dimensions, or number of packages which may be used to enclose any commodity;

(2) regulate the placement upon any package containing any commodity, or upon any label affixed to such commodity, of any printed matter stating or representing by implication that such commodity is offered for retail sale at a price lower than the ordinary and customary retail sale price or that a retail sale price advantage is accorded to purchasers thereof by reason of the size of that package or the quantity of its contents;

(3) require that the label on each package of a consumer commodity (other than one which is a food within the meaning of section 321(f) of Title 21) bear (A) the common or usual name of such consumer commodity, if any, and (B) in case such consumer commodity consists of two or more ingredients, the common or usual name of each such ingredient listed in order of decreasing predominance, but nothing in this paragraph shall be deemed to require that any trade secret be divulged; or

(4) prevent the nonfunctional-slack-fill of packages containing consumer commodities.

For purposes of paragraph (4) of this subsection, a package shall be deemed to be nonfunctionally slack-filled if it is filled to substantially less than its capacity for reasons other than (A) protection of the contents of such package or (B) the requirements of machines used for enclosing the contents in such package.

(d) Development by manufacturers, packers, and distributors of voluntary product standards

Whenever the Secretary of Commerce determines that there is undue proliferation of the weights or masses, measures, or quantities in which any consumer commodity or reasonably comparable consumer commodities are being distributed in packages for sale at retail and such undue proliferation impairs the reasonable ability of consumers to make value comparisons with respect to such consumer commodity or commodities, he shall request manufacturers, packers, and distributors of the commodity or commodities to participate in the development of a voluntary product standard for such commodity or commodities under the procedures for the development of voluntary products standards established by the Secretary pursuant to section 272 of this title. Such procedures shall provide adequate manufacturer, packer, distributor, and consumer representation.

(e) Report and recommendations to Congress upon industry failure to develop or abide by voluntary product standards

If (1) after one year after the date on which the Secretary of Commerce first makes the request of manufacturers, packers, and distributors to participate in the development of a voluntary product standard as provided in subsection (d) of this section, he determines that such a standard will not be published pursuant to the provisions of such subsection (d), or (2) if such a standard is published and the Secretary of Commerce determines that it has not been observed, he shall promptly report such determination to the Congress with a statement of the efforts that have been made under the voluntary standards program and his recommendation as to whether Congress should enact legislation providing regulatory authority to deal with the situation in question.

§ 1455. Procedure for promulgation of regulations

(a) Hearings by Secretary of Health and Human Services

Regulations promulgated by the Secretary under section 1453 or 1454 of this title shall be promulgated, and shall be subject to judicial review, pursuant to the provisions of subsections (e), (f), and (g) of section 371 of Title 21. Hearings authorized or required for the promulgation of any such regulations by the Secretary shall be conducted by the Secretary or by such officer or employee of the Department of Health and Human Services as he may designate for that purpose.

(b) Judicial review; hearings by Federal Trade Commission

Regulations promulgated by the Commission under section 1453 or 1454 of this title shall be promulgated, and shall be subject to judicial review, by proceedings taken in conformity with the provisions of subsections (e), (f), and (g) of section 371 of Title 21 in the same manner, and with the same effect, as if such proceedings were taken by the Secretary pursuant to subsection (a) of this section. Hearings authorized or required for the promulgation of any such regulations by the Commission shall be conducted by the Commission or by such officer or employee of the Commission as the Commission may designate for that purpose.

(c) Cooperation with other departments and agencies

In carrying into effect the provisions of this chapter, the Secretary and the Commission are authorized to cooperate with any department or agency of the United States, with any State, Commonwealth, or possession of the United States, and with any department, agency, or political subdivision of any such State, Commonwealth, or possession.

(d) Returnable or reusable glass containers for beverages

No regulation adopted under this chapter shall preclude the continued use of returnable or reusable glass containers for beverages in inventory or with the trade as of the effective date of this Act, nor shall any regulation under this chapter preclude the orderly disposal of packages in inventory or with the trade as of the effective date of such regulation.

§ 1456. Enforcement

(a) Misbranded consumer commodities

Any consumer commodity which is a food, drug, device, or cosmetic, as each such term is defined by section 321 of Title 21, and which is introduced or delivered for introduction into commerce in violation of any of the provisions of this chapter, or the regulations issued pursuant to this chapter, shall be deemed to be misbranded within the meaning of sections 331 to 337 of Title 21, but the provisions of section 333 of Title 21 shall have no application to any violation of section 1452 of this title.

(b) Unfair or deceptive acts or practices in commerce

Any violation of any of the provisions of this chapter, or the regulations issued pursuant to this chapter, with respect to any consumer commodity which is not a food, drug, device, or cosmetic, shall constitute an unfair or deceptive act or practice in commerce in violation of section 45(a) of this title and shall be subject to enforcement under section 45(b) of this title.

(c) Imports

In the case of any imports into the United States of any consumer commodity covered by this chapter, the provisions of sections 1453 and 1454 of this title shall be enforced by the Secretary of the Treasury pursuant to section 381(a) and (b) of Title 21.

§ 1457. Annual reports to Congress; submission dates

Each officer or agency required or authorized by this chapter to promulgate regulations for the packaging or labeling of any consumer commodity, shall transmit to the Congress each year a report containing a full and complete description of the activities of that officer or agency for the administration and enforcement of this chapter during the preceding fiscal year. All agencies except the Department of Health and Human Services and the Federal Trade Commission shall submit their reports in January of each year. The Department of Health and Human Services shall include this report in its annual report to Congress on activities under the Federal Food, Drug, and Cosmetic Act [21 U.S.C.A.

§ 301 et seq.] and the Federal Trade Commission shall include this report in the Commission's annual report to Congress.

§ 1458. Cooperation with state authorities; transmittal of regulations to states; noninterference with existing programs

(a) A copy of each regulation promulgated under this chapter shall be transmitted promptly to the Secretary of Commerce, who shall (1) transmit copies thereof to all appropriate State officers and agencies, and (2) furnish to such State officers and agencies information and assistance to promote to the greatest practicable extent uniformity in State and Federal regulation of the labeling of consumer commodities.

(b) Nothing contained in this section shall be construed to impair or otherwise interfere with any program carried into effect by the Secretary of Health and Human Services under other provisions of law in cooperation with State governments or agencies, instrumentalities, or political subdivisions thereof.

§ 1459. Definitions

For the purposes of this chapter—

(a) The term "consumer commodity", except as otherwise specifically provided by this subsection, means any food, drug, device, or cosmetic (as those terms are defined by the Federal Food, Drug, and Cosmetic Act), and any other article, product, or commodity of any kind or class which is customarily produced or distributed for sale through retail sales agencies or instrumentalities for consumption by individuals, or use by individuals for purposes of personal care or in the performance of services ordinarily rendered within the household, and which usually is consumed or expended in the course of such consumption or use. Such term does not include—

(1) any meat or meat product, poultry or poultry product, or tobacco or tobacco product;

(2) any commodity subject to packaging or labeling requirements imposed by the Secretary of Agriculture pursuant to the Federal Insecticide, Fungicide, and Rodenticide Act, or the provisions of the eighth paragraph under the heading "Bureau of Animal Industry" of the Act of March 4, 1913 [37 Stat. 832–833; 21 U.S.C.A. §§ 151–157], commonly known as the Virus–Serum–Toxin Act;

(3) any drug subject to the provisions of section 503(b)(1) or 506 of the Federal Food, Drug, and Cosmetic Act [21 U.S.C.A. §§ 353(b)(1) and 356];

(4) any beverage subject to or complying with packaging or labeling requirements imposed under the Federal Alcohol Administration Act [27 U.S.C.A. §§ 201 et seq.]; or

(5) any commodity subject to the provisions of the Federal Seed Act [7 U.S.C.A. §§ 1551–1610].

(b) The term "package" means any container or wrapping in which any consumer commodity is enclosed for use in the delivery or display of that consumer commodity to retail purchasers, but does not include—

(1) shipping containers or wrappings used solely for the transportation of any consumer commodity in bulk or in quantity to manufacturers, packers, or processors, or to wholesale or retail distributors thereof;

(2) shipping containers or outer wrappings used by retailers to ship or deliver any commodity to retail customers if such containers and wrappings bear no printed matter pertaining to any particular commodity; or

(3) containers subject to the provisions of the Act of August 3, 1912 [37 Stat. 250, as amended; 15 U.S.C.A. §§ 231–233], or the Act of March 4, 1915 [38 Stat. 1186, as amended; 15 U.S.C.A. §§ 234–236].

(c) The term "label" means any written, printed, or graphic matter affixed to any consumer commodity or affixed to or appearing upon a package containing any consumer commodity.

(d) The term "person" includes any firm, corporation, or association.

(e) The term "commerce" means (1) commerce between any State, the District of Columbia, the Commonwealth of Puerto Rico, or any territory or possession of the United States, and any place outside thereof, and (2) commerce within the District of Columbia or within any territory or possession of the United States not organized with a legislative body, but shall not include exports to foreign countries.

(f) The term "principal display panel" means that part of a label that is most likely to be displayed, presented, shown, or examined under normal and customary conditions of display for retail sale.

§ 1460. Savings provisions

Nothing contained in this chapter shall be construed to repeal, invalidate, or supersede—

(a) the Federal Trade Commission Act or any statute defined therein as an antitrust Act;

(b) the Federal Food, Drug, and Cosmetic Act; or

(c) the Federal Hazardous Substances Labeling Act.

§ **1461.** Effect upon State law

It is hereby declared that it is the express intent of Congress to supersede any and all laws of the States or political subdivisions thereof insofar as they may now or hereafter provide for the labeling of the net quantity of contents of the package of any consumer commodity covered by this chapter which are less stringent than or require information different from the requirements of section 1453 of this title or regulations promulgated pursuant thereto.

FEDERAL TRADE COMMISSION ACT

TITLE 15, U.S.C.A.

§ **53.** **False advertisements; injunctions and restraining orders**

(a) Power of Commission; jurisdiction of courts

Whenever the Commission has reason to believe—

(1) that any person, partnership, or corporation is engaged in, or is about to engage in, the dissemination or the causing of the dissemination of any advertisement in violation of section 52 of this title, and

(2) that the enjoining thereof pending the issuance of a complaint by the Commission under section 45 of this title, and until such complaint is dismissed by the Commission or set aside by the court on review, or the order of the Commission to cease and desist made thereon has become final within the meaning of section 45 of this title, would be to the interest of the public,

the Commission by any of its attorneys designated by it for such purpose may bring suit in a district court of the United States or in the United States court of any Territory, to enjoin the dissemination or the causing of the dissemination of such advertisement. Upon proper showing a temporary injunction or restraining order shall be granted without bond. Any suit may be brought where such person, partnership, or corporation resides or transacts business, or wherever venue is proper under section 1391 of Title 28. In addition, the court may, if the court determines that the interests of justice require that any other person, partnership, or corporation should be a party in such suit, cause such other person, partnership, or corporation to be added as a party without regard to whether venue is otherwise proper in the district in which the suit is brought. In any suit under this section, process may be served on any person, partnership, or corporation wherever it may be found.

(b) Temporary restraining orders; preliminary injunctions

Whenever the Commission has reason to believe—

(1) that any person, partnership, or corporation is violating, or is about to violate, any provision of law enforced by the Federal Trade Commission, and

(2) that the enjoining thereof pending the issuance of a complaint by the Commission and until such complaint is dismissed by the Commission or set aside by the court on review, or until the order of the Commission made thereon has become final, would be in the interest of the public—

the Commission by any of its attorneys designated by it for such purpose may bring suit in a district court of the United States to enjoin any such act or practice. Upon a proper showing that, weighing the equities and considering the Commission's likelihood of ultimate success, such action would be in the public interest, and after notice to the defendant, a temporary restraining order or a preliminary injunction may be granted without bond: Provided, however, That if a complaint is not filed within such period (not exceeding 20 days) as may be specified by the court after issuance of the temporary restraining order or preliminary injunction, the order or injunction shall be dissolved by the court and be of no further force and effect: Provided further, That in proper cases the Commission may seek, and after proper proof, the court may issue, a permanent injunction. Any suit may be brought where such person, partnership, or corporation resides or transacts business, or wherever venue is proper under section 1391 of Title 28. In addition, the court may, if the court determines that the interests of justice require that any other person, partnership, or corporation should be a party in such suit, cause such other person, partnership, or corporation to be added as a party without regard to whether venue is otherwise proper in the district in which the suit is brought. In any suit under this section, process may be served on any person, partnership, or corporation wherever it may be found.

(c) Service of process; proof of service

Any process of the Commission under this section may be served by any person duly authorized by the Commission—

(1) by delivering a copy of such process to the person to be served, to a member of the partnership to be served, or to the president, secretary, or other executive officer or a director of the corporation to be served;

(2) by leaving a copy of such process at the residence or the principal office or place of business of such person, partnership, or corporation; or

(3) by mailing a copy of such process by registered mail or certified mail addressed to such person, partnership, or corporation at his, or her, or its residence, principal office, or principal place or business.

The verified return by the person serving such process setting forth the manner of such service shall be proof of the same.

(d) Exception of periodical publications

Whenever it appears to the satisfaction of the court in the case of a newspaper, magazine, periodical, or other publication, published at regular intervals—

(1) that restraining the dissemination of a false advertisement in any particular issue of such publication would delay the delivery of such issue after the regular time therefor, and

(2) that such delay would be due to the method by which the manufacture and distribution of such publication is customarily conducted by the publisher in accordance with sound business practice, and not to any method or device adopted for the evasion of this section or to prevent or delay the issuance of an injunction or restraining order with respect to such false advertisement or any other advertisement.

The court shall exclude such issue from the operation of the restraining order or injunction.

§ 54. Same; penalties

(a) Imposition of penalties

Any person, partnership, or corporation who violates any provision of section 52(a) of this title shall, if the use of the commodity advertised may be injurious to health because of results from such use under the conditions prescribed in the advertisement thereof, or under such conditions as are customary or usual, or if such violation is with intent to defraud or mislead, be guilty of a misdemeanor, and upon conviction shall be punished by a fine of not more than $5,000 or by imprisonment for not more than six months, or by both such fine and imprisonment; except that if the conviction is for a violation committed after a first conviction of such person, partnership, or corporation, for any violation of such section, punishment shall be by a fine of not more than $10,000 or by imprisonment for not more than one year, or by both such fine and imprisonment: Provided, That for the purposes of this section meats and meat food products duly inspected, marked, and labeled in accordance with rules and regulations issued under the Meat Inspection Act, shall be conclusively presumed not injurious to health at the time the same leave official "establishments."

(b) Exception of advertising medium or agency

No publisher, radio-broadcast licensee, or agency or medium for the dissemination of advertising, except the manufacturer, packer, distributor, or seller of the commodity to which the false advertisement relates, shall be liable under this section by reason of the dissemination by him of any false advertisement, unless he has refused, on the request of the Commission, to furnish the Commission the name and post-office address of the manufacturer, packer, distributor, seller, or advertising agency, residing in the United States, who caused him to disseminate such advertisement. No advertising agency shall be liable under this section by reason of the causing by it of the dissemination of any false advertisement, unless it has refused, on the request of the Commission, to furnish the Commission the name and post-office address of the manufacturer, packer, distributor, or seller, residing in the United States, who caused it to cause the dissemination of such advertisement.

§ 55. Additional definitions

For the purposes of sections 52 to 54 of this title—

(a) False advertisement

(1) The term "false advertisement" means an advertisement, other than labeling, which is misleading in a material respect; and in determining whether any advertisement is misleading, there shall be taken into account (among other things) not only representations made or suggested by statement, word, design, device, sound, or any combination thereof, but also the extent to which the advertisement fails to reveal facts material in the light of such representations or material with respect to consequences which may result from the use of the commodity to which the advertisement relates under the conditions prescribed in said advertisement, or under such conditions as are customary or usual. No advertisement of a drug shall be deemed to be false if it is disseminated only to members of the medical profession, contains no false representation of a material fact, and includes, or is accompanied in each instance by truthful disclosure of, the formula showing quantitatively each ingredient of such drug.

(2) In the case of oleomargarine or margarine an advertisement shall be deemed misleading in a material respect if in such advertisement representations are made or suggested by statement, word, grade designation, design, device, symbol, sound, or any combination thereof, that such oleomargarine or margarine is a dairy product, except that nothing contained herein shall prevent a truthful, accurate, and full statement in any such advertisement of all the ingredients contained in such oleomargarine or margarine.

(b) Food

The term "food" means (1) articles used for food or drink for man or other animals, (2) chewing gum, and (3) articles used for components of any such article.

(c) Drug

The term "drug" means (1) articles recognized in the official United States Pharmacopoeia, official Homeopathic Pharmacopoeia of the United States, or official National Formulary, or any supplement to any of them; and (2) articles intended for use in the diagnosis, cure, mitigation, treatment, or prevention of disease in man or other animals; and (3) articles (other than food) intended to affect the structure or any function of the body of man or other animals; and (4) articles intended for use as a component of any article specified in clauses (1), (2), or (3); but does not include devices or their components, parts, or accessories.

(d) Device

The term "device" (except when used in subsection (a) of this section) means an instrument, apparatus, implement, machine, contrivance, implant, in vitro reagent, or other similar or related article, including any component, part, or accessory, which is—

(1) recognized in the official National Formulary, or the United States Pharmacopeia, or any supplement to them,

(2) intended for use in the diagnosis of disease or other conditions, or in the cure, mitigation, treatment, or prevention of disease, in man or other animals, or

(3) intended to affect the structure or any function of the body of man or other animals, and

which does not achieve any of its principal intended purposes through chemical action within or on the body of man or other animals and which is not depended upon being metabolized for the achievement of any of its principal intended purposes.

(e) Cosmetic

The term "cosmetic" means (1) articles to be rubbed, poured, sprinkled, or sprayed on, introduced into, or otherwise applied to the human body or any part thereof intended for cleansing, beautifying, promoting attractiveness, or altering the appearance, and (2) articles intended for use as a component of any such article; except that such term shall not include soap.

(f) Oleomargarine or margarine

For the purposes of this section and section 347 of Title 21, the term "oleomargarine" or "margarine" includes—

(1) all substances, mixtures, and compounds known as oleomargarine or margarine;

(2) all substances, mixtures, and compounds which have a consistence similar to that of butter and which contain any edible oils or fats other than milk fat if made in imitation or semblance of butter.

ADMINISTRATIVE PROCEDURE ACT

TITLE 5, U.S.C.A.

§ 551. Definitions

For the purpose of this subchapter—

(1) "agency" means each authority of the Government of the United States, whether or not it is within or subject to review by another agency, but does not include—

    (A) the Congress;

    (B) the courts of the United States;

    (C) the governments of the territories or possessions of the United States;

    (D) the government of the District of Columbia; or except as to the requirements of section 552 of this title—

    (E) agencies composed of representatives of the parties or of representatives of organizations of the parties to the disputes determined by them;

    (F) courts martial and military commissions;

    (G) military authority exercised in the field in time of war or in occupied territory; or

    (H) functions conferred by sections 1738, 1739, 1743, and 1744 of title 12; chapter 2 of title 41; subchapter II of chapter 471 of title 49; or sections 1884, 1891–1902, and former section 1641(b)(2), of title 50, appendix;

(2) "person" includes an individual, partnership, corporation, association, or public or private organization other than an agency;

(3) "party" includes a person or agency named or admitted as a party, or properly seeking and entitled as of right to be admitted as a party, in an agency proceeding, and a person or agency admitted by an agency as a party for limited purposes;

(4) "rule" means the whole or a part of an agency statement of general or particular applicability and future effect designed to implement, interpret, or prescribe law or policy or describing the organization, procedure, or practice requirements of an agency and includes the approval or prescription for the future of rates, wages, corporate or financial structures or reorganizations thereof, prices, facilities, appliances, services or allowances therefor or of valuations, costs, or accounting, or practices bearing on any of the foregoing;

(5) "rule making" means agency process for formulating, amending, or repealing a rule;

(6) "order" means the whole or a part of a final disposition, whether affirmative, negative, injunctive, or declaratory in form, of an agency in a matter other than rule making but including licensing;

(7) "adjudication" means agency process for the formulation of an order;

(8) "license" includes the whole or a part of an agency permit, certificate, approval, registration, charter, membership, statutory exemption or other form of permission;

(9) "licensing" includes agency process respecting the grant, renewal, denial, revocation, suspension, annulment, withdrawal, limitation, amendment, modification, or conditioning of a license;

(10) "sanction" includes the whole or a part of an agency—

(A) prohibition, requirement, limitation, or other condition affecting the freedom of a person;

(B) withholding of relief;

(C) imposition of penalty or fine;

(D) destruction, taking, seizure, or withholding of property;

(E) assessment of damages, reimbursement, restitution, compensation, costs, charges, or fees;

(F) requirement, revocation, or suspension of a license; or

(G) taking other compulsory or restrictive action;

(11) "relief" includes the whole or a part of an agency—

(A) grant of money, assistance, license, authority, exemption, exception, privilege, or remedy;

(B) recognition of a claim, right, immunity, privilege, exemption, or exception; or

(C) taking of other action on the application or petition of, and beneficial to, a person;

(12) "agency proceeding" means an agency process as defined by paragraphs (5), (7), and (9) of this section;

(13) "agency action" includes the whole or a part of an agency rule, order, license, sanction, relief, or the equivalent or denial thereof, or failure to act; and

(14) "ex parte communication" means an oral or written communication not on the public record with respect to which reasonable prior notice to all parties is not given, but it shall not include requests for status reports on any matter or proceeding covered by this subchapter.

FREEDOM OF INFORMATION ACT

§ 552.　Public information; agency rules, opinions, orders, records, and proceedings

(a) Each agency shall make available to the public information as follows:

(1) Each agency shall separately state and currently publish in the Federal Register for the guidance of the public—

(A) descriptions of its central and field organization and the established places at which, the employees (and in the case of a uniformed service, the members) from whom, and the methods whereby, the public may obtain information, make submittals or requests, or obtain decisions;

(B) statements of the general course and method by which its functions are channeled and determined, including the nature and requirements of all formal and informal procedures available;

(C) rules of procedure, descriptions of forms available or the places at which forms may be obtained, and instructions as to the scope and contents of all papers, reports, or examinations;

(D) substantive rules of general applicability adopted as authorized by law, and statements of general policy or interpretations of general applicability formulated and adopted by the agency; and

(E) each amendment, revision, or repeal of the foregoing.

Except to the extent that a person has actual and timely notice of the terms thereof, a person may not in any manner be required to resort to, or be adversely affected by, a matter required to be published in the Federal Register and not so published. For the purpose of this paragraph, matter reasonably available to the class of persons affected thereby is deemed published in the Federal Register when incorporated by reference therein with the approval of the Director of the Federal Register.

(2) Each agency, in accordance with published rules, shall make available for public inspection and copying—

(A) final opinions, including concurring and dissenting opinions, as well as orders, made in the adjudication of cases;

(B) those statements of policy and interpretations which have been adopted by the agency and are not published in the Federal Register; and

(C) administrative staff manuals and instructions to staff that affect a member of the public;

unless the materials are promptly published and copies offered for sale. To the extent required to prevent a clearly unwarranted invasion of personal privacy, an agency may delete identifying details when it makes available or publishes an opinion, statement of policy, interpretation, or staff manual or instruction. However, in each case the justification for the deletion shall be explained fully in writing. Each agency shall also maintain and make available for public inspection and copying current indexes providing identifying information for the public as to any matter issued, adopted, or promulgated after July 4, 1967, and required by this paragraph to be made available or published. Each agency shall promptly publish, quarterly or more frequently, and distribute (by sale or otherwise) copies of each index or supplements thereto unless it determines by order published in the Federal Register that the publication would be unnecessary and impracticable, in which case the agency shall nonetheless provide copies of such index on request at a cost not to exceed the direct cost of duplication. A final order, opinion, statement of policy, interpretation, or staff manual or instruction that affects a member of the public may be relied on, used, or cited as precedent by an agency against a party other than an agency only if—

(i) it has been indexed and either made available or published as provided by this paragraph; or

(ii) the party has actual and timely notice of the terms thereof.

(3) Except with respect to the records made available under paragraphs (1) and (2) of this subsection, each agency, upon any request for records which (A) reasonably describes such records and (B) is made in accordance with published rules stating the time, place, fees (if any), and procedures to be followed, shall make the records promptly available to any person.

(4)(A)(i) In order to carry out the provisions of this section, each agency shall promulgate regulations, pursuant to notice and receipt of public comment, specifying the schedule of fees applicable to the processing of requests under this section and establishing procedures and guidelines for determining when such fees should be waived or reduced. Such schedule shall conform to the guidelines which shall be promulgated, pursuant to notice and receipt of public comment, by the Director of the Office of Management and Budget and which shall provide for a uniform schedule of fees for all agencies.

(ii) Such agency regulations shall provide that—

(I) fees shall be limited to reasonable standard charges for document search, duplication, and review, when records are requested for commercial use;

(II) fees shall be limited to reasonable standard charges for document duplication when records are not sought for commercial use and the request is made by an educational or noncommercial scientific institution, whose purpose is scholarly or scientific research; or a representative of the news media; and

(III) for any request not described in (I) or (II), fees shall be limited to reasonable standard charges for document search and duplication.

(iii) Documents shall be furnished without any charge or at a charge reduced below the fees established under clause (ii) if disclosure of the information is in the public interest because it is likely to contribute significantly to public understanding of the operations or activities of the government and is not primarily in the commercial interest of the requester.

(iv) Fee schedules shall provide for the recovery of only the direct costs of search, duplication, or review. Review costs shall include only the direct costs incurred during the initial examination of a document for the purposes of determining whether the documents must be disclosed under this section and for the purposes of withholding any portions exempt from disclosure under this section. Review costs may not include any costs incurred in resolving issues of law or policy that may be raised in the course of processing a request under this section. No fee may be charged by any agency under this section—

(I) if the costs of routine collection and processing of the fee are likely to equal or exceed the amount of the fee; or

(II) for any request described in clause (ii)(II) or (III) of this subparagraph for the first two hours of search time or for the first one hundred pages of duplication.

(v) No agency may require advance payment of any fee unless the requester has previously failed to pay fees in a timely fashion, or the agency has determined that the fee will exceed $250.

(vi) Nothing in this subparagraph shall supersede fees chargeable under a statute specifically providing for setting the level of fees for particular types of records.

(vii) In any action by a requester regarding the waiver of fees under this section, the court shall determine the matter de novo: Provided, That the court's review of the matter shall be limited to the record before the agency.

(B) On complaint, the district court of the United States in the district in which the complainant resides, or has his principal place of business, or in which the agency records are situated, or in the District of Columbia, has jurisdiction to enjoin the agency from withholding agency records and to order the production of any agency records improperly withheld from the complainant. In such a case the court shall determine the matter de novo, and may examine the contents of such agency records in camera to determine whether such records or any part thereof shall be withheld under any of the exemptions set forth in subsection (b) of this section, and the burden is on the agency to sustain its action.

(C) Notwithstanding any other provision of law, the defendant shall serve an answer or otherwise plead to any complaint made under this subsection within thirty days after service upon the defendant of the pleading in which such complaint is made, unless the court otherwise directs for good cause shown.

[(D) Repealed. Pub.L. 98–620, Title IV, § 402(2), Nov. 8, 1984, 98 Stat. 3357]

(E) The court may assess against the United States reasonable attorney fees and other litigation costs reasonably incurred in any case under this section in which the complainant has substantially prevailed.

(F) Whenever the court orders the production of any agency records improperly withheld from the complainant and assesses against the United States reasonable attorney fees and other litigation costs, and the court additionally issues a written finding that the circumstances surrounding the withholding raise questions whether agency personnel acted arbitrarily or capriciously with respect to the withholding, the Special Counsel shall promptly initiate a proceeding to determine whether disciplinary action is warranted against the officer or employee who was primarily responsible for the withholding. The Special Counsel, after investigation and consideration of the evidence submitted, shall submit his findings and recommendations to the administrative authority of the agency concerned and shall send copies of the findings and recommendations to the officer or employee or his representative. The administrative authority shall take the corrective action that the Special Counsel recommends.

(G) In the event of noncompliance with the order of the court, the district court may punish for contempt the responsible employee, and in the case of a uniformed service, the responsible member.

(5) Each agency having more than one member shall maintain and make available for public inspection a record of the final votes of each member in every agency proceeding.

(6)(A) Each agency, upon any request for records made under paragraph (1), (2), or (3) of this subsection, shall—

(i) determine within ten days (excepting Saturdays, Sundays, and legal public holidays) after the receipt of any such request whether to comply with such request and shall immediately notify the person making such request of such determination and the reasons therefor, and of the right of such person to appeal to the head of the agency any adverse determination; and

(ii) make a determination with respect to any appeal within twenty days (excepting Saturdays, Sundays, and legal public holidays) after the receipt of such appeal. If on appeal the denial of the request for records is in whole or in part upheld, the agency shall notify the person making such request of the provisions for judicial review of that determination under paragraph (4) of this subsection.

(B) In unusual circumstances as specified in this subparagraph, the time limits prescribed in either clause (i) or clause (ii) of subparagraph (A) may be extended by written notice to the person making such request setting forth the reasons for such extension and the date on which a determination is expected to be dispatched. No such notice shall specify a date that would result in an extension for more than ten working days. As used in this subparagraph, "unusual circumstances" means, but only to the extent reasonably necessary to the proper processing of the particular request—

(i) the need to search for and collect the requested records from field facilities or other establishments that are separate from the office processing the request;

(ii) the need to search for, collect, and appropriately examine a voluminous amount of separate and distinct records which are demanded in a single request; or

(iii) the need for consultation, which shall be conducted with all practicable speed, with another agency having a substantial interest in the determination of the request or among two or more components of the agency having substantial subject-matter interest therein.

(C) Any person making a request to any agency for records under paragraph (1), (2), or (3) of this subsection shall be deemed to have exhausted his administrative remedies with respect to such request if the agency fails to comply with the applicable time limit provisions of this paragraph. If the Government can show exceptional circumstances exist and that the agency is exercising due diligence in responding to the request, the court may retain jurisdiction and allow the agency additional time to complete its review of the records. Upon any determination by an agency to comply with a request for records, the records shall be made promptly available to such person making such request. Any notification of denial of any request for records under this subsection shall set forth the names and titles or positions of each person responsible for the denial of such request.

(b) This section does not apply to matters that are—

(1)(A) specifically authorized under criteria established by an Executive order to be kept secret in the interest of national defense or foreign policy and (B) are in fact properly classified pursuant to such Executive order;

(2) related solely to the internal personnel rules and practices of an agency;

(3) specifically exempted from disclosure by statute (other than section 552b of this title), provided that such statute (A) requires that the matters be withheld from the public in such a manner as to leave no discretion on the issue, or (B) establishes particular criteria for withholding or refers to particular types of matters to be withheld;

(4) trade secrets and commercial or financial information obtained from a person and privileged or confidential;

(5) inter-agency or intra-agency memorandums or letters which would not be available by law to a party other than an agency in litigation with the agency;

(6) personnel and medical files and similar files the disclosure of which would constitute a clearly unwarranted invasion of personal privacy;

(7) records or information compiled for law enforcement purposes, but only to the extent that the production of such law enforcement records or information (A) could reasonably be expected to interfere with enforcement proceedings, (B) would deprive a person of a right to a fair trial or an impartial adjudication, (C) could reasonably be expected to constitute an unwarranted invasion of personal privacy, (D) could reasonably be expected to disclose the identity of a confidential source, including a State, local, or foreign agency or authority or any private institution which furnished information on a confidential basis, and, in the case of a record or information compiled by criminal law enforcement authority in the course of a criminal investigation or by an agency conducting a lawful national security intelligence investigation, information furnished by a confidential source, (E) would disclose techniques and procedures for law enforcement investigations or prosecutions, or would disclose guidelines for law enforcement investigations or prosecutions if such disclosure could reasonably be expected to risk circumvention of the law, or (F) could reasonably be expected to endanger the life or physical safety of any individual;

(8) contained in or related to examination, operating, or condition reports prepared by, on behalf of, or for the use of an agency responsible for the regulation or supervision of financial institutions; or

(9) geological and geophysical information and data, including maps, concerning wells.

Any reasonable segregable portion of a record shall be provided to any person requesting such record after deletion of the portions which are exempt under this subsection.

(c)(1) Whenever a request is made which involves access to records described in subsection (b)(7)(A) and—

(A) the investigation or proceeding involves a possible violation of criminal law; and

(B) there is reason to believe that (i) the subject of the investigation or proceeding is not aware of its pendency, and (ii) disclosure of the existence of the records could reasonably be expected to interfere with enforcement proceedings.

The agency may, during only such time as that circumstance continues, treat the records as not subject to the requirements of this section.

(2) Whenever informant records maintained by a criminal law enforcement agency under an informant's name or personal identifier are requested by a third party according to the informant's name or personal identifier, the agency may treat the records as not subject to the requirements of this section unless the informant's status as an informant has been officially confirmed.

(3) Whenever a request is made which involves access to records maintained by the Federal Bureau of Investigation pertaining to foreign intelligence or counterintelligence, or international terrorism, and the existence of the records is classified information as provided in subsection (b)(1), the Bureau may, as long as the existence of the records remains classified information, treat the records as not subject to the requirements of this section.

(d) This section does not authorize withholding of information or limit the availability of records to the public, except as specifically stated in this section. This section is not authority to withhold information from Congress.

(e) On or before March 1 of each calendar year, each agency shall submit a report covering the preceding calendar year to the Speaker of the House of Representatives and President of the Senate for referral to the appropriate committees of the Congress. The report shall include—

(1) the number of determinations made by such agency not to comply with requests for records made to such agency under subsection (a) and the reasons for each such determination;

(2) the number of appeals made by persons under subsection (a)(6), the result of such appeals, and the reason for the action upon each appeal that results in a denial of information;

(3) the names and titles or positions of each person responsible for the denial of records requested under this section, and the number of instances of participation for each;

(4) the results of each proceeding conducted pursuant to subsection (a)(4)(F), including a report of the disciplinary action taken against the officer or employee who was primarily responsible for improperly withholding records or an explanation of why disciplinary action was not taken;

(5) a copy of every rule made by such agency regarding this section;

(6) a copy of the fee schedule and the total amount of fees collected by the agency for making records available under this section; and

(7) such other information as indicates efforts to administer fully this section.

The Attorney General shall submit an annual report on or before March 1 of each calendar year which shall include for the prior calendar year a listing of the number of cases arising under this section, the exemption involved in each case, the disposition of such case, and the cost, fees, and penalties assessed under subsections (a)(4)(E), (F), and (G). Such report shall also include a description of the efforts undertaken by the Department of Justice to encourage agency compliance with this section.

(f) For purposes of this section, the term "agency" as defined in section 551(1) of this title includes any executive department, military department, Government corporation, Government controlled corporation, or other establishment in the executive branch of the Government (including the Executive Office of the President), or any independent regulatory agency.

GOVERNMENT IN THE SUNSHINE ACT

§ 552b. Open meetings

(a) For purposes of this section—

(1) the term "agency" means any agency, as defined in section 552(e) of this title, headed by a collegial body composed of two or more individual members, a majority of whom are appointed to such position by the President with the advice and consent of the Senate, and any subdivision thereof authorized to act on behalf of the agency;

(2) the term "meeting" means the deliberations of at least the number of individual agency members required to take action on

behalf of the agency where such deliberations determine or result in the joint conduct or disposition of official agency business, but does not include deliberations required or permitted by subsection (d) or (e); and

(3) the term "member" means an individual who belongs to a collegial body heading an agency.

(b) Members shall not jointly conduct or dispose of agency business other than in accordance with this section. Except as provided in subsection (c), every portion of every meeting of an agency shall be open to public observation.

(c) Except in a case where the agency finds that the public interest requires otherwise, the second sentence of subsection (b) shall not apply to any portion of an agency meeting, and the requirements of subsections (d) and (e) shall not apply to any information pertaining to such meeting otherwise required by this section to be disclosed to the public, where the agency properly determines that such portion or portions of its meeting or the disclosure of such information is likely to—

(1) disclose matters that are (A) specifically authorized under criteria established by an Executive order to be kept secret in the interests of national defense or foreign policy and (B) in fact properly classified pursuant to such Executive order;

(2) relate solely to the internal personnel rules and practices of an agency;

(3) disclose matters specifically exempted from disclosure by statute (other than section 552 of this title), provided that such statute (A) requires that the matters be withheld from the public in such a manner as to leave no discretion on the issue, or (B) establishes particular criteria for withholding or refers to particular types of matters to be withheld;

(4) disclose trade secrets and commercial or financial information obtained from a person and privileged or confidential;

(5) involve accusing any person of a crime, or formally censuring any person;

(6) disclose information of a personal nature where disclosure would constitute a clearly unwarranted invasion of personal privacy;

(7) disclose investigatory records compiled for law enforcement purposes, or information which if written would be contained in such records, but only to the extent that the production of such records or information would (A) interfere with enforcement proceedings, (B) deprive a person of a right to a fair trial or an impartial adjudication, (C) constitute an unwarranted invasion of personal privacy, (D) disclose the identity of a confidential source and, in the case of a record compiled by a criminal law enforcement authority in the course of a criminal investigation, or by an agency

conducting a lawful national security intelligence investigation, confidential information furnished only by the confidential source, (E) disclose investigative techniques and procedures, or (F) endanger the life or physical safety of law enforcement personnel;

(8) disclose information contained in or related to examination, operating, or condition reports prepared by, on behalf of, or for the use of an agency responsible for the regulation or supervision of financial institutions;

(9) disclose information the premature disclosure of which would—

(A) in the case of an agency which regulates currencies, securities, commodities, or financial institutions, be likely to (i) lead to significant financial speculation in currencies, securities, or commodities, or (ii) significantly endanger the stability of any financial institution; or

(B) in the case of any agency, be likely to significantly frustrate implementation of a proposed agency action, except that subparagraph (B) shall not apply in any instance where the agency has already disclosed to the public the content or nature of its proposed action, or where the agency is required by law to make such disclosure on its own initiative prior to taking final agency action on such proposal; or

(10) specifically concern the agency's issuance of a subpena, or the agency's participation in a civil action or proceeding, an action in a foreign court or international tribunal, or an arbitration, or the initiation, conduct, or disposition by the agency of a particular case of formal agency adjudication pursuant to the procedures in section 554 of this title or otherwise involving a determination on the record after opportunity for a hearing.

(d)(1) Action under subsection (c) shall be taken only when a majority of the entire membership of the agency (as defined in subsection (a)(1))votes to take such action. A separate vote of the agency members shall be taken with respect to each agency meeting a portion or portions of which are proposed to be closed to the public pursuant to subsection (c), or with respect to any information which is proposed to be withheld under subsection (c). A single vote may be taken with respect to a series of meetings, a portion or portions of which are proposed to be closed to the public, or with respect to any information concerning such series of meetings, so long as each meeting in such series involves the same particular matters and is scheduled to be held no more than thirty days after the initial meeting in such series. The vote of each agency member participating in such vote shall be recorded and no proxies shall be allowed.

(2) Whenever any person whose interests may be directly affected by a portion of a meeting requests that the agency close such portion to

the public for any of the reasons referred to in paragraph (5), (6), or (7) of subsection (c), the agency, upon request of any one of its members, shall vote by recorded vote whether to close such meeting.

(3) Within one day of any vote taken pursuant to paragraph (1) or (2), the agency shall make publicly available a written copy of such vote reflecting the vote of each member on the question. If a portion of a meeting is to be closed to the public, the agency shall, within one day of the vote taken pursuant to paragraph (1) or (2) of this subsection, make publicly available a full written explanation of its action closing the portion together with a list of all persons expected to attend the meeting and their affiliation.

(4) Any agency, a majority of whose meetings may properly be closed to the public pursuant to paragraph (4), (8), (9)(A), or (10) of subsection (c), or any combination thereof, may provide by regulation for the closing of such meetings or portions thereof in the event that a majority of the members of the agency votes by recorded vote at the beginning of such meeting, or portion thereof, to close the exempt portion or portions of the meeting, and a copy of such vote, reflecting the vote of each member on the question, is made available to the public. The provisions of paragraphs (1), (2), and (3) of this subsection and subsection (e) shall not apply to any portion of a meeting to which such regulations apply: Provided, That the agency shall, except to the extent that such information is exempt from disclosure under the provisions of subsection (c), provide the public with public announcement of the time, place, and subject matter of the meeting and of each portion thereof at the earliest practicable time.

(e)(1) In the case of each meeting, the agency shall make public announcement, at least one week before the meeting, of the time, place, and subject matter of the meeting, whether it is to be open or closed to the public, and the name and phone number of the official designated by the agency to respond to requests for information about the meeting. Such announcement shall be made unless a majority of the members of the agency determines by a recorded vote that agency business requires that such meeting be called at an earlier date, in which case the agency shall make public announcement of the time, place, and subject matter of such meeting, and whether open or closed to the public, at the earliest practicable time.

(2) The time or place of a meeting may be changed following the public announcement required by paragraph (1) only if the agency publicly announces such change at the earliest practicable time. The subject matter of a meeting, or the determination of the agency to open or close a meeting, or portion of a meeting, to the public, may be changed following the public announcement required by this subsection only if (A) a majority of the entire membership of the agency determines by a recorded vote that agency business so requires and that no earlier announcement of the change was possible, and (B) the agency publicly

announces such change and the vote of each member upon such change at the earliest practicable time.

(3) Immediately following each public announcement required by this subsection, notice of the time, place, and subject matter of a meeting, whether the meeting is open or closed, any change in one of the preceding, and the name and phone number of the official designated by the agency to respond to requests for information about the meeting, shall also be submitted for publication in the Federal Register.

(f)(1) For every meeting closed pursuant to paragraphs (1) through (10) of subsection (c), the General Counsel or chief legal officer of the agency shall publicly certify that, in his or her opinion, the meeting may be closed to the public and shall state each relevant exemptive provision. A copy of such certification, together with a statement from the presiding officer of the meeting setting forth the time and place of the meeting, and the persons present, shall be retained by the agency. The agency shall maintain a complete transcript or electronic recording adequate to record fully the proceedings of each meeting, or portion of a meeting, closed to the public, except that in the case of a meeting, or portion of a meeting, closed to the public pursuant to paragraph (8), (9)(A), or (10) of subsection (c), the agency shall maintain either such a transcript or recording, or a set of minutes. Such minutes shall fully and clearly describe all matters discussed and shall provide a full and accurate summary of any actions taken, and the reasons therefor, including a description of each of the views expressed on any item and the record of any rollcall vote (reflecting the vote of each member on the question). All documents considered in connection with any action shall be identified in such minutes.

(2) The agency shall make promptly available to the public, in a place easily accessible to the public, the transcript, electronic recording, or minutes (as required by paragraph (1))of the discussion of any item on the agenda, or of any item of the testimony of any witness received at the meeting, except for such item or items of such discussion or testimony as the agency determines to contain information which may be withheld under subsection (c). Copies of such transcript, or minutes, or a transcription of such recording disclosing the identity of each speaker, shall be furnished to any person at the actual cost of duplication or transcription. The agency shall maintain a complete verbatim copy of the transcript, a complete copy of the minutes, or a complete electronic recording of each meeting, or portion of a meeting, closed to the public, for a period of at least two years after such meeting, or until one year after the conclusion of any agency proceeding with respect to which the meeting or portion was held, whichever occurs later.

(g) Each agency subject to the requirements of this section shall, within 180 days after the date of enactment of this section, following consultation with the Office of the Chairman of the Administrative Conference of the United States and published notice in the Federal

Register of at least thirty days and opportunity for written comment by any person, promulgate regulations to implement the requirements of subsections (b) through (f) of this section. Any person may bring a proceeding in the United States District Court for the District of Columbia to require an agency to promulgate such regulations if such agency has not promulgated such regulations within the time period specified herein. Subject to any limitations of time provided by law, any person may bring a proceeding in the United States Court of Appeals for the District of Columbia to set aside agency regulations issued pursuant to this subsection that are not in accord with the requirements of subsections (b) through (f) of this section and to require the promulgation of regulations that are in accord with such subsections.

(h)(1) The district courts of the United States shall have jurisdiction to enforce the requirements of subsections (b) through (f) of this section by declaratory judgment, injunctive relief, or other relief as may be appropriate. Such actions may be brought by any person against an agency prior to, or within sixty days after, the meeting out of which the violation of this section arises, except that if public announcement of such meeting is not initially provided by the agency in accordance with the requirements of this section, such action may be instituted pursuant to this section at any time prior to sixty days after any public announcement of such meeting. Such actions may be brought in the district court of the United States for the district in which the agency meeting is held or in which the agency in question has its headquarters, or in the District Court for the District of Columbia. In such actions a defendant shall serve his answer within thirty days after the service of the complaint. The burden is on the defendant to sustain his action. In deciding such cases the court may examine in camera any portion of the transcript, electronic recording, or minutes of a meeting closed to the public, and may take such additional evidence as it deems necessary. The court, having due regard for orderly administration and the public interest, as well as the interests of the parties, may grant such equitable relief as it deems appropriate, including granting an injunction against future violations of this section or ordering the agency to make available to the public such portion of the transcript, recording, or minutes of a meeting as is not authorized to be withheld under subsection (c) of this section.

(2) Any Federal court otherwise authorized by law to review agency action may, at the application of any person properly participating in the proceeding pursuant to other applicable law, inquire into violations by the agency of the requirements of this section and afford such relief as it deems appropriate. Nothing in this section authorizes any Federal court having jurisdiction solely on the basis of paragraph (1) to set aside, enjoin, or invalidate any agency action (other than an action to close a meeting or to withhold information under this section) taken or dis-

cussed at any agency meeting out of which the violation of this section arose.

(i) The court may assess against any party reasonable attorney fees and other litigation costs reasonably incurred by any other party who substantially prevails in any action brought in accordance with the provisions of subsection (g) or (h) of this section, except that costs may be assessed against the plaintiff only where the court finds that the suit was initiated by the plaintiff primarily for frivolous or dilatory purposes. In the case of assessment of costs against an agency, the costs may be assessed by the court against the United States.

(j) Each agency subject to the requirements of this section shall annually report to Congress regarding its compliance with such requirements, including a tabulation of the total number of agency meetings open to the public, the total number of meetings closed to the public, the reasons for closing such meetings, and a description of any litigation brought against the agency under this section, including any costs assessed against the agency in such litigation (whether or not paid by the agency).

(k) Nothing herein expands or limits the present rights of any person under section 552 of this title, except that the exemptions set forth in subsection (c) of this section shall govern in the case of any request made pursuant to section 552 to copy or inspect the transcripts, recordings, or minutes described in subsection (f) of this section. The requirements of chapter 33 of title 44, United States Code, shall not apply to the transcripts, recordings, and minutes described in subsection (f) of this section.

(*l*) This section does not constitute authority to withhold any information from Congress, and does not authorize the closing of any agency meeting or portion thereof required by any other provision of law to be open.

(m) Nothing in this section authorizes any agency to withhold from any individual any record, including transcripts, recordings, or minutes required by this section, which is otherwise accessible to such individual under section 552a of this title.

§ 553. Rule making

(a) This section applies, according to the provisions thereof, except to the extent that there is involved—

(1) a military or foreign affairs function of the United States; or

(2) a matter relating to agency management or personnel or to public property, loans, grants, benefits, or contracts.

(b) General notice of proposed rule making shall be published in the Federal Register, unless persons subject thereto are named and either personally served or otherwise have actual notice thereof in accordance with law. The notice shall include—

(1) a statement of the time, place, and nature of public rule making proceedings;

(2) reference to the legal authority under which the rule is proposed; and

(3) either the terms or substance of the proposed rule or a description of the subjects and issues involved.

Except when notice or hearing is required by statute, this subsection does not apply—

(A) to interpretative rules, general statements of policy, or rules of agency organization, procedure, or practice; or

(B) when the agency for good cause finds (and incorporates the finding and a brief statement of reasons therefor in the rules issued) that notice and public procedure thereon are impracticable, unnecessary, or contrary to the public interest.

(c) After notice required by this section, the agency shall give interested persons an opportunity to participate in the rule making through submission of written data, views, or arguments with or without opportunity for oral presentation. After consideration of the relevant matter presented, the agency shall incorporate in the rules adopted a concise general statement of their basis and purpose. When rules are required by statute to be made on the record after opportunity for an agency hearing, sections 556 and 557 of this title apply instead of this subsection.

(d) The required publication or service of a substantive rule shall be made not less than 30 days before its effective date, except—

(1) a substantive rule which grants or recognizes an exemption or relieves a restriction;

(2) interpretative rules and statements of policy; or

(3) as otherwise provided by the agency for good cause found and published with the rule.

(e) Each agency shall give an interested person the right to petition for the issuance, amendment, or repeal of a rule.

§ 554. Adjudications

(a) This section applies, according to the provisions thereof, in every case of adjudication required by statute to be determined on the record after opportunity for an agency hearing, except to the extent that there is involved—

(1) a matter subject to a subsequent trial of the law and the facts de novo in a court;

(2) the selection or tenure of an employee, except a administrative law judge appointed under section 3105 of this title;

(3) proceedings in which decisions rest solely on inspections, tests, or elections;

(4) the conduct of military or foreign affairs functions;

(5) cases in which an agency is acting as an agent for a court; or

(6) the certification of worker representatives.

(b) Persons entitled to notice of an agency hearing shall be timely informed of—

(1) the time, place, and nature of the hearing;

(2) the legal authority and jurisdiction under which the hearing is to be held; and

(3) the matters of fact and law asserted.

When private persons are the moving parties, other parties to the proceeding shall give prompt notice of issues controverted in fact or law; and in other instances agencies may by rule require responsive pleading. In fixing the time and place for hearings, due regard shall be had for the convenience and necessity of the parties or their representatives.

(c) The agency shall give all interested parties opportunity for—

(1) the submission and consideration of facts, arguments, offers of settlement, or proposals of adjustment when time, the nature of the proceeding, and the public interest permit; and

(2) to the extent that the parties are unable so to determine a controversy by consent, hearing and decision on notice and in accordance with sections 556 and 557 of this title.

(d) The employee who presides at the reception of evidence pursuant to section 556 of this title shall make the recommended decision or initial decision required by section 557 of this title, unless he becomes unavailable to the agency. Except to the extent required for the disposition of ex parte matters as authorized by law, such an employee may not—

(1) consult a person or party on a fact in issue, unless on notice and opportunity for all parties to participate; or

(2) be responsible to or subject to the supervision or direction of an employee or agent engaged in the performance of investigative or prosecuting functions for an agency.

An employee or agent engaged in the performance of investigative or prosecuting functions for an agency in a case may not, in that or a factually related case, participate or advise in the decision, recommended decision, or agency review pursuant to section 557 of this title, except as witness or counsel in public proceedings. This subsection does not apply—

(A) in determining applications for initial licenses;

(B) to proceedings involving the validity or application of rates, facilities, or practices of public utilities or carriers; or

(C) to the agency or a member or members of the body comprising the agency.

(e) The agency, with like effect as in the case of other orders, and in its sound discretion, may issue a declaratory order to terminate a controversy or remove uncertainty.

§ 555. Ancillary matters

(a) This section applies, according to the provisions thereof, except as otherwise provided by this subchapter.

(b) A person compelled to appear in person before an agency or representative thereof is entitled to be accompanied, represented, and advised by counsel or, if permitted by the agency, by other qualified representative. A party is entitled to appear in person or by or with counsel or other duly qualified representative in an agency proceeding. So far as the orderly conduct of public business permits, an interested person may appear before an agency or its responsible employees for the presentation, adjustment, or determination of an issue, request, or controversy in a proceeding, whether interlocutory, summary, or other-wise, or in connection with an agency function. With due regard for the convenience and necessity of the parties or their representatives and within a reasonable time, each agency shall proceed to conclude a matter presented to it. This subsection does not grant or deny a person who is not a lawyer the right to appear for or represent others before an agency or in an agency proceeding.

(c) Process, requirement of a report, inspection, or other investiga-tive act or demand may not be issued, made, or enforced except as authorized by law. A person compelled to submit data or evidence is entitled to retain or, on payment of lawfully prescribed costs, procure a copy or transcript thereof, except that in a nonpublic investigatory proceeding the witness may for good cause be limited to inspection of the official transcript of his testimony.

(d) Agency subpenas authorized by law shall be issued to a party on request and, when required by rules of procedure, on a statement or showing of general relevance and reasonable scope of the evidence sought. On contest, the court shall sustain the subpena or similar process or demand to the extent that it is found to be in accordance with law. In a proceeding for enforcement, the court shall issue an order requiring the appearance of the witness or the production of the evidence or data within a reasonable time under penalty of punishment for contempt in case of contumacious failure to comply.

(e) Prompt notice shall be given of the denial in whole or in part of a written application, petition, or other request of an interested person made in connection with any agency proceeding. Except in affirming a prior denial or when the denial is self-explanatory, the notice shall be accompanied by a brief statement of the grounds for denial.

§ 556. Hearings; presiding employees; powers and duties; burden of proof; evidence; record as basis of decision

(a) This section applies, according the provisions thereof, to hearings required by section 553 or 554 of this title to be conducted in accordance with this section.

(b) There shall preside at the taking of evidence—

(1) the agency;

(2) one or more members of the body which comprises the agency; or

(3) one or more administrative law judges appointed under section 3105 of this title.

This subchapter does not supersede the conduct of specified classes of proceedings, in whole or in part, by or before boards or other employees specially provided for by or designated under statute. The functions of presiding employees and of employees participating in decisions in accordance with section 557 of this title shall be conducted in an impartial manner. A presiding or participating employee may at any time disqualify himself. On the filing in good faith of a timely and sufficient affidavit of personal bias or other disqualification of a presiding or participating employee, the agency shall determine the matter as a part of the record and decision in the case.

(c) Subject to published rules of the agency and within its powers, employees presiding at hearings may—

(1) administer oaths and affirmations;

(2) issue subpenas authorized by law;

(3) rule on offers of proof and receive relevant evidence;

(4) take depositions or have depositions taken when the ends of justice would be served;

(5) regulate the course of the hearing;

(6) hold conferences for the settlement or simplification of the issues by consent of the parties or by the use of alternative means of dispute resolution as provided in subchapter IV of this chapter;

(7) inform the parties as to the availability of one or more alternative means of dispute resolution, and encourage use of such methods;

(8) require the attendance at any conference held pursuant to paragraph (6) of at least one representative of each party who has authority to negotiate concerning resolution of issues in controversy;

(9) dispose of procedural requests or similar matters;

(10) make or recommend decisions in accordance with section 557 of this title; and

(11) take other action authorized by agency rule consistent with this subchapter.

(d) Except as otherwise provided by statute, the proponent of a rule or order has the burden of proof. Any oral or documentary evidence may be received, but the agency as a matter of policy shall provide for the exclusion of irrelevant, immaterial, or unduly repetitious evidence. A sanction may not be imposed or rule or order issued except on consideration of the whole record or those parts thereof cited by a party and supported by and in accordance with the reliable, probative, and substantial evidence. The agency may, to the extent consistent with the interests of justice and the policy of the underlying statutes administered by the agency, consider a violation of section 557(d) of this title sufficient grounds for a decision adverse to a party who has knowingly committed such violation or knowingly caused such violation to occur. A party is entitled to present his case or defense by oral or documentary evidence, to submit rebuttal evidence, and to conduct such cross-examination as may be required for a full and true disclosure of the facts. In rule making or determining claims for money or benefits or applications for initial licenses an agency may, when a party will not be prejudiced thereby, adopt procedures for the submission of all or part of the evidence in written form.

(e) The transcript of testimony and exhibits, together with all papers and requests filed in the proceeding, constitutes the exclusive record for decision in accordance with section 557 of this title and, on payment of lawfully prescribed costs, shall be made available to the parties. When an agency decision rests on official notice of a material fact not appearing in the evidence in the record, a party is entitled, on timely request, to an opportunity to show the contrary.

§ 557. Initial decisions; conclusiveness; review by agency; submissions by parties; contents of decisions; record

(a) This section applies, according to the provisions thereof, when a hearing is required to be conducted in accordance with section 556 of this title.

(b) When the agency did not preside at the reception of the evidence, the presiding employee or, in cases not subject to section 554(d) of this title, an employee qualified to preside at hearings pursuant to section 556 of this title, shall initially decide the case unless the agency requires, either in specific cases or by general rule, the entire record to be certified to it for decision. When the presiding employee makes an initial decision, that decision then becomes the decision of the agency without further proceedings unless there is an appeal to, or review on motion of, the agency within time provided by rule. On appeal from or review of the initial decision, the agency has all the powers which it would have in making the initial decision except as it may limit the issues on notice or by rule. When the agency makes the decision without having presided at the reception of the evidence, the presiding employee or an employee qualified to preside at hearings pursuant to section 556 of this title shall first recommend a decision, except that in rule making or determining applications for initial licenses—

(1) instead thereof the agency may issue a tentative decision or one of its responsible employees may recommend a decision; or

(2) this procedure may be omitted in a case in which the agency finds on the record that due and timely execution of its functions imperatively and unavoidably so requires.

(c) Before a recommended, initial, or tentative decision, or a decision on agency review of the decision of subordinate employees, the parties are entitled to a reasonable opportunity to submit for the consideration of the employees participating in the decisions—

(1) proposed findings and conclusions; or

(2) exceptions to the decisions or recommended decisions of subordinate employees or to tentative agency decisions; and

(3) supporting reasons for the exceptions or proposed findings or conclusions.

The record shall show the ruling on each finding, conclusion, or exception presented. All decisions, including initial, recommended, and tentative decisions, are a part of the record and shall include a statement of—

(A) findings and conclusions, and the reasons or basis therefor, on all the material issues of fact, law, or discretion presented on the record; and

(B) the appropriate rule, order, sanction, relief, or denial thereof.

(d)(1) In any agency proceeding which is subject to subsection (a) of this section, except to the extent required for the disposition of ex parte matters as authorized by law—

(A) no interested person outside the agency shall make or knowingly cause to be made to any member of the body comprising the agency, administrative law judge, or other employee who is or may reasonably be expected to be involved in the decisional process of the proceeding, an ex parte communication relevant to the merits of the proceeding;

(B) no member of the body comprising the agency, administrative law judge, or other employee who is or may reasonably be expected to be involved in the decisional process of the proceeding, shall make or knowingly cause to be made to any interested person outside the agency an ex parte communication relevant to the merits of the proceeding;

(C) a member of the body comprising the agency, administrative law judge, or other employee who is or may reasonably be expected to be involved in the decisional process of such proceeding who receives, or who makes or knowingly causes to be made, a communication prohibited by this subsection shall place on the public record of the proceeding:

(i) all such written communications;

(ii) memoranda stating the substance of all such oral communications; and

(iii) all written responses, and memoranda stating the substance of all oral responses, to the materials described in clauses (i) and (ii) of this subparagraph;

(D) upon receipt of a communication knowingly made or knowingly caused to be made by a party in violation of this subsection, the agency, administrative law judge, or other employee presiding at the hearing may, to the extent consistent with the interests of justice and the policy of the underlying statutes, require the party to show cause why his claim or interest in the proceeding should not be dismissed, denied, disregarded, or otherwise adversely affected on account of such violation; and

(E) the prohibitions of this subsection shall apply beginning at such time as the agency may designate, but in no case shall they begin to apply later than the time at which a proceeding is noticed for hearing unless the person responsible for the communication has knowledge that it will be noticed, in which case the prohibitions shall apply beginning at the time of his acquisition of such knowledge.

(2) This subsection does not constitute authority to withhold information from Congress.

§ 558. Imposition of sanctions; determination of applications for licenses; suspension, revocation, and expiration of licenses

(a) This section applies, according to the provisions thereof, to the exercise of a power or authority.

(b) A sanction may not be imposed or a substantive rule or order issued except within jurisdiction delegated to the agency and as authorized by law.

(c) When application is made for a license required by law, the agency, with due regard for the rights and privileges of all the interested parties or adversely affected persons and within a reasonable time, shall set and complete proceedings required to be conducted in accordance with sections 556 and 557 of this title or other proceedings required by law and shall make its decision. Except in cases of willfulness or those in which public health, interest, or safety requires otherwise, the withdrawal, suspension, revocation, or annulment of a license is lawful only if, before the institution of agency proceedings therefor, the licensee has been given—

    (1) notice by the agency in writing of the facts or conduct which may warrant the action; and

    (2) opportunity to demonstrate or achieve compliance with all lawful requirements.

When the licensee has made timely and sufficient application for a renewal or a new license in accordance with agency rules, a license with reference to an activity of a continuing nature does not expire until the application has been finally determined by the agency.

§ 559. Effect on other laws; effect of subsequent statute

This subchapter, chapter 7, and sections 1305, 3105, 3344, 4301(2)(E), 5372, and 7521 of this title, and the provisions of section 5335(a)(B) of this title that relate to administrative law judges, do not limit or repeal additional requirements imposed by statute or otherwise recognized by law. Except as otherwise required by law, requirements or privileges relating to evidence or procedure apply equally to agencies and persons. Each agency is granted the authority necessary to comply with the requirements of this subchapter through the issuance of rules or otherwise. Subsequent statute may not be held to supersede or modify this subchapter, chapter 7, sections 1305, 3105, 3344, 4301(2)(E), 5372, or 7521 of this title, or the provisions of section 5335(a)(B) of this title that relate to administrative law judges, except to the extent that it does so expressly.

NEGOTIATED RULEMAKING ACT

§ 561. Purpose

The purpose of this subchapter is to establish a framework for the conduct of negotiated rulemaking, consistent with section 553 of this title, to encourage agencies to use the process when it enhances the informal rulemaking process. Nothing in this subchapter should be construed as an attempt to limit innovation and experimentation with the negotiated rulemaking process or with other innovative rulemaking procedures otherwise authorized by law.

§ 562. Definitions

For the purposes of this subchapter, the term—

(1) "agency" has the same meaning as in section 551(1) of this title;

(2) "consensus" means unanimous concurrence among the interests represented on a negotiated rulemaking committee established under this subchapter, unless such committee—

    (A) agrees to define such term to mean a general but not unanimous concurrence; or

    (B) agrees upon another specified definition;

(3) "convener" means a person who impartially assists an agency in determining whether establishment of a negotiated rulemaking committee is feasible and appropriate in a particular rulemaking;

(4) "facilitator" means a person who impartially aids in the discussions and negotiations among the members of a negotiated rulemaking committee to develop a proposed rule;

(5) "interest" means, with respect to an issue or matter, multiple parties which have a similar point of view or which are likely to be affected in a similar manner;

(6) "negotiated rulemaking" means rulemaking through the use of a negotiated rulemaking committee;

(7) "negotiated rulemaking committee" or "committee" means an advisory committee established by an agency in accordance with this subchapter and the Federal Advisory Committee Act to consider and discuss issues for the purpose of reaching a consensus in the development of a proposed rule;

(8) "party" has the same meaning as in section 551(3) of this title;

(9) "person" has the same meaning as in section 551(2) of this title;

(10) "rule" has the same meaning as in section 551(4) of this title; and

(11) "rulemaking" means "rule making" as that term is defined in section 551(5) of this title.

§ 563. Determination of need for negotiated rulemaking committee

(a) Determination of need by the agency.—An agency may establish a negotiated rulemaking committee to negotiate and develop a proposed rule, if the head of the agency determines that the use of the negotiated rulemaking procedure is in the public interest. In making such a determination, the head of the agency shall consider whether—

(1) there is a need for a rule;

(2) there are a limited number of identifiable interests that will be significantly affected by the rule;

§ 564. Publication of notice; applications for membership on committees

(a) Publication of notice.—If, after considering the report of a convener or conducting its own assessment, an agency decides to establish a negotiated rulemaking committee, the agency shall publish in the Federal Register and, as appropriate, in trade or other specialized publications, a notice which shall include—

(1) an announcement that the agency intends to establish a negotiated rulemaking committee to negotiate and develop a proposed rule;

(2) a description of the subject and scope of the rule to be developed, and the issues to be considered;

(3) a list of the interests which are likely to be significantly affected by the rule;

(4) a list of the persons proposed to represent such interests and the person or persons proposed to represent the agency;

(5) a proposed agenda and schedule for completing the work of the committee, including a target date for publication by the agency of a proposed rule for notice and comment;

(6) a description of administrative support for the committee to be provided by the agency, including technical assistance;

(7) a solicitation for comments on the proposal to establish the committee, and the proposed membership of the negotiated rulemaking committee; and

(8) an explanation of how a person may apply or nominate another person for membership on the committee, as provided under subsection (b).

(b) Applications for membership or committee.—Persons who will be significantly affected by a proposed rule and who believe that their interests will not be adequately represented by any person specified in a notice under subsection (a)(4) may apply for, or nominate another person for, membership on the negotiated rulemaking committee to represent such interests with respect to the proposed rule. Each application or nomination shall include—

(1) the name of the applicant or nominee and a description of the interests such person shall represent;

(2) evidence that the applicant or nominee is authorized to represent parties related to the interests the person proposes to represent;

(3) a written commitment that the applicant or nominee shall actively participate in good faith in the development of the rule under consideration; and

(4) the reasons that the persons specified in the notice under subsection (a)(4) do not adequately represent the interests of the person submitting the application or nomination.

(c) Period for submission of comments and applications.—The agency shall provide for a period of at least 30 calendar days for the submission of comments and applications under this section.

§ 565. Establishment of committee

(a) Establishment.—

(1) Determination to establish committee.—If after considering comments and applications submitted under section 564, the agency determines that a negotiated rulemaking committee can adequately represent the interests that will be significantly affected by a proposed rule and that it is feasible and appropriate in the particular rulemaking, the agency may establish a negotiated rulemaking committee. In establishing and administering such a committee, the agency shall comply with the Federal Advisory Committee Act with respect to such committee, except as otherwise provided in this subchapter.

(2) Determination not to establish committee.—If after considering such comments and applications, the agency decides not to establish a negotiated rulemaking committee, the agency shall promptly publish notice of such decision and the reasons therefor in the Federal Register and, as appropriate, in trade or other specialized publications, a copy of which shall be sent to any person who applied for, or nominated another person for membership on the negotiated rulemaking committee to represent such interests with respect to the proposed rule.

(b) Membership.—The agency shall limit membership on a negotiated rulemaking committee to 25 members, unless the agency head determines that a greater number of members is necessary for the functioning of the committee or to achieve balanced membership. Each committee shall include at least one person representing the agency.

(c) Administrative Support.—The agency shall provide appropriate administrative support to the negotiated rulemaking committee, including technical assistance.

§ 566. Conduct of committee activity

(a) Duties of Committee.—Each negotiated rulemaking committee established under this subchapter shall consider the matter proposed by the agency for consideration and shall attempt to reach a consensus concerning a proposed rule with respect to such matter and any other matter the committee determines is relevant to the proposed rule.

(b) Representatives of Agency on Committee.—The person or persons representing the agency on a negotiated rulemaking committee shall participate in the deliberations and activities of the committee with the same rights and responsibilities as other members of the committee, and shall be authorized to fully represent the agency in the discussions and negotiations of the committee.

(c) Selecting Facilitator.—Notwithstanding section 10(e) of the Federal Advisory Committee Act, an agency may nominate either a person from the Federal Government or a person from outside the Federal Government to serve as a facilitator for the negotiations of the committee, subject to the approval of the committee by consensus. If the committee does not approve the nominee of the agency for facilitator, the agency shall submit a substitute nomination. If a committee does not approve any nominee of the agency for facilitator, the committee shall select by consensus a person to serve as facilitator. A person designated to represent the agency in substantive issues may not serve as facilitator or otherwise chair the committee.

(d) Duties of Facilitator.—A facilitator approved or selected by a negotiated rulemaking committee shall—

　　(1) chair the meetings of the committee in an impartial manner;

　　(2) impartially assist the members of the committee in conducting discussions and negotiations; and

　　(3) manage the keeping of minutes and records as required under section 10(b) and (c) of the Federal Advisory Committee Act, except that any personal notes and materials of the facilitator or of the members of a committee shall not be subject to section 552 of this title.

(e) Committee Procedures.—A negotiated rulemaking committee established under this subchapter may adopt procedures for the operation of the committee. No provision of section 553 of this title shall apply to the procedures of a negotiated rulemaking committee.

(f) Report of Committee.—If a committee reaches a consensus on a proposed rule, at the conclusion of negotiations the committee shall transmit to the agency that established the committee a report containing the proposed rule. If the committee does not reach a consensus on a proposed rule, the committee may transmit to the agency a report specifying any areas in which the committee reached a consensus. The committee may include in a report any other information, recommendations, or materials that the committee considers appropriate. Any committee member may include as an addendum to the report additional information, recommendations, or materials.

(g) Records of Committee.—In addition to the report required by subsection (f), a committee shall submit to the agency the records required under section 10(b) and (c) of the Federal Advisory Committee Act.

§ 567. Termination of committee

A negotiated rulemaking committee shall terminate upon promulgation of the final rule under consideration, unless the committee's charter contains an earlier termination date or the agency, after consulting the committee, or the committee itself specifies an earlier termination date.

§ 568. Services, facilities, and payment of committee member expenses

(a) Services of Conveners and Facilitators.—

(1) In general.—An agency may employ or enter into contracts for the services of an individual or organization to serve as a convener or facilitator for a negotiated rulemaking committee under this subchapter, or may use the services of a Government employee to act as a convener or a facilitator for such a committee.

(2) Determination of conflicting interests.—An agency shall determine whether a person under consideration to serve as convener or facilitator of a committee under paragraph (1) has any financial or other interest that would preclude such person from serving in an impartial and independent manner.

(b) Services and Facilities of Other Entities.—For purposes of this subchapter, an agency may use the services and facilities of other Federal agencies and public and private agencies and instrumentalities with the consent of such agencies and instrumentalities, and with or without reimbursement to such agencies and instrumentalities, and may accept voluntary and uncompensated services without regard to the provisions of section 1342 of title 31. The Federal Mediation and Conciliation Service may provide services and facilities, with or without reimbursement, to assist agencies under this subchapter, including furnishing conveners, facilitators, and training in negotiated rulemaking.

(c) Expenses of Committee Members.—Members of a negotiated rulemaking committee shall be responsible for their own expenses of participation in such committee, except that an agency may, in accordance with section 7(d) of the Federal Advisory Committee Act, pay for a member's reasonable travel and per diem expenses, expenses to obtain technical assistance, and a reasonable rate of compensation, if—

(1) such member certifies a lack of adequate financial resources to participate in the committee; and

(2) the agency determines that such member's participation in the committee is necessary to assure an adequate representation of the member's interest.

(d) Status of Member as Federal Employee.—A member's receipt of funds under this section or section 569 shall not conclusively determine for purposes of sections 202 through 209 of title 18 whether that member is an employee of the United States Government.

§ 569. Role of the Administrative Conference of the United States and other entities

(a) Consultation by Agencies.—An agency may consult with the Administrative Conference of the United States or other public or private individuals or organizations for information and assistance in forming a negotiated rulemaking committee and conducting negotiations on a proposed rule.

(b) Roster of Potential Conveners and Facilitators.—The Administrative Conference of the United States, in consultation with the Federal Mediation and Conciliation Service, shall maintain a roster of individuals who have acted as or are interested in serving as conveners or facilitators in negotiated rulemaking proceedings. The roster shall include individuals from government agencies and private groups, and shall be made available upon request. Agencies may also use rosters maintained by other public or private individuals or organizations.

(c) Procedures to Obtain Conveners and Facilitators.—

(1) Procedures.—The Administrative Conference of the United States shall develop procedures which permit agencies to obtain the services of conveners and facilitators on an expedited basis.

(2) Payment for services.—Payment for the services of conveners or facilitators shall be made by the agency using the services, unless the Chairman of the Administrative Conference agrees to pay for such services under subsection (f).

(d) Compilation of Data on Negotiated Rulemaking; Report to Congress.—

(1) Compilation of data.—The Administrative Conference of the United States shall compile and maintain data related to negotiated rulemaking and shall act as a clearinghouse to assist agencies and parties participating in negotiated rulemaking proceedings.

(2) Submission of information by agencies.—Each agency engaged in negotiated rulemaking shall provide to the Administrative Conference of the United States a copy of any reports submitted to the agency by negotiated rulemaking committees under section 566 and such additional information as necessary to enable the Administrative Conference of the United States to comply with this subsection.

(3) Reports to congress.—The Administrative Conference of the United States shall review and analyze the reports and information received under this subsection and shall transmit a biennial report to the Committee on Governmental Affairs of the Senate and the appropriate committees of the House of Representatives that—

(A) provides recommendations for effective use by agencies of negotiated rulemaking; and

(B) describes the nature and amounts of expenditures made by the Administrative Conference of the United States to accomplish the purposes of this subchapter.

(e) Training in Negotiated Rulemaking.—The Administrative Conference of the United States is authorized to provide training in negotiated rulemaking techniques and procedures for personnel of the Federal Government either on a reimbursable or nonreimbursable basis. Such training may be extended to private individuals on a reimbursable basis.

(f) Payment of Expenses of Agencies.—The Chairman of the Administrative Conference of the United States is authorized to pay, upon request of an agency, all or part of the expenses of establishing a negotiated rulemaking committee and conducting a negotiated rulemaking. Such expenses may include, but are not limited to—

(1) the costs of conveners and facilitators;

(2) the expenses of committee members determined by the agency to be eligible for assistance under section 568(c); and

(3) training costs.

Determinations with respect to payments under this section shall be at the discretion of such Chairman in furthering the use by Federal agencies of negotiated rulemaking.

(g) Use of Funds of the Conference.—The Administrative Conference of the United States may apply funds received under section 595(c)(12) of this title to carry out the purposes of this subchapter.

§ 570. Judicial review

Any agency action relating to establishing, assisting, or terminating a negotiated rulemaking committee under this subchapter shall not be subject to judicial review. Nothing in this section shall bar judicial review of a rule if such judicial review is otherwise provided by law. A rule which is the product of negotiated rulemaking and is subject to judicial review shall not be accorded any greater deference by a court than a rule which is the product of other rulemaking procedures.

ALTERNATIVE DISPUTE RESOLUTION ACT

§ 571. Definitions

For the purposes of this subchapter, the term—

(1) "agency" has the same meaning as in section 551(1) of this title;

(2) "administrative program" includes a Federal function which involves protection of the public interest and the determination of rights, privileges, and obligations of private persons through rule making, adjudication, licensing, or investigation, as those terms are used in subchapter II of this chapter;

(3) "alternative means of dispute resolution" means any procedure that is used, in lieu of an adjudication as defined in section 551(7) of this title, to resolve issues in controversy, including, but not limited to, settlement negotiations, conciliation, facilitation, mediation, factfinding, minitrials, and arbitration, or any combination thereof;

(4) "award" means any decision by an arbitrator resolving the issues in controversy;

(5) "dispute resolution communication" means any oral or written communication prepared for the purposes of a dispute resolution proceeding,including any memoranda, notes or work product of the neutral, parties or nonparty participant; except that a written agreement to enter into a dispute resolution proceeding, or final written agreement or arbitral award reached as a result of a dispute resolution proceeding, is not a dispute resolution communication;

(6) "dispute resolution proceeding" means any process in which an alternative means of dispute resolution is used to resolve an issue in controversy in which a neutral is appointed and specified parties participate;

(7) "in confidence" means, with respect to information, that the information is provided—

(A) with the expressed intent of the source that it not be disclosed; or

(B) under circumstances that would create the reasonable expectation on behalf of the source that the information will not be disclosed;

(8) "issue in controversy" means an issue which is material to a decision concerning an administrative program of an agency, and with which there is disagreement—

(A) between an agency and persons who would be substantially affected by the decision; or

(B) between persons who would be substantially affected by the decision, except that such term shall not include any matter specified under section 2302 or 7121(c) of this title;

(9) "neutral" means an individual who, with respect to an issue in controversy, functions specifically to aid the parties in resolving the controversy;

(10) "party" means—

(A) for a proceeding with named parties, the same as in section 551(3) of this title; and

(B) for a proceeding without named parties, a person who will be significantly affected by the decision in the proceeding and who participates in the proceeding;

(11) "person" has the same meaning as in section 551(2) of this title; and

(12) "roster" means a list of persons qualified to provide services as neutrals.

§ 572. General authority

(a) An agency may use a dispute resolution proceeding for the resolution of an issue in controversy that relates to an administrative program, if the parties agree to such proceeding.

(b) An agency shall consider not using a dispute resolution proceeding if—

(1) a definitive or authoritative resolution of the matter is required for precedential value, and such a proceeding is not likely to be accepted generally as an authoritative precedent;

(2) the matter involves or may bear upon significant questions of Government policy that require additional procedures before a final resolution may be made, and such a proceeding would not likely serve to develop a recommended policy for the agency;

(3) maintaining established policies is of special importance, so that variations among individual decisions are not increased and such a proceeding would not likely reach consistent results among individual decisions;

(4) the matter significantly affects persons or organizations who are not parties to the proceeding;

(5) a full public record of the proceeding is important, and a dispute resolution proceeding cannot provide such a record; and

(6) the agency must maintain continuing jurisdiction over the matter with authority to alter the disposition of the matter in the light of changed circumstances, and a dispute resolution proceeding would interfere with the agency's fulfilling that requirement.

(c) Alternative means of dispute resolution authorized under this subchapter are voluntary procedures which supplement rather than limit other available agency dispute resolution techniques.

§ 573. Neutrals

(a) A neutral may be a permanent or temporary officer or employee of the Federal Government or any other individual who is acceptable to the parties to a dispute resolution proceeding. A neutral shall have no official, financial, or personal conflict of interest with respect to the issues in controversy, unless such interest is fully disclosed in writing to all parties and all parties agree that the neutral may serve.

(b) A neutral who serves as a conciliator, facilitator, or mediator serves at the will of the parties.

(c) In consultation with the Federal Mediation and Conciliation Service, other appropriate Federal agencies, and professional organizations experienced in matters concerning dispute resolution, the Administrative Conference of the United States shall—

(1) establish standards for neutrals (including experience, training, affiliations, diligence, actual or potential conflicts of interest, and other qualifications) to which agencies may refer;

(2) maintain a roster of individuals who meet such standards and are otherwise qualified to act as neutrals, which shall be made available upon request;

(3) enter into contracts for the services of neutrals that may be used by agencies on an elective basis in dispute resolution proceedings; and

(4) develop procedures that permit agencies to obtain the services of neutrals on an expedited basis.

(d) An agency may use the services of one or more employees of other agencies to serve as neutrals in dispute resolution proceedings. The agencies may enter into an interagency agreement that provides for the reimbursement by the user agency or the parties of the full or partial cost of the services of such an employee.

(e) Any agency may enter into a contract with any person on a roster established under subsection (c)(2) or a roster maintained by other public or private organizations, or individual for services as a neutral, or for training in connection with alternative means of dispute resolution. The parties in a dispute resolution proceeding shall agree on compensation for the neutral that is fair and reasonable to the Government.

§ 574. Confidentiality

(a) Except as provided in subsections (d) and (e), a neutral in a dispute resolution proceeding shall not voluntarily disclose or through discovery or compulsory process be required to disclose any information concerning any dispute resolution communication or any communication provided in confidence to the neutral, unless—

(1) all parties to the dispute resolution proceeding and the neutral consent in writing, and, if the dispute resolution communication was provided by a nonparty participant, that participant also consents in writing;

(2) the dispute resolution communication has already been made public;

(3) the dispute resolution communication is required by statute to be made public, but a neutral should make such communication public only if no other person is reasonably available to disclose the communication; or

(4) a court determines that such testimony or disclosure is necessary to—

    (A) prevent a manifest injustice;

    (B) help establish a violation of law; or

    (C) prevent harm to the public health or safety,

of sufficient magnitude in the particular case to outweigh the integrity of dispute resolution proceedings in general by reducing the confidence of parties in future cases that their communications will remain confidential.

(b) A party to a dispute resolution proceeding shall not voluntarily disclose or through discovery or compulsory process be required to disclose any information concerning any dispute resolution communication, unless—

(1) the communication was prepared by the party seeking disclosure;

(2) all parties to the dispute resolution proceeding consent in writing;

(3) the dispute resolution communication has already been made public;

(4) the dispute resolution communication is required by statute to be made public;

(5) a court determines that such testimony or disclosure is necessary to—

    (A) prevent a manifest injustice;

    (B) help establish a violation of law; or

    (C) prevent harm to the public health and safety,

of sufficient magnitude in the particular case to outweigh the integrity of dispute resolution proceedings in general by reducing the confidence of parties in future cases that their communications will remain confidential;

(6) the dispute resolution communication is relevant to determining the existence or meaning of an agreement or award that resulted from the dispute resolution proceeding or to the enforcement of such an agreement or award; or

(7) the dispute resolution communication was provided to or was available to all parties to the dispute resolution proceeding.

(c) Any dispute resolution communication that is disclosed in violation of subsection (a) or (b), shall not be admissible in any proceeding relating to the issues in controversy with respect to which the communication was made.

(d) The parties may agree to alternative confidential procedures for disclosures by a neutral. Upon such agreement the parties shall inform the neutral before the commencement of the dispute resolution proceeding of any modifications to the provisions of subsection (a) that will govern the confidentiality of the dispute resolution proceeding. If the parties do not so inform the neutral, subsection (a) shall apply.

(e) If a demand for disclosure, by way of discovery request or other legal process, is made upon a neutral regarding a dispute resolution communication, the neutral shall make reasonable efforts to notify the parties and any affected nonparty participants of the demand. Any party or affected nonparty participant who receives such notice and within 15 calendar days does not offer to defend a refusal of the neutral to disclose the requested information shall have waived any objection to such disclosure.

(f) Nothing in this section shall prevent the discovery or admissibility of any evidence that is otherwise discoverable, merely because the evidence was presented in the course of a dispute resolution proceeding.

(g) Subsections (a) and (b) shall have no effect on the information and data that are necessary to document an agreement reached or order issued pursuant to a dispute resolution proceeding.

(h) Subsections (a) and (b) shall not prevent the gathering of information for research or educational purposes, in cooperation with other agencies, governmental entities, or dispute resolution programs, so long as the parties and the specific issues in controversy are not identifiable.

(i) Subsections (a) and (b) shall not prevent use of a dispute resolution communication to resolve a dispute between the neutral in a dispute resolution proceeding and a party to or participant in such proceeding, so long as such dispute resolution communication is disclosed only to the extent necessary to resolve such dispute.

(j) This section shall not be considered a statute specifically exempting disclosure under section 552(b)(3) of this title.

§ 575. Authorization of arbitration

(a)(1) Arbitration may be used as an alternative means of dispute resolution whenever all parties consent. Consent may be obtained either before or after an issue in controversy has arisen. A party may agree to—

(A) submit only certain issues in controversy to arbitration;　or

(B) arbitration on the condition that the award must be within a range of possible outcomes.

(2) Any arbitration agreement that sets forth the subject matter submitted to the arbitrator shall be in writing.

(3) An agency may not require any person to consent to arbitration as a condition of entering into a contract or obtaining a benefit.

(b) An officer or employee of an agency may offer to use arbitration for the resolution of issues in controversy, if such officer or employee—

(1) has authority to enter into a settlement concerning the matter;　or

(2) is otherwise specifically authorized by the agency to consent to the use of arbitration.

§ 576. Enforcement of arbitration agreements

An agreement to arbitrate a matter to which this subchapter applies is enforceable pursuant to section 4 of title 9, and no action brought to enforce such an agreement shall be dismissed nor shall relief therein be denied on the grounds that it is against the United States or that the United States is an indispensable party.

§ 577. Arbitrators

(a) The parties to an arbitration proceeding shall be entitled to participate in the selection of the arbitrator.

(b) The arbitrator shall be a neutral who meets the criteria of section 573 of this title.

§ 578. Authority of the arbitrator

An arbitrator to whom a dispute is referred under this subchapter may—

(1) regulate the course of and conduct arbitral hearings;

(2) administer oaths and affirmations;

(3) compel the attendance of witnesses and production of evidence at the hearing under the provisions of section 7 of title 9 only to the extent the agency involved is otherwise authorized by law to do so;　and

(4) make awards.

§ 579. Arbitration proceedings

(a) The arbitrator shall set a time and place for the hearing on the dispute and shall notify the parties not less than 5 days before the hearing.

(b) Any party wishing a record of the hearing shall—

(1) be responsible for the preparation of such record;

(2) notify the other parties and the arbitrator of the preparation of such record;

(3) furnish copies to all identified parties and the arbitrator; and

(4) pay all costs for such record, unless the parties agree otherwise or the arbitrator determines that the costs should be apportioned.

(c)(1) The parties to the arbitration are entitled to be heard, to present evidence material to the controversy, and to cross-examine witnesses appearing at the hearing.

(2) The arbitrator may, with the consent of the parties, conduct all or part of the hearing by telephone, television, computer, or other electronic means, if each party has an opportunity to participate.

(3) The hearing shall be conducted expeditiously and in an informal manner.

(4) The arbitrator may receive any oral or documentary evidence, except that irrelevant, immaterial, unduly repetitious, or privileged evidence may be excluded by the arbitrator.

(5) The arbitrator shall interpret and apply relevant statutory and regulatory requirements, legal precedents, and policy directives.

(d) No interested person shall make or knowingly cause to be made to the arbitrator an unauthorized ex parte communication relevant to the merits of the proceeding, unless the parties agree otherwise. If a communication is made in violation of this subsection, the arbitrator shall ensure that a memorandum of the communication is prepared and made a part of the record, and that an opportunity for rebuttal is allowed. Upon receipt of a communication made in violation of this subsection, the arbitrator may, to the extent consistent with the interests of justice and the policies underlying this subchapter, require the offending party to show cause why the claim of such party should not be resolved against such party as a result of the improper conduct.

(e) The arbitrator shall make the award within 30 days after the close of the hearing, or the date of the filing of any briefs authorized by the arbitrator, whichever date is later, unless—

(1) the parties agree to some other time limit; or

(2) the agency provides by rule for some other time limit.

§ 580. Arbitration awards

(a)(1) Unless the agency provides otherwise by rule, the award in an arbitration proceeding under this subchapter shall include a brief, informal discussion of the factual and legal basis for the award, but formal findings of fact or conclusions of law shall not be required.

(2) The prevailing parties shall file the award with all relevant agencies, along with proof of service on all parties.

(b) The award in an arbitration proceeding shall become final 30 days after it is served on all parties. Any agency that is a party to the proceeding may extend this 30–day period for an additional 30–day period by serving a notice of such extension on all other parties before the end of the first 30–day period.

(c) The head of any agency that is a party to an arbitration proceeding conducted under this subchapter is authorized to terminate the arbitration proceeding or vacate any award issued pursuant to the proceeding before the award becomes final by serving on all other parties a written notice to that effect, in which case the award shall be null and void. Notice shall be provided to all parties to the arbitration proceeding of any request by a party, nonparty participant or other person that the agency head terminate the arbitration proceeding or vacate the award. An employee or agent engaged in the performance of investigative or prosecuting functions for an agency may not, in that or a factually related case, advise in a decision under this subsection to terminate an arbitration proceeding or to vacate an arbitral award, except as witness or counsel in public proceedings.

(d) A final award is binding on the parties to the arbitration proceeding, and may be enforced pursuant to sections 9 through 13 of title 9. No action brought to enforce such an award shall be dismissed nor shall relief therein be denied on the grounds that it is against the United States or that the United States is an indispensable party.

(e) An award entered under this subchapter in an arbitration proceeding may not serve as an estoppel in any other proceeding for any issue that was resolved in the proceeding. Such an award also may not be used as precedent or otherwise be considered in any factually unrelated proceeding, whether conducted under this subchapter, by an agency, or in a court, or in any other arbitration proceeding.

(f) An arbitral award that is vacated under subsection (c) shall not be admissible in any proceeding relating to the issues in controversy with respect to which the award was made.

(g) If an agency head vacates an award under subsection (c), a party to the arbitration (other than the United States) may within 30 days of such action petition the agency head for an award of fees and other expenses (as defined in section 504(b)(1)(A) of this title) incurred in connection with the arbitration proceeding. The agency head shall award the petitioning party those fees and expenses that would not have been incurred in the absence of such arbitration proceeding, unless the agency head or his or her designee finds that special circumstances make such an award unjust. The procedures for reviewing applications for awards shall, where appropriate, be consistent with those set forth in subsection (a)(2) and (3) of section 504 of this title. Such fees and

338

expenses shall be paid from the funds of the agency that vacated the award.

§ 581. Judicial Review

(a) Notwithstanding any other provision of law, any person adversely affected or aggrieved by an award made in an arbitration proceeding conducted under this subchapter may bring an action for review of such award only pursuant to the provisions of sections 9 through 13 of title 9.

(b)(1) A decision by an agency to use or not to use a dispute resolution proceeding under this subchapter shall be committed to the discretion of the agency and shall not be subject to judicial review, except that arbitration shall be subject to judicial review under section 10(b) of title 9.

(2) A decision by the head of an agency under section 580 to terminate an arbitration proceeding or vacate an arbitral award shall be committed to the discretion of the agency and shall not be subject to judicial review.

§ 582. Compilation of information

The Chairman of the Administrative Conference of the United States shall compile and maintain data on the use of alternative means of dispute resolution in conducting agency proceedings. Agencies shall, upon the request of the Chairman of the Administrative Conference of the United States, supply such information as is required to enable the Chairman to comply with this section.

§ 583. Support services

For the purposes of this subchapter, an agency may use (with or without reimbursement) the services and facilities of other Federal agencies, public and private organizations and agencies, and individuals, with the consent of such agencies, organizations, and individuals. An agency may accept voluntary and uncompensated services for purposes of this subchapter without regard to the provisions of section 1342 of title 31.

REGULATORY FLEXIBILITY ACT

§ 601. Definitions

For purposes of this chapter—

(1) the term "agency" means an agency as defined in section 551(1) of this title;

(2) the term "rule" means any rule for which the agency publishes a general notice of proposed rulemaking pursuant to section 553(b) of this title, or any other law, including any rule of general applicability

governing Federal grants to State and local governments for which the agency provides an opportunity for notice and public comment, except that the term "rule" does not include a rule of particular applicability relating to rates, wages, corporate or financial structures or reorganizations thereof, prices, facilities, appliances, services, or allowances therefor or to valuations, costs or accounting, or practices relating to such rates, wages, structures, prices, appliances, services, or allowances;

(3) the term "small business" has the same meaning as the term "small business concern" under section 3 of the Small Business Act, unless an agency, after consultation with the Office of Advocacy of the Small Business Administration and after opportunity for public comment, establishes one or more definitions of such term which are appropriate to the activities of the agency and publishes such definition(s) in the Federal Register;

(4) the term "small organization" means any not-for-profit enterprise which is independently owned and operated and is not dominant in its field, unless an agency establishes, after opportunity for public comment, one or more definitions of such term which are appropriate to the activities of the agency and publishes such definition(s) in the Federal Register;

(5) the term "small governmental jurisdiction" means governments of cities, counties, towns, townships, villages, school districts, or special districts, with a population of less than fifty thousand, unless an agency establishes, after opportunity for public comment, one or more definitions of such term which are appropriate to the activities of the agency and which are based on such factors as location in rural or sparsely populated areas or limited revenues due to the population of such jurisdiction, and publishes such definition(s) in the Federal Register; and

(6) the term "small entity" shall have the same meaning as the terms "small business", "small organization" and "small governmental jurisdiction" defined in paragraphs (3), (4) and (5) of this section.

§ 602. Regulatory agenda

(a) During the months of October and April of each year, each agency shall publish in the Federal Register a regulatory flexibility agenda which shall contain—

(1) a brief description of the subject area of any rule which the agency expects to propose or promulgate which is likely to have a significant economic impact on a substantial number of small entities;

(2) a summary of the nature of any such rule under consideration for each subject area listed in the agenda pursuant to paragraph (1), the objectives and legal basis for the issuance of the rule, and an approximate schedule for completing action on any rule for

which the agency has issued a general notice of proposed rulemaking, and

(3) the name and telephone number of an agency official knowledgeable concerning the items listed in paragraph (1).

(b) Each regulatory flexibility agenda shall be transmitted to the Chief Counsel for Advocacy of the Small Business Administration for comment, if any.

(c) Each agency shall endeavor to provide notice of each regulatory flexibility agenda to small entities or their representatives through direct notification or publication of the agenda in publications likely to be obtained by such small entities and shall invite comments upon each subject area on the agenda.

(d) Nothing in this section precludes an agency from considering or acting on any matter not included in a regulatory flexibility agenda, or requires an agency to consider or act on any matter listed in such agenda.

§ 603. Initial regulatory flexibility analysis

(a) Whenever an agency is required by section 553 of this title, or any other law, to publish general notice of proposed rulemaking for any proposed rule, the agency shall prepare and make available for public comment an initial regulatory flexibility analysis. Such analysis shall describe the impact of the proposed rule on small entities. The initial regulatory flexibility analysis or a summary shall be published in the Federal Register at the time of the publication of general notice of proposed rulemaking for the rule. The agency shall transmit a copy of the initial regulatory flexibility analysis to the Chief Counsel for Advocacy of the Small Business Administration.

(b) Each initial regulatory flexibility analysis required under this section shall contain—

(1) a description of the reasons why action by the agency is being considered;

(2) a succinct statement of the objectives of, and legal basis for, the proposed rule;

(3) a description of and where feasible, an estimate of the number of small entities to which the proposed rule will apply;

(4) a description of the projected reporting, recordkeeping and other compliance requirements of the proposed rule, including an estimate of the classes of small entities which will be subject to the requirement and the type of professional skills necessary for preparation of the report or record;

(5) an identification, to the extent practicable, of all relevant Federal rules which may duplicate, overlap or conflict with the proposed rule.

(c) Each initial regulatory flexibility analysis shall also contain a description by any significant alternatives to the proposed rule which accomplish the stated objectives of applicable statutes and which minimize any significant economic impact of the proposed rule on small entities. Consistent with the stated objectives of applicable statutes, the analysis shall discuss significant alternatives such as—

(1) the establishment of differing compliance or reporting requirements or timetables that take into account the resources available to small entities;

(2) the clarification, consolidation, or simplification of compliance and reporting requirements under the rule for such small entities;

(3) the use of performance rather than design standards; and

(4) an exemption from coverage of the rule, or any part thereof, for such small entities.

§ 604. Final regulatory flexibility analysis

(a) When an agency promulgates a final rule under section 553 of this title, after being required by that section or any other law to publish a general notice of proposed rulemaking, the agency shall prepare a final regulatory flexibility analysis. Each final regulatory flexibility analysis shall contain—

(1) a succinct statement of the need for, and the objectives of, the rule;

(2) a summary of the issues raised by the public comments in response to the initial regulatory flexibility analysis, a summary of the assessment of the agency of such issues, and a statement of any changes made in the proposed rule as a result of such comments; and

(3) a description of each of the significant alternatives to the rule consistent with the stated objectives of applicable statutes and designed to minimize any significant economic impact of the rule on small entities which was considered by the agency, and a statement of the reasons why each one of such alternatives was rejected.

(b) The agency shall make copies of the final regulatory flexibility analysis available to members of the public and shall publish in the Federal Register at the time of publication of the final rule under section 553 of this title a statement describing how the public may obtain such copies.

§ 605. Avoidance of duplicative or unnecessary analyses

(a) Any Federal agency may perform the analyses required by sections 602, 603, and 604 of this title in conjunction with or as a part of any other agenda or analysis required by any other law if such other analysis satisfies the provisions of such sections.

(b) Sections 603 and 604 of this title shall not apply to any proposed or final rule if the head of the agency certifies that the rule will not, if promulgated, have a significant economic impact on a substantial number of small entities. If the head of the agency makes a certification under the preceding sentence, the agency shall publish such certification in the Federal Register, at the time of publication of general notice of proposed rulemaking for the rule or at the time of publication of the final rule, along with a succinct statement explaining the reasons for such certification, and provide such certification and statement to the Chief Counsel for Advocacy of the Small Business Administration.

(c) In order to avoid duplicative action, an agency may consider a series of closely related rules as one rule for the purposes of sections 602, 603, 604 and 610 of this title.

§ 606. Effect on other law

The requirements of sections 603 and 604 of this title do not alter in any manner standards otherwise applicable by law to agency action.

§ 607. Preparation of analyses

In complying with the provisions of sections 603 and 604 of this title, an agency may provide either a quantifiable or numerical description of the effects of a proposed rule or alternatives to the proposed rule, or more general descriptive statements if quantification is not practicable or reliable.

§ 608. Procedure for waiver or delay of completion

(a) An agency head may waive or delay the completion of some or all of the requirements of section 603 of this title by publishing in the Federal Register, not later than the date of publication of the final rule, a written finding, with reasons therefor, that the final rule is being promulgated in response to an emergency that makes compliance or timely compliance with the provisions of section 603 of this title impracticable.

(b) Except as provided in section 605(b), an agency head may not waive the requirements of section 604 of this title. An agency head may delay the completion of the requirements of section 604 of this title for a period of not more than one hundred and eighty days after the date of publication in the Federal Register of a final rule by publishing in the Federal Register, not later than such date of publication, a written finding, with reasons therefor, that the final rule is being promulgated in response to an emergency that makes timely compliance with the provisions of section 604 of this title impracticable. If the agency has not prepared a final regulatory analysis pursuant to section 604 of this title within one hundred and eighty days from the date of publication of the final rule, such rule shall lapse and have no effect. Such rule shall not be repromulgated until a final regulatory flexibility analysis has been completed by the agency.

§ 609. Procedures for gathering comments

When any rule is promulgated which will have a significant economic impact on a substantial number of small entities, the head of the agency promulgating the rule or the official of the agency with statutory responsibility for the promulgation of the rule shall assure that small entities have been given an opportunity to participate in the rulemaking for the rule through techniques such as—

(1) the inclusion in an advanced notice of proposed rulemaking, if issued, of a statement that the proposed rule may have a significant economic effect on a substantial number of small entities;

(2) the publication of general notice of proposed rulemaking in publications likely to be obtained by small entities;

(3) the direct notification of interested small entities;

(4) the conduct of open conferences or public hearings concerning the rule for small entities; and

(5) the adoption or modification of agency procedural rules to reduce the cost or complexity of participation in the rulemaking by small entities.

§ 610. Periodic review of rules

(a) Within one hundred and eighty days after the effective date of this chapter, each agency shall publish in the Federal Register a plan for the periodic review of the rules issued by the agency which have or will have a significant economic impact upon a substantial number of small entities. Such plan may be amended by the agency at any time by publishing the revision in the Federal Register. The purpose of the review shall be to determine whether such rules should be continued without change, or should be amended or rescinded, consistent with the stated objectives of applicable statutes, to minimize any significant economic impact of the rules upon a substantial number of such small entities. The plan shall provide for the review of all such agency rules existing on the effective date of this chapter within ten years of that date and for the review of such rules adopted after the effective date of this chapter within ten years of the publication of such rules as the final rule. If the head of the agency determines that completion of the review of existing rules is not feasible by the established date, he shall so certify in a statement published in the Federal Register and may extend the completion date by one year at a time for a total of not more than five years.

(b) In reviewing rules to minimize any significant economic impact of the rule on a substantial number of small entities in a manner consistent with the stated objectives of applicable statutes, the agency shall consider the following factors—

(1) the continued need for the rule;

(2) the nature of complaints or comments received concerning the rule from the public;

(3) the complexity of the rule;

(4) the extent to which the rule overlaps, duplicates or conflicts with other Federal rules, and, to the extent feasible, with State and local governmental rules; and

(5) the length of time since the rule has been evaluated or the degree to which technology, economic conditions, or other factors have changed in the area affected by the rule.

(c) Each year, each agency shall publish in the Federal Register a list of the rules which have a significant economic impact on a substantial number of small entities, which are to be reviewed pursuant to this section during the succeeding twelve months. The list shall include a brief description of each rule and the need for and legal basis of such rule and shall invite public comment upon the rule.

§ 611. Judicial review

(a) Except as otherwise provided in subsection (b), any determination by an agency concerning the applicability of any of the provisions of this chapter to any action of the agency shall not be subject to judicial review.

(b) Any regulatory flexibility analysis prepared under sections 603 and 604 of this title and the compliance or noncompliance of the agency with the provisions of this chapter shall not be subject to judicial review. When an action for judicial review of a rule is instituted, any regulatory flexibility analysis for such rule shall constitute part of the whole record of agency action in connection with the review.

§ 612. Reports and intervention rights

(a) The Chief Counsel for Advocacy of the Small Business Administration shall monitor agency compliance with this chapter and shall report at least annually thereon to the President and to the Committees on the Judiciary of the Senate and House of Representatives, the Select Committee on Small Business of the Senate, and the Committee on Small Business of the House of Representatives.

(b) The Chief Counsel for Advocacy of the Small Business Administration is authorized to appear as amicus curiae in any action brought in a court of the United States to review a rule. In any such action, the Chief Counsel is authorized to present his views with respect to the effect of the rule on small entities.

(c) A court of the United States shall grant the application of the Chief Counsel for Advocacy of the Small Business Administration to appear in any such action for the purposes described in subsection (b).

JUDICIAL REVIEW

§ 701. Application; definitions

(a) This chapter applies, according to the provisions thereof, except to the extent that—

    (1) statutes preclude judicial review; or

    (2) agency action is committed to agency discretion by law.

(b) For the purpose of this chapter—

    (1) "agency" means each authority of the Government of the United States, whether or not it is within or subject to review by another agency, but does not include—

        (A) the Congress;

        (B) the courts of the United States;

        (C) the governments of the territories or possessions of the United States;

        (D) the government of the District of Columbia;

        (E) agencies composed of representatives of the parties or of representatives of organizations of the parties to the disputes determined by them;

        (F) courts martial and military commissions;

        (G) military authority exercised in the field in time of war or in occupied territory; or

        (H) functions conferred by sections 1738, 1739, 1743, and 1744 of title 12; chapter 2 of title 41; subchapter II of chapter 471 of title 49; or sections 1884, 1891–1902, and former section 1641(b)(2), of title 50, appendix; and

    (2) "person", "rule", "order", "license", "sanction", "relief", and "agency action" have the meanings given them by section 551 of this title.

§ 702. Right of review

A person suffering legal wrong because of agency action, or adversely affected or aggrieved by agency action within the meaning of a relevant statute, is entitled to judicial review thereof. An action in a court of the United States seeking relief other than money damages and stating a claim that an agency or an officer or employee thereof acted or failed to act in an official capacity or under color of legal authority shall not be dismissed nor relief therein be denied on the ground that it is against the United States or that the United States is an indispensable party. The United States may be named as a defendant in any such action, and a judgment or decree may be entered against the United States: Provided, That any mandatory or injunctive decree shall specify the Federal officer or officers (by name or by title), and their successors in office, personally responsible for compliance. Nothing herein (1) affects other limitations on judicial review or the power or duty of the court to dismiss any action or deny relief on any other appropriate legal or equitable ground; or (2) confers authority to grant relief if any other statute that grants consent to suit expressly or impliedly forbids the relief which is sought.

§ 703. Form and venue of proceeding

The form of proceeding for judicial review is the special statutory review proceeding relevant to the subject matter in a court specified by statute or, in the absence or inadequacy thereof, any applicable form of legal action, including actions for declaratory judgments or writs of prohibitory or mandatory injunction or habeas corpus, in a court of competent jurisdiction. If no special statutory review proceeding is applicable, the action for judicial review may be brought against the United States, the agency by its official title, or the appropriate officer. Except to the extent that prior, adequate, and exclusive opportunity for judicial review is provided by law, agency action is subject to judicial review in civil or criminal proceedings for judicial enforcement.

§ 704. Actions reviewable

Agency action made reviewable by statute and final agency action for which there is no other adequate remedy in a court are subject to judicial review. A preliminary, procedural, or intermediate agency action or ruling not directly reviewable is subject to review on the review of the final agency action. Except as otherwise expressly required by statute, agency action otherwise final is final for the purposes of this section whether or not there has been presented or determined an application for a declaratory order, for any form of reconsideration, or, unless the agency otherwise requires by rule and provides that the action meanwhile is inoperative, for an appeal to superior agency authority.

§ 705. Relief pending review

When an agency finds that justice so requires, it may postpone the effective date of action taken by it, pending judicial review. On such conditions as may be required and to the extent necessary to prevent irreparable injury, the reviewing court, including the court to which a case may be taken on appeal from or on application for certiorari or other writ to a reviewing court, may issue all necessary and appropriate process to postpone the effective date of an agency action or to preserve status or rights pending conclusion of the review proceedings.

§ 706. Scope of review

To the extent necessary to decision and when presented, the reviewing court shall decide all relevant questions of law, interpret constitutional and statutory provisions, and determine the meaning or applicability of the terms of an agency action. The reviewing court shall—

(1) compel agency action unlawfully withheld or unreasonably delayed; and

(2) hold unlawful and set aside agency action, findings, and conclusions found to be—

(A) arbitrary, capricious, an abuse of discretion, or otherwise not in accordance with law;

(B) contrary to constitutional right, power, privilege, or immunity;

(C) in excess of statutory jurisdiction, authority, or limitations, or short of statutory right;

(D) without observance of procedure required by law;

(E) unsupported by substantial evidence in a case subject to sections 556 and 557 of this title or otherwise reviewed on the record of an agency hearing provided by statute; or

(F) unwarranted by the facts to the extent that the facts are subject to trial de novo by the reviewing court.

In making the foregoing determinations, the court shall review the whole record or those parts of it cited by a party, and due account shall be taken of the rule of prejudicial error.

†